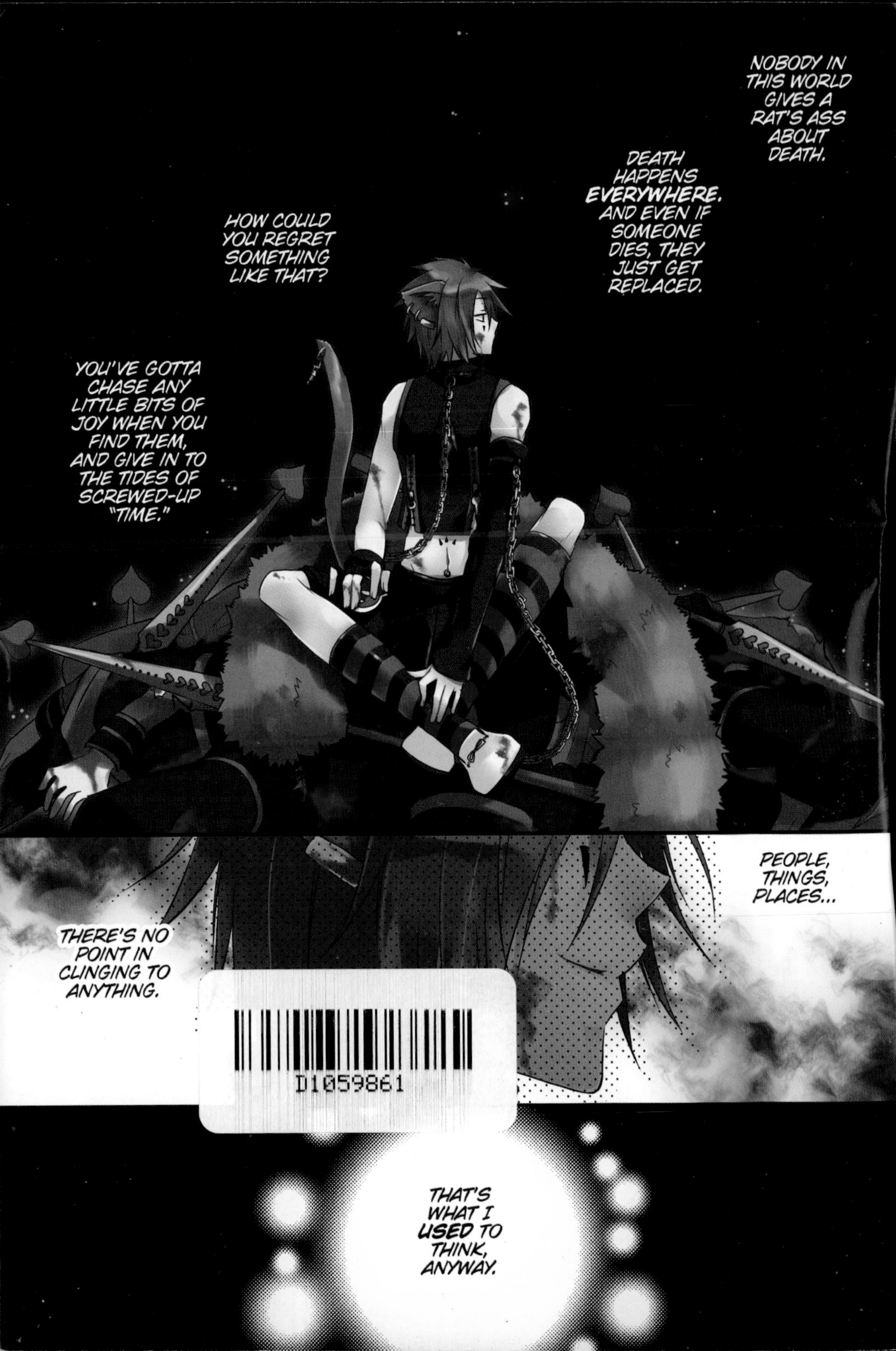
NOBODY IN THIS WORLD GIVES A RAT'S ASS ABOUT DEATH.
DEATH HAPPENS **EVERYWHERE.** AND EVEN IF SOMEONE DIES, THEY JUST GET REPLACED.
HOW COULD YOU REGRET SOMETHING LIKE THAT?
YOU'VE GOTTA CHASE ANY LITTLE BITS OF JOY WHEN YOU FIND THEM, AND GIVE IN TO THE TIDES OF SCREWED-UP "TIME."
PEOPLE, THINGS, PLACES...
THERE'S NO POINT IN CLINGING TO ANYTHING.
THAT'S WHAT I **USED** TO THINK, ANYWAY.

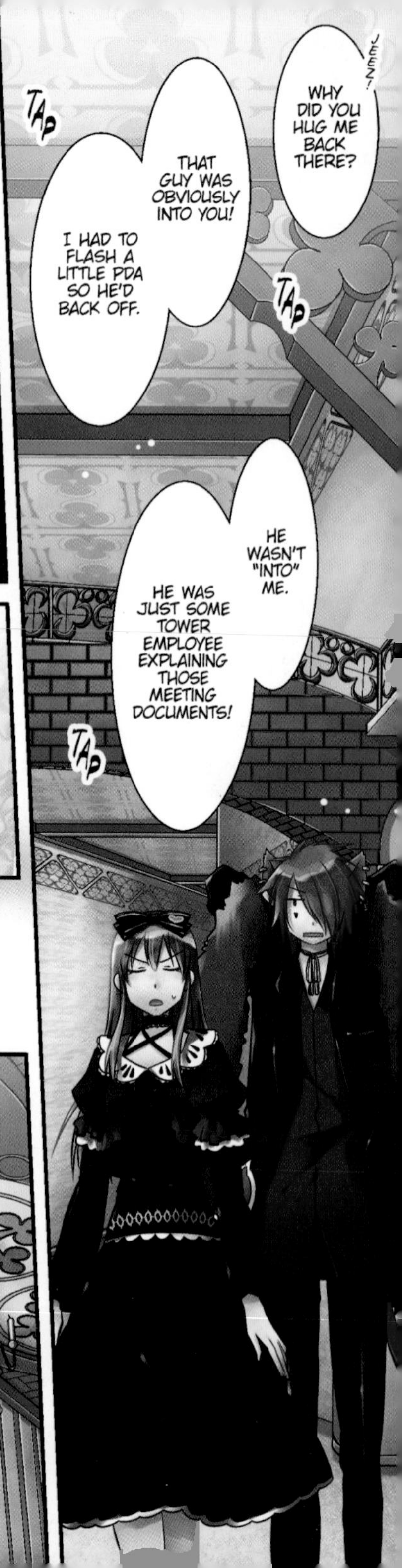
JEEZ!
WHY DID YOU HUG ME BACK THERE?
TAP
THAT GUY WAS OBVIOUSLY INTO YOU!
I HAD TO FLASH A LITTLE PDA SO HE'D BACK OFF.
TAP
HE WASN'T "INTO" ME.
HE WAS JUST SOME TOWER EMPLOYEE EXPLAINING THOSE MEETING DOCUMENTS!
TAP

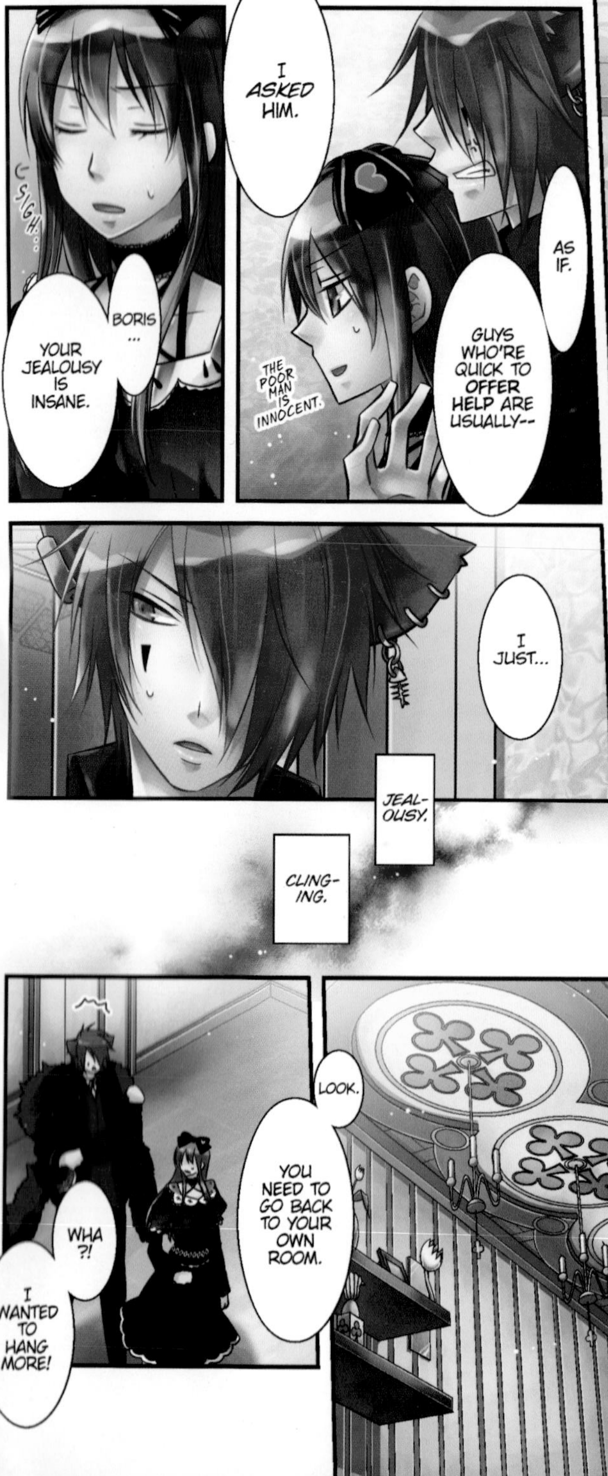
I ASKED HIM.
AS IF.
GUYS WHO'RE QUICK TO OFFER HELP ARE USUALLY--
THE POOR MAN IS INNOCENT.
SIGH...
BORIS...
YOUR JEALOUSY IS INSANE.
I JUST...
JEAL-OUSY.
CLING-ING.
LOOK.
YOU NEED TO GO BACK TO YOUR OWN ROOM.
WHA ?!
I WANTED TO HANG MORE!

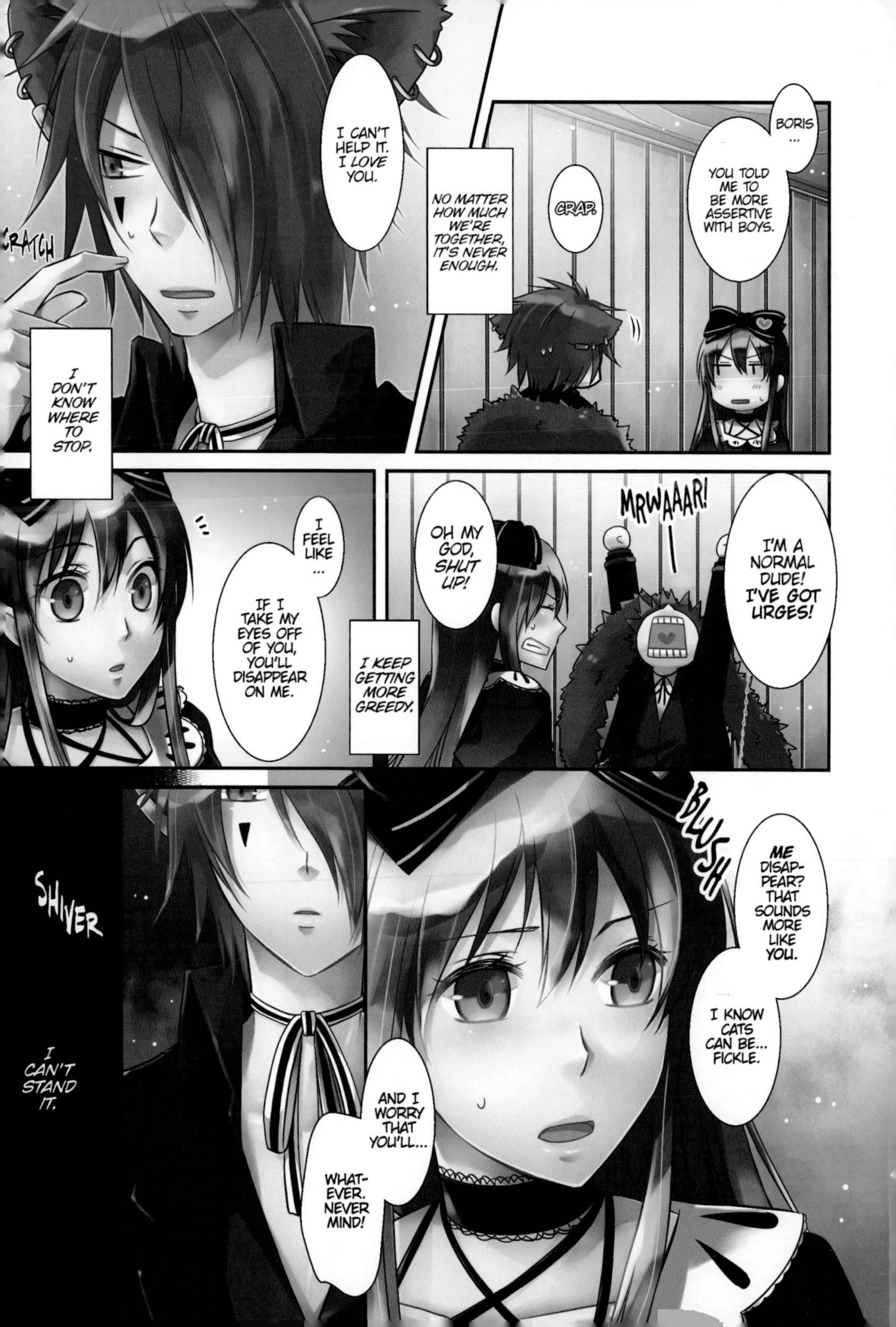
BORIS ...
YOU TOLD ME TO BE MORE ASSERTIVE WITH BOYS.
CRAP.
NO MATTER HOW MUCH WE'RE TOGETHER, IT'S NEVER ENOUGH.
I CAN'T HELP IT. I LOVE YOU.
CRATCH
I DON'T KNOW WHERE TO STOP.
MRWAAAR!
I'M A NORMAL DUDE! I'VE GOT URGES!
OH MY GOD, SHUT UP!
I KEEP GETTING MORE GREEDY.
I FEEL LIKE ...
IF I TAKE MY EYES OFF OF YOU, YOU'LL DISAPPEAR ON ME.
BLUSH
ME DISAPPEAR? THAT SOUNDS MORE LIKE YOU.
I KNOW CATS CAN BE... FICKLE.
AND I WORRY THAT YOU'LL...
WHATEVER. NEVER MIND!
SHIVER
I CAN'T STAND IT.

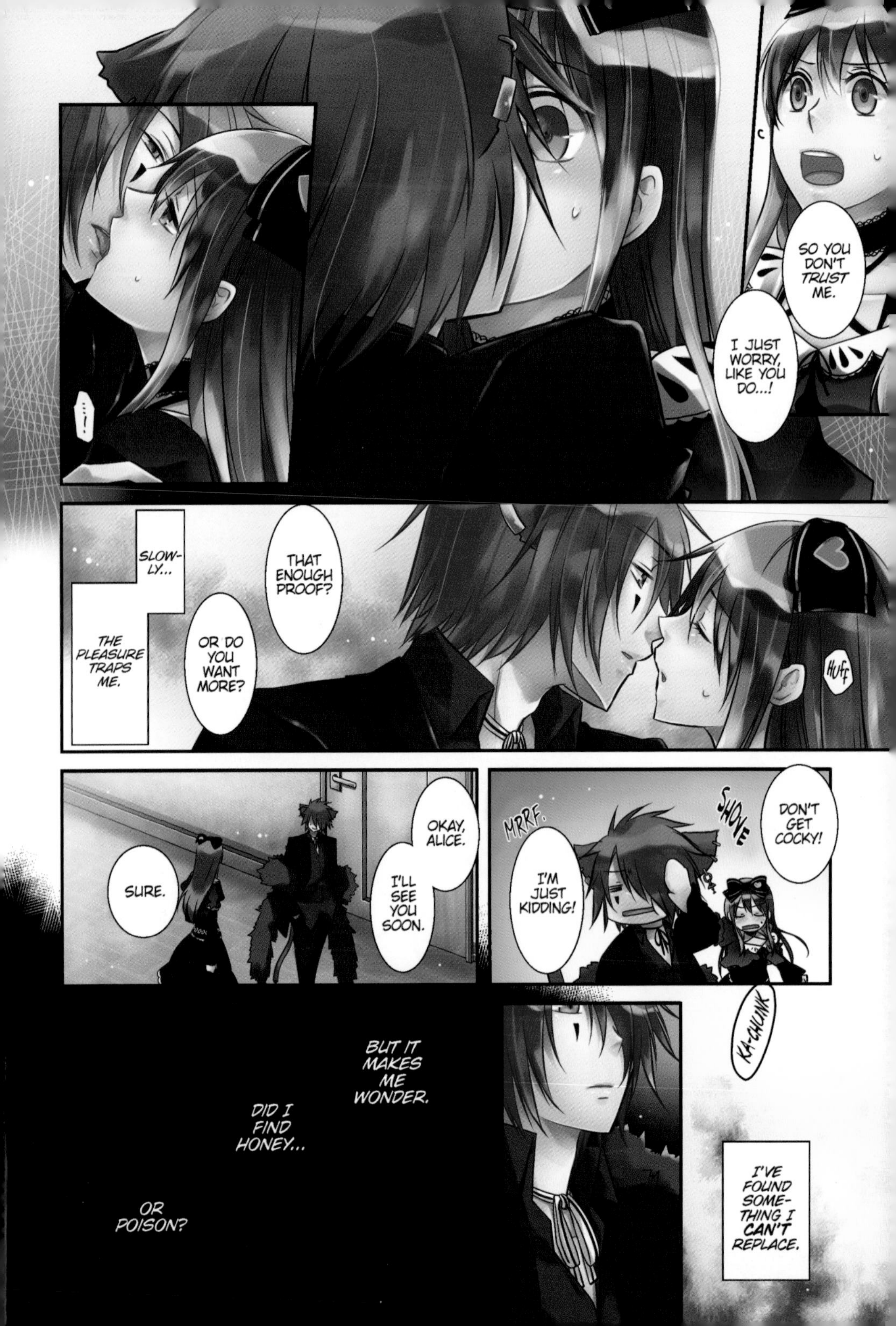
SO YOU DON'T TRUST ME.
I JUST WORRY, LIKE YOU DO...!
...!
HUFF
THAT ENOUGH PROOF?
OR DO YOU WANT MORE?
SLOWLY...
THE PLEASURE TRAPS ME.
DON'T GET COCKY!
SHOVE
MRRF.
I'M JUST KIDDING!
OKAY, ALICE.
I'LL SEE YOU SOON.
SURE.
KA-CHUNK
I'VE FOUND SOMETHING I CAN'T REPLACE.
BUT IT MAKES ME WONDER.
DID I FIND HONEY...
OR POISON?

Alice in the Country of Clover ~Cheshire Cat Waltz~ 4

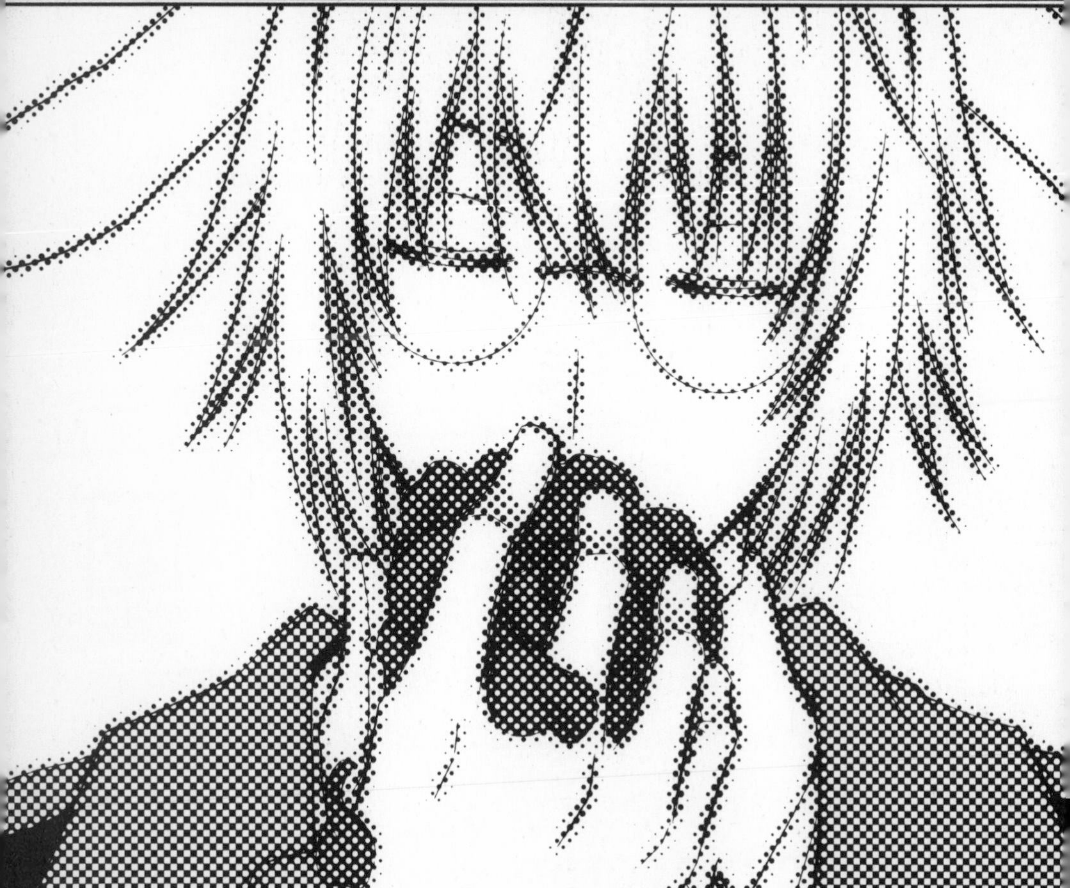

Mamenosuke Fujimaru

藤丸 豆ノ介

Alice IN THE COUNTRY OF Clover
CHESHIRE CAT WALTZ
VOLUME 4

story by **QuinRose**

art by **Mamenosuke Fujimaru**

STAFF CREDITS

translation	**Angela Liu**
adaptation	**Lianne Sentar**
lettering	**Roland Amago**
layout	**Bambi Eloriaga-Amago**
cover design	**Nicky Lim**
copy editor	**Shanti Whitesides**
editor	**Adam Arnold**
publisher	**Jason DeAngelis**
	Seven Seas Entertainment

ALICE IN THE COUNTRY OF CLOVER: CHESHIRE CAT WALTZ VOL. 4
Copyright © Mamenosuke Fujimaru / QuinRose 2010
First published in Japan in 2010 by ICHIJINSHA Inc., Tokyo.
English translation rights arranged with ICHIJINSHA Inc., Tokyo, Japan.

ISBN: 978-1-937867-10-2

Printed in Canada

First Printing: March 2013

10 9 8 7 6 5 4 3 2 1

FOLLOW US ONLINE: www.gomanga.com

READING DIRECTIONS

This book reads from **right to left**, Japanese style.
If this is your first time reading manga, you start
reading from the top right panel on each page and
take it from there. If you get lost, just follow the
numbered diagram here. It may seem backwards
at first, but you'll get the hang of it! Have fun!!

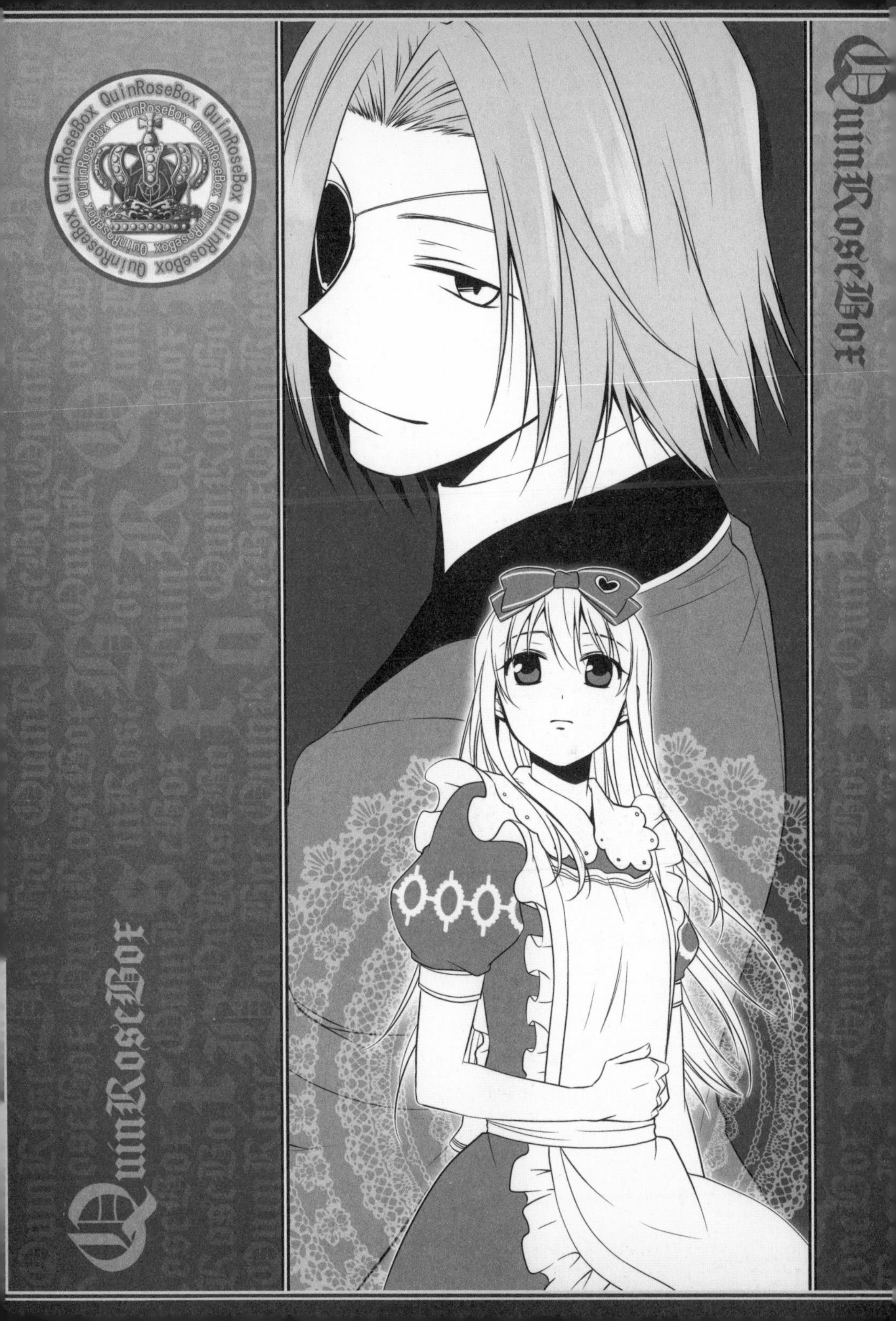
QuinRoseBox
QuinRoseBox

Alice in the Country of Clover
クローバーの国の
アリス
~Wonderful Wonder World~

- STORY -

In *Alice in the Country of Clover*, the game starts with Alice having not fallen in love, but still deciding to stay in Wonderland.

She's acquainted with all the characters from the previous game, *Alice in the Country of Hearts*.

Since love would now start from a place of friendship rather than passion with a new stranger, she can experience a different type of romance from that in the previous game. Her dynamic with the characters is different through this friendship—characters can't always be forceful with her, and in many ways it's more comfortable to grow intimate. The relationships *between* the Ones With Duties have also become more of a factor.

In this game, the story focuses on the mafia. Alice attends the suited meetings (forcefully) and gets involved in various gunfights (forcefully), among other things.

Land fluctuations, sea creatures in the forest, and whispering doors—it's a game more fantastic and more eerie than the first.

Will our everywoman Alice be able to have a romantic relationship in a world devoid of common sense?

Alice in the Country of Clover Character Information

Elliot March
VA: Tsuguo Mogami

Blood's right-hand man has a criminal past... and a temperamental present. But he's not as bad as he used to be, so that's something. Joining Blood has been good(?) for him.

Blood Dupre
VA: Katsuyuki Konishi

The head of the mafia Hatter Family, Blood is a cunning yet moody puppet-master. Alice now has the pleasure of having him for a landlord.

Alice Liddell
VA: Rie Kugimiya

A normal girl with a bit of a chip on her shoulder. Deciding to stay in the Wonderland she was carried to, she's adapted to her strange new lifestyle.

Vivaldi
VA: Yuuko Kaida

The beautiful Queen of Hearts has an unrivaled temper—which is really saying something in Wonderland. Although a picture-perfect Mad Queen, she cares for Alice as if Alice were her little sister...or a very interesting plaything.

Tweedle Dum
VA: Jun Fukuyama

The second "Bloody Twin" is equally cute and equally scary. In Clover, Dum can also turn into an adult.

Tweedle Dee
VA: Jun Fukuyama

One of the "Bloody Twin" gatekeepers of the Hatter territory, Dee can be cute when he's not being terrifying. In Clover, he sometimes turns into an adult.

Boris Airay
VA: Noriaki Sugiyama

This riddle-loving cat has a signature smirk—and in Clover, a new toy. One of his favorite pastimes is giving the Sleepy Mouse a hard time.

Ace
VA: Daisuke Hirakawa

The unlucky knight of Hearts was a former subordinate of Vivaldi and is perpetually lost. Even though he's depressed to be separated from his friend and boss Julius, he stays positive and tries to overcome it with a smile. He seems like a classic nice guy... or is he?

Peter White
VA: Kouki Miyata

The Prime Minister of Heart Castle—who has rabbit ears growing out of his head—invited (kidnapped) Alice to Wonderland. He loves Alice and hates everything else. His cruel, irrational actions are disturbing, but he acts like a completely different person (rabbit?) when in the throes of his love for Alice.

Gray Ringmarc
VA: Kazuya Nakai

Nightmare's subordinate in Clover. He used to have strong social ambition and considered assassinating Nightmare... but since Nightmare was such a useless boss, Gray couldn't help but feel sorry for him and ended up a dedicated assistant. He's a sound thinker with a strong work ethic. He's also highly skilled with his blades, rivaling even Ace.

Nightmare Gottschalk
VA: Tomokazu Sugita

A sickly nightmare who hates the hospital and needles. He has the power to read people's thoughts and enter dreams. Even though he likes to shut himself away in dreams, Gray drags him out to sulk from time to time. He technically holds a high position and has many subordinates, but since he can't even take care of his own health, he leaves most things to Gray.

Pierce Villiers
VA: Souichirou Hoshi

New to Clover, Pierce is an insomniac mouse who drinks too much coffee. He loves Nightmare (who can help him sleep) and hates Boris (who terrifies him). He dislikes Blood and Vivaldi for discarding coffee in favor of tea. He likes Elliot and Peter well enough, since rabbits aren't natural predators of mice.

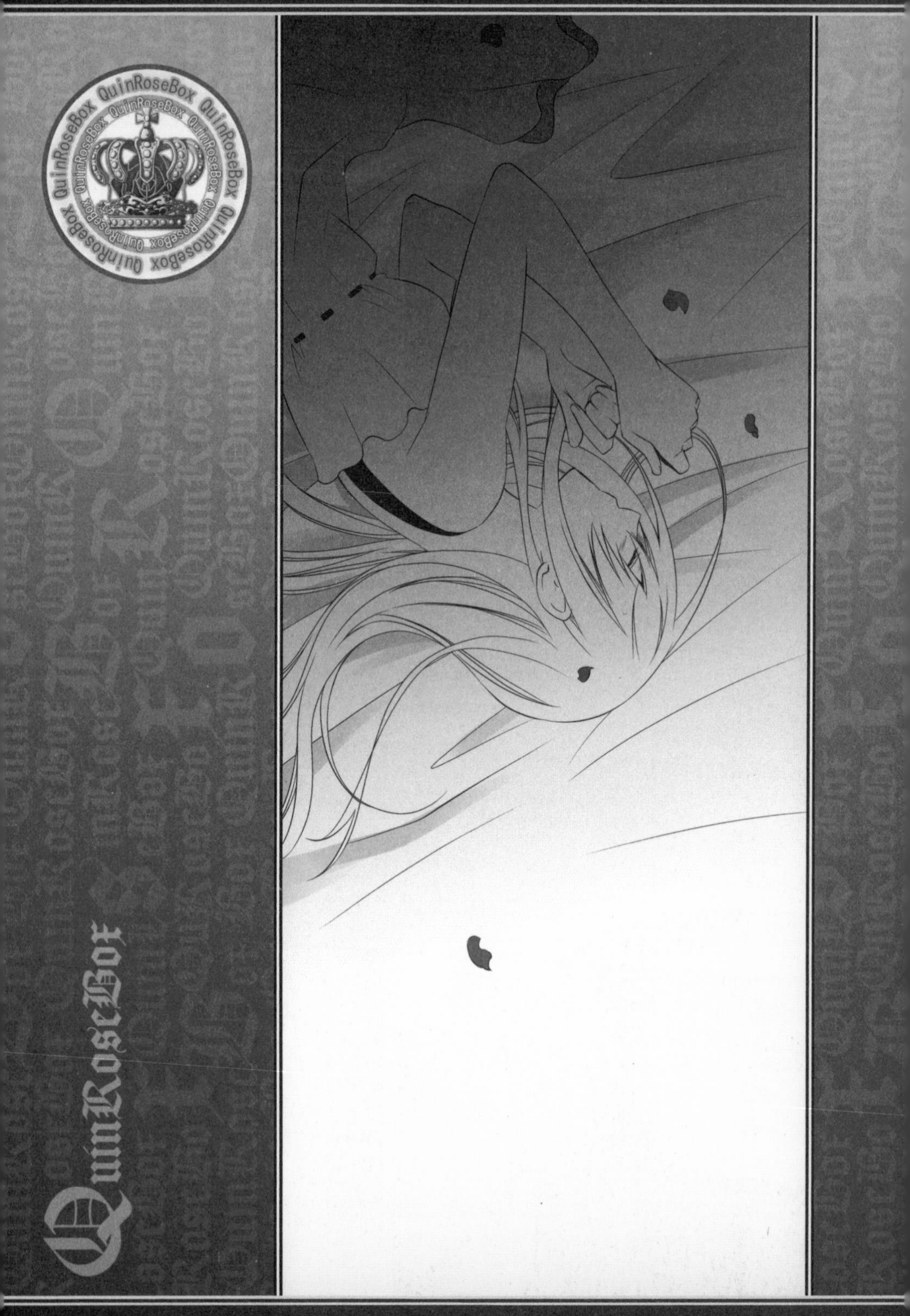
QuinRoseBox

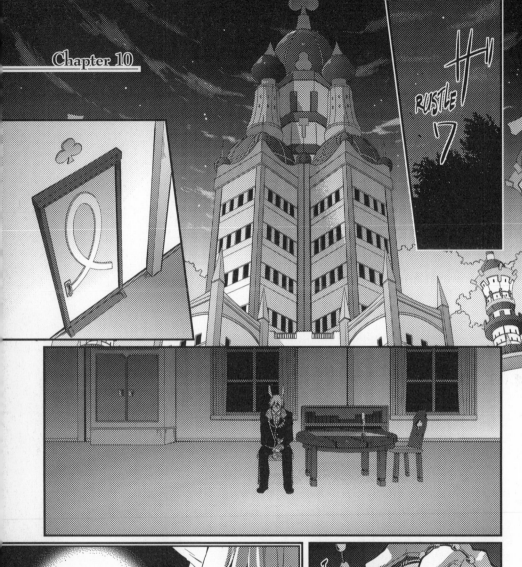

Chapter 10

RUSTLE

SHE'S DREAMING.

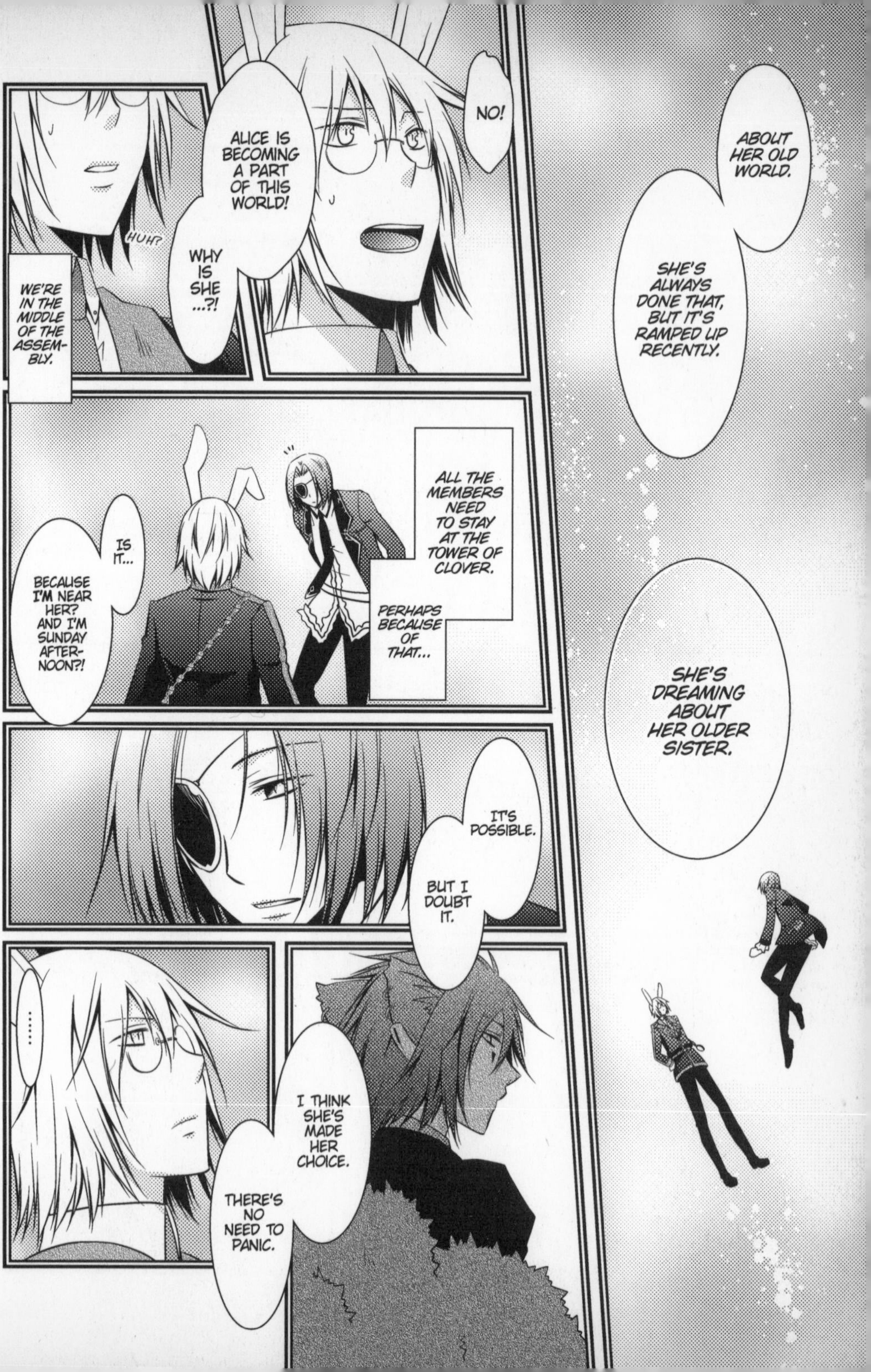
ABOUT HER OLD WORLD.
SHE'S ALWAYS DONE THAT, BUT IT'S RAMPED UP RECENTLY.
SHE'S DREAMING ABOUT HER OLDER SISTER.
NO!
ALICE IS BECOMING A PART OF THIS WORLD!
WHY IS SHE ...?!
HUH?
WE'RE IN THE MIDDLE OF THE ASSEMBLY.
ALL THE MEMBERS NEED TO STAY AT THE TOWER OF CLOVER.
PERHAPS BECAUSE OF THAT...
IS IT...
BECAUSE I'M NEAR HER? AND I'M SUNDAY AFTERNOON?!
IT'S POSSIBLE.
BUT I DOUBT IT.
I THINK SHE'S MADE HER CHOICE.
THERE'S NO NEED TO PANIC.
......

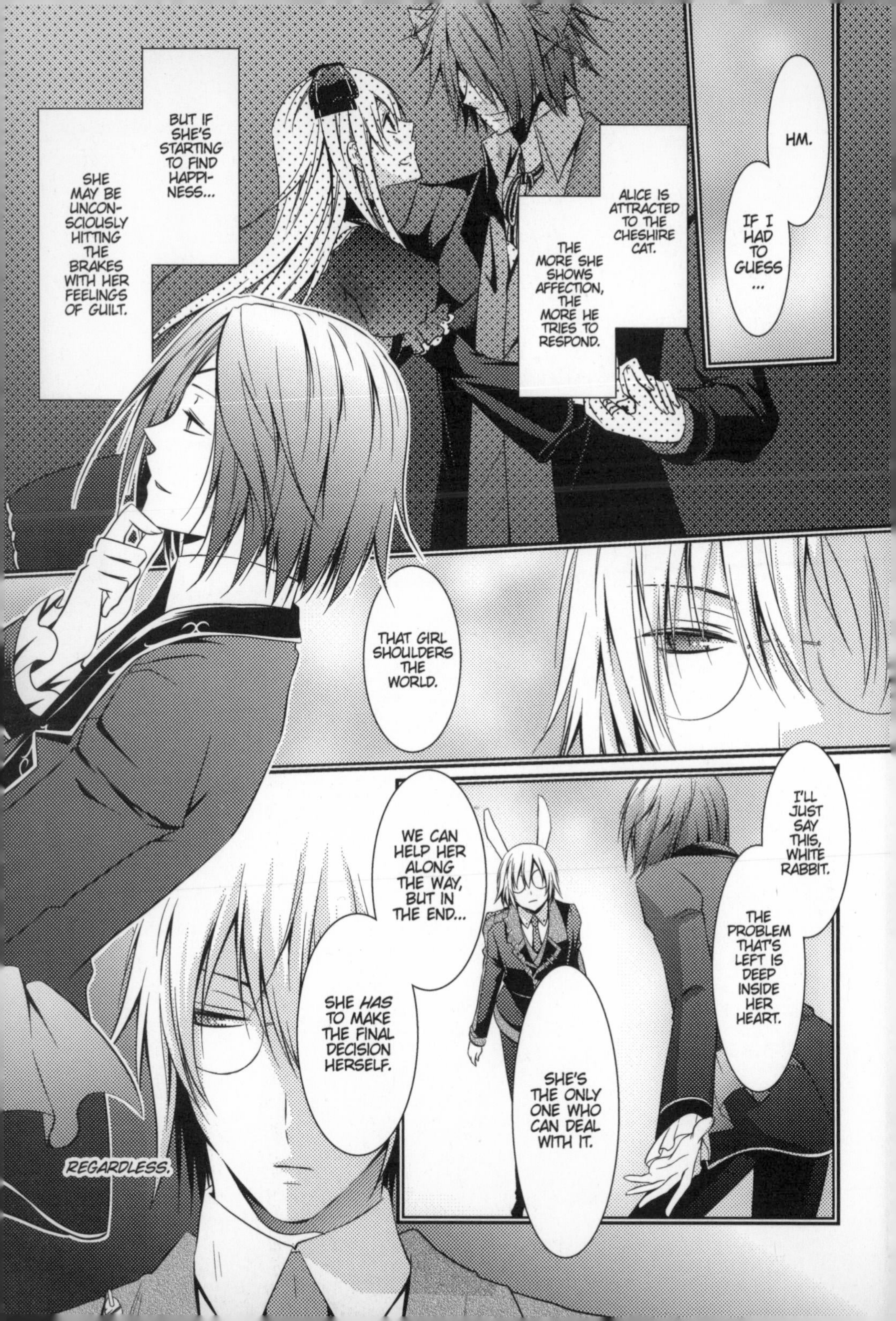
HM.
IF I HAD TO GUESS...
ALICE IS ATTRACTED TO THE CHESHIRE CAT.
THE MORE SHE SHOWS AFFECTION, THE MORE HE TRIES TO RESPOND.
BUT IF SHE'S STARTING TO FIND HAPPINESS...
SHE MAY BE UNCONSCIOUSLY HITTING THE BRAKES WITH HER FEELINGS OF GUILT.
THAT GIRL SHOULDERS THE WORLD.
I'LL JUST SAY THIS, WHITE RABBIT.
THE PROBLEM THAT'S LEFT IS DEEP INSIDE HER HEART.
SHE'S THE ONLY ONE WHO CAN DEAL WITH IT.
WE CAN HELP HER ALONG THE WAY, BUT IN THE END...
SHE *HAS* TO MAKE THE FINAL DECISION HERSELF.
REGARDLESS.

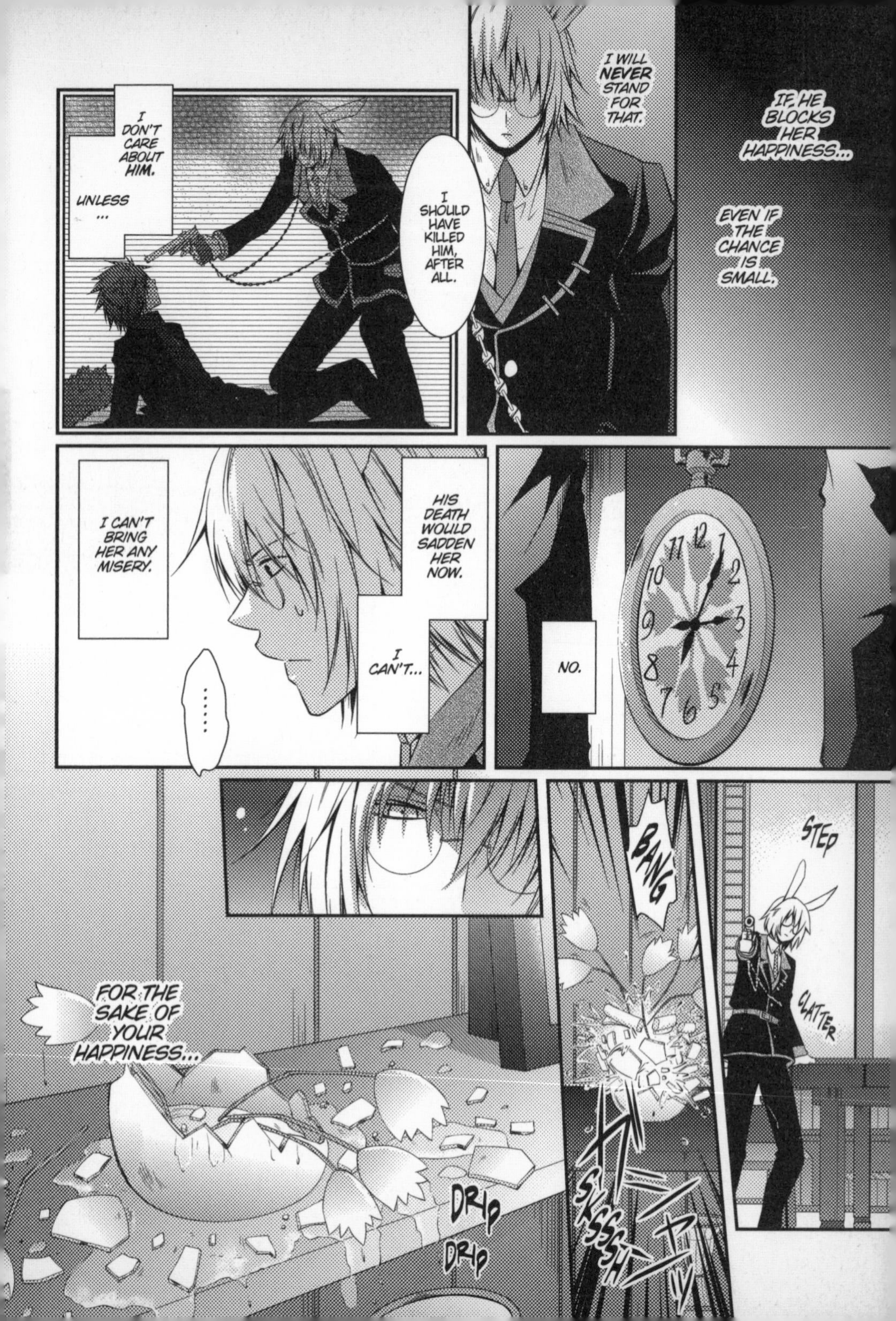
IF HE BLOCKS HER HAPPINESS...
EVEN IF THE CHANCE IS SMALL.
I WILL NEVER STAND FOR THAT.
I SHOULD HAVE KILLED HIM, AFTER ALL.
I DON'T CARE ABOUT HIM.
UNLESS ...
NO.
HIS DEATH WOULD SADDEN HER NOW.
I CAN'T BRING HER ANY MISERY.
I CAN'T...
......
STEP
CLATTER
BANG
FOR THE SAKE OF YOUR HAPPINESS...
DRIP
DRIP
SKSSSH

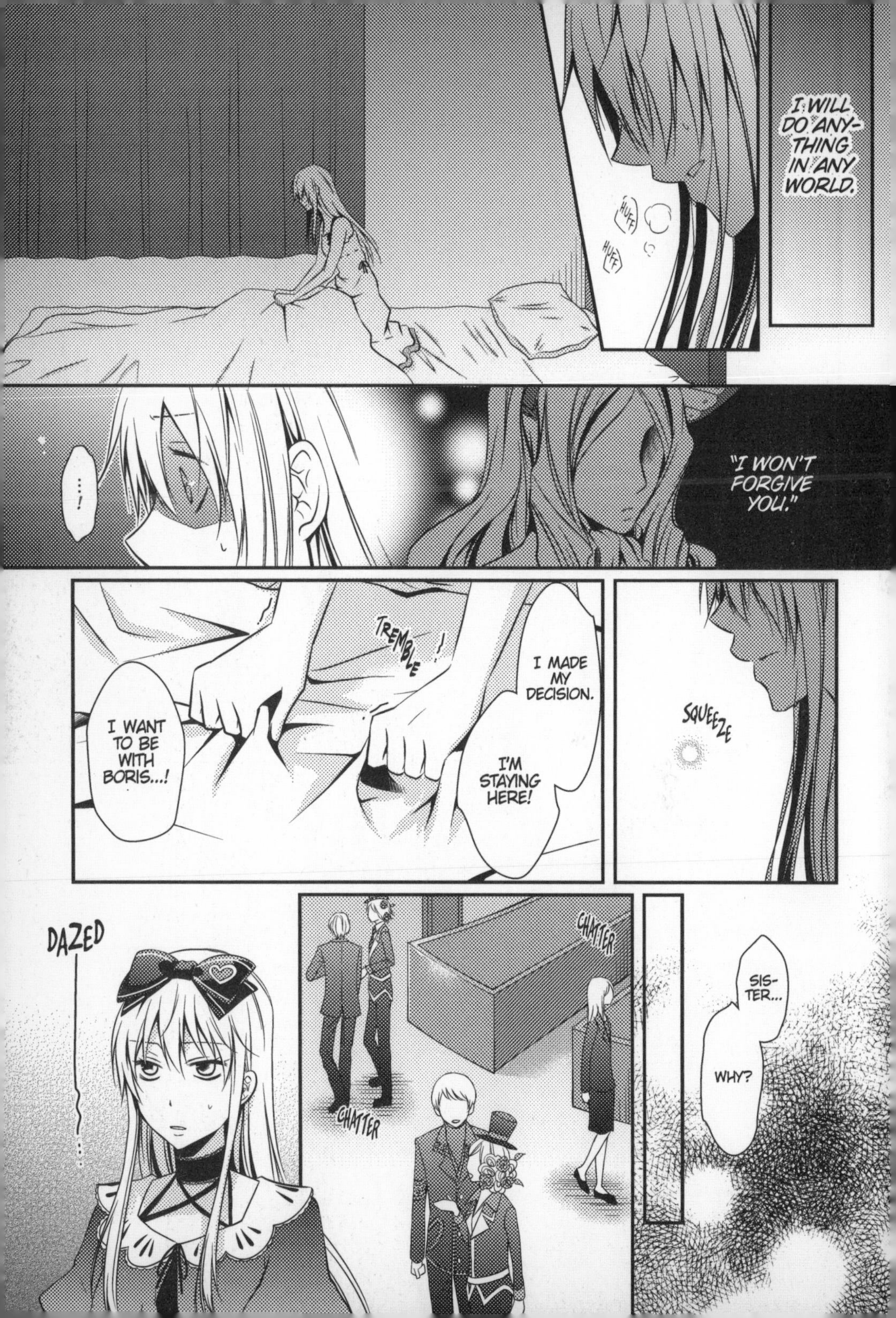
I WILL DO ANY-THING IN ANY WORLD.
HUFF
HUFF
"I WON'T FORGIVE YOU."
...!
SQUEEZE
TREMBLE
I MADE MY DECISION.
I'M STAYING HERE!
I WANT TO BE WITH BORIS...!
SIS-TER...
WHY?
CHATTER
CHATTER
DAZED
......

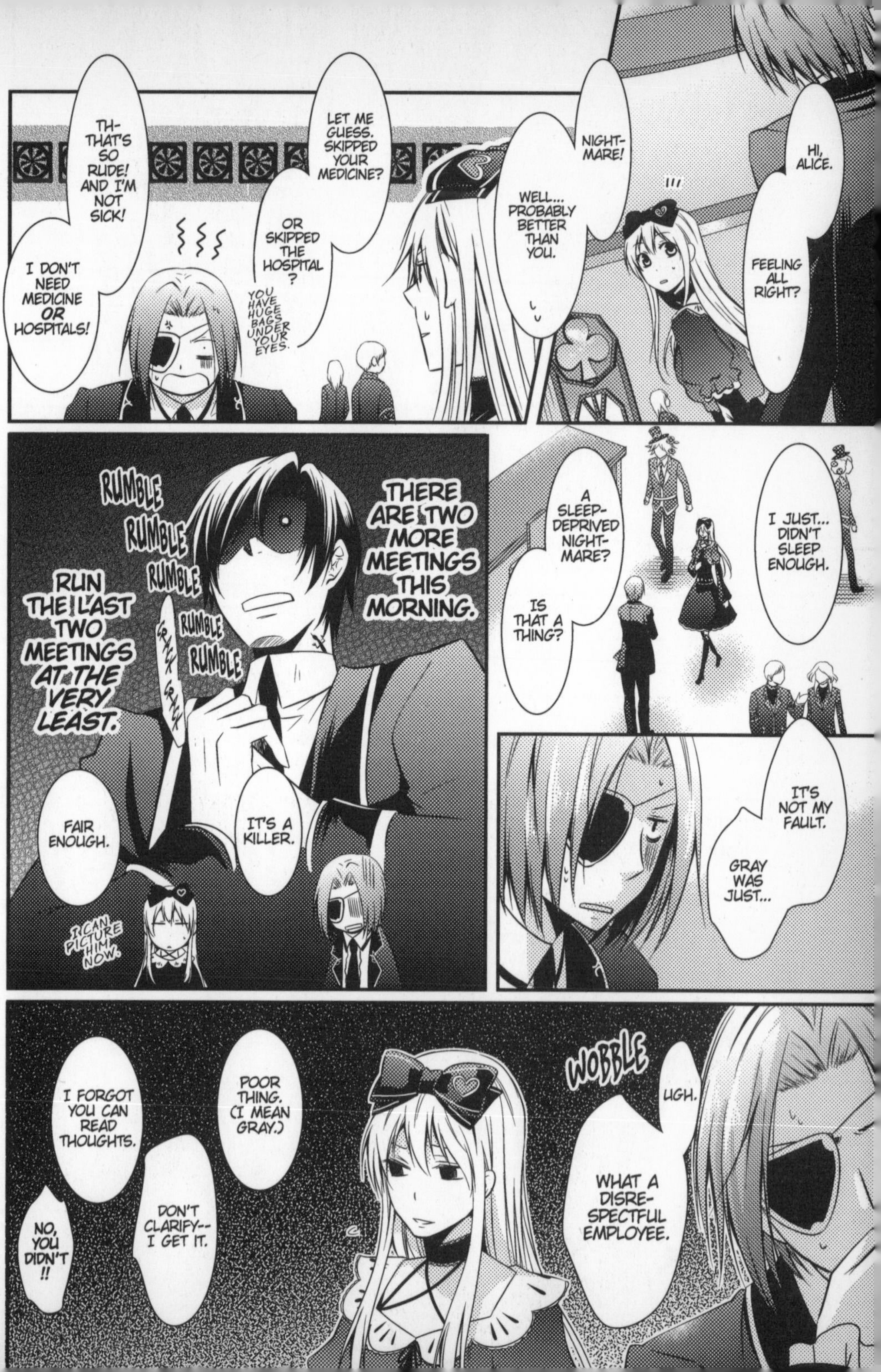
HI, ALICE.
FEELING ALL RIGHT?
NIGHT-MARE!
WELL... PROBABLY BETTER THAN YOU.
LET ME GUESS. SKIPPED YOUR MEDICINE?
OR SKIPPED THE HOSPITAL?
YOU HAVE HUGE BAGS UNDER YOUR EYES.
TH-THAT'S SO RUDE! AND I'M NOT SICK!
I DON'T NEED MEDICINE OR HOSPITALS!
I JUST... DIDN'T SLEEP ENOUGH.
A SLEEP-DEPRIVED NIGHT-MARE?
IS THAT A THING?
IT'S NOT MY FAULT.
GRAY WAS JUST...
THERE ARE TWO MORE MEETINGS THIS MORNING.
RUMBLE RUMBLE RUMBLE RUMBLE RUMBLE
CRACK CRACK
RUN THE LAST TWO MEETINGS AT THE VERY LEAST.
IT'S A KILLER.
FAIR ENOUGH.
I CAN PICTURE HIM, NOW.
WOBBLE
UGH.
WHAT A DISRE-SPECTFUL EMPLOYEE.
POOR THING. (I MEAN GRAY.)
I FORGOT YOU CAN READ THOUGHTS.
DON'T CLARIFY-- I GET IT.
NO, YOU DIDN'T!!

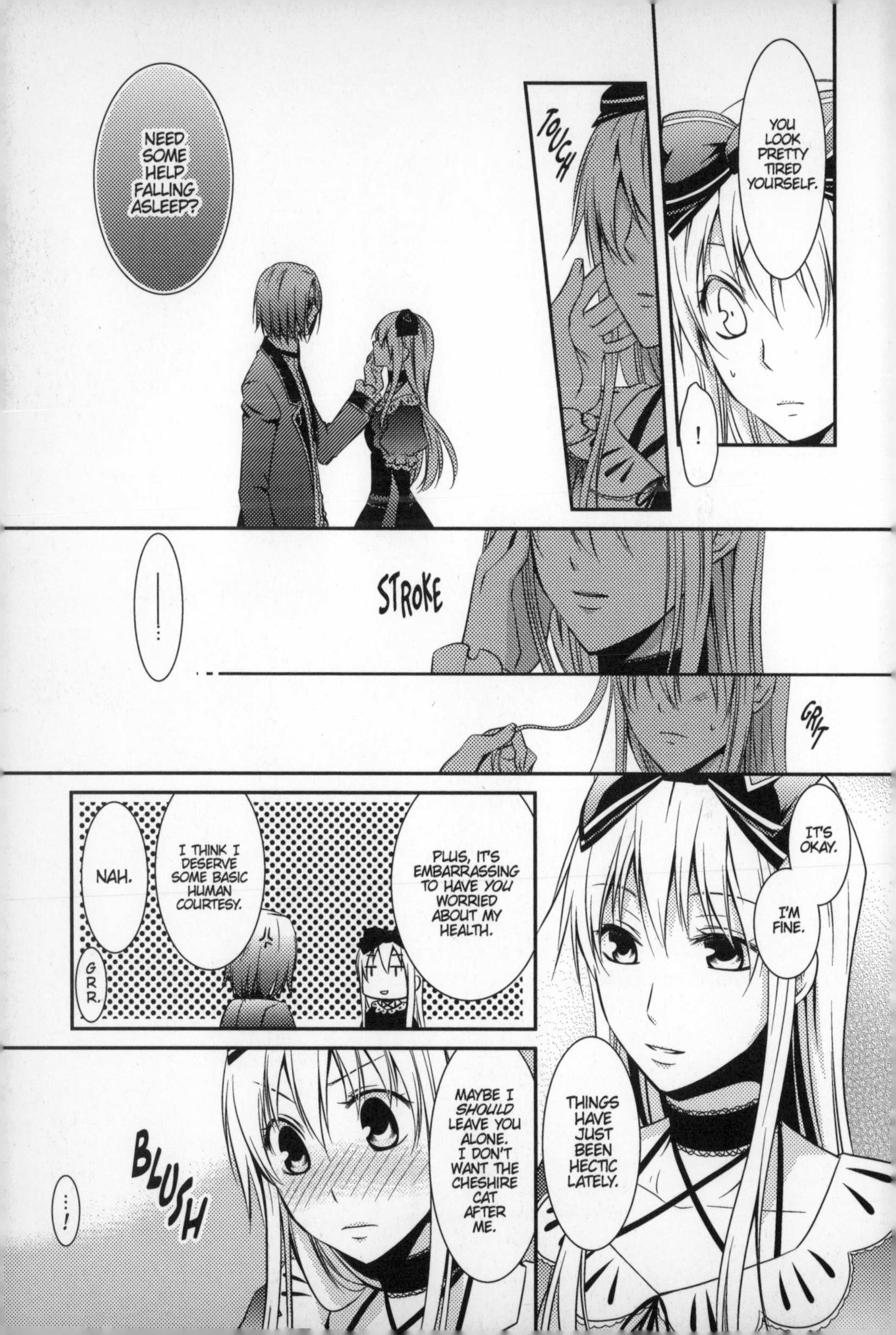
YOU LOOK PRETTY TIRED YOURSELF.
!
TOUCH
NEED SOME HELP FALLING ASLEEP?
STROKE
—!…
GRIT
IT'S OKAY.
I'M FINE.
THINGS HAVE JUST BEEN HECTIC LATELY.
PLUS, IT'S EMBARRASSING TO HAVE *YOU* WORRIED ABOUT MY HEALTH.
I THINK I DESERVE SOME BASIC HUMAN COURTESY.
NAH.
GRR.
MAYBE I *SHOULD* LEAVE YOU ALONE. I DON'T WANT THE CHESHIRE CAT AFTER ME.
BLUSH
…!

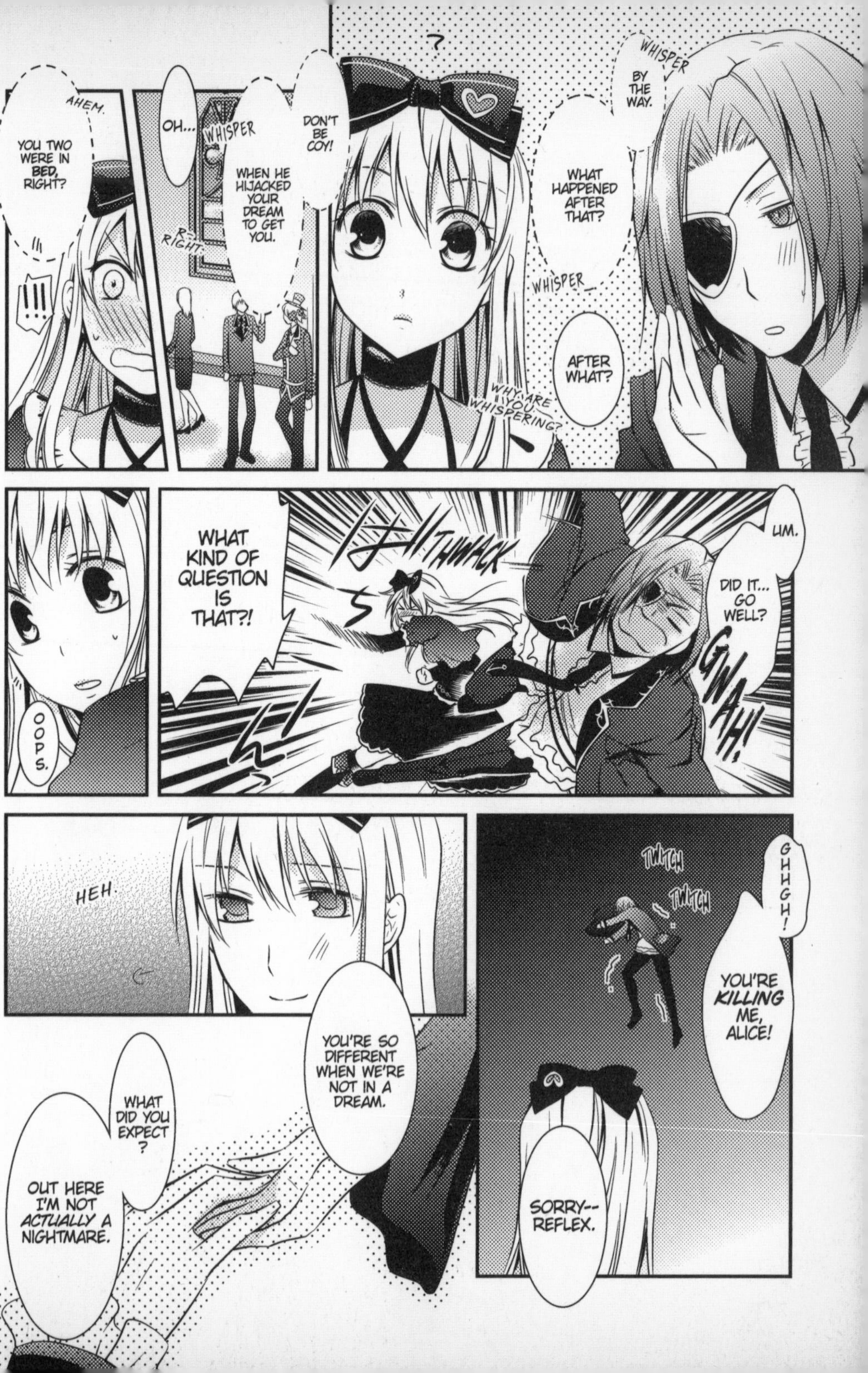
?
WHISPER
BY THE WAY.
WHAT HAPPENED AFTER THAT?
WHISPER
AFTER WHAT?
WHY ARE YOU WHISPERING?
DON'T BE COY!
WHISPER
WHEN HE HIJACKED YOUR DREAM TO GET YOU.
OH...
R-RIGHT.
AHEM.
YOU TWO WERE IN BED, RIGHT?
!!!
UM.
DID IT... GO WELL?
WHAT KIND OF QUESTION IS THAT?!
THWACK
GWAH!
OOPS.
GHHGH!
TWITCH
TWITCH
YOU'RE KILLING ME, ALICE!
SORRY-- REFLEX.
HEH.
YOU'RE SO DIFFERENT WHEN WE'RE NOT IN A DREAM.
WHAT DID YOU EXPECT?
OUT HERE I'M NOT ACTUALLY A NIGHTMARE.

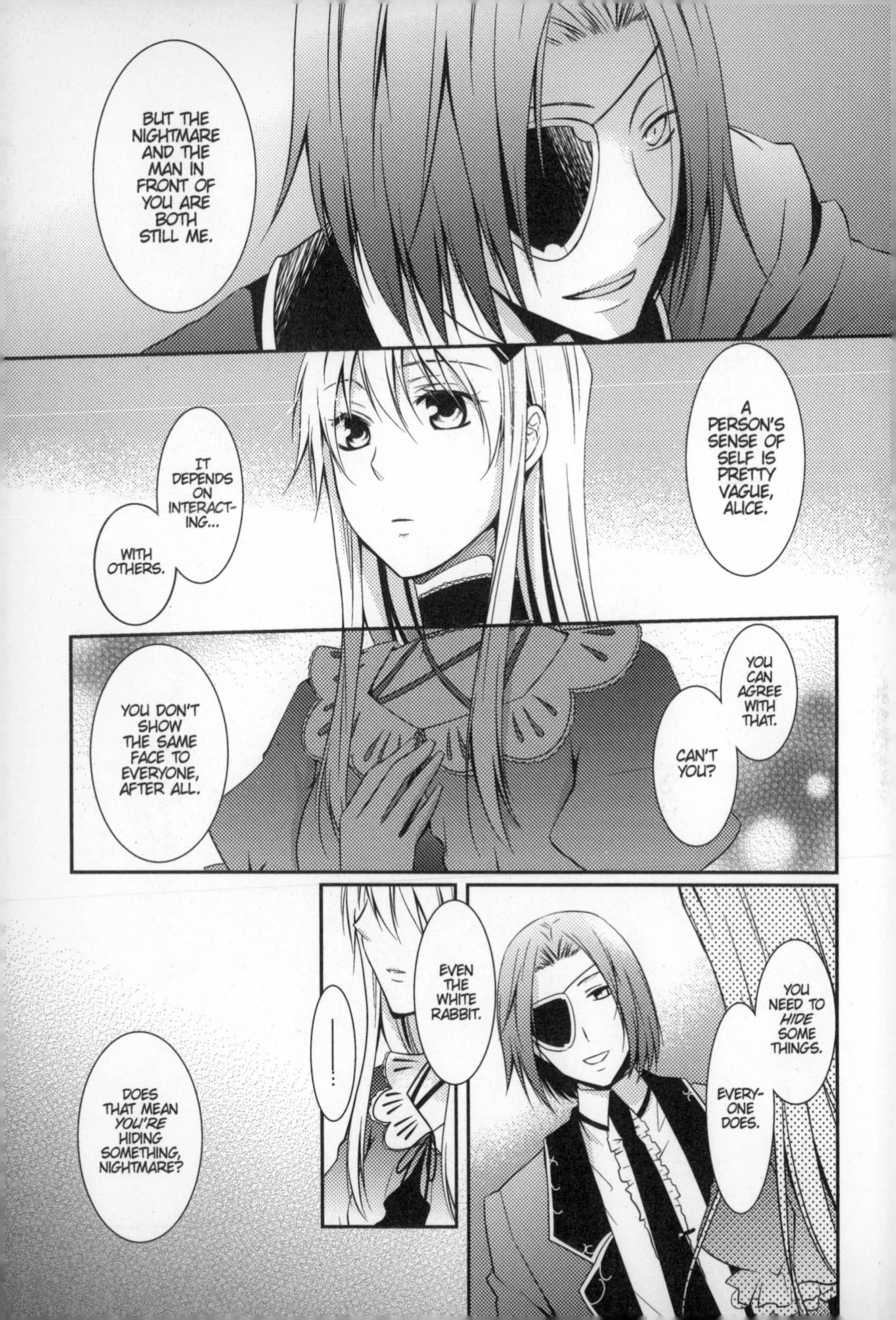
BUT THE NIGHTMARE AND THE MAN IN FRONT OF YOU ARE BOTH STILL ME.
A PERSON'S SENSE OF SELF IS PRETTY VAGUE, ALICE.
IT DEPENDS ON INTERACTING...
WITH OTHERS.
YOU CAN AGREE WITH THAT.
CAN'T YOU?
YOU DON'T SHOW THE SAME FACE TO EVERYONE, AFTER ALL.
YOU NEED TO *HIDE* SOME THINGS.
EVERYONE DOES.
EVEN THE WHITE RABBIT.
...!
DOES THAT MEAN *YOU'RE* HIDING SOMETHING, NIGHTMARE?

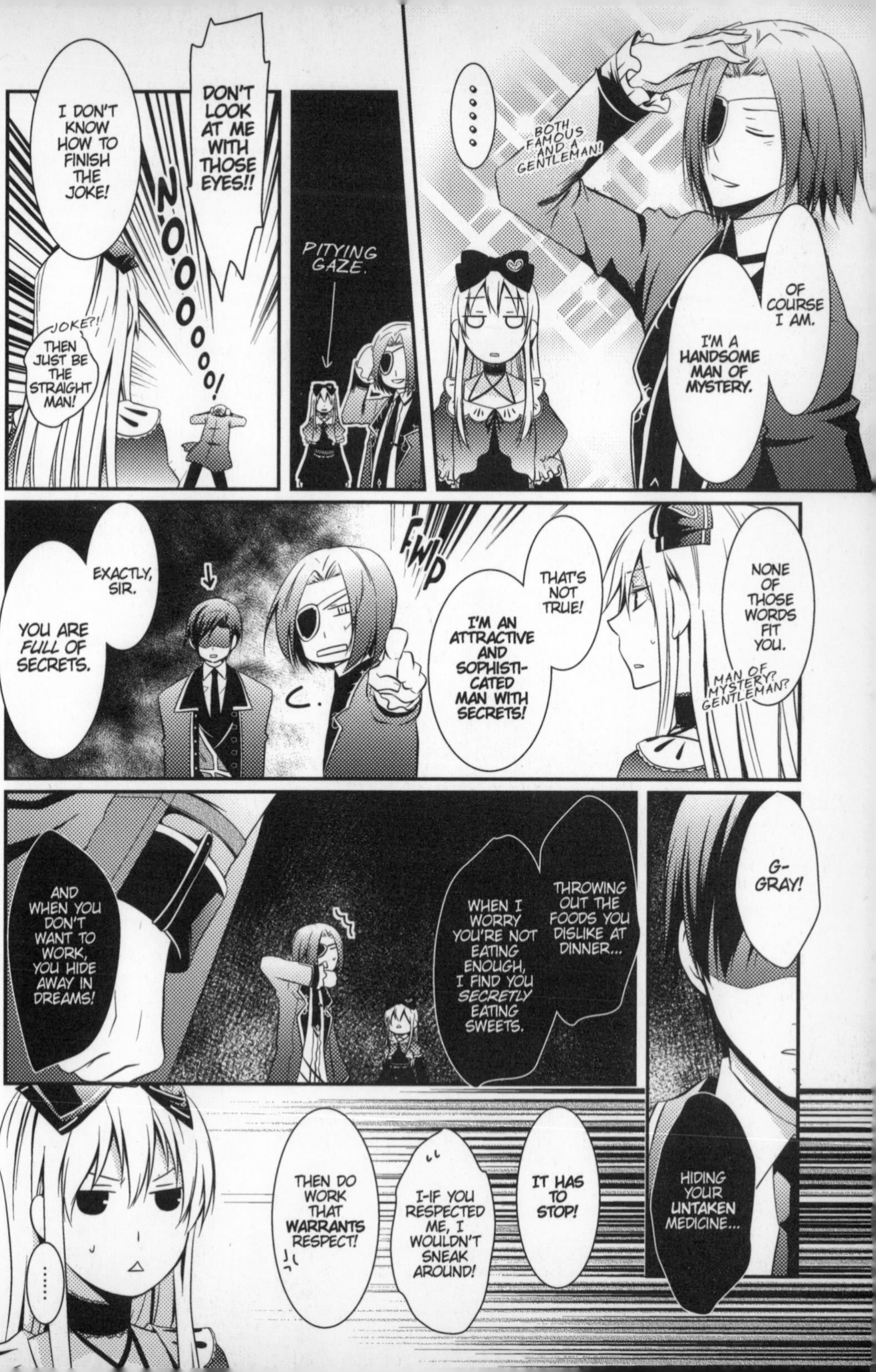

OF COURSE I AM.
I'M A HANDSOME MAN OF MYSTERY.
BOTH FAMOUS AND A GENTLEMAN!
.....
PITYING GAZE.
DON'T LOOK AT ME WITH THOSE EYES!!
NOOOOOOO!
I DON'T KNOW HOW TO FINISH THE JOKE!
JOKE?! THEN JUST BE THE STRAIGHT MAN!
NONE OF THOSE WORDS FIT YOU.
MAN OF MYSTERY? GENTLEMAN?
FWP
THAT'S NOT TRUE!
I'M AN ATTRACTIVE AND SOPHISTICATED MAN WITH SECRETS!
EXACTLY, SIR.
YOU ARE FULL OF SECRETS.
G-GRAY!
HIDING YOUR UNTAKEN MEDICINE...
THROWING OUT THE FOODS YOU DISLIKE AT DINNER...
WHEN I WORRY YOU'RE NOT EATING ENOUGH, I FIND YOU SECRETLY EATING SWEETS.
AND WHEN YOU DON'T WANT TO WORK, YOU HIDE AWAY IN DREAMS!
IT HAS TO STOP!
I-IF YOU RESPECTED ME, I WOULDN'T SNEAK AROUND!
THEN DO WORK THAT WARRANTS RESPECT!
......

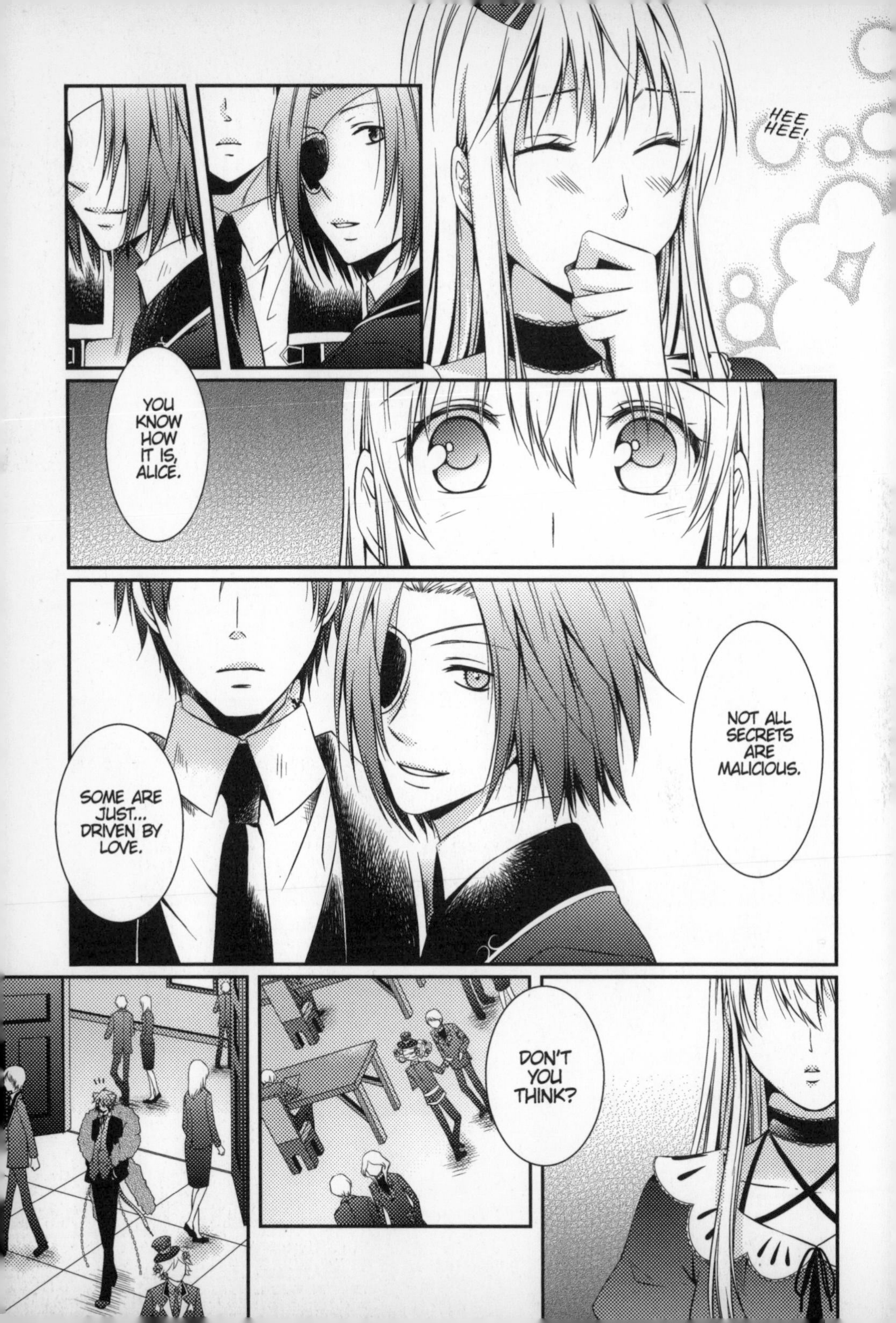
HEE HEE!
YOU KNOW HOW IT IS, ALICE.
NOT ALL SECRETS ARE MALICIOUS.
SOME ARE JUST... DRIVEN BY LOVE.
DON'T YOU THINK?

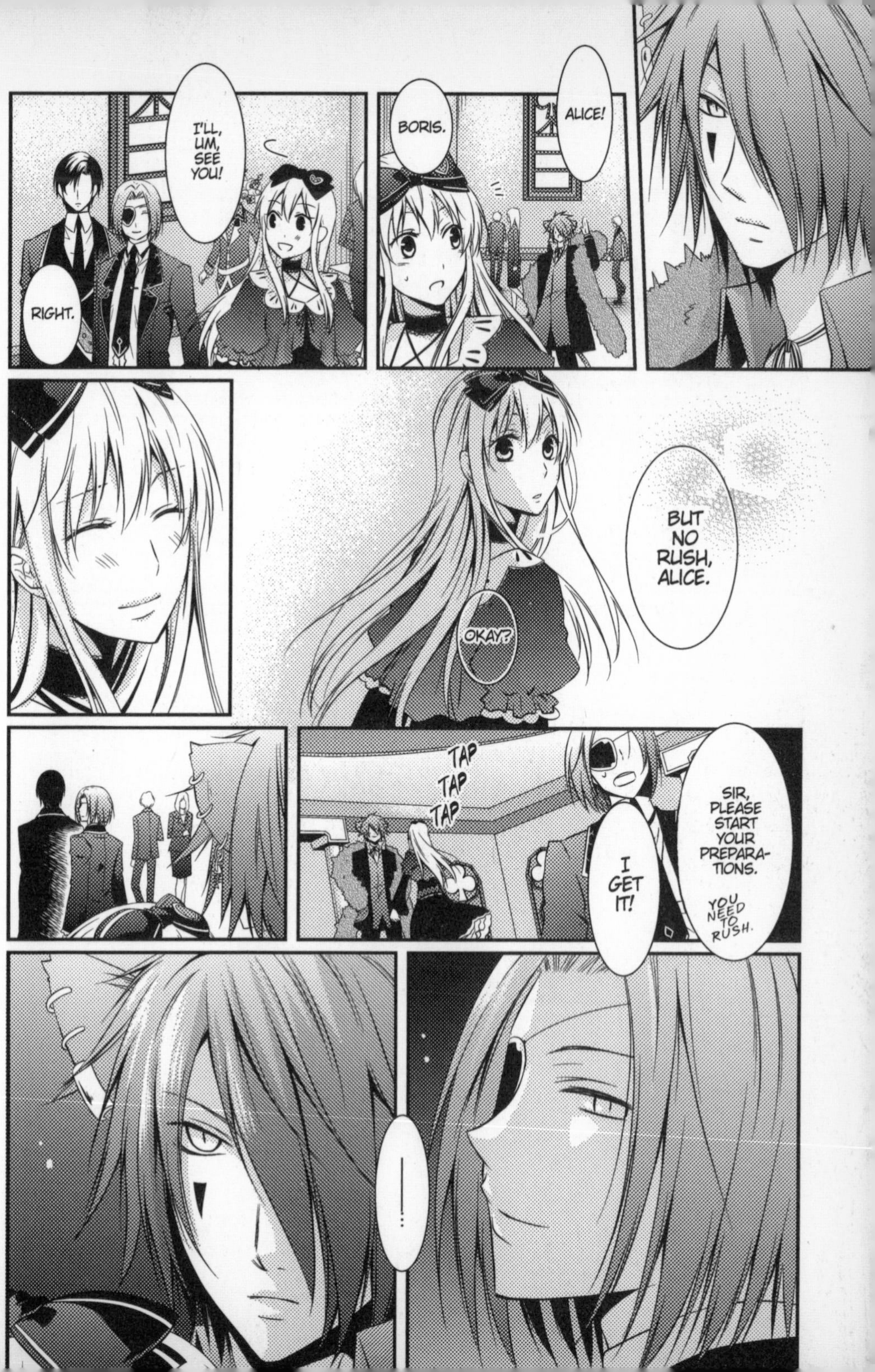
ALICE!
BORIS.
I'LL, UM, SEE YOU!
RIGHT.
BUT NO RUSH, ALICE.
OKAY?
SIR, PLEASE START YOUR PREPARATIONS.
YOU NEED TO RUSH.
I GET IT!
TAP TAP TAP
......!

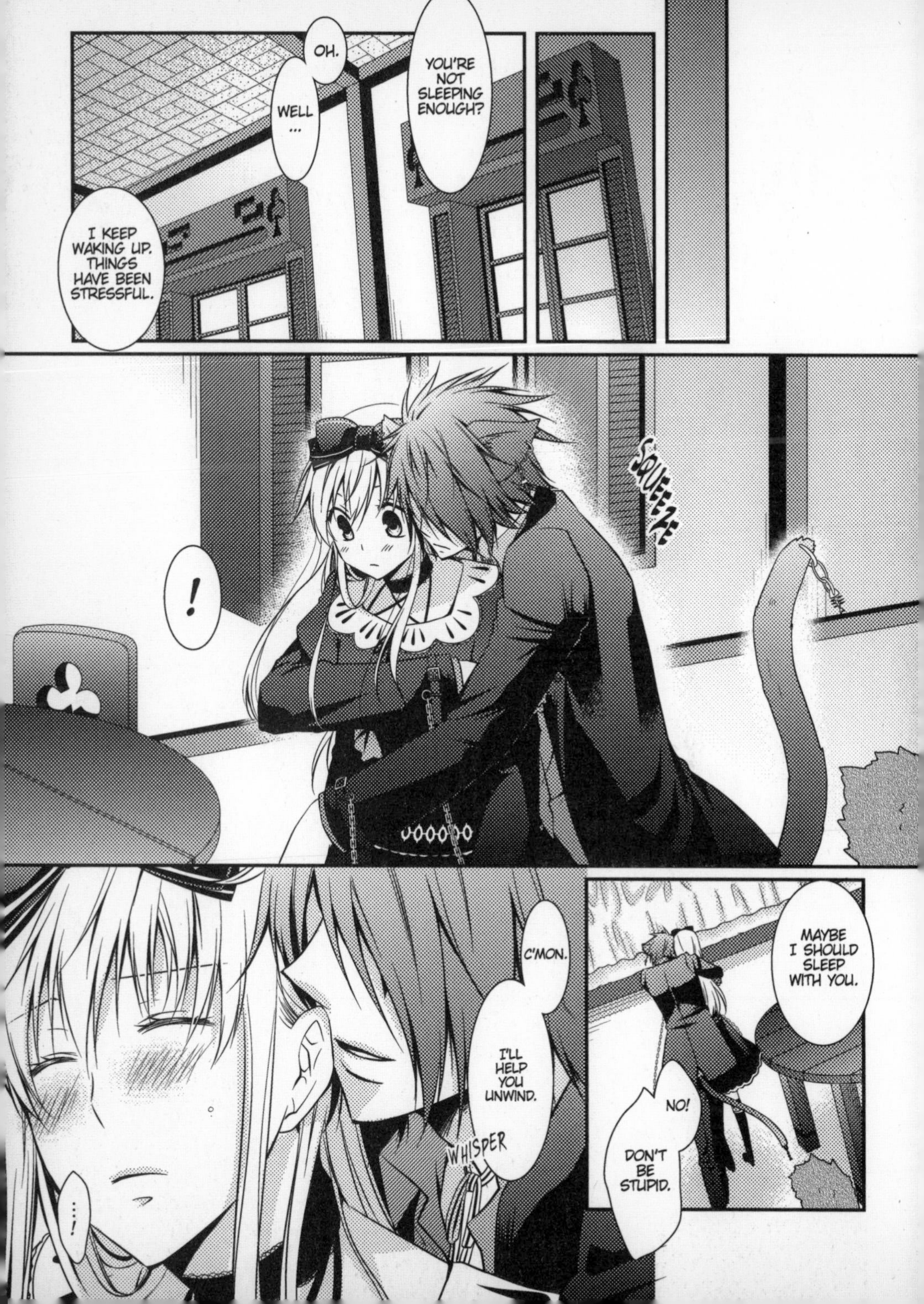
YOU'RE NOT SLEEPING ENOUGH?
OH.
WELL ...
I KEEP WAKING UP. THINGS HAVE BEEN STRESSFUL.
SQUEEZE
!
MAYBE I SHOULD SLEEP WITH YOU.
NO!
DON'T BE STUPID.
C'MON.
I'LL HELP YOU UNWIND.
WHISPER
...!

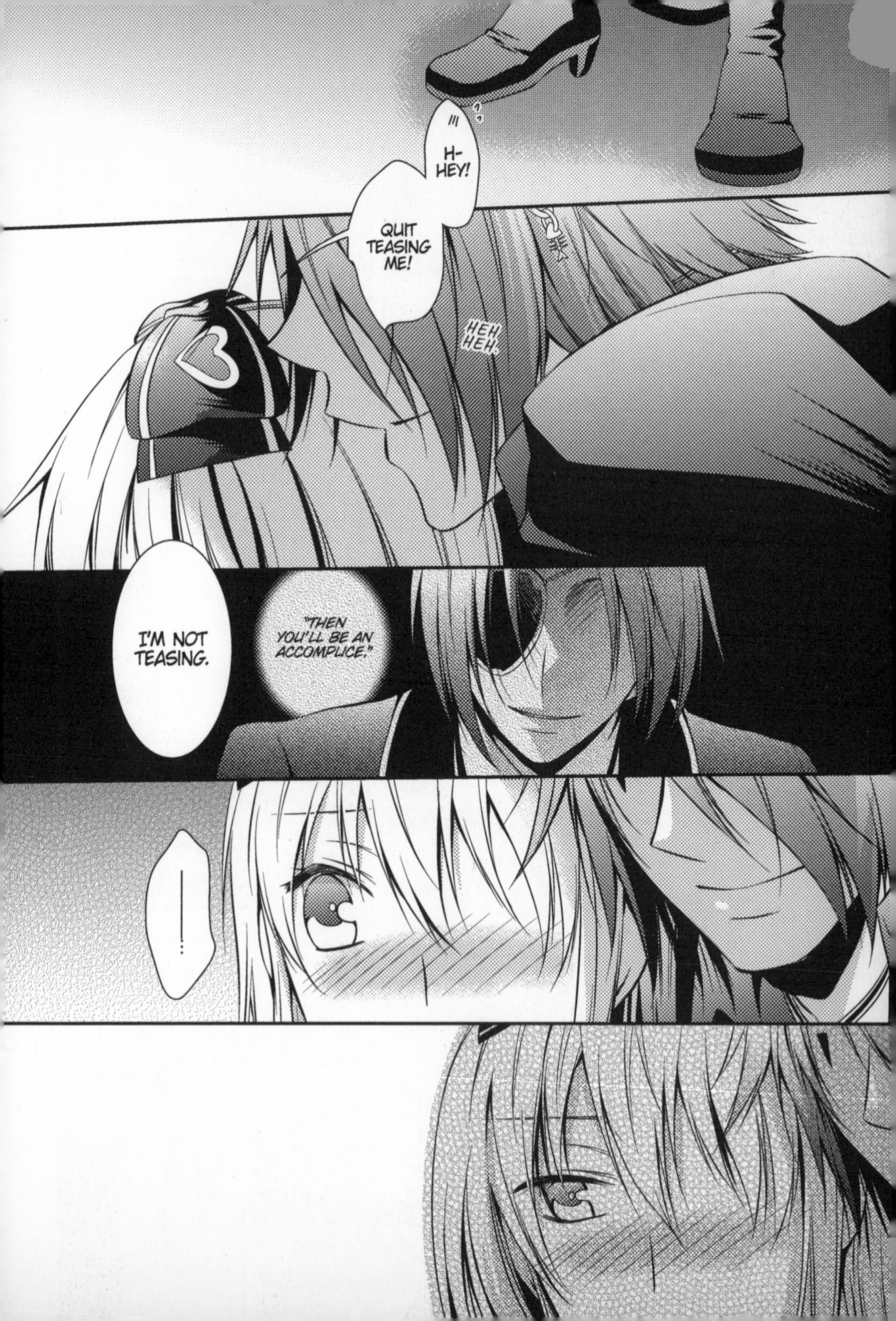
///
H- HEY!
QUIT TEASING ME!
HEH HEH.
"THEN YOU'LL BE AN ACCOMPLICE."
I'M NOT TEASING.
!...

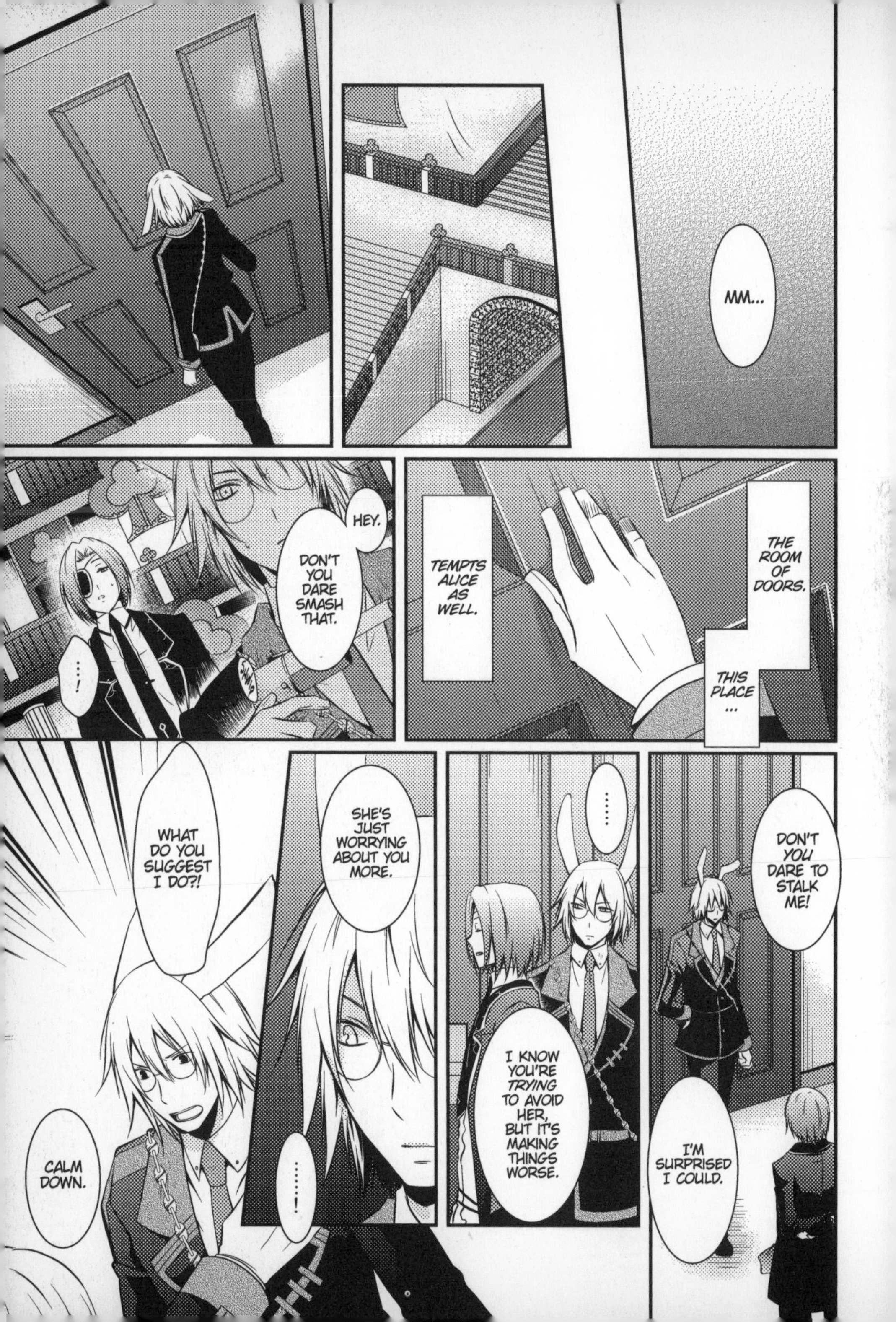
MM...
THE ROOM OF DOORS.
THIS PLACE ...
TEMPTS ALICE AS WELL.
HEY.
DON'T YOU DARE SMASH THAT.
...!
DON'T YOU DARE TO STALK ME!
I'M SURPRISED I COULD.
......
I KNOW YOU'RE TRYING TO AVOID HER, BUT IT'S MAKING THINGS WORSE.
SHE'S JUST WORRYING ABOUT YOU MORE.
......!
WHAT DO YOU SUGGEST I DO?!
CALM DOWN.

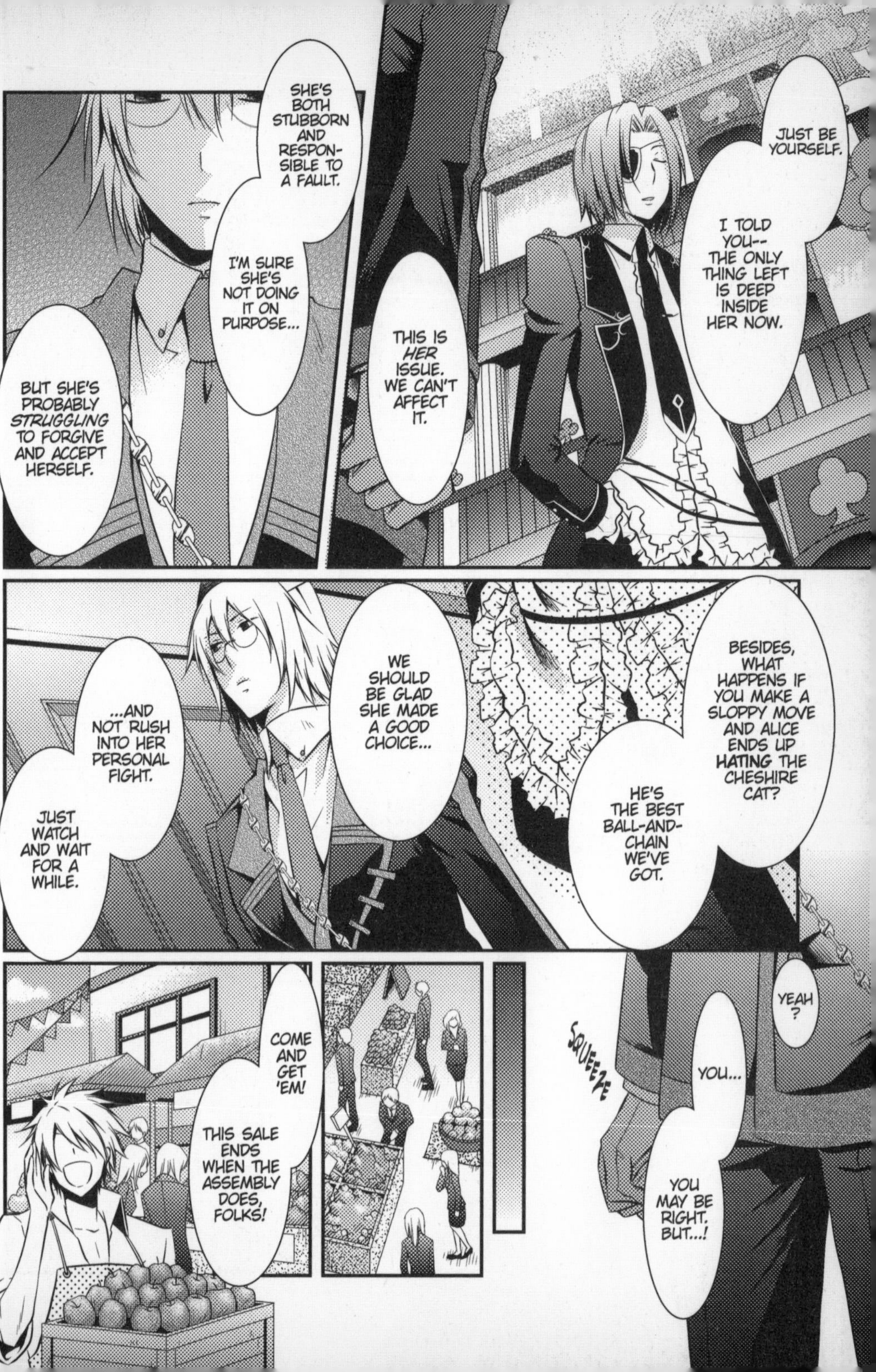
JUST BE YOURSELF.
I TOLD YOU-- THE ONLY THING LEFT IS DEEP INSIDE HER NOW.
THIS IS *HER* ISSUE. WE CAN'T AFFECT IT.
SHE'S BOTH STUBBORN AND RESPONSIBLE TO A FAULT.
I'M SURE SHE'S NOT DOING IT ON PURPOSE...
BUT SHE'S PROBABLY *STRUGGLING* TO FORGIVE AND ACCEPT HERSELF.
BESIDES, WHAT HAPPENS IF YOU MAKE A SLOPPY MOVE AND ALICE ENDS UP **HATING** THE CHESHIRE CAT?
HE'S THE BEST BALL-AND-CHAIN WE'VE GOT.
WE SHOULD BE GLAD SHE MADE A GOOD CHOICE...
...AND NOT RUSH INTO HER PERSONAL FIGHT.
JUST WATCH AND WAIT FOR A WHILE.
YEAH?
SQUEEZE
YOU...
YOU MAY BE RIGHT. BUT...!
COME AND GET 'EM!
THIS SALE ENDS WHEN THE ASSEMBLY DOES, FOLKS!

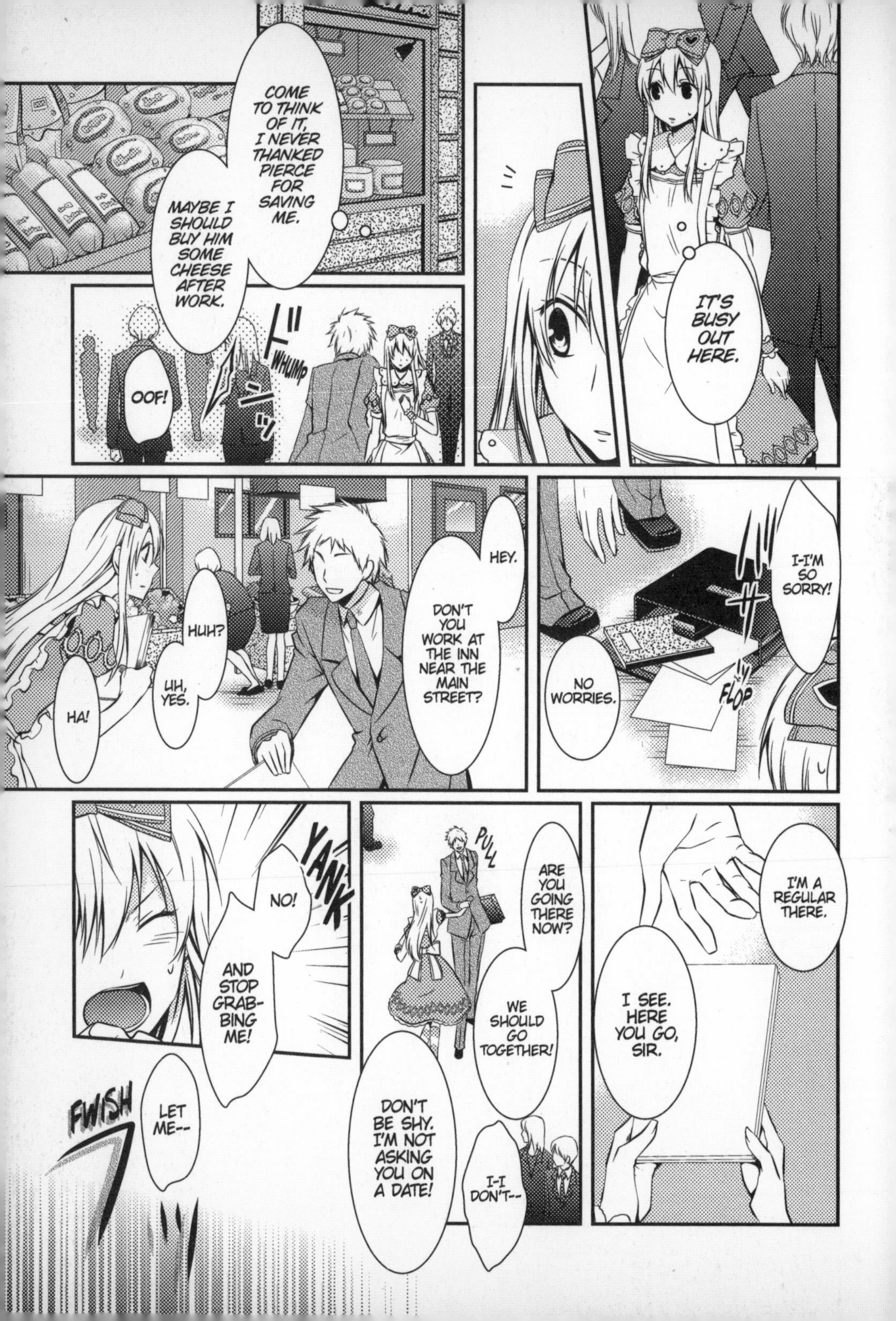
IT'S BUSY OUT HERE.
COME TO THINK OF IT, I NEVER THANKED PIERCE FOR SAVING ME.
MAYBE I SHOULD BUY HIM SOME CHEESE AFTER WORK.
WHUMP
OOF!
I-I'M SO SORRY!
NO WORRIES.
FLOP
HEY.
DON'T YOU WORK AT THE INN NEAR THE MAIN STREET?
HUH?
UH, YES.
HA!
I'M A REGULAR THERE.
I SEE. HERE YOU GO, SIR.
PULL
ARE YOU GOING THERE NOW?
WE SHOULD GO TOGETHER!
I-I DON'T--
DON'T BE SHY. I'M NOT ASKING YOU ON A DATE!
YANK
NO!
AND STOP GRABBING ME!
LET ME--
FWISH

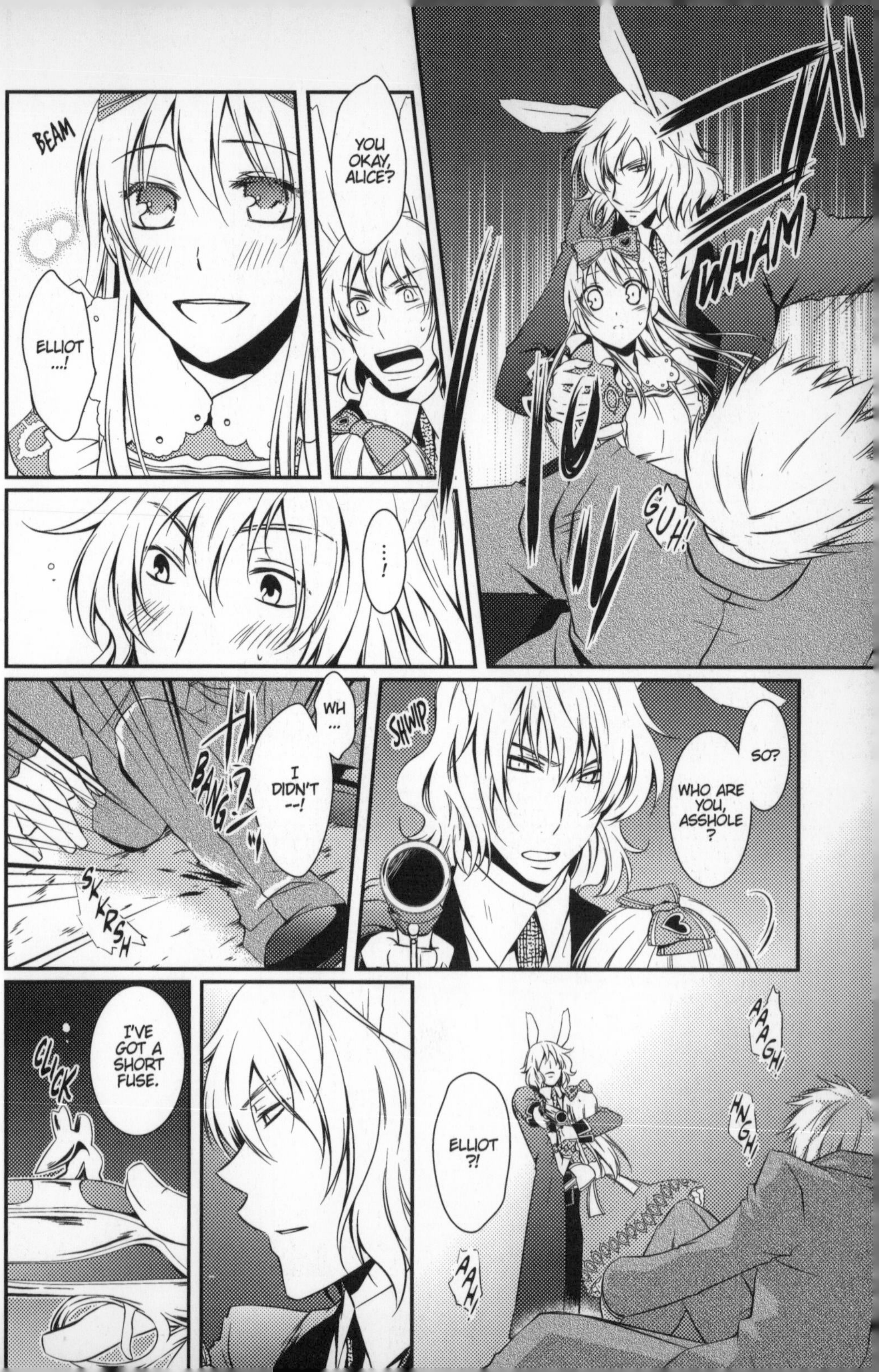
WHAM
GUH!
YOU OKAY, ALICE?
BEAM
ELLIOT ...!
...!
SHWIP
SO?
WHO ARE YOU, ASSHOLE?
WH ...
I DIDN'T --!
BANG!
SKRSH
AAAGH!
HNGH!
ELLIOT ?!
AAH
I'VE GOT A SHORT FUSE.
CLICK

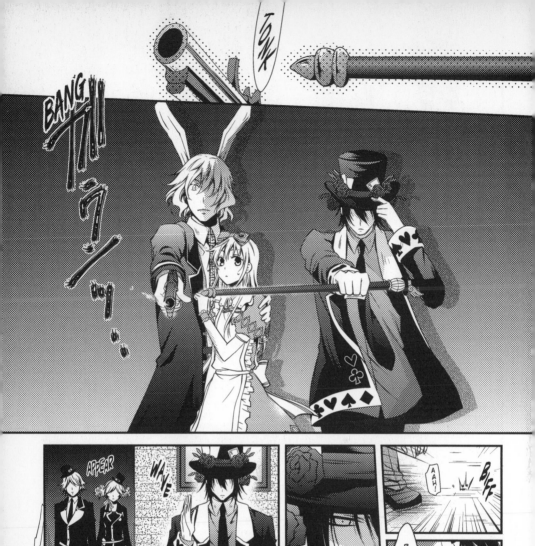

BANG

TONK

APPEAR

WAVE

THRASH

HUH?!

KICK

ELLIOT.

YEAH.

NO!

ST-STOP!

AAH!

BIFF

BLOOD.

SLIDE

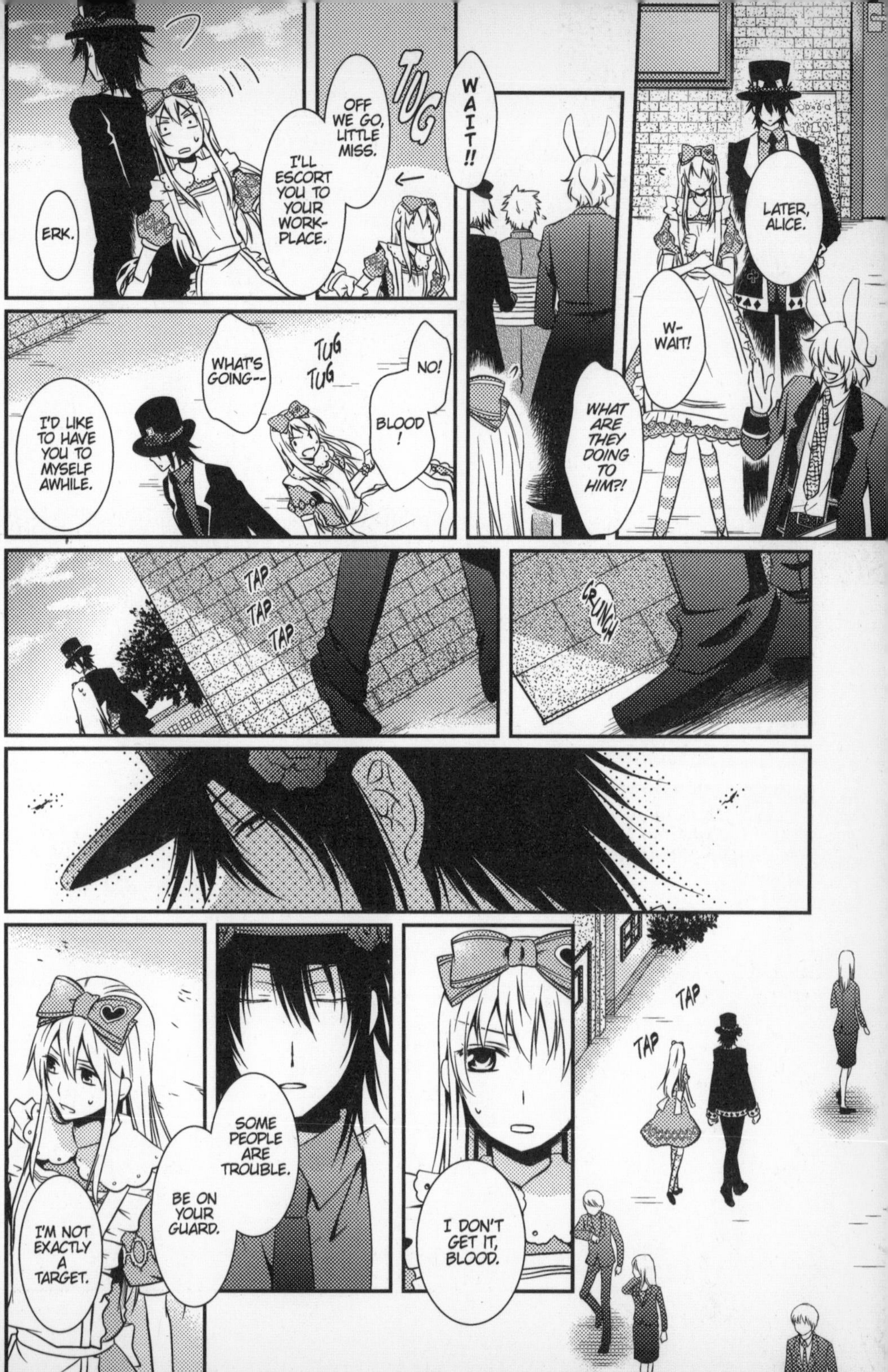
LATER, ALICE.
W-WAIT!
WHAT ARE THEY DOING TO HIM?!
WAIT!!
TUG
OFF WE GO, LITTLE MISS.
I'LL ESCORT YOU TO YOUR WORK-PLACE.
ERK.
NO!
BLOOD!
TUG TUG
WHAT'S GOING--
I'D LIKE TO HAVE YOU TO MYSELF AWHILE.
CRUNCH
TAP TAP TAP
TAP
TAP
I DON'T GET IT, BLOOD.
SOME PEOPLE ARE TROUBLE.
BE ON YOUR GUARD.
I'M NOT EXACTLY A TARGET.

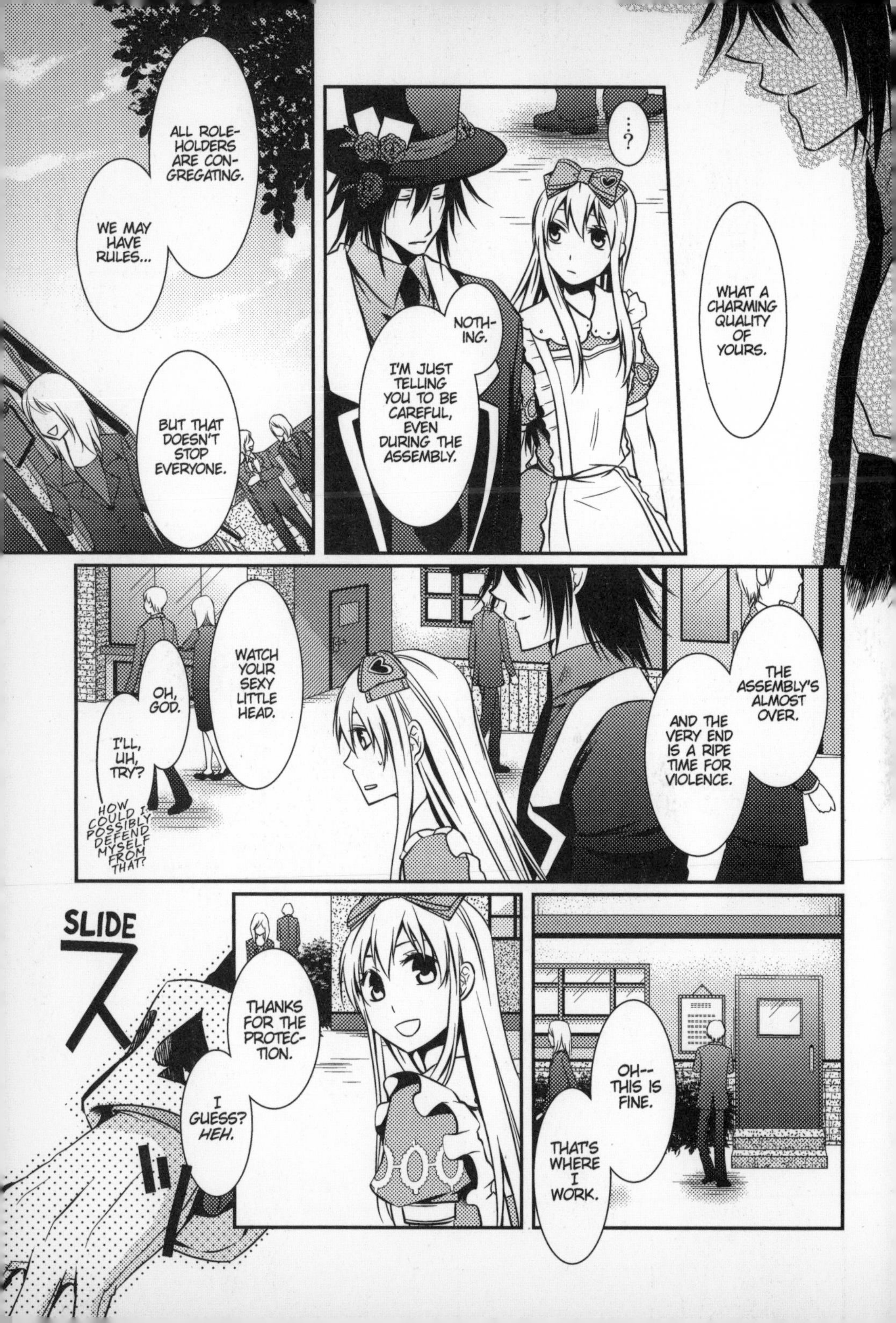
WHAT A CHARMING QUALITY OF YOURS.
...?
NOTHING.
I'M JUST TELLING YOU TO BE CAREFUL, EVEN DURING THE ASSEMBLY.
ALL ROLE-HOLDERS ARE CONGREGATING.
WE MAY HAVE RULES...
BUT THAT DOESN'T STOP EVERYONE.
THE ASSEMBLY'S ALMOST OVER.
AND THE VERY END IS A RIPE TIME FOR VIOLENCE.
WATCH YOUR SEXY LITTLE HEAD.
OH, GOD.
I'LL, UH, TRY?
HOW COULD I POSSIBLY DEFEND MYSELF FROM THAT?
OH-- THIS IS FINE.
THAT'S WHERE I WORK.
THANKS FOR THE PROTECTION.
I GUESS? HEH.
SLIDE
ス

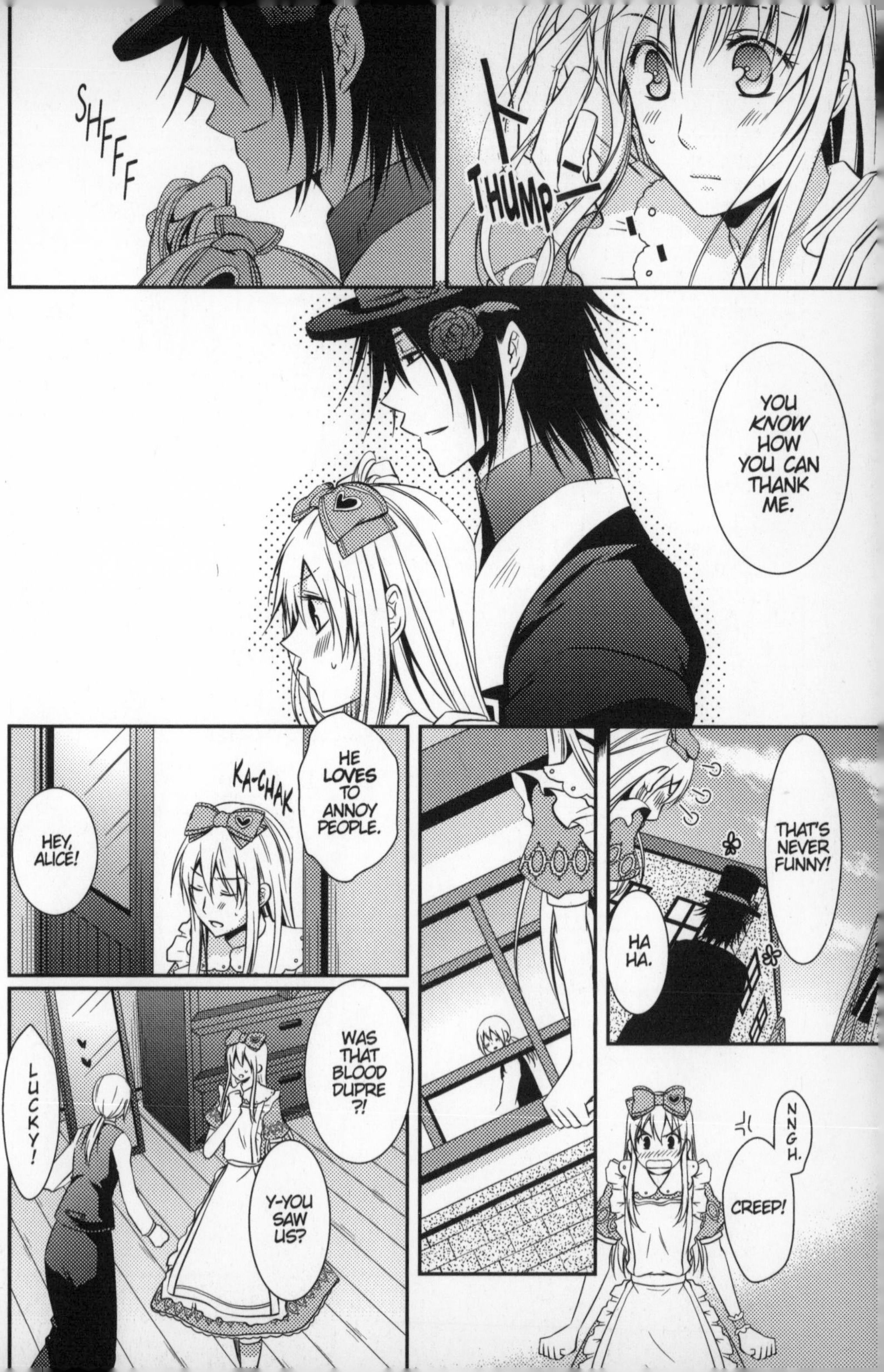
THUMP
SHFFFF
YOU KNOW HOW YOU CAN THANK ME.
THAT'S NEVER FUNNY!
HA HA.
NNGH.
CREEP!
HE LOVES TO ANNOY PEOPLE.
KA-CHAK
HEY, ALICE!
WAS THAT BLOOD DUPRE?!
LUCKY!
Y-YOU SAW US?

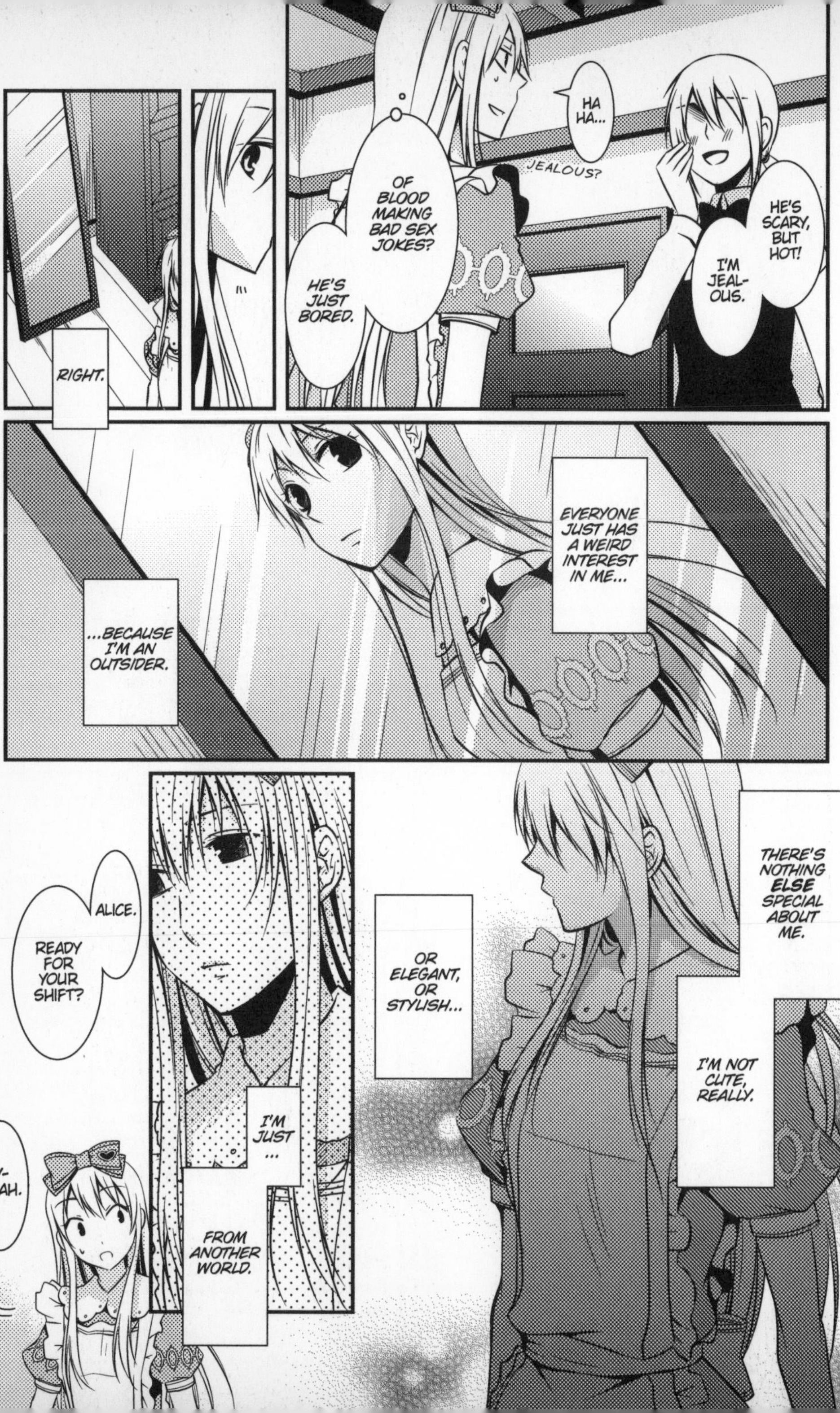
HE'S SCARY, BUT HOT!
I'M JEAL-OUS.
HA HA...
JEALOUS?
OF BLOOD MAKING BAD SEX JOKES?
HE'S JUST BORED.
RIGHT.
EVERYONE JUST HAS A WEIRD INTEREST IN ME...
...BECAUSE I'M AN OUTSIDER.
THERE'S NOTHING ELSE SPECIAL ABOUT ME.
I'M NOT CUTE, REALLY.
OR ELEGANT, OR STYLISH...
I'M JUST ...
FROM ANOTHER WORLD.
ALICE.
READY FOR YOUR SHIFT?
Y-YEAH.

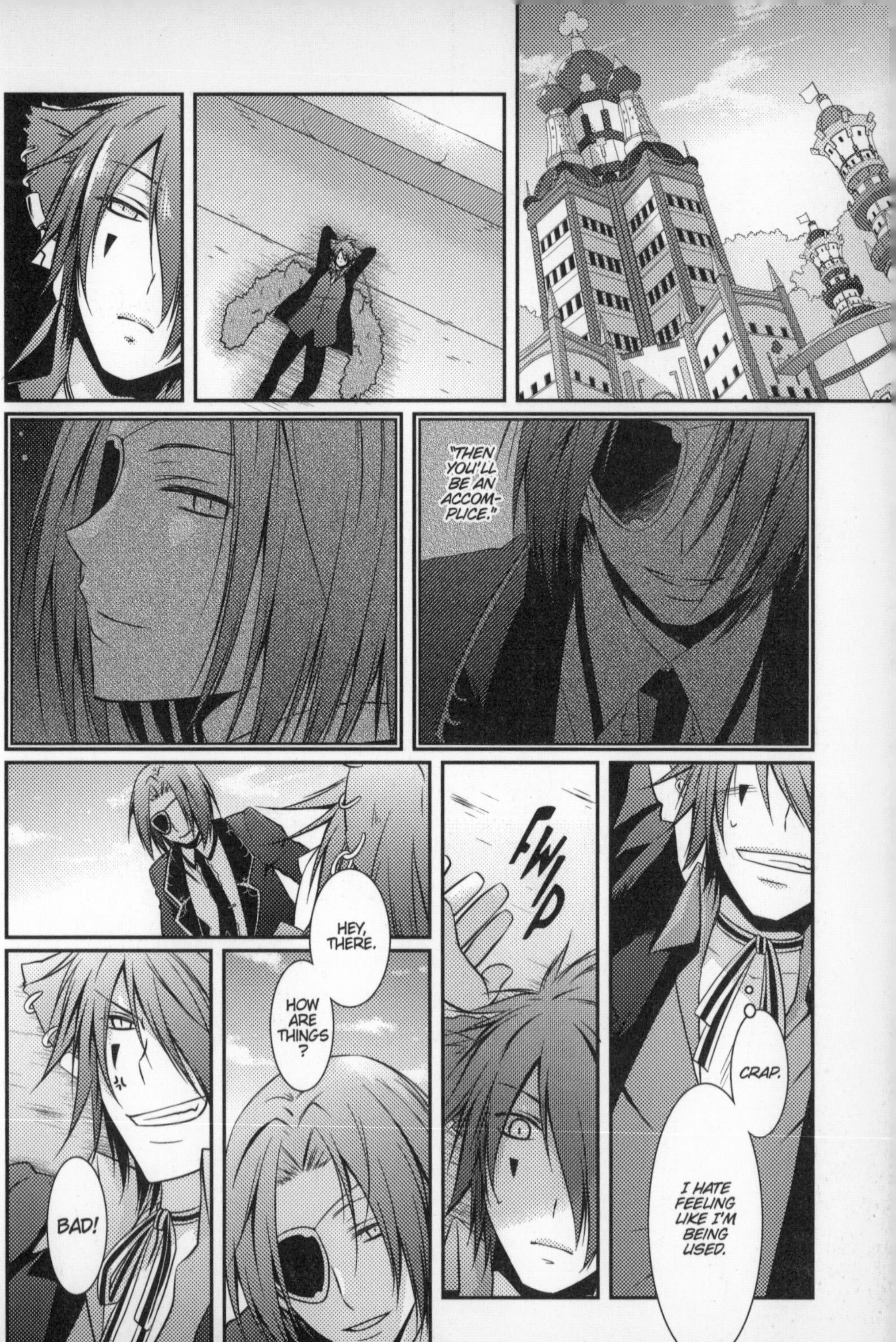
"THEN YOU'LL BE AN ACCOMPLICE."
CRAP.
I HATE FEELING LIKE I'M BEING USED.
FWIP
HEY, THERE.
HOW ARE THINGS?
BAD!

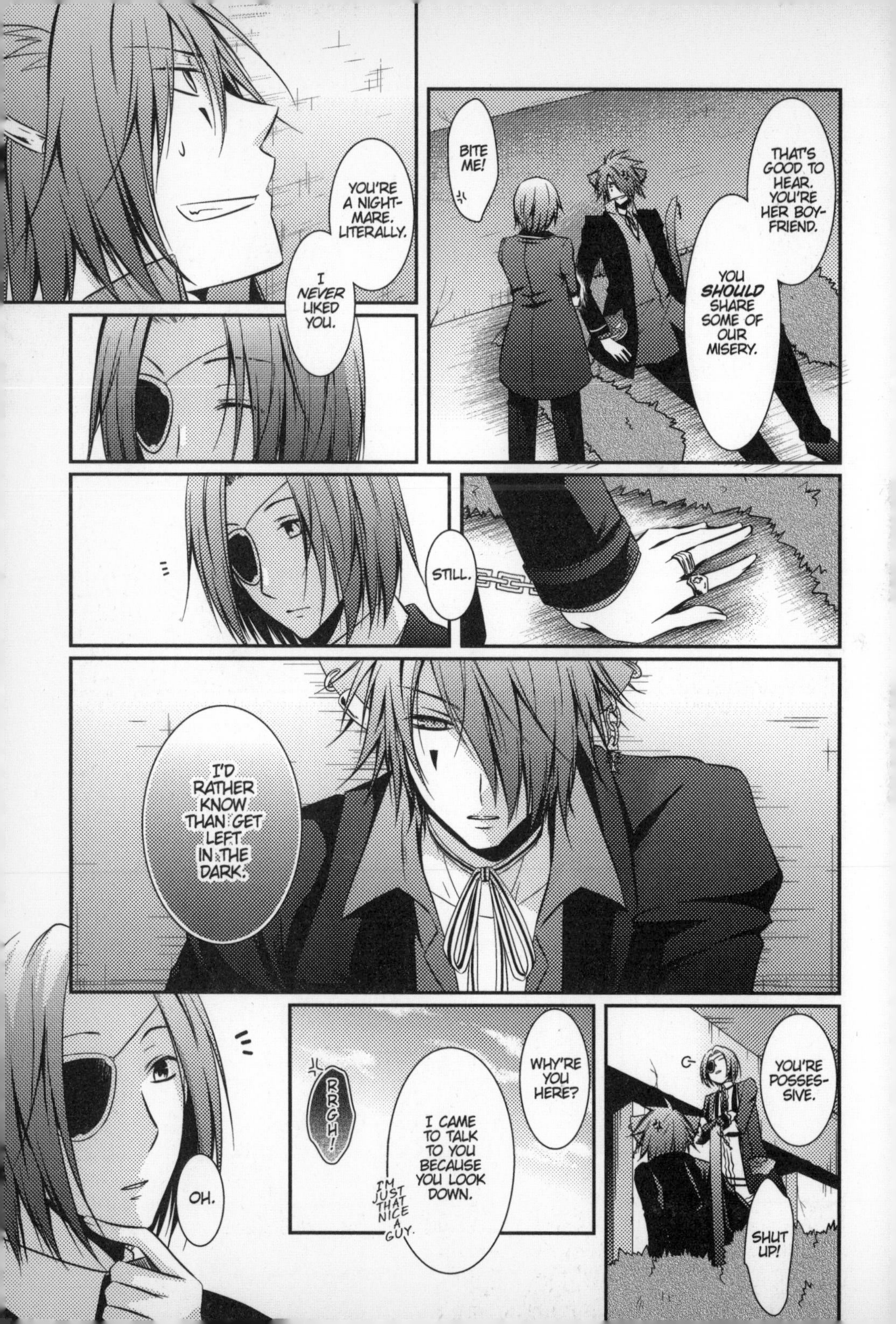
THAT'S GOOD TO HEAR. YOU'RE HER BOY-FRIEND.
YOU SHOULD SHARE SOME OF OUR MISERY.
BITE ME!
YOU'RE A NIGHT-MARE. LITERALLY.
I NEVER LIKED YOU.
STILL.
I'D RATHER KNOW THAN GET LEFT IN THE DARK.
YOU'RE POSSES-SIVE.
SHUT UP!
WHY'RE YOU HERE?
I CAME TO TALK TO YOU BECAUSE YOU LOOK DOWN.
I'M JUST THAT NICE A GUY.
RRGH!
OH.

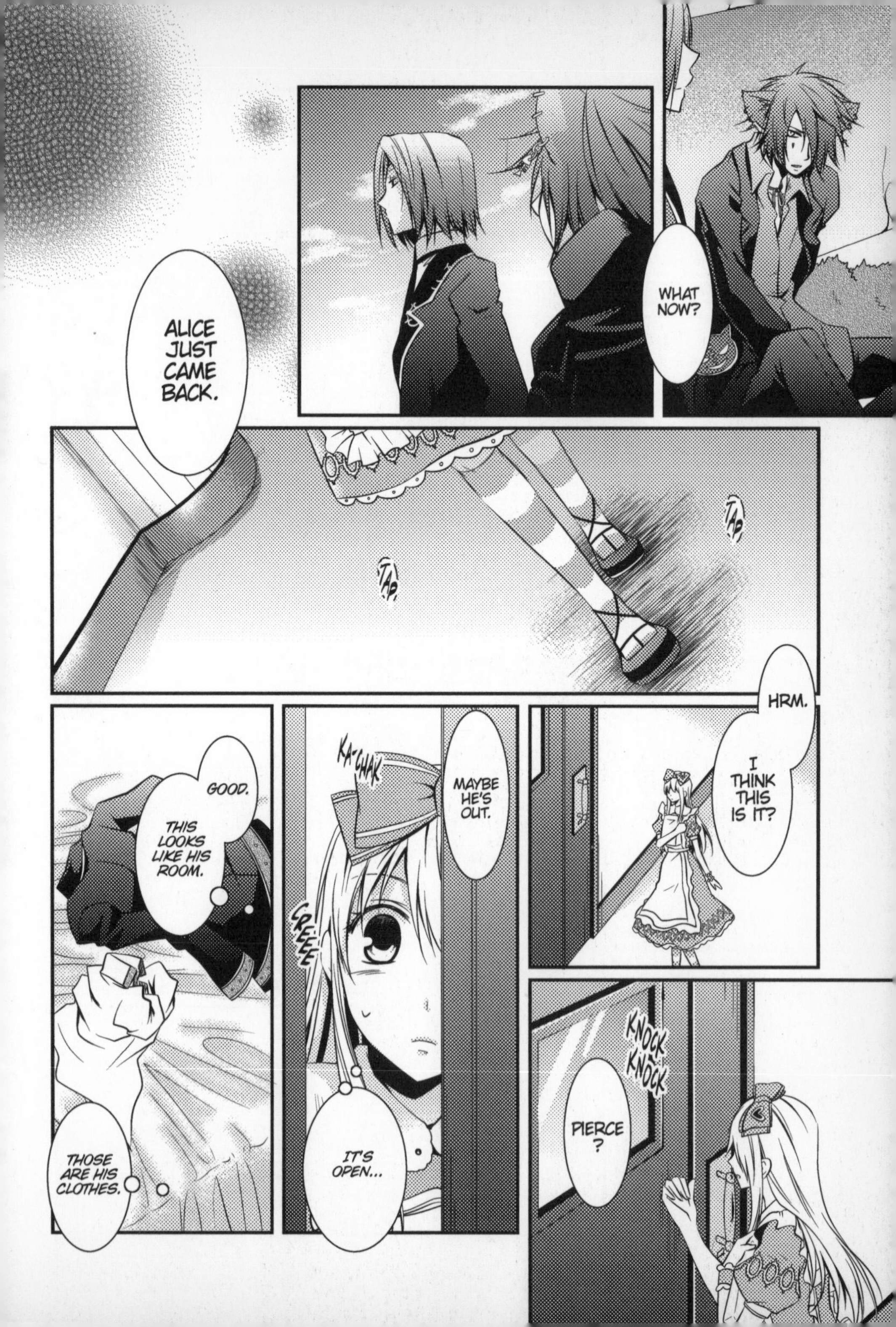
WHAT NOW?
ALICE JUST CAME BACK.
TAP
TAP
HRM.
I THINK THIS IS IT?
KNOCK KNOCK
PIERCE?
KA-CHAK
MAYBE HE'S OUT.
CREEEE
IT'S OPEN...
GOOD.
THIS LOOKS LIKE HIS ROOM.
THOSE ARE HIS CLOTHES.

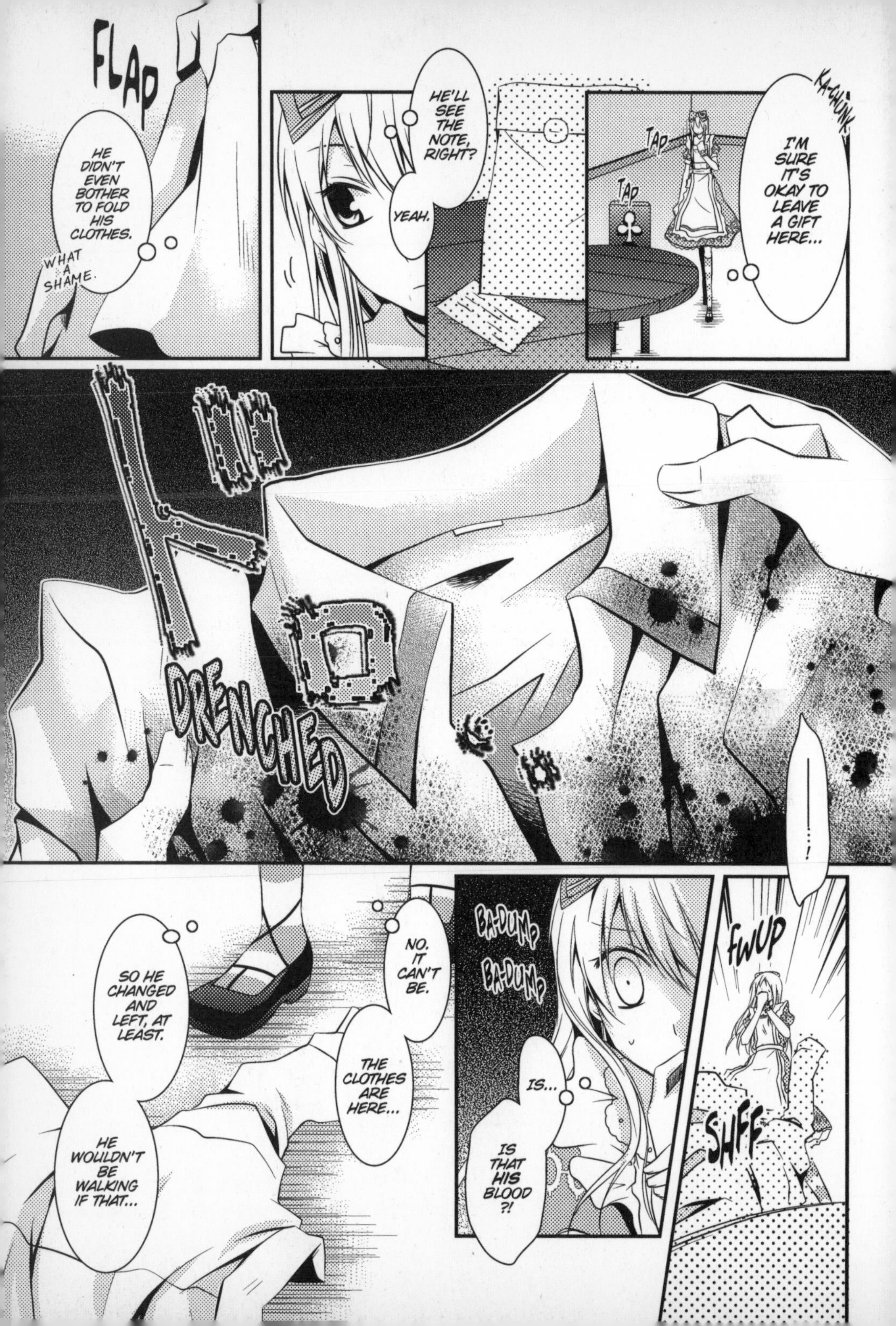
KA-CHUNK
TAP
TAP
I'M SURE IT'S OKAY TO LEAVE A GIFT HERE...
HE'LL SEE THE NOTE, RIGHT?
YEAH.
FLAP
HE DIDN'T EVEN BOTHER TO FOLD HIS CLOTHES.
WHAT A SHAME.
DRENCHED
...!
FWUP
SHFF
BA-DUMP
BA-DUMP
IS...
IS THAT HIS BLOOD?!
SO HE CHANGED AND LEFT, AT LEAST.
NO. IT CAN'T BE.
THE CLOTHES ARE HERE...
HE WOULDN'T BE WALKING IF THAT...

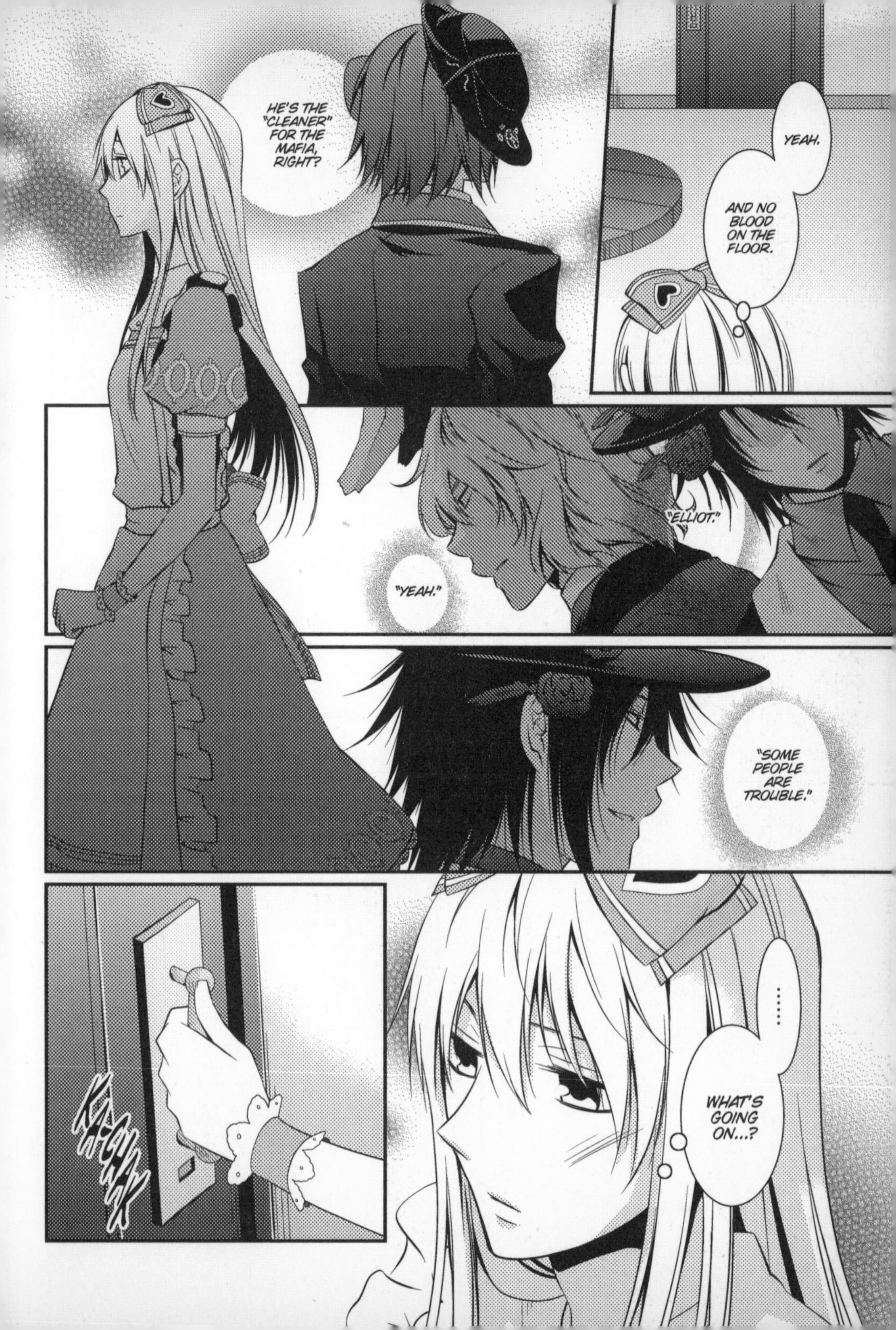

YEAH.
AND NO BLOOD ON THE FLOOR.
HE'S THE "CLEANER" FOR THE MAFIA, RIGHT?
"ELLIOT."
"YEAH."
"SOME PEOPLE ARE TROUBLE."
......
WHAT'S GOING ON...?
KACHAK

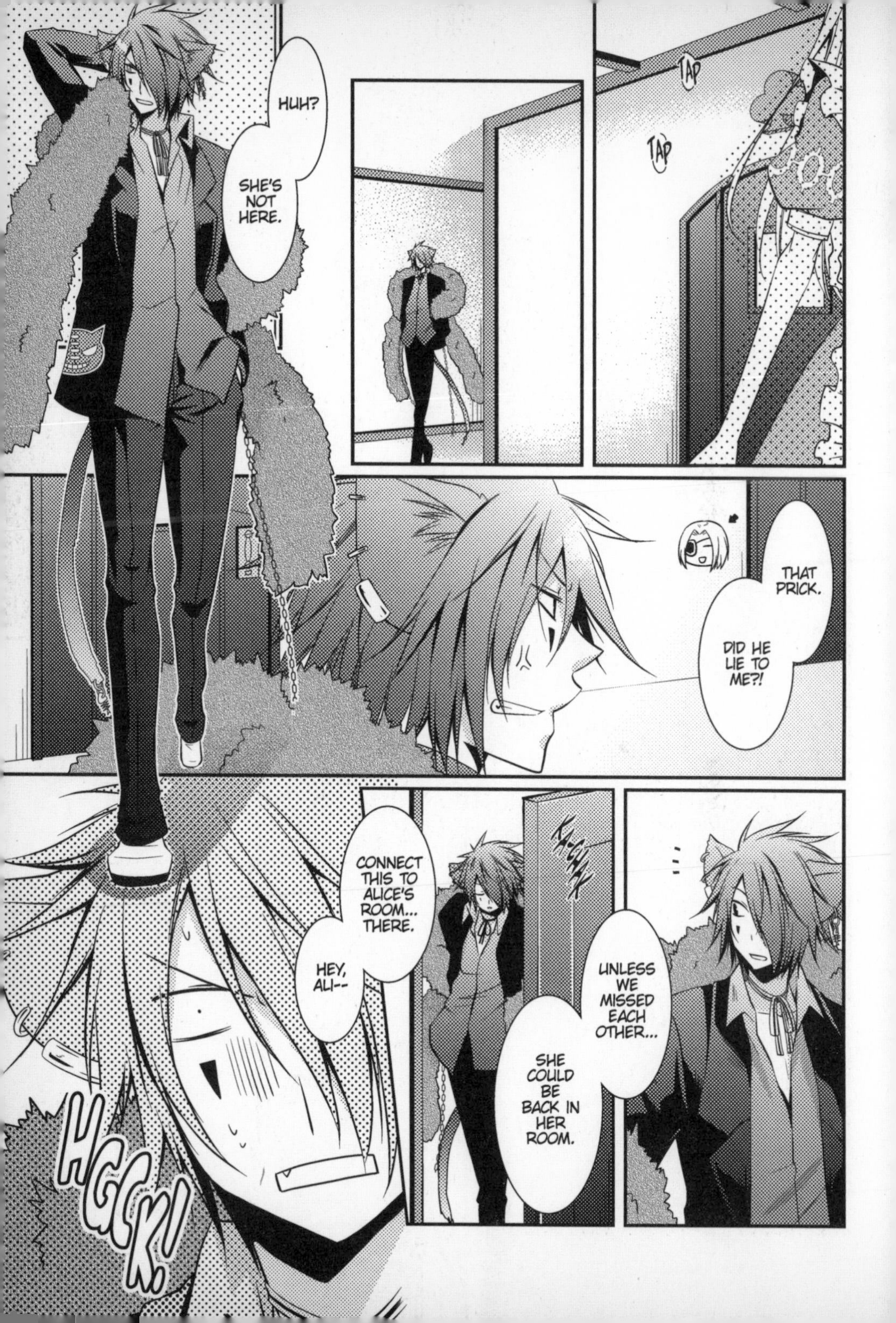
TAP
TAP
HUH?
SHE'S NOT HERE.
THAT PRICK.
DID HE LIE TO ME?!
...
UNLESS WE MISSED EACH OTHER...
SHE COULD BE BACK IN HER ROOM.
KA-CHUNK
CONNECT THIS TO ALICE'S ROOM... THERE.
HEY, ALI--
HGCK!

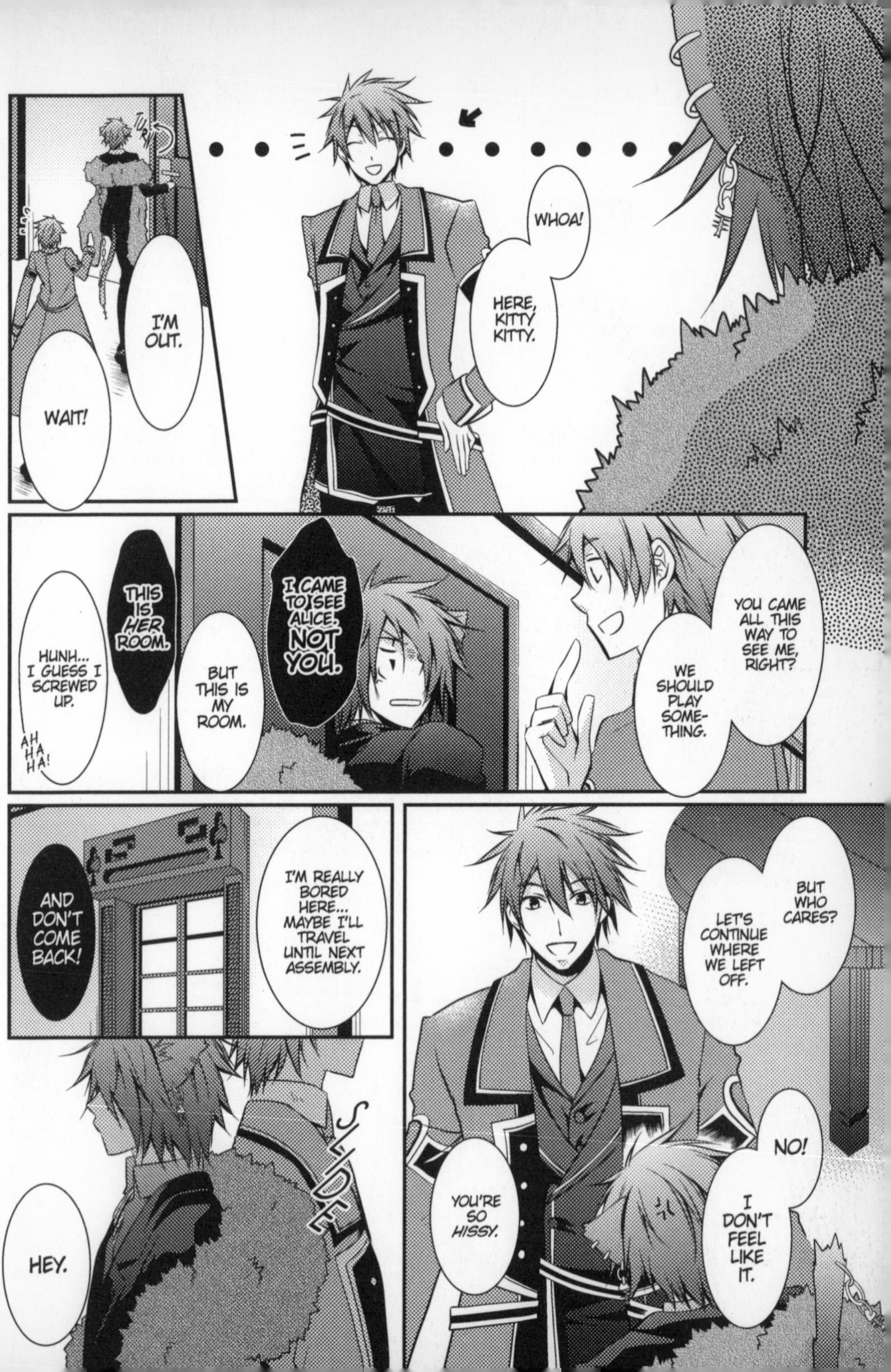
WHOA!
HERE, KITTY KITTY.
I'M OUT.
WAIT!
YOU CAME ALL THIS WAY TO SEE ME, RIGHT?
WE SHOULD PLAY SOME-THING.
I CAME TO SEE ALICE, NOT YOU.
BUT THIS IS MY ROOM.
THIS IS HER ROOM.
HUNH... I GUESS I SCREWED UP.
AH HA HA!
BUT WHO CARES?
LET'S CONTINUE WHERE WE LEFT OFF.
NO!
I DON'T FEEL LIKE IT.
YOU'RE SO HISSY.
I'M REALLY BORED HERE... MAYBE I'LL TRAVEL UNTIL NEXT ASSEMBLY.
AND DON'T COME BACK!
SLIDE
HEY.

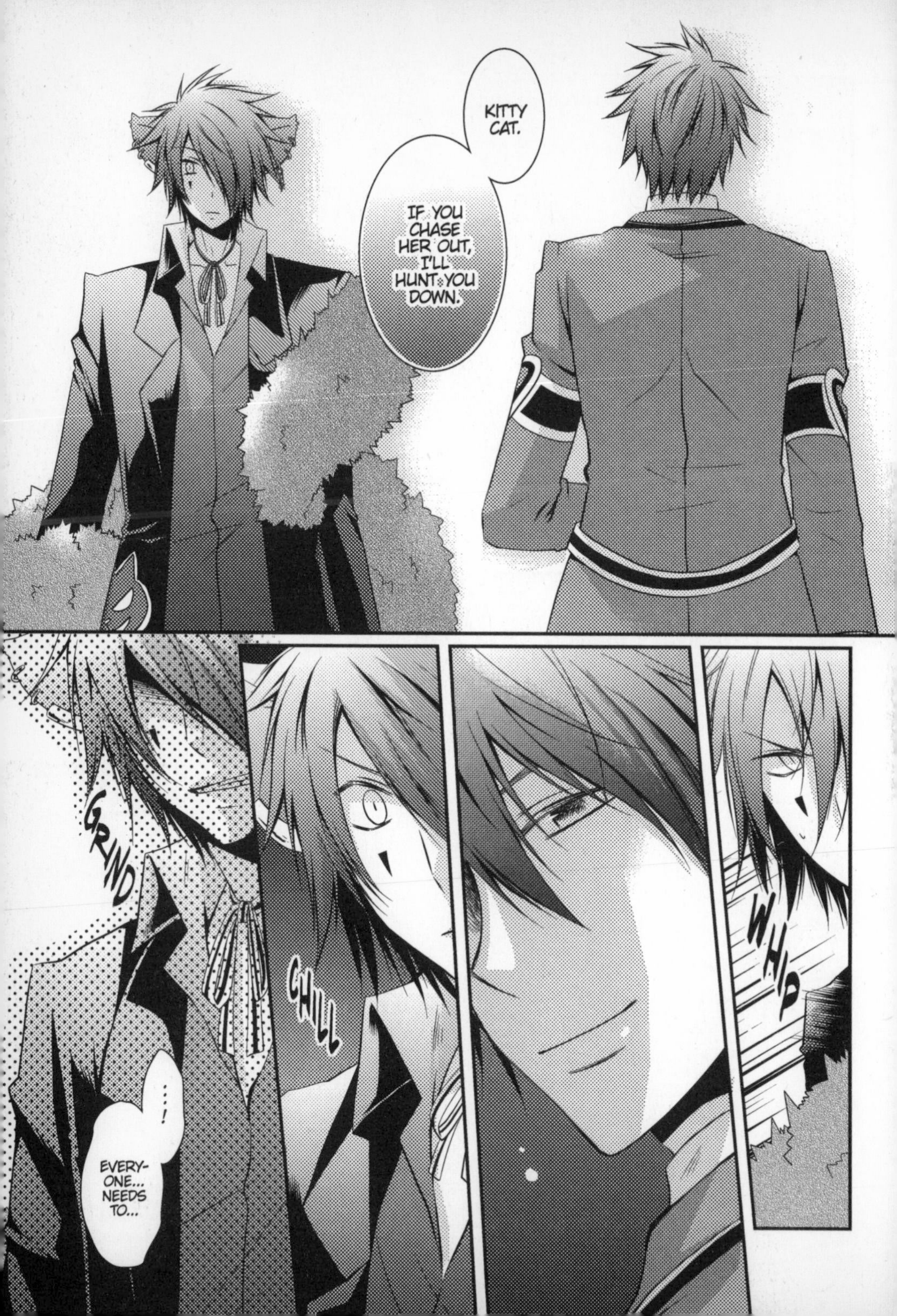
KITTY CAT.
IF YOU CHASE HER OUT, I'LL HUNT YOU DOWN.
WHIP
CHILL
GRIND
...!
EVERY-ONE... NEEDS TO...

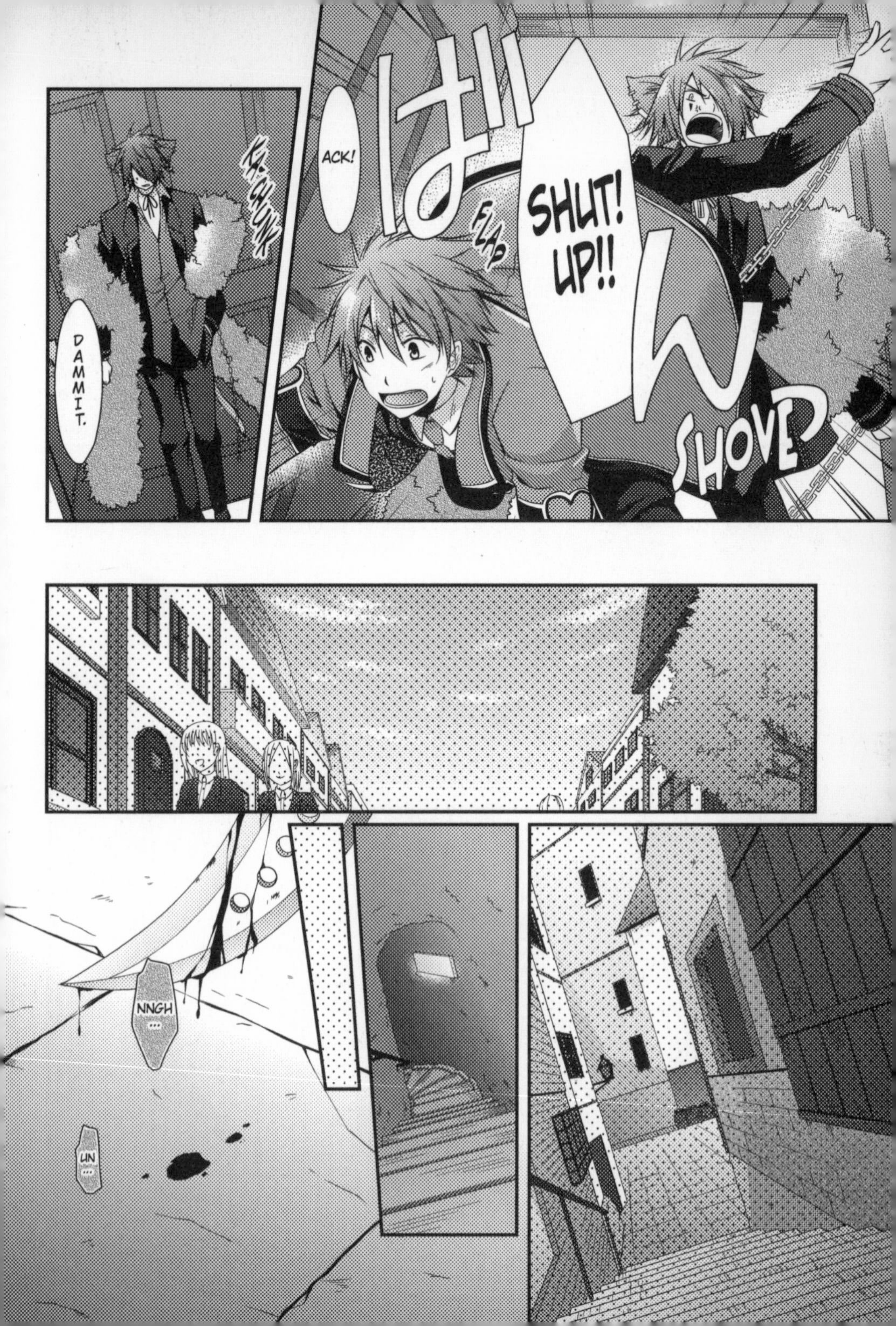

SHUT! UP!!
ばん
SHOVE
FLAP
ACK!
KA-CHUNK
DAMMIT.
NNGH...
UN...

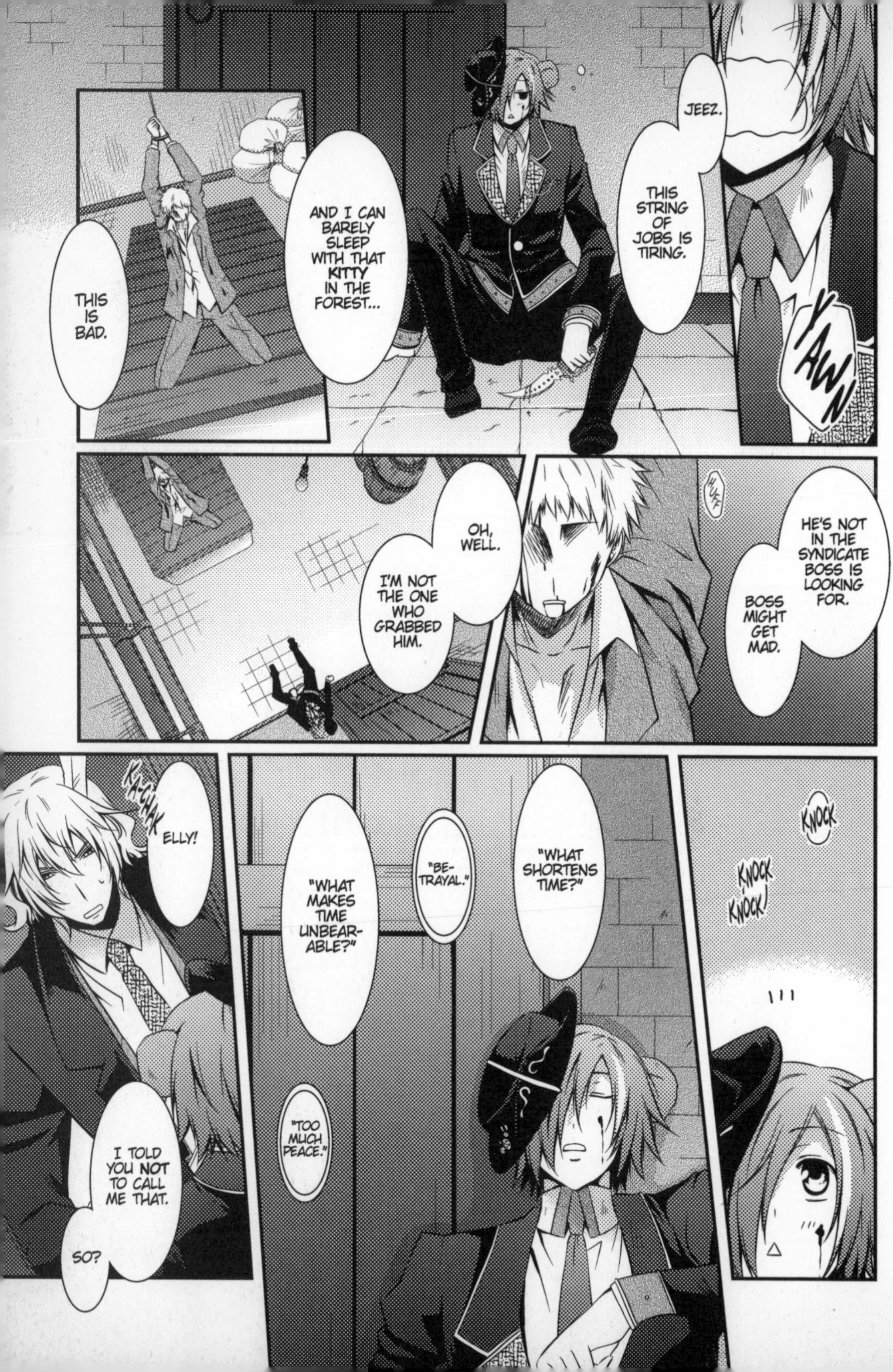
JEEZ.
THIS STRING OF JOBS IS TIRING.
YAWN
AND I CAN BARELY SLEEP WITH THAT KITTY IN THE FOREST...
THIS IS BAD.
HUFF
HE'S NOT IN THE SYNDICATE BOSS IS LOOKING FOR.
BOSS MIGHT GET MAD.
OH, WELL.
I'M NOT THE ONE WHO GRABBED HIM.
KNOCK
KNOCK KNOCK!
"WHAT SHORTENS TIME?"
"BE-TRAYAL."
"WHAT MAKES TIME UNBEARABLE?"
"TOO MUCH PEACE."
KA-CHAK
ELLY!
I TOLD YOU NOT TO CALL ME THAT.
SO?

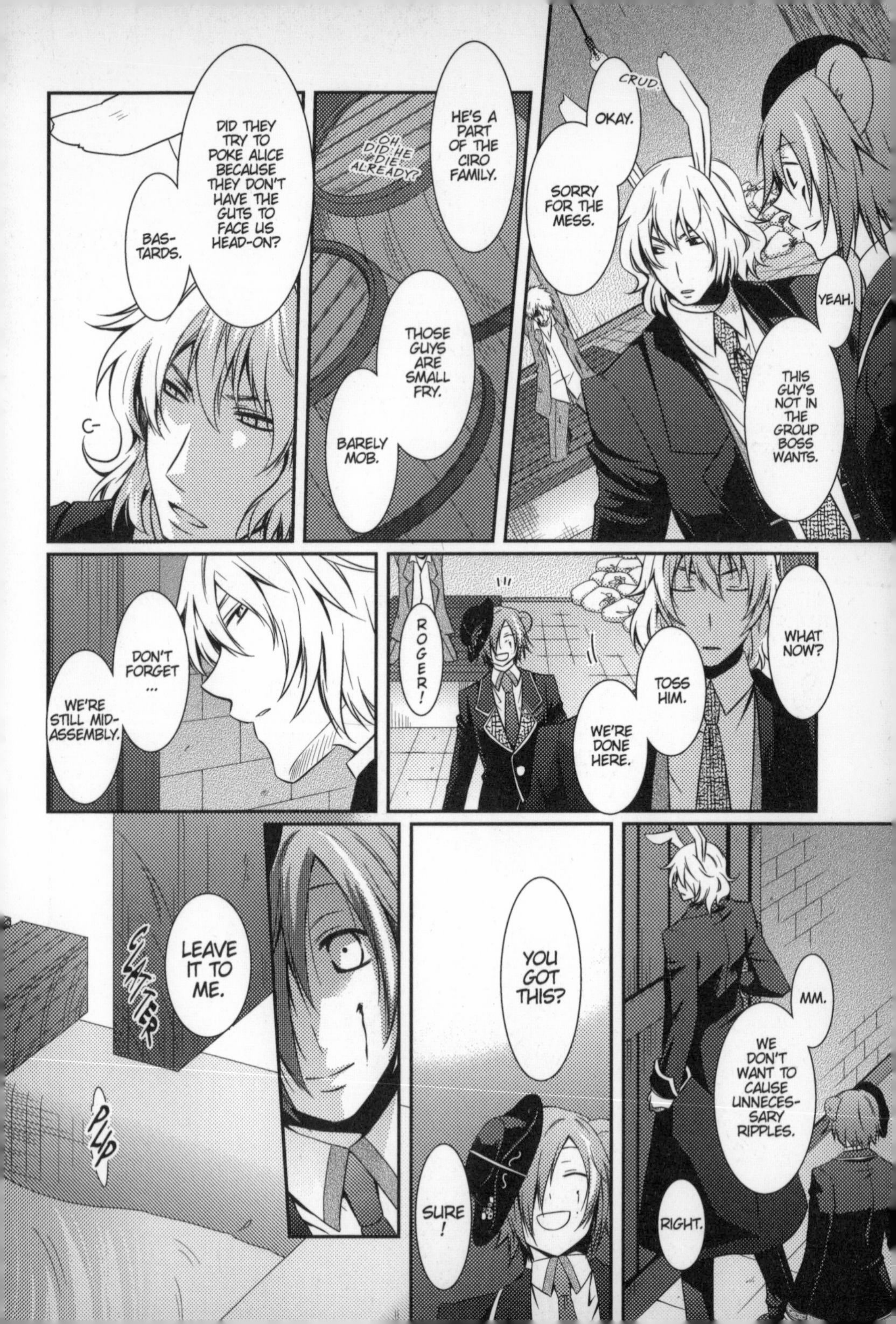
YEAH.
THIS GUY'S NOT IN THE GROUP BOSS WANTS.
CRUD.
OKAY.
SORRY FOR THE MESS.
HE'S A PART OF THE CIRO FAMILY.
OH DID HE DIE ALREADY?
THOSE GUYS ARE SMALL FRY.
BARELY MOB.
DID THEY TRY TO POKE ALICE BECAUSE THEY DON'T HAVE THE GUTS TO FACE US HEAD-ON?
BAS-TARDS.
C-
WHAT NOW?
TOSS HIM.
WE'RE DONE HERE.
ROGER!
DON'T FORGET...
WE'RE STILL MID-ASSEMBLY.
MM.
WE DON'T WANT TO CAUSE UNNECES-SARY RIPPLES.
RIGHT.
YOU GOT THIS?
SURE!
LEAVE IT TO ME.
CLATTER
PLIP

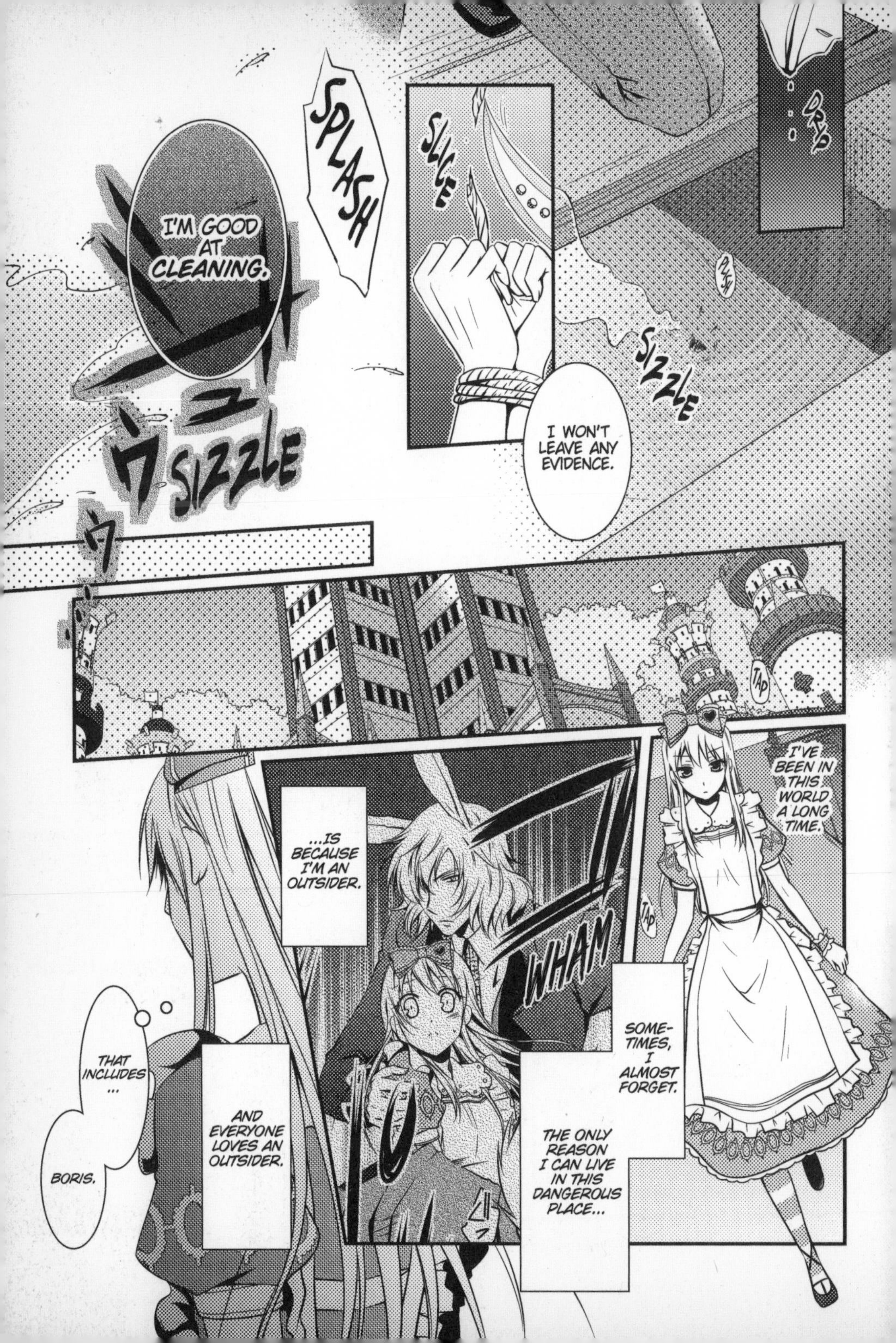
DRIP
PLISH
SIZZLE
I WON'T LEAVE ANY EVIDENCE.
SLICE
SPLASH
I'M GOOD AT CLEANING.
SIZZLE
TAP
I'VE BEEN IN THIS WORLD A LONG TIME.
TAP
SOME-TIMES, I ALMOST FORGET.
THE ONLY REASON I CAN LIVE IN THIS DANGEROUS PLACE...
...IS BECAUSE I'M AN OUTSIDER.
WHAM
AND EVERYONE LOVES AN OUTSIDER.
THAT INCLUDES...
BORIS.

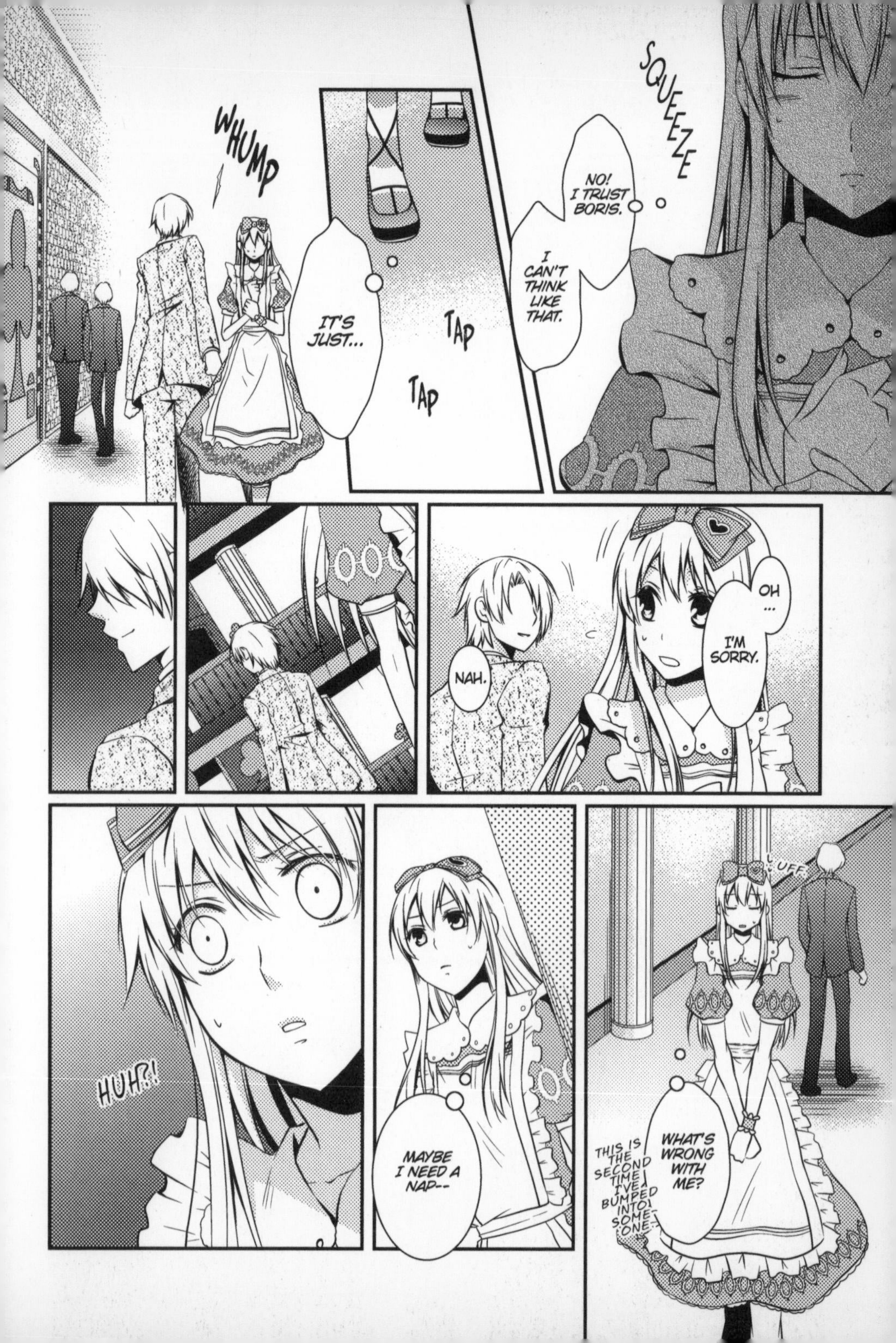
SQUEEZE
NO! I TRUST BORIS.
I CAN'T THINK LIKE THAT.
IT'S JUST...
TAP
TAP
WHUMP
OH... I'M SORRY.
NAH.
WHAT'S WRONG WITH ME?
THIS IS THE SECOND TIME I'VE BUMPED INTO SOMEONE.
MAYBE I NEED A NAP--
HUH?!

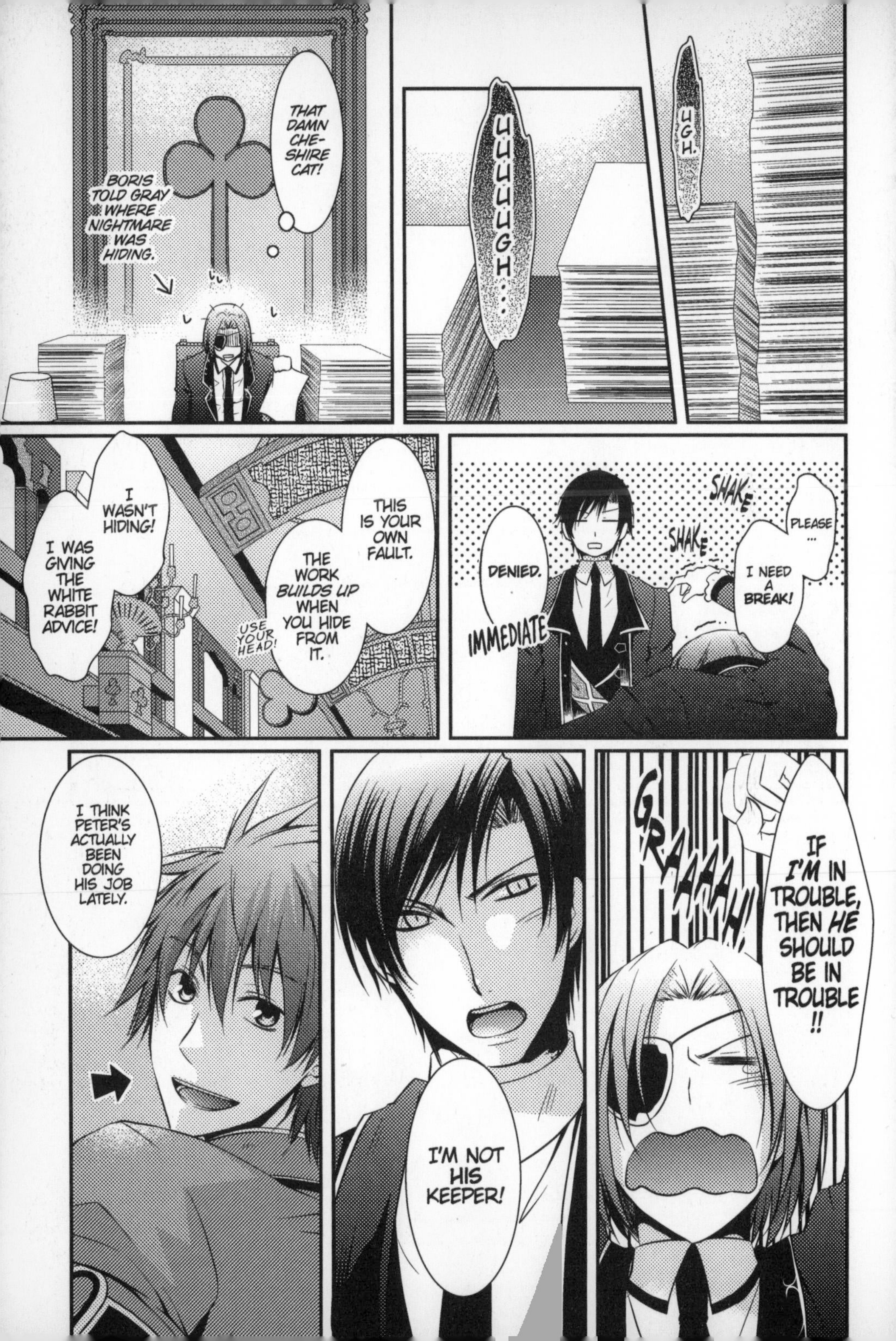
UGH.
UUUUUGH...
THAT DAMN CHESHIRE CAT!
BORIS TOLD GRAY WHERE NIGHTMARE WAS HIDING.
PLEASE... I NEED A BREAK!
SHAKE SHAKE
DENIED.
IMMEDIATE
THIS IS YOUR OWN FAULT.
THE WORK BUILDS UP WHEN YOU HIDE FROM IT.
USE YOUR HEAD!
I WASN'T HIDING! I WAS GIVING THE WHITE RABBIT ADVICE!
GRAAAAAH!
IF I'M IN TROUBLE, THEN HE SHOULD BE IN TROUBLE!!
I'M NOT HIS KEEPER!
I THINK PETER'S ACTUALLY BEEN DOING HIS JOB LATELY.

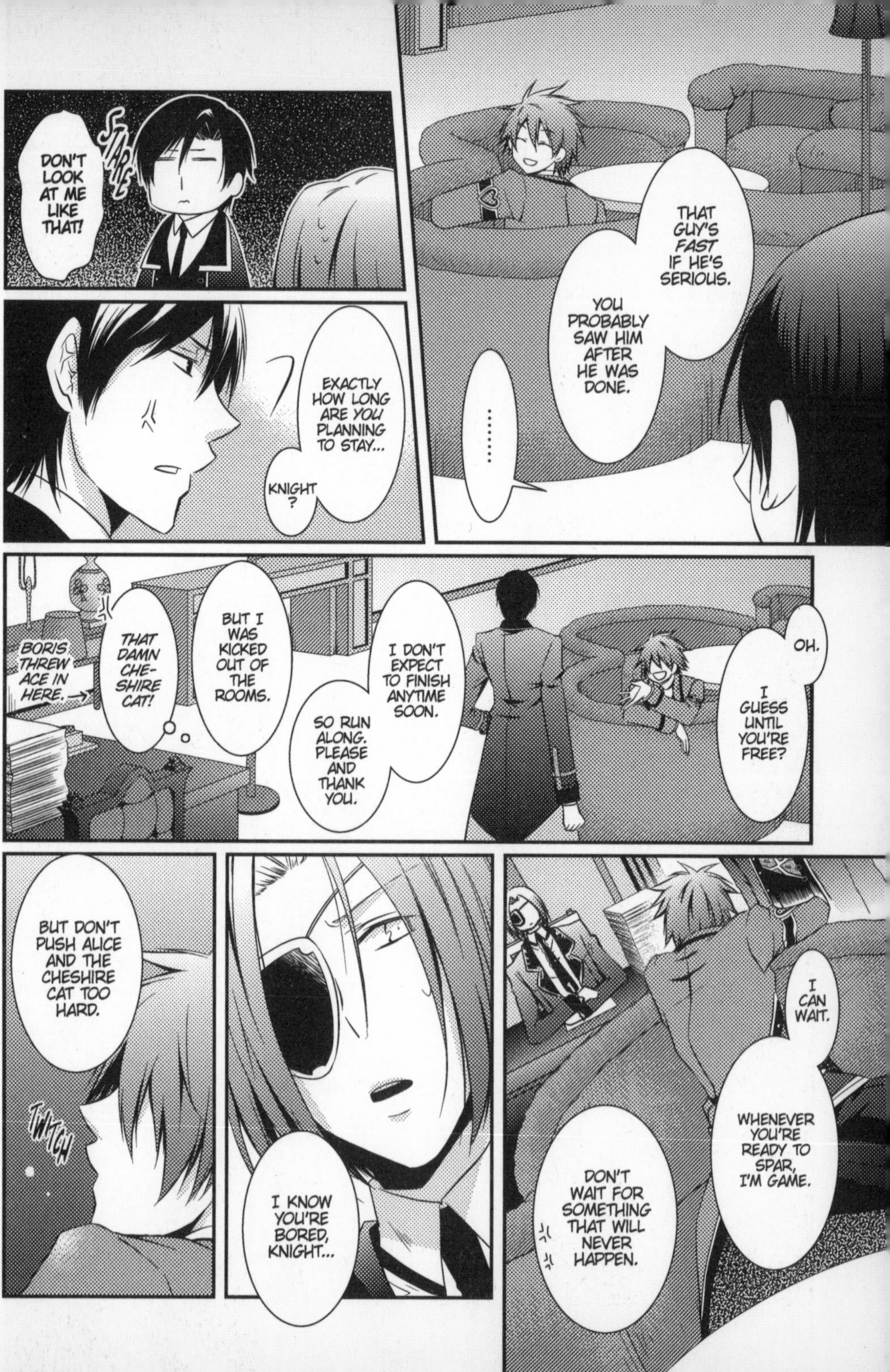
THAT GUY'S *FAST* IF HE'S SERIOUS.
YOU PROBABLY SAW HIM AFTER HE WAS DONE.
......
STARE
DON'T LOOK AT ME LIKE THAT!
EXACTLY HOW LONG ARE *YOU* PLANNING TO STAY...
KNIGHT?
OH.
I GUESS UNTIL YOU'RE FREE?
I DON'T EXPECT TO FINISH ANYTIME SOON.
SO RUN ALONG. PLEASE AND THANK YOU.
BUT I WAS KICKED OUT OF THE ROOMS.
THAT DAMN CHESHIRE CAT!
BORIS THREW ACE IN HERE. →
I CAN WAIT.
WHENEVER YOU'RE READY TO SPAR, I'M GAME.
DON'T WAIT FOR SOMETHING THAT WILL NEVER HAPPEN.
I KNOW YOU'RE BORED, KNIGHT...
BUT DON'T PUSH ALICE AND THE CHESHIRE CAT TOO HARD.
TWITCH

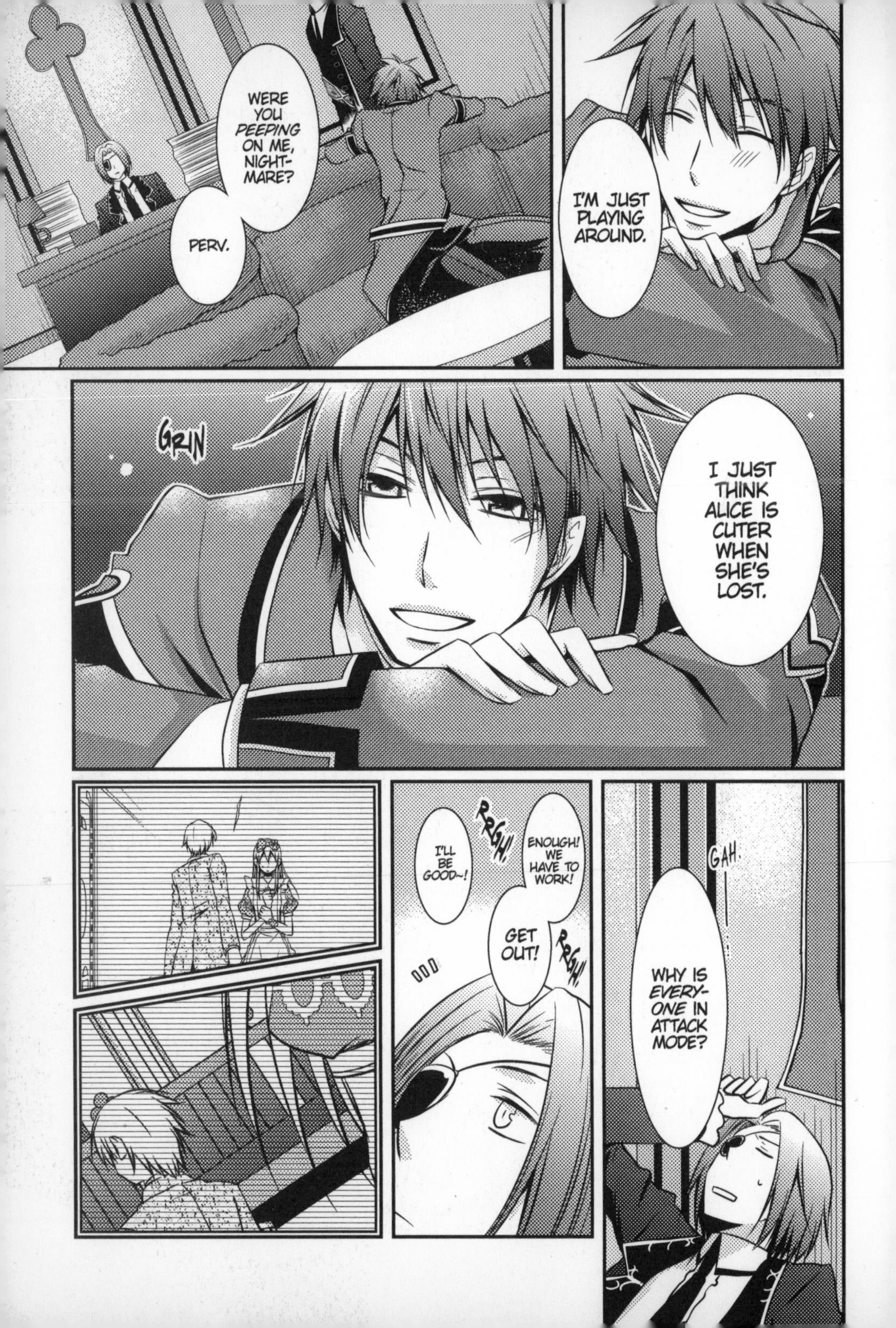

I'M JUST PLAYING AROUND.
WERE YOU *PEEPING* ON ME, NIGHT-MARE?
PERV.
I JUST THINK ALICE IS CUTER WHEN SHE'S LOST.
GRIN
GAH
WHY IS *EVERY-ONE* IN ATTACK MODE?
RRGH!
ENOUGH! WE HAVE TO WORK!
I'LL BE GOOD~!
RRGH!
GET OUT!

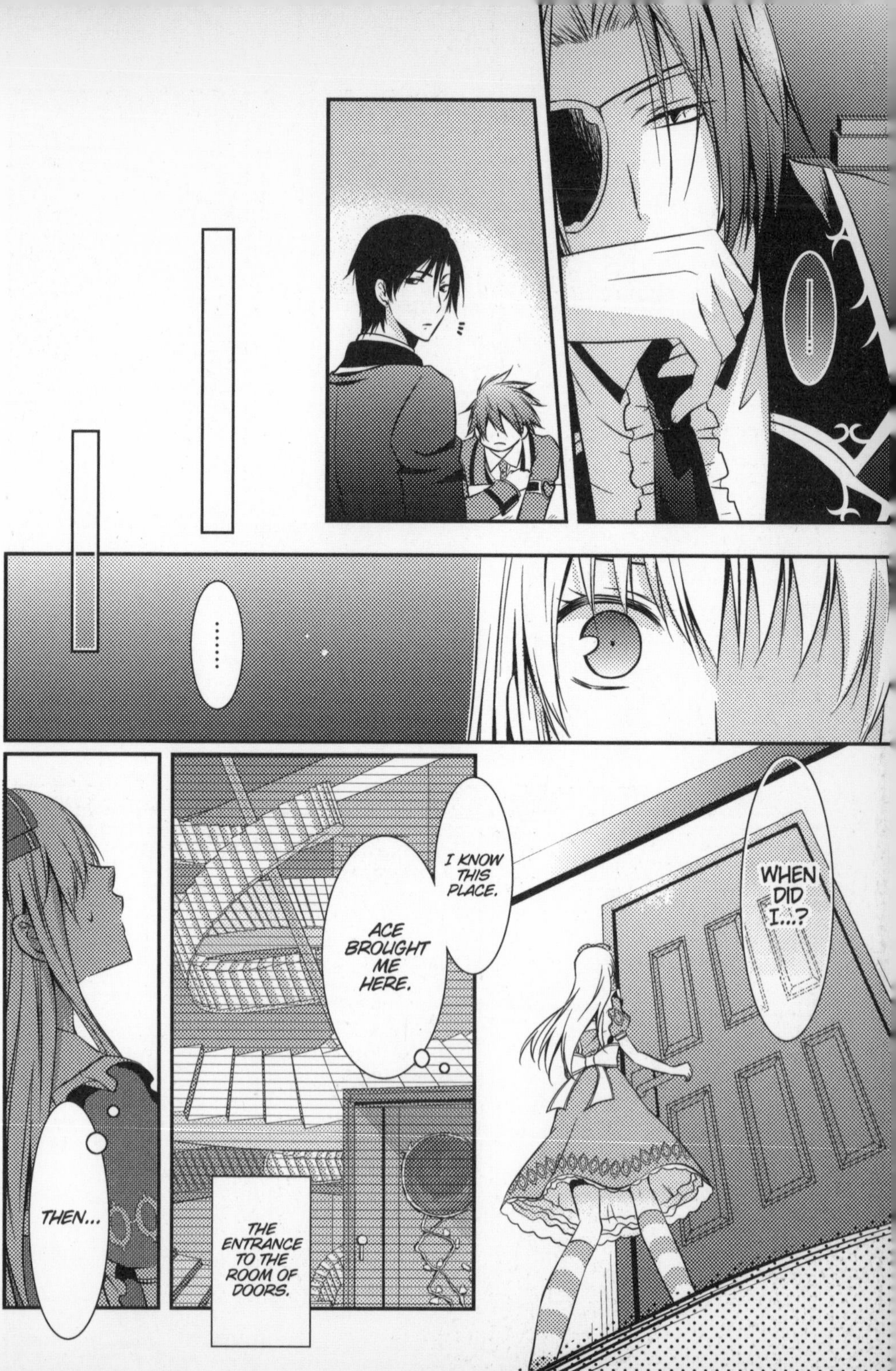
!
......
WHEN DID I...?
I KNOW THIS PLACE.
ACE BROUGHT ME HERE.
THE ENTRANCE TO THE ROOM OF DOORS.
THEN...

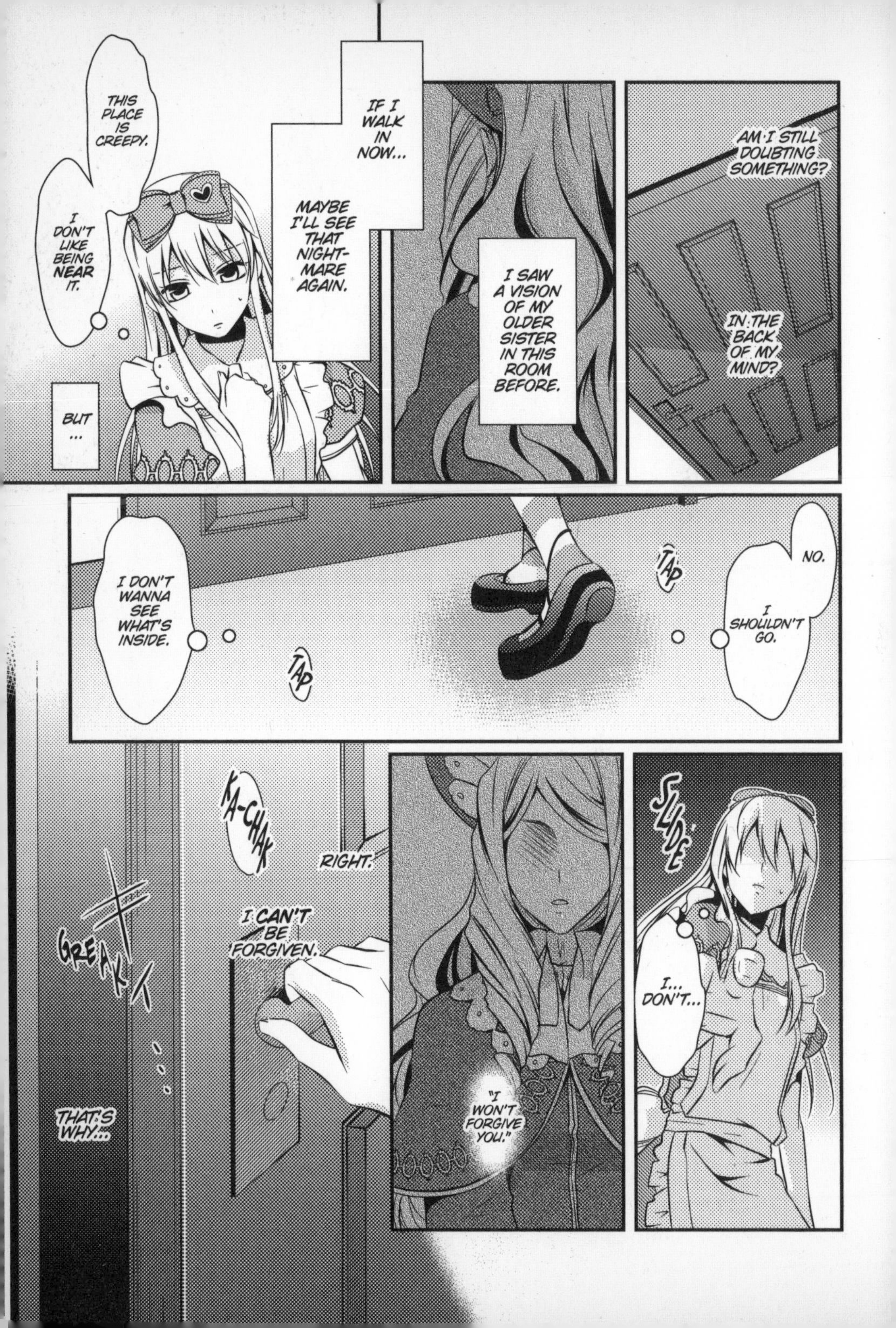
AM I STILL DOUBTING SOMETHING?
IN THE BACK OF MY MIND?
I SAW A VISION OF MY OLDER SISTER IN THIS ROOM BEFORE.
IF I WALK IN NOW...
MAYBE I'LL SEE THAT NIGHTMARE AGAIN.
THIS PLACE IS CREEPY.
I DON'T LIKE BEING NEAR IT.
BUT ...
NO.
I SHOULDN'T GO.
TAP
TAP
I DON'T WANNA SEE WHAT'S INSIDE.
SLIDE
I... DON'T...
"I WON'T FORGIVE YOU."
KA-CHAK
RIGHT.
I CAN'T BE FORGIVEN.
CREAK
...
THAT'S WHY...

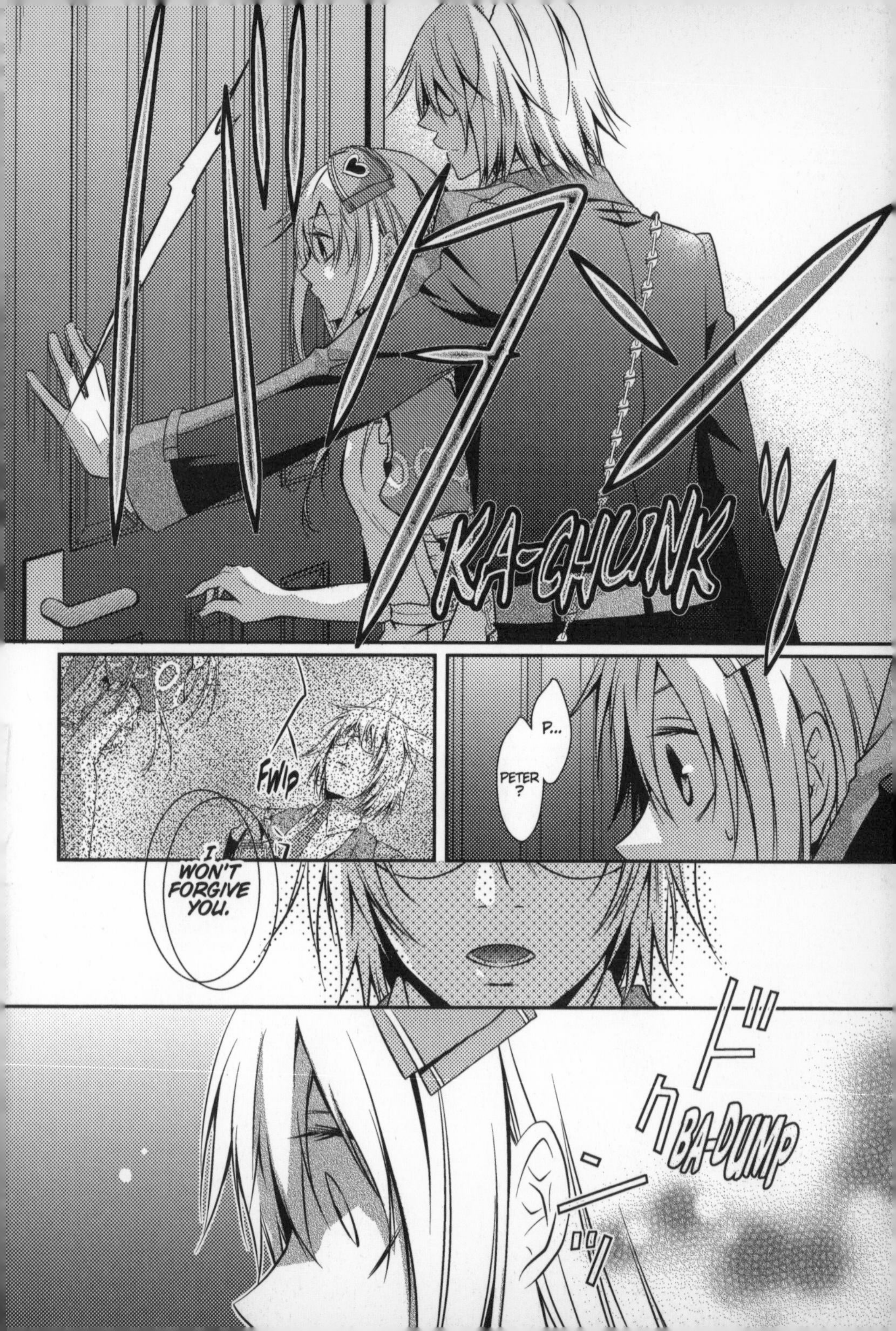
KA-CHUNK
P...
PETER?
FWIP
I WON'T FORGIVE YOU.
BA-DUMP

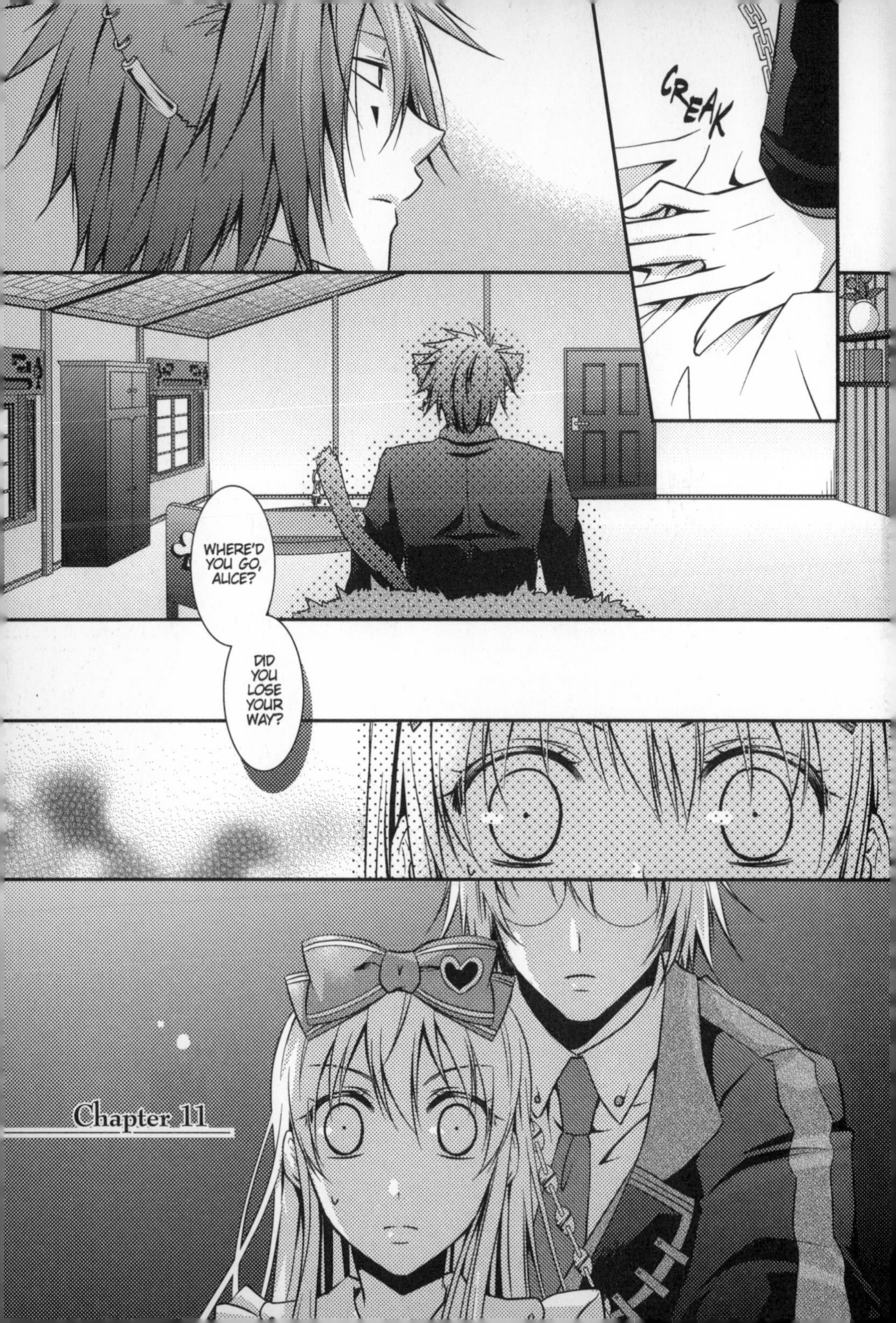
CREAK
WHERE'D YOU GO, ALICE?
DID YOU LOSE YOUR WAY?
Chapter 11

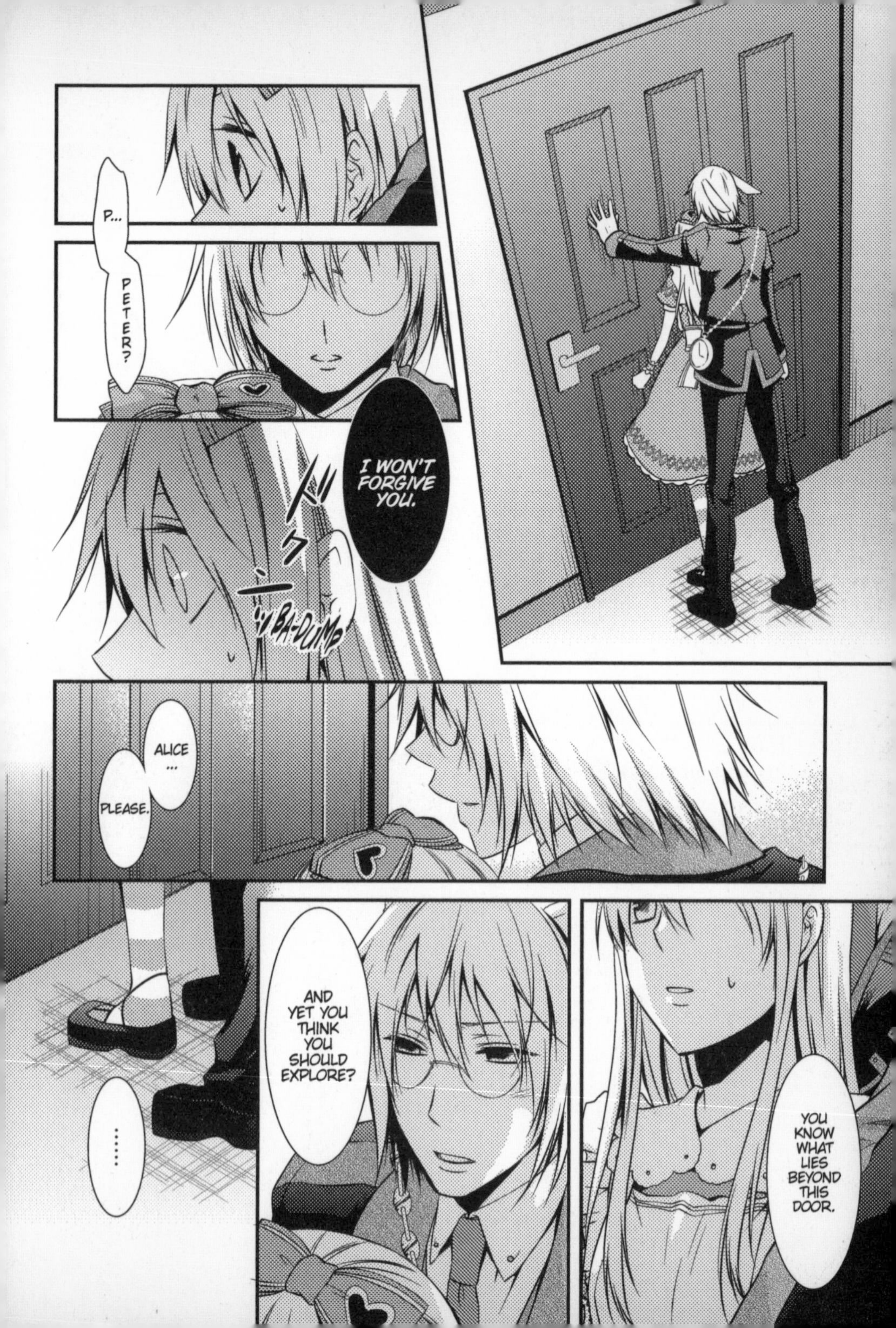
P...
PETER?
I WON'T FORGIVE YOU.
BA-DUMP
ALICE...
PLEASE.
YOU KNOW WHAT LIES BEYOND THIS DOOR.
AND YET YOU THINK YOU SHOULD EXPLORE?
......

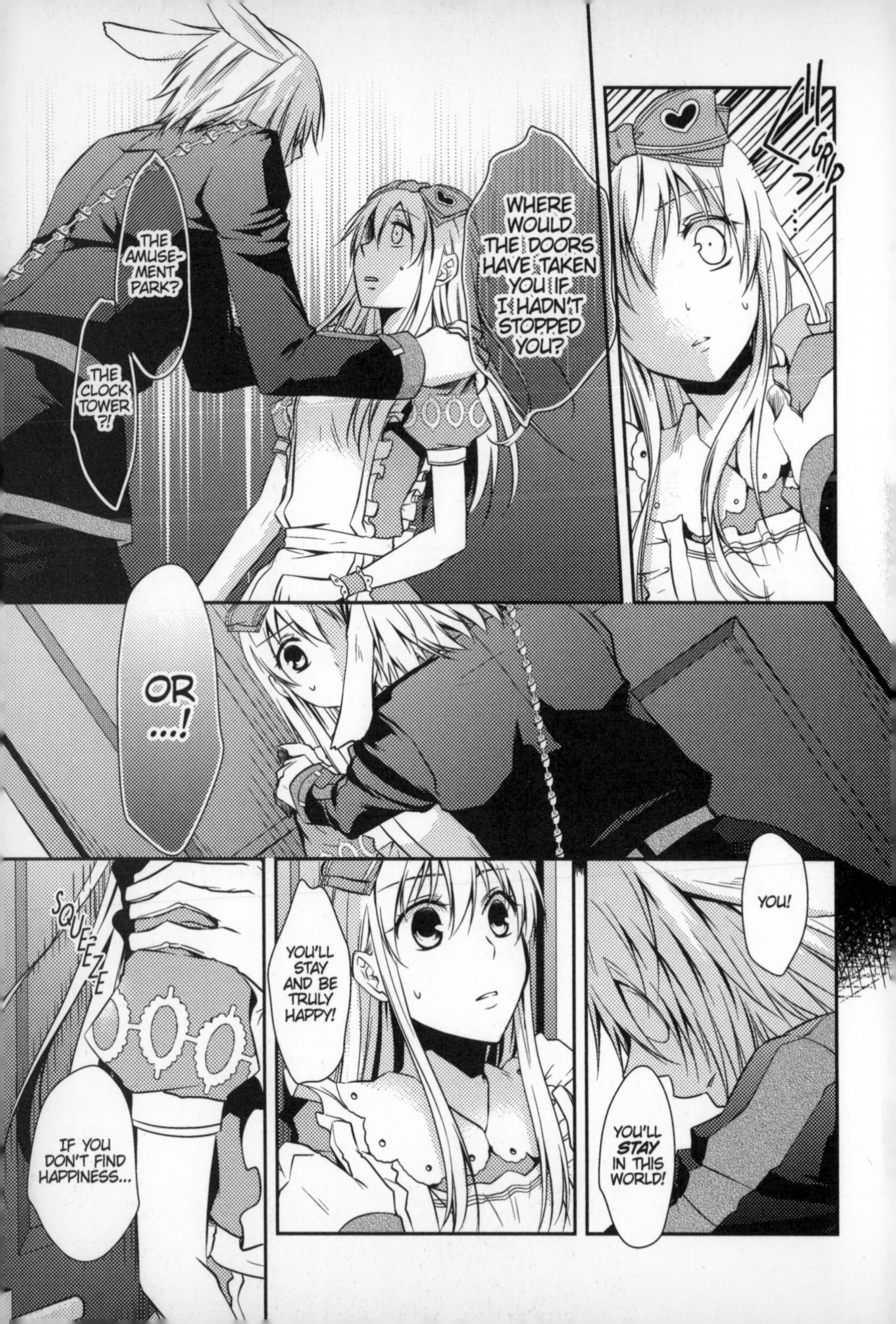
GRIP
?!
WHERE WOULD THE DOORS HAVE TAKEN YOU IF I HADN'T STOPPED YOU?
THE AMUSEMENT PARK?
THE CLOCK TOWER?!
OR ...!
YOU!
YOU'LL STAY IN THIS WORLD!
YOU'LL STAY AND BE TRULY HAPPY!
SQUEEZE
IF YOU DON'T FIND HAPPINESS...

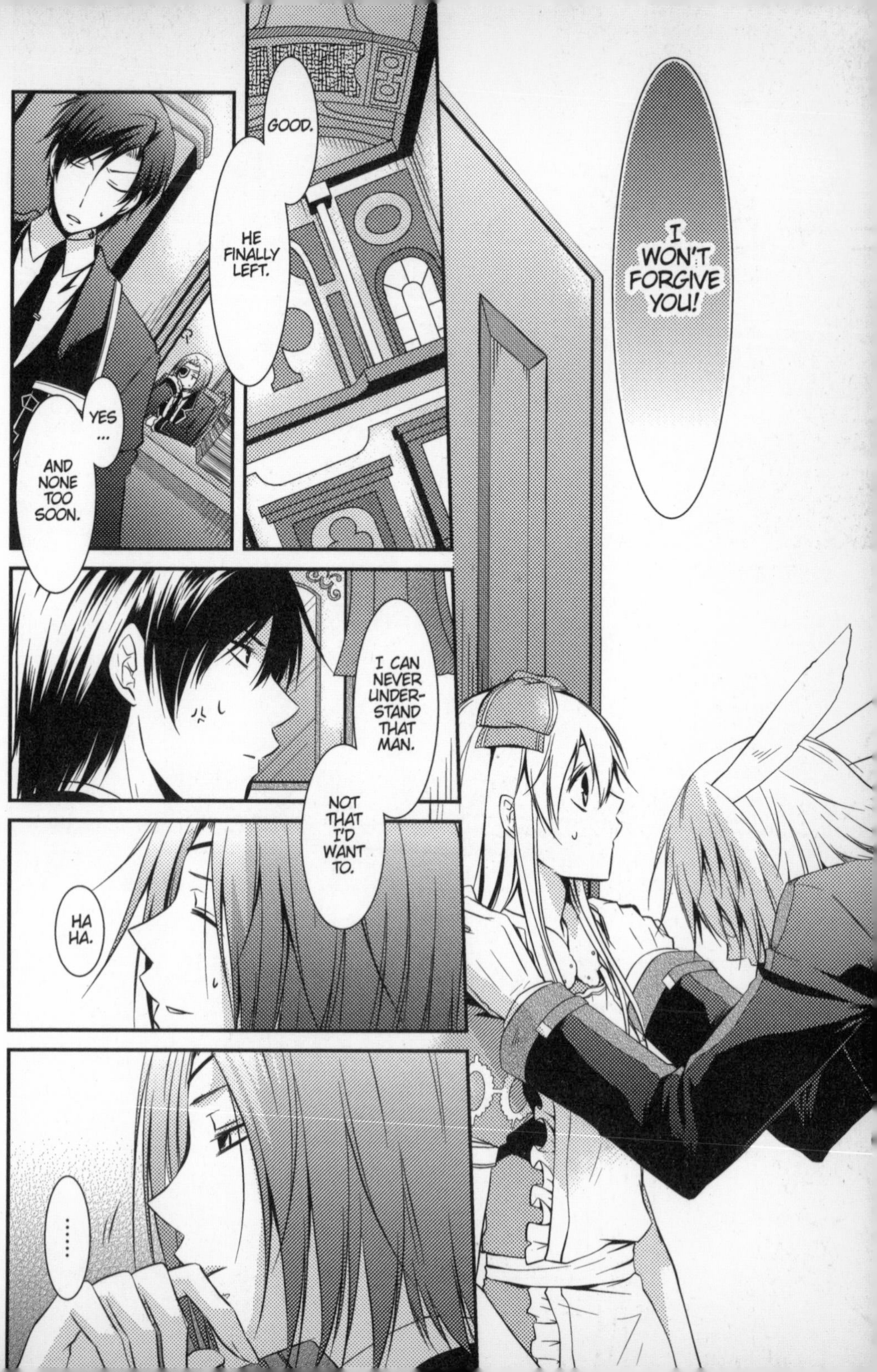
I WON'T FORGIVE YOU!
GOOD.
HE FINALLY LEFT.
YES ...
AND NONE TOO SOON.
I CAN NEVER UNDER-STAND THAT MAN.
NOT THAT I'D WANT TO.
HA HA.
......

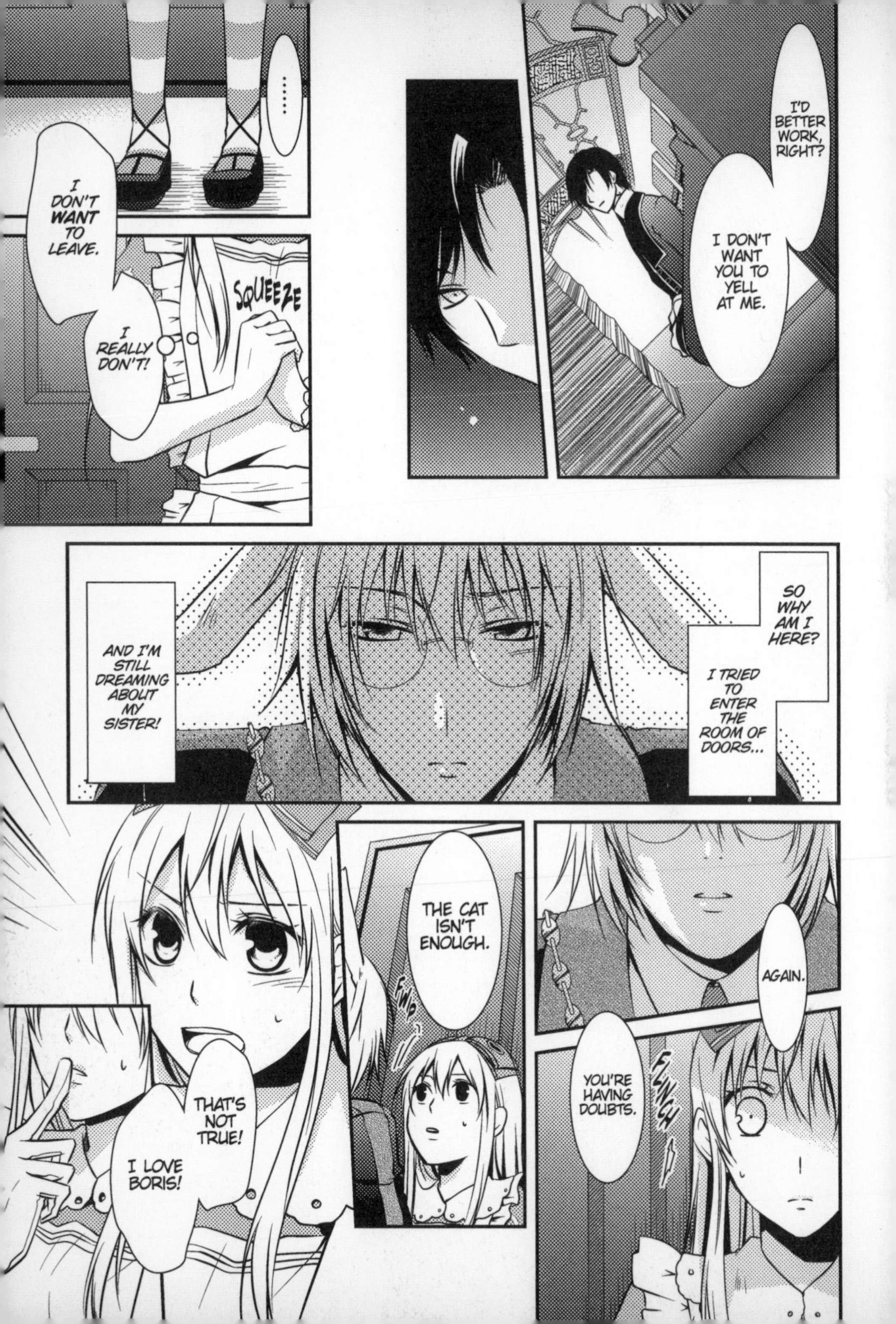
I'D BETTER WORK, RIGHT?
I DON'T WANT YOU TO YELL AT ME.
......
I DON'T WANT TO LEAVE.
SQUEEZE
I REALLY DON'T!
SO WHY AM I HERE?
I TRIED TO ENTER THE ROOM OF DOORS...
AND I'M STILL DREAMING ABOUT MY SISTER!
AGAIN.
YOU'RE HAVING DOUBTS.
FLINCH
!
THE CAT ISN'T ENOUGH.
FWIP
THAT'S NOT TRUE!
I LOVE BORIS!

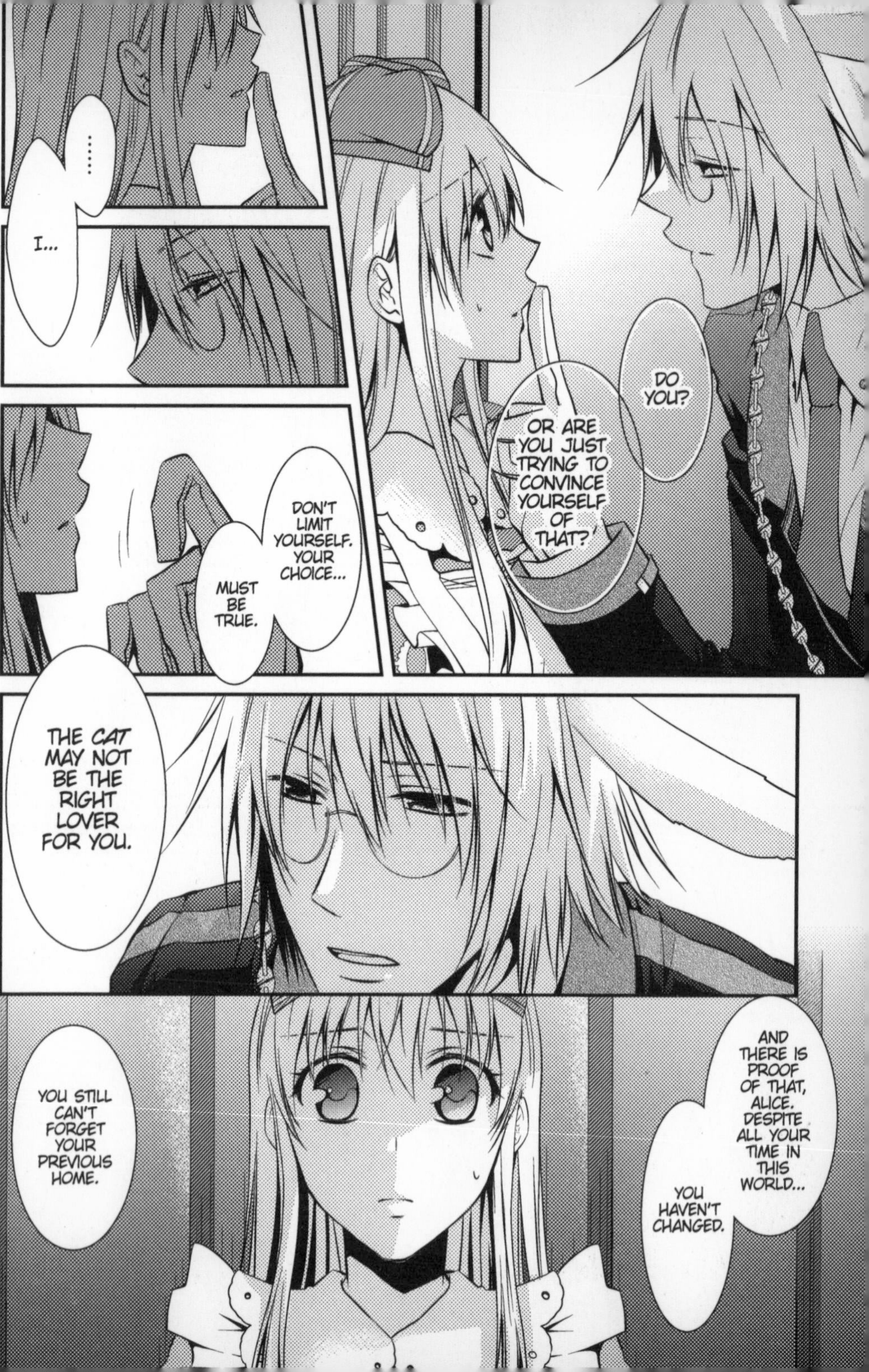
DO YOU?
OR ARE YOU JUST TRYING TO CONVINCE YOURSELF OF THAT?
......
I...
DON'T LIMIT YOURSELF. YOUR CHOICE...
MUST BE TRUE.
THE CAT MAY NOT BE THE RIGHT LOVER FOR YOU.
AND THERE IS PROOF OF THAT, ALICE. DESPITE ALL YOUR TIME IN THIS WORLD...
YOU HAVEN'T CHANGED.
YOU STILL CAN'T FORGET YOUR PREVIOUS HOME.

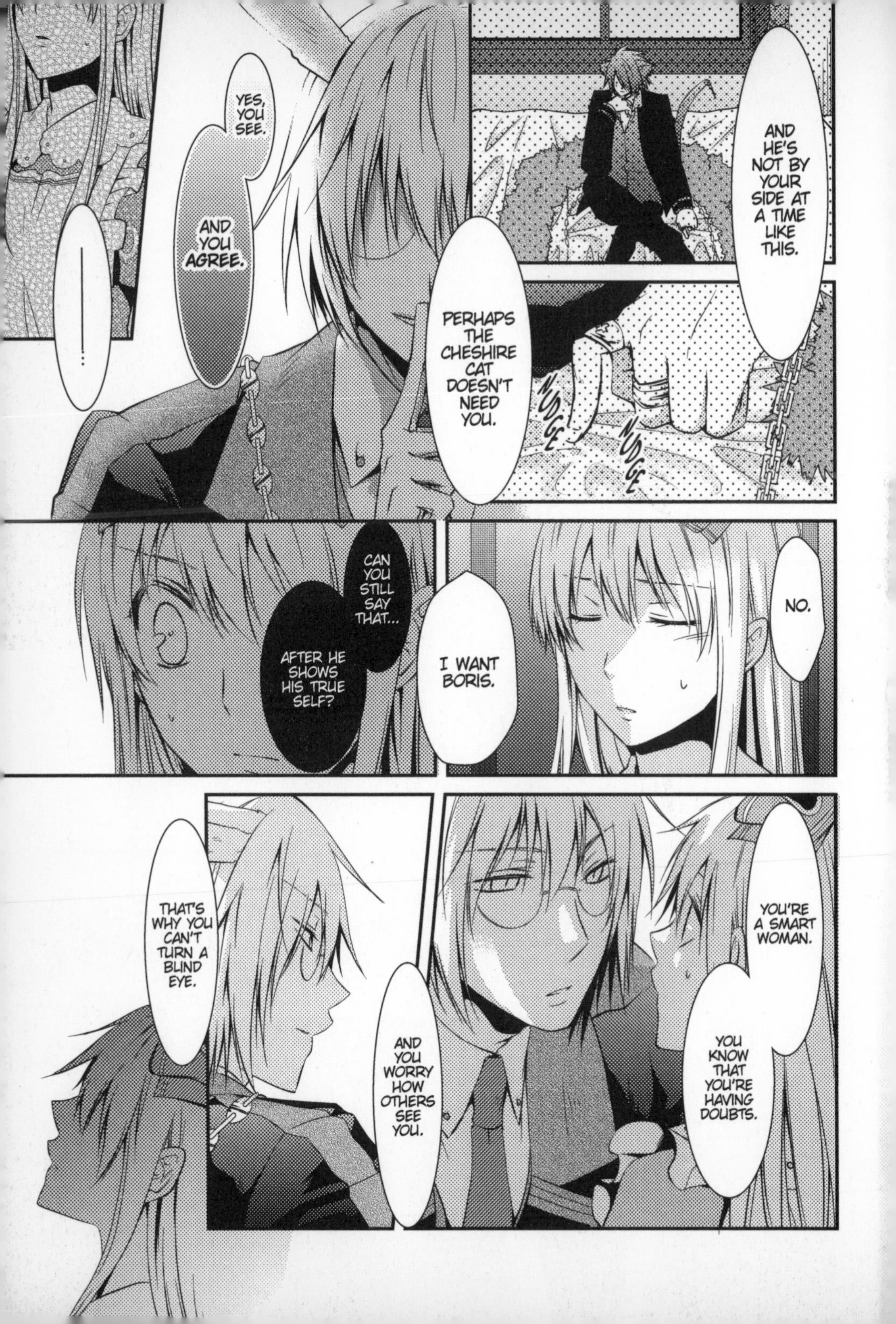
AND HE'S NOT BY YOUR SIDE AT A TIME LIKE THIS.
NUDGE
NUDGE
PERHAPS THE CHESHIRE CAT DOESN'T NEED YOU.
YES, YOU SEE.
AND YOU AGREE.
......
NO.
I WANT BORIS.
CAN YOU STILL SAY THAT...
AFTER HE SHOWS HIS TRUE SELF?
YOU'RE A SMART WOMAN.
YOU KNOW THAT YOU'RE HAVING DOUBTS.
AND YOU WORRY HOW OTHERS SEE YOU.
THAT'S WHY YOU CAN'T TURN A BLIND EYE.

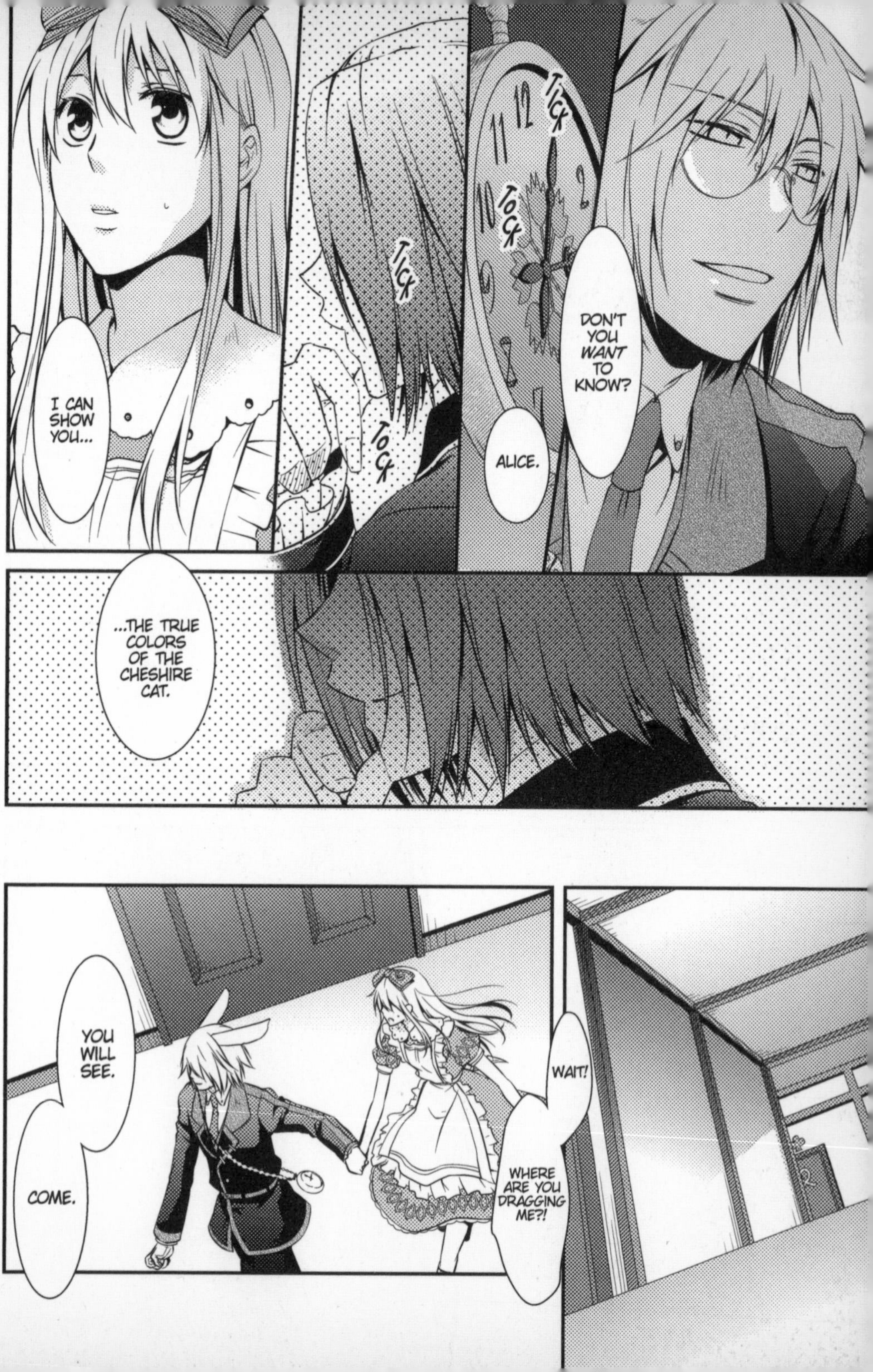
DON'T YOU WANT TO KNOW?
ALICE.
TICK
TOCK
TICK
TOCK
I CAN SHOW YOU...
...THE TRUE COLORS OF THE CHESHIRE CAT.
WAIT!
WHERE ARE YOU DRAGGING ME?!
YOU WILL SEE.
COME.

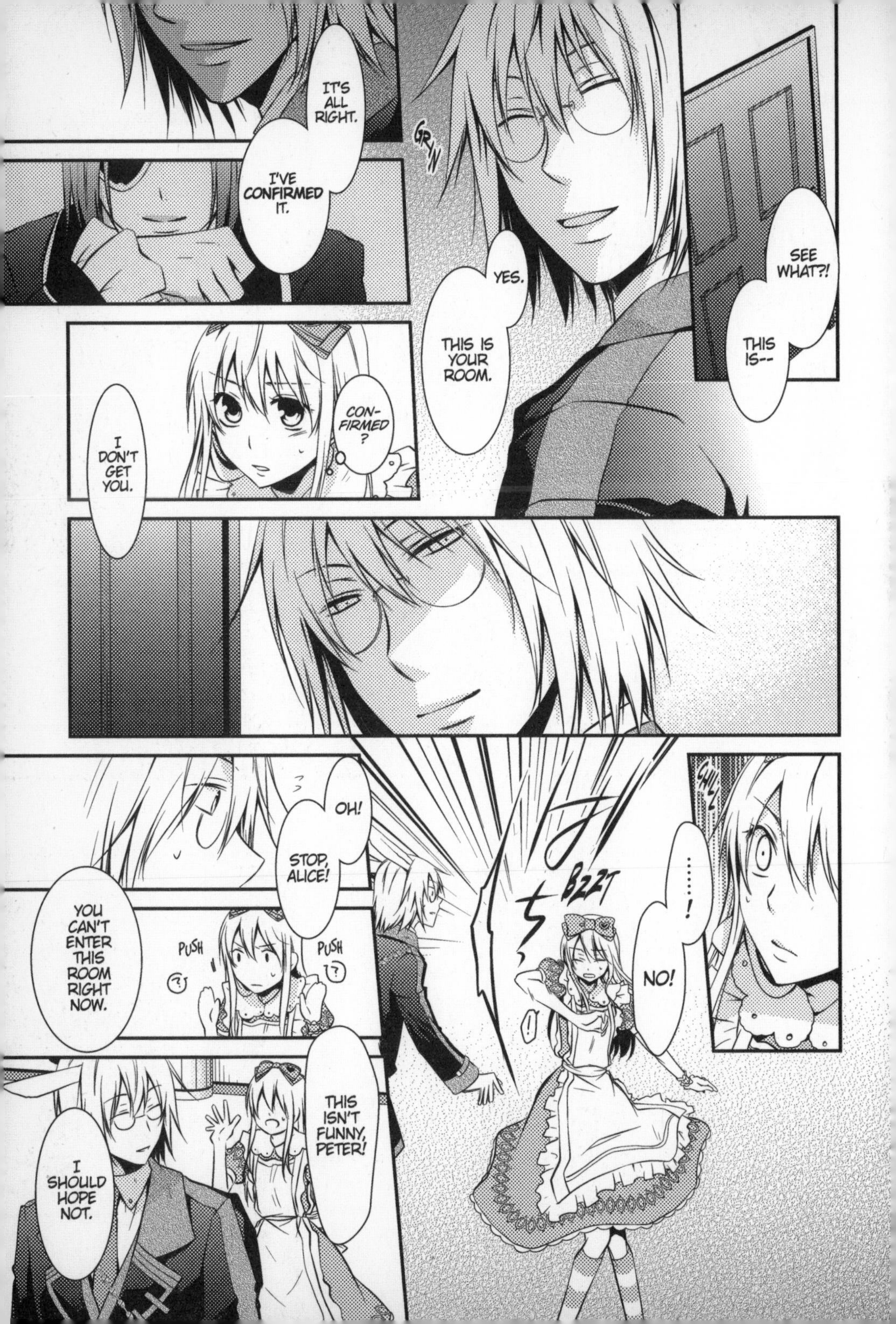
SEE WHAT?!
THIS IS--
GRIN
YES.
THIS IS YOUR ROOM.
IT'S ALL RIGHT.
I'VE CONFIRMED IT.
CON-FIRMED?
I DON'T GET YOU.
CHILL
......!
NO!
BZZT
OH!
STOP, ALICE!
YOU CAN'T ENTER THIS ROOM RIGHT NOW.
PUSH
PUSH
THIS ISN'T FUNNY, PETER!
I SHOULD HOPE NOT.

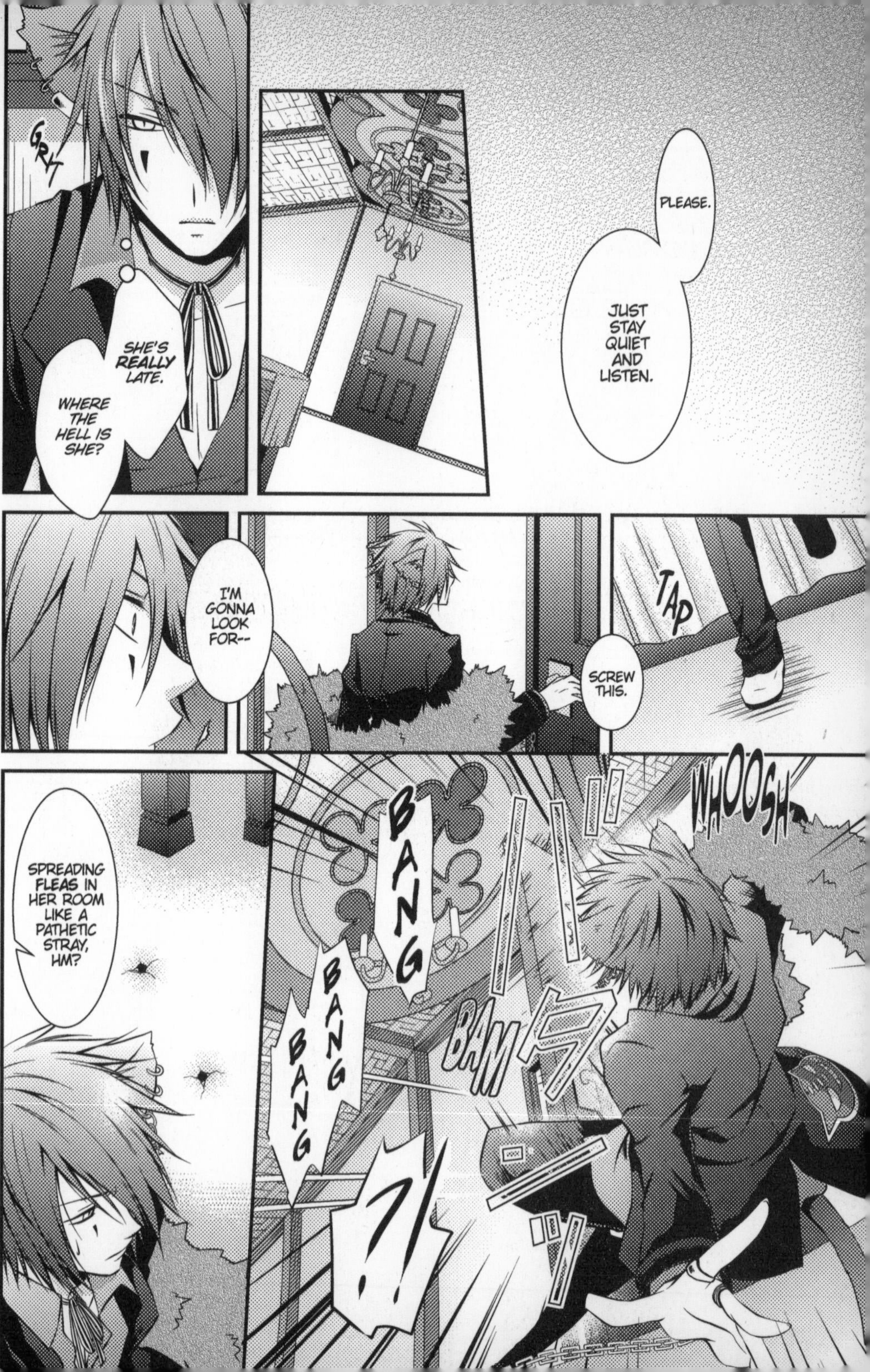
PLEASE.
JUST STAY QUIET AND LISTEN.
GRYT
SHE'S REALLY LATE.
WHERE THE HELL IS SHE?
TAP
I'M GONNA LOOK FOR--
SCREW THIS.
WHOOSH
BANG
BANG
BANG
BANG
BAM
?!
SPREADING FLEAS IN HER ROOM LIKE A PATHETIC STRAY, HM?

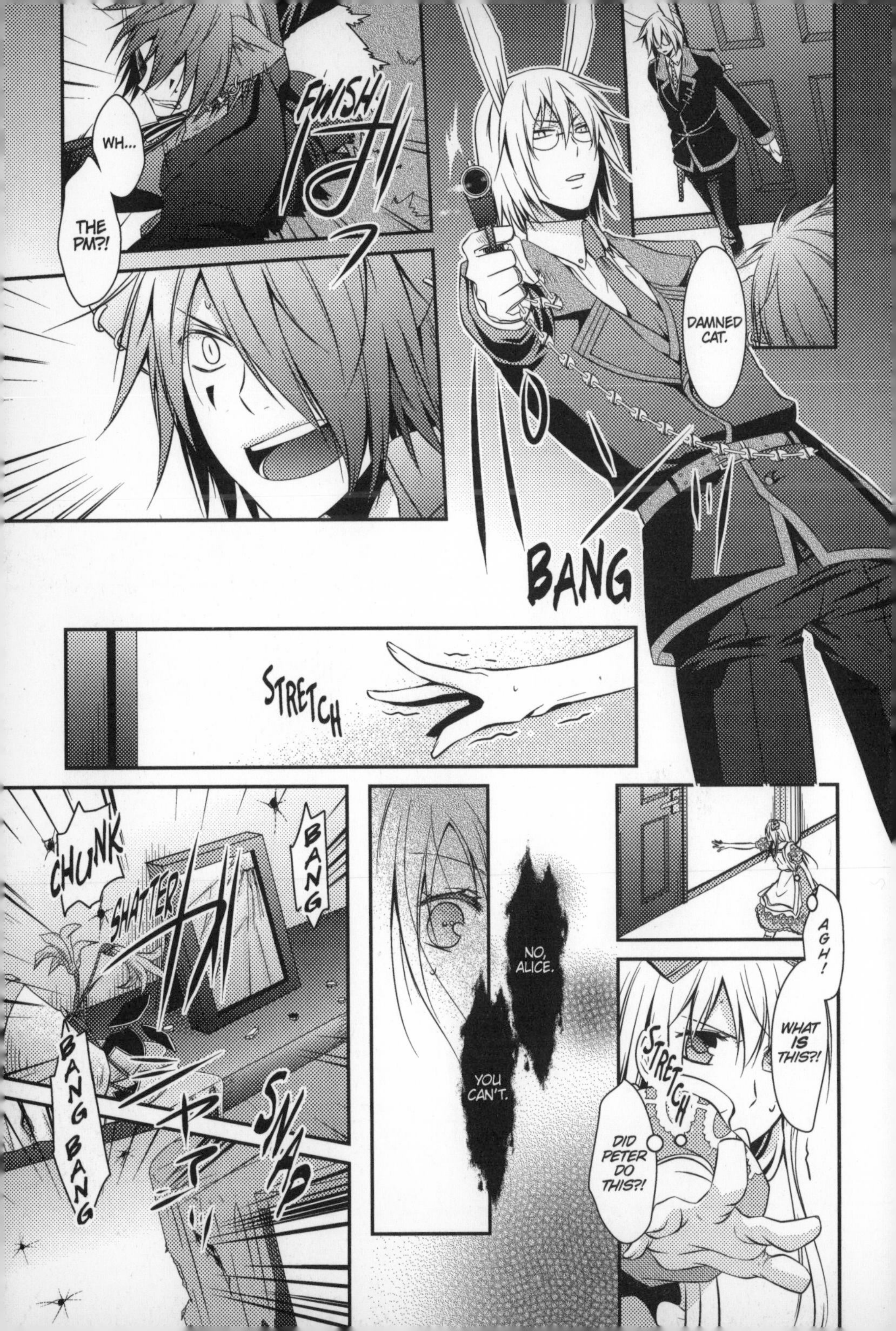
DAMNED CAT.
BANG
FWISH
WH...
THE PM?!
STRETCH
AGH!
WHAT IS THIS?!
STRETCH
DID PETER DO THIS?!
NO, ALICE.
YOU CAN'T.
BANG BANG
CHUNK
SHATTER
SNAP
BANG BANG

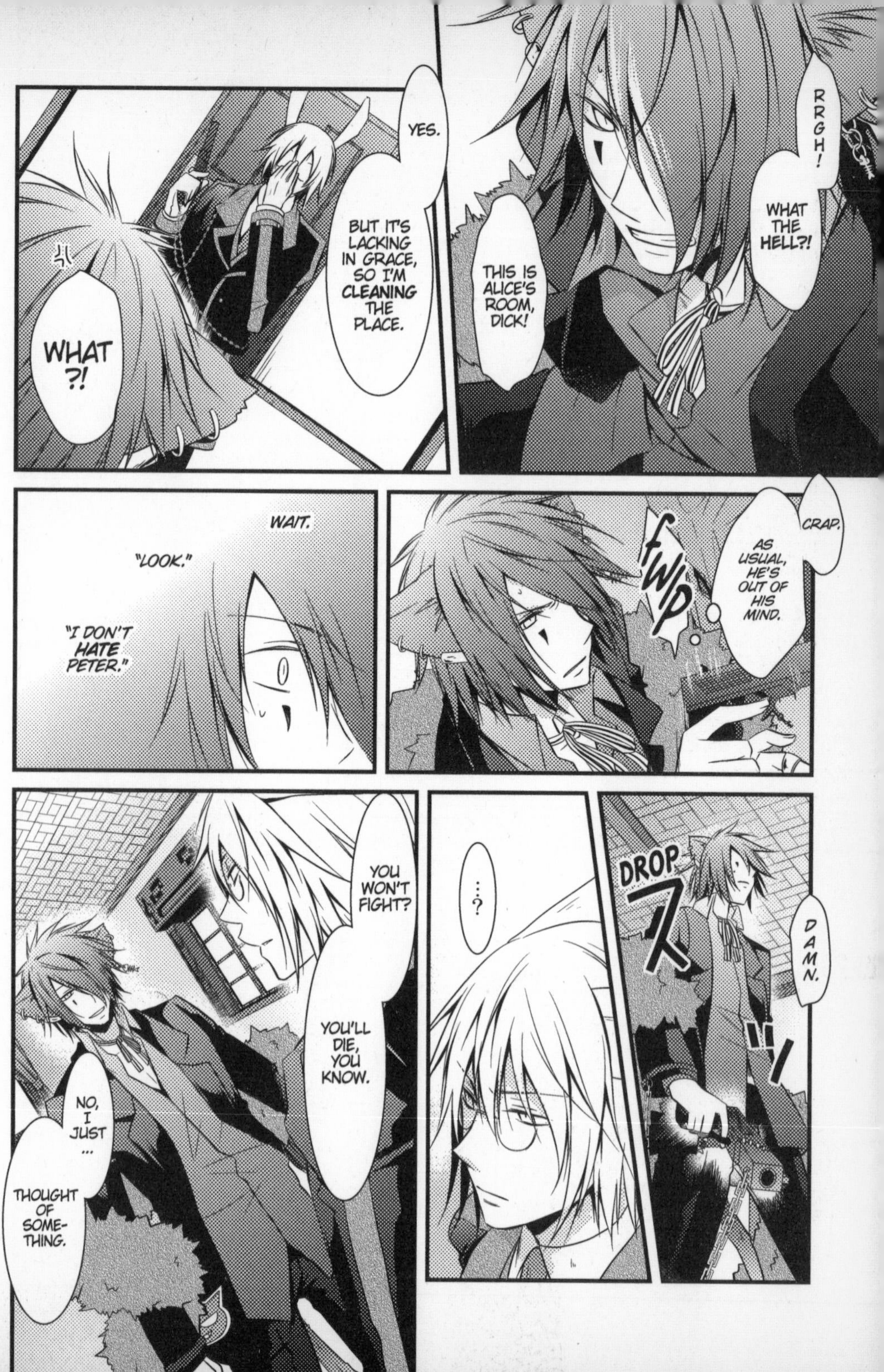

RRGH!
WHAT THE HELL?!
THIS IS ALICE'S ROOM, DICK!
YES.
BUT IT'S LACKING IN GRACE, SO I'M CLEANING THE PLACE.
WHAT?!
CRAP.
AS USUAL, HE'S OUT OF HIS MIND.
FWIP
WAIT.
"LOOK."
"I DON'T HATE PETER."
DROP
DAMN.
...?
YOU WON'T FIGHT?
YOU'LL DIE, YOU KNOW.
NO, I JUST ...
THOUGHT OF SOME-THING.

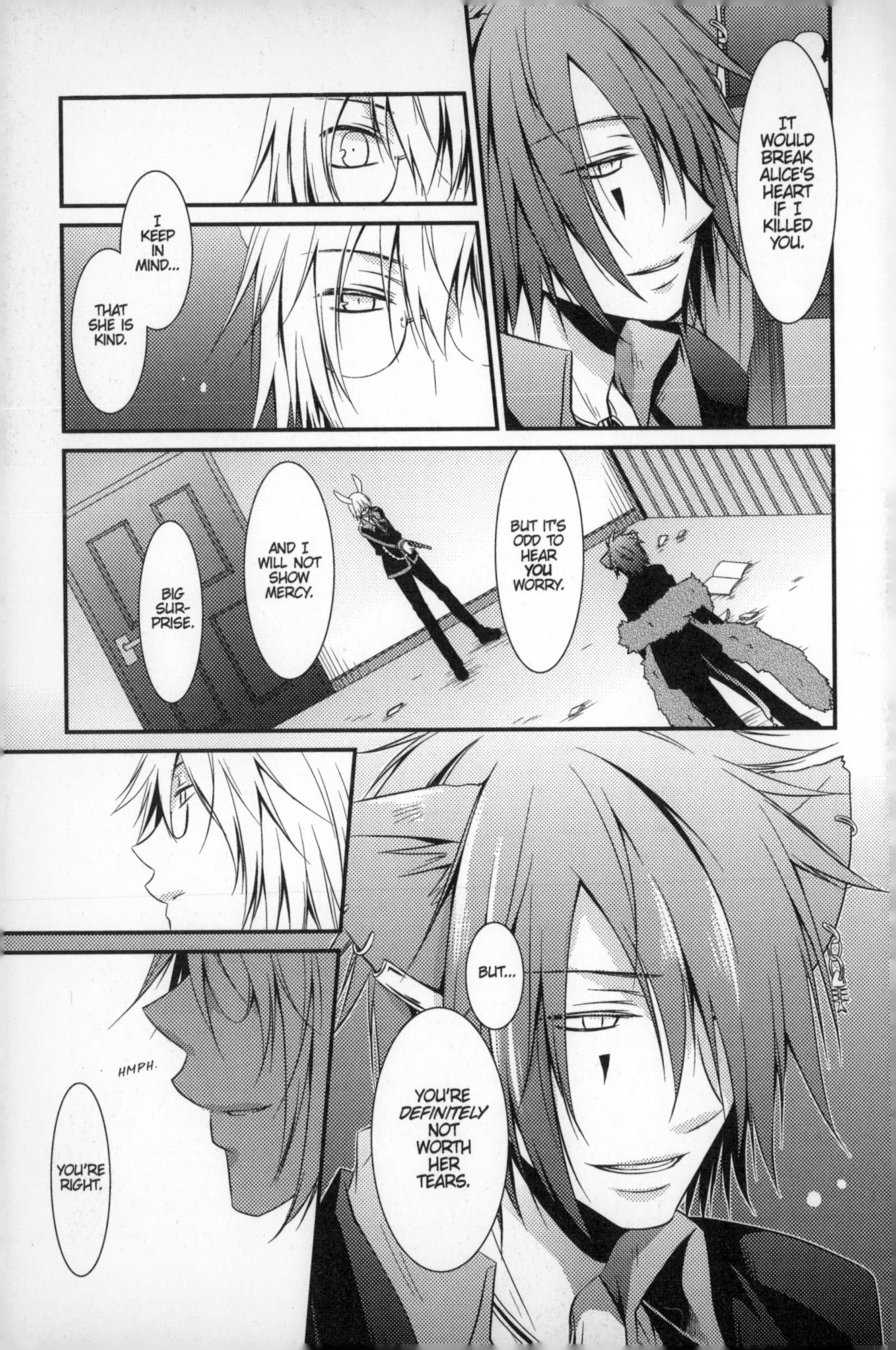
IT WOULD BREAK ALICE'S HEART IF I KILLED YOU.
I KEEP IN MIND...
THAT SHE IS KIND.
BUT IT'S ODD TO HEAR *YOU* WORRY.
AND I WILL NOT SHOW MERCY.
BIG SURPRISE.
BUT...
YOU'RE *DEFINITELY* NOT WORTH HER TEARS.
HMPH.
YOU'RE RIGHT.

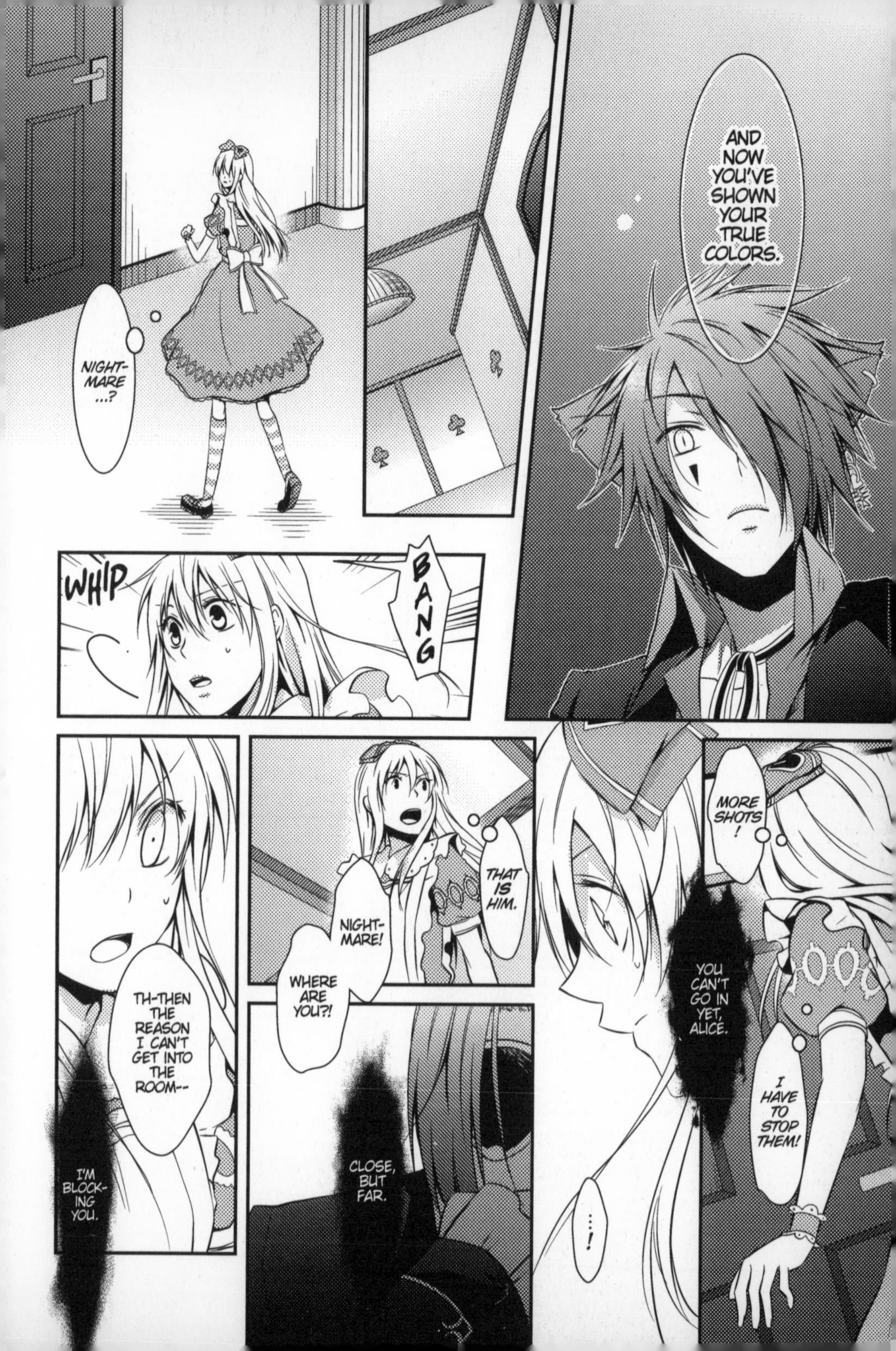

AND NOW YOU'VE SHOWN YOUR TRUE COLORS.
NIGHT-MARE ...?
BANG
WHIP
MORE SHOTS!
YOU CAN'T GO IN YET, ALICE.
I HAVE TO STOP THEM!
...!
THAT IS HIM.
NIGHT-MARE!
WHERE ARE YOU?!
CLOSE, BUT FAR.
TH-THEN THE REASON I CAN'T GET INTO THE ROOM--
I'M BLOCK-ING YOU.

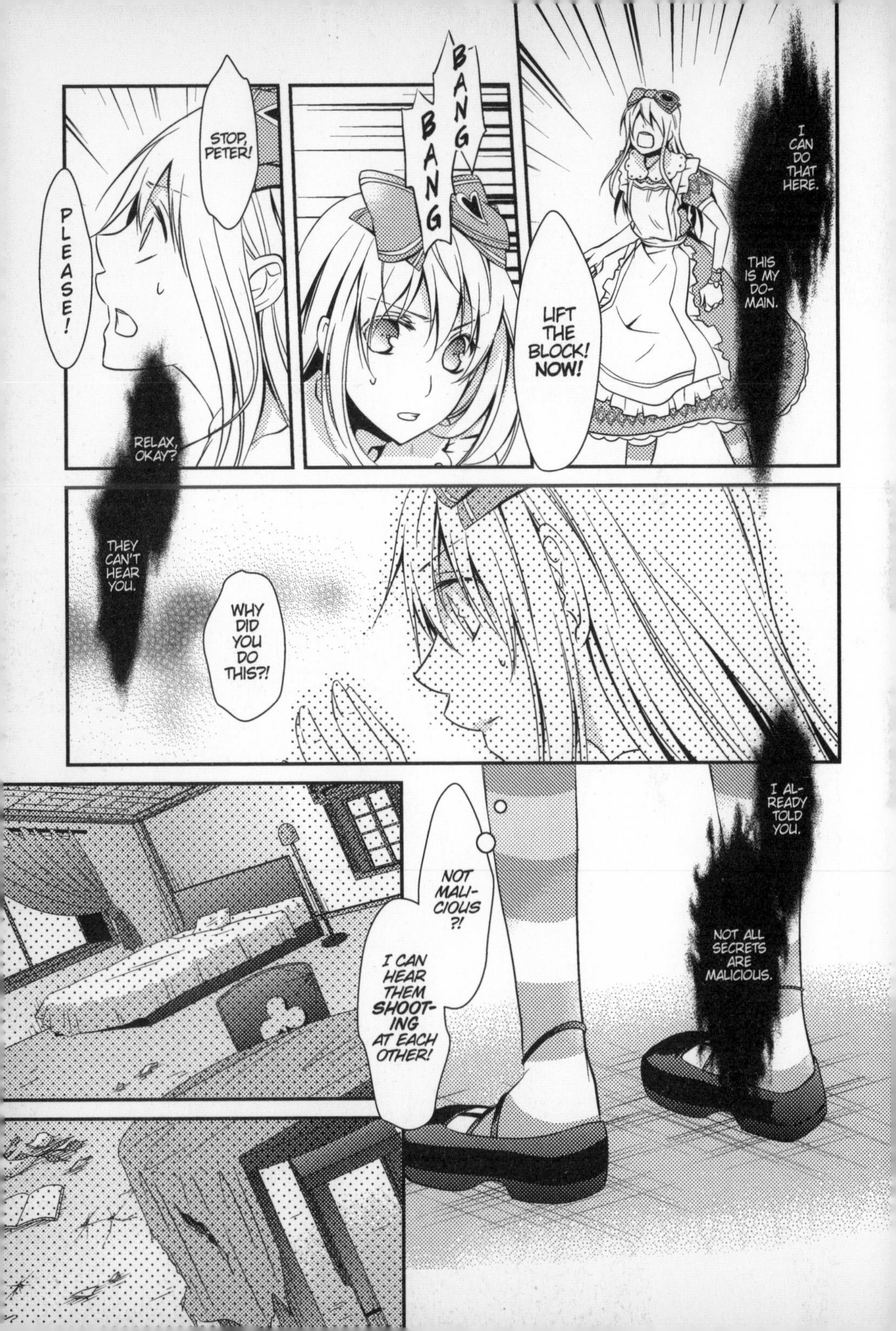
LIFT THE BLOCK! NOW!
I CAN DO THAT HERE.
THIS IS MY DO-MAIN.
BANG
BANG
BANG
STOP, PETER!
PLEASE!
RELAX, OKAY?
WHY DID YOU DO THIS?!
THEY CAN'T HEAR YOU.
I AL-READY TOLD YOU.
NOT ALL SECRETS ARE MALICIOUS.
NOT MALI-CIOUS?!
I CAN HEAR THEM SHOOT-ING AT EACH OTHER!

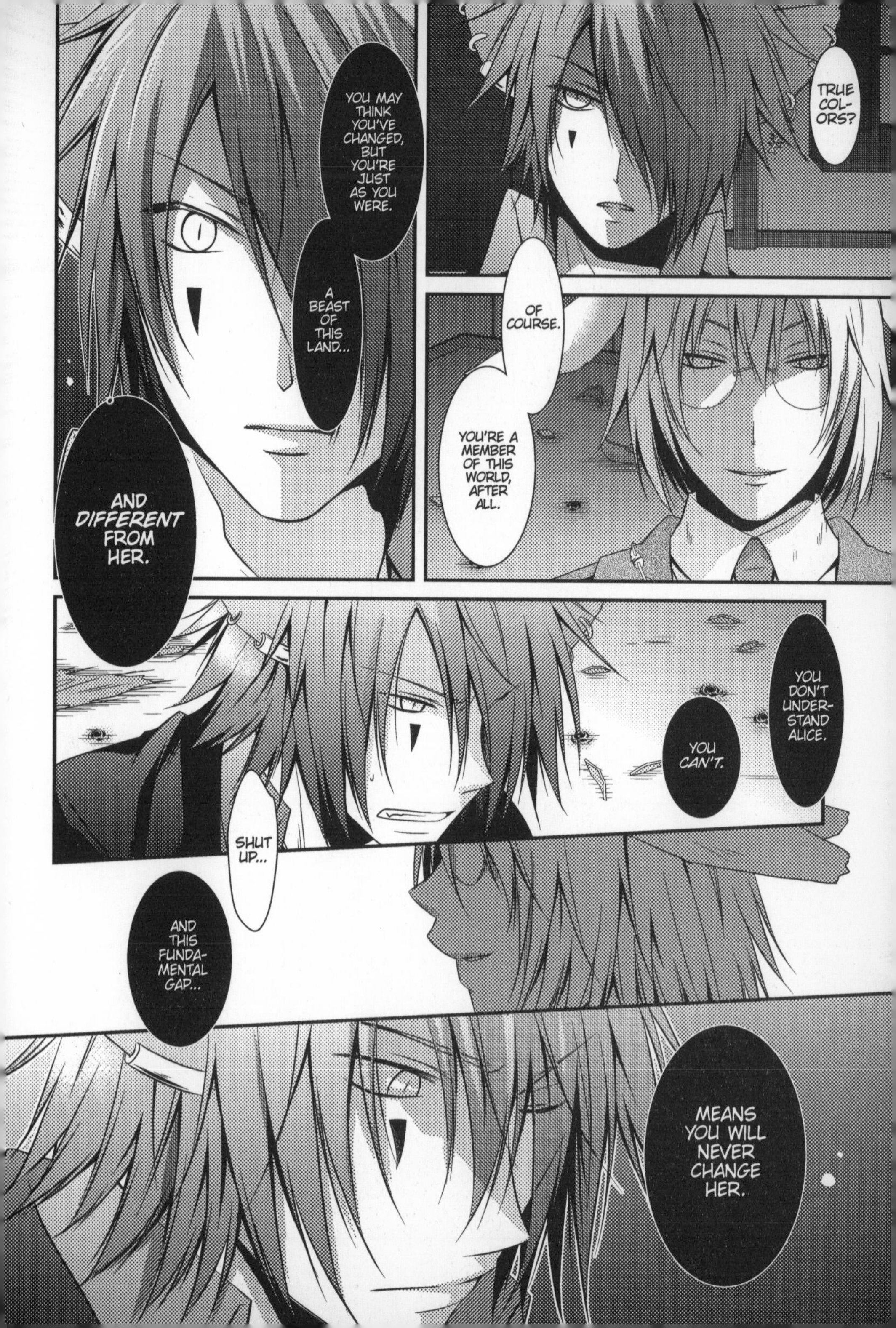
TRUE COL-ORS?
OF COURSE.
YOU'RE A MEMBER OF THIS WORLD, AFTER ALL.
YOU MAY THINK YOU'VE CHANGED, BUT YOU'RE JUST AS YOU WERE.
A BEAST OF THIS LAND...
AND *DIFFERENT* FROM HER.
YOU DON'T UNDER-STAND ALICE.
YOU *CAN'T.*
SHUT UP...
AND THIS FUNDA-MENTAL GAP...
MEANS YOU WILL NEVER CHANGE HER.

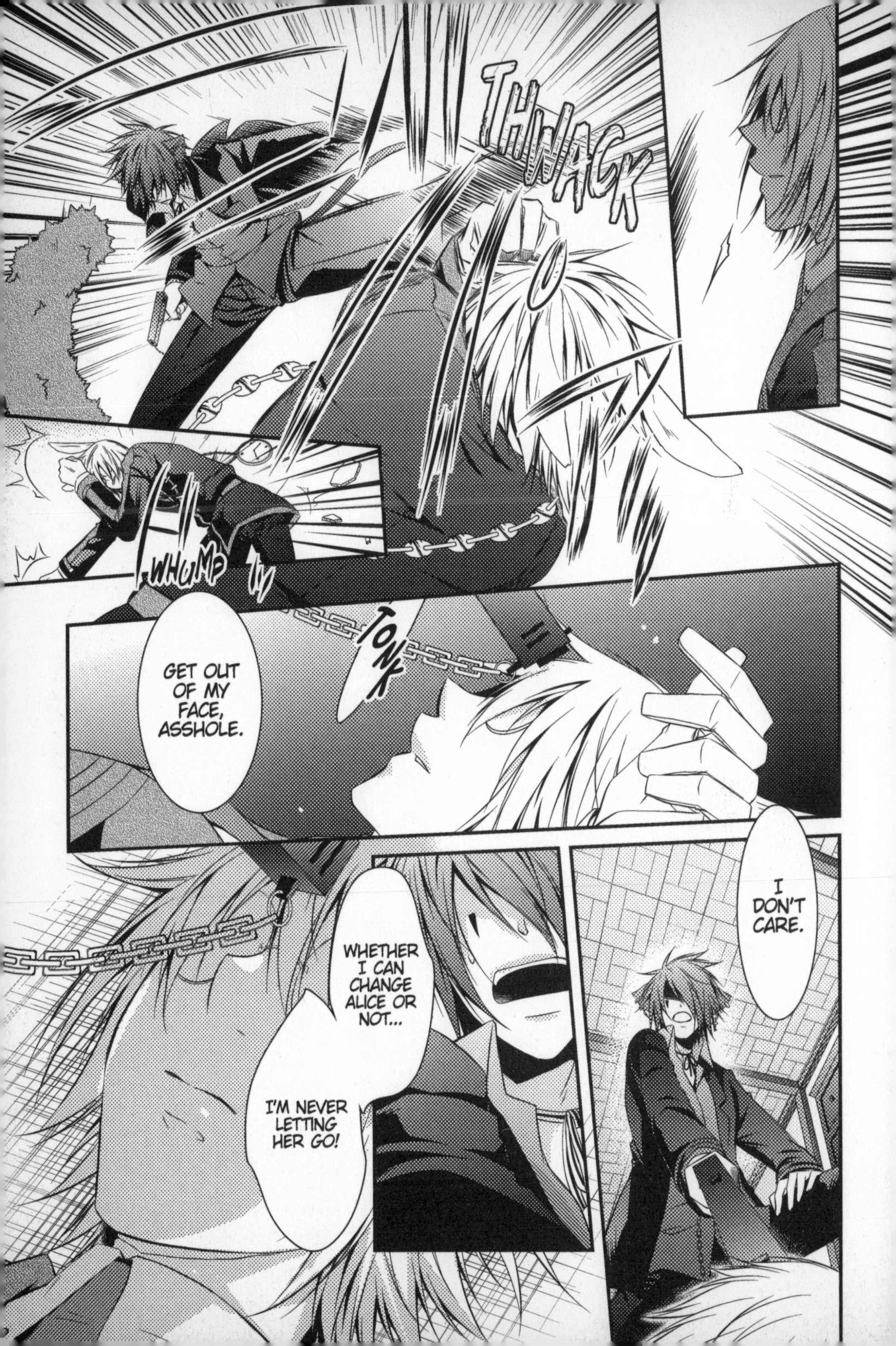
THWACK
WHUMP
TONK
GET OUT OF MY FACE, ASSHOLE.
I DON'T CARE.
WHETHER I CAN CHANGE ALICE OR NOT...
I'M NEVER LETTING HER GO!

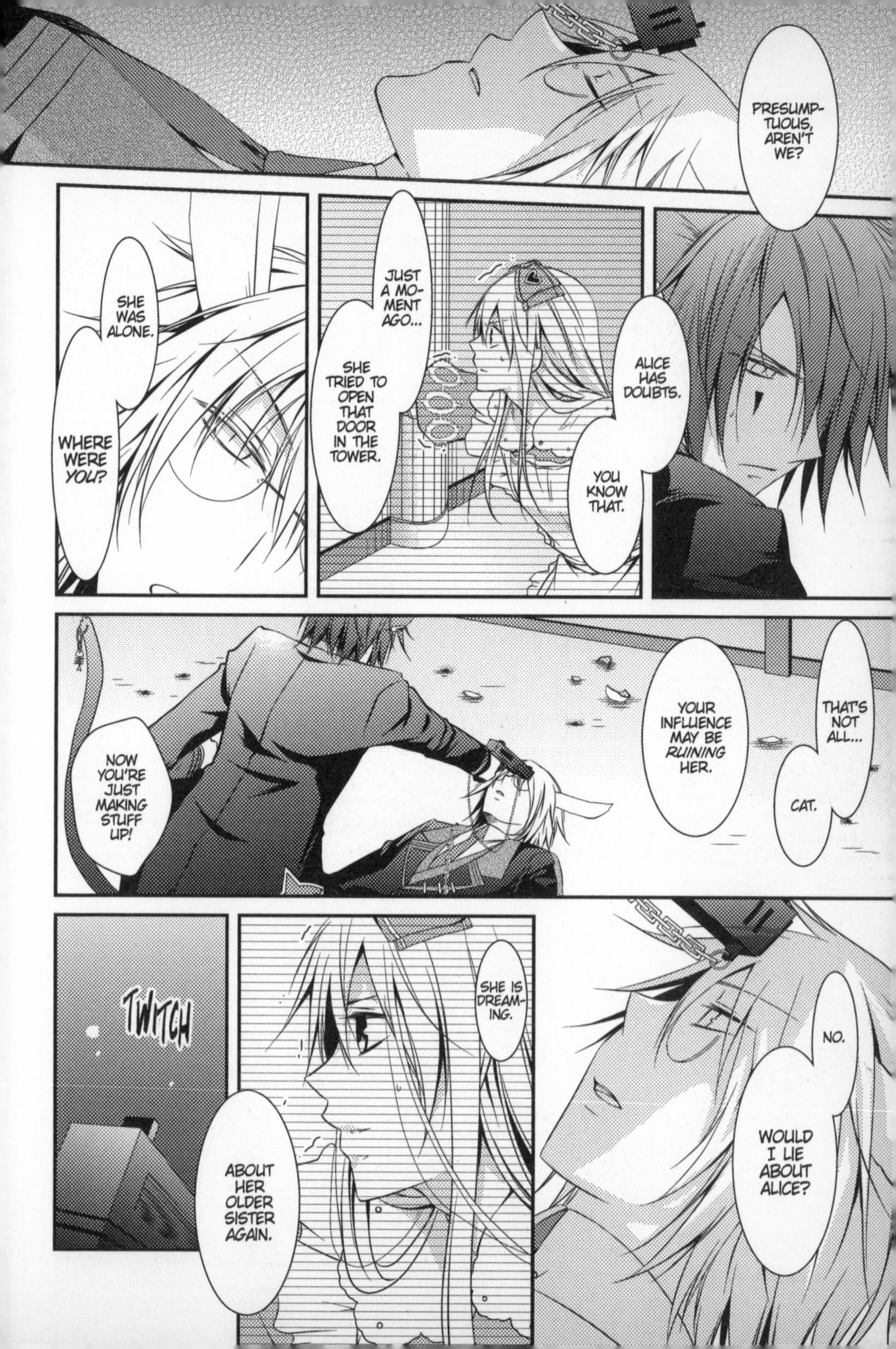
PRESUMPTUOUS, AREN'T WE?
ALICE HAS DOUBTS.
YOU KNOW THAT.
JUST A MOMENT AGO...
SHE TRIED TO OPEN THAT DOOR IN THE TOWER.
SHE WAS ALONE.
WHERE WERE *YOU*?
THAT'S NOT ALL...
CAT.
YOUR INFLUENCE MAY BE *RUINING* HER.
NOW YOU'RE JUST MAKING STUFF UP!
NO.
WOULD I LIE ABOUT ALICE?
SHE IS DREAMING.
ABOUT HER OLDER SISTER AGAIN.
TWITCH

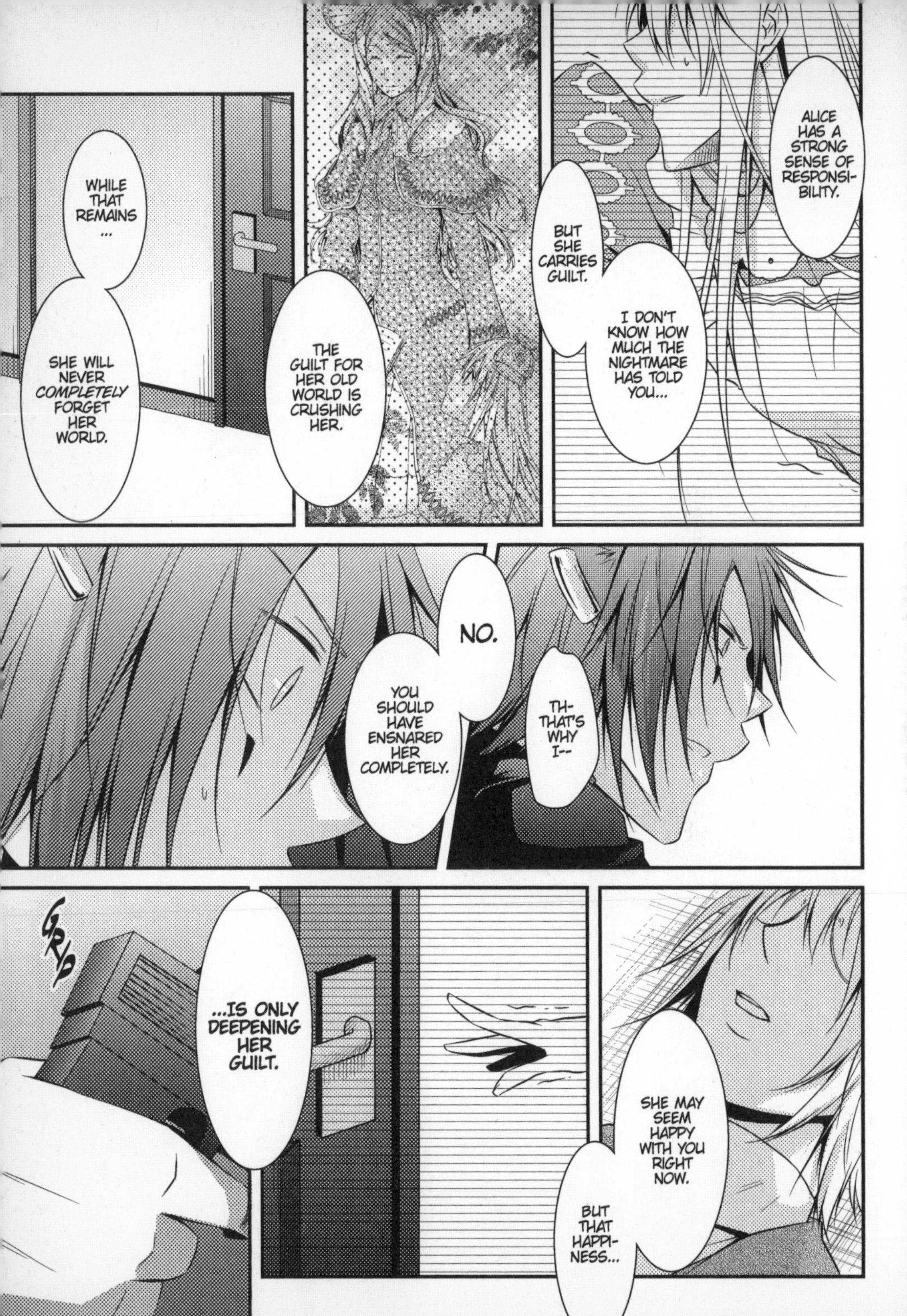
ALICE HAS A STRONG SENSE OF RESPONSI-BILITY.
BUT SHE CARRIES GUILT.
I DON'T KNOW HOW MUCH THE NIGHTMARE HAS TOLD YOU...
THE GUILT FOR HER OLD WORLD IS CRUSHING HER.
WHILE THAT REMAINS ...
SHE WILL NEVER COMPLETELY FORGET HER WORLD.
TH-THAT'S WHY I--
NO.
YOU SHOULD HAVE ENSNARED HER COMPLETELY.
SHE MAY SEEM HAPPY WITH YOU RIGHT NOW.
BUT THAT HAPPI-NESS...
...IS ONLY DEEPENING HER GUILT.
GRIP

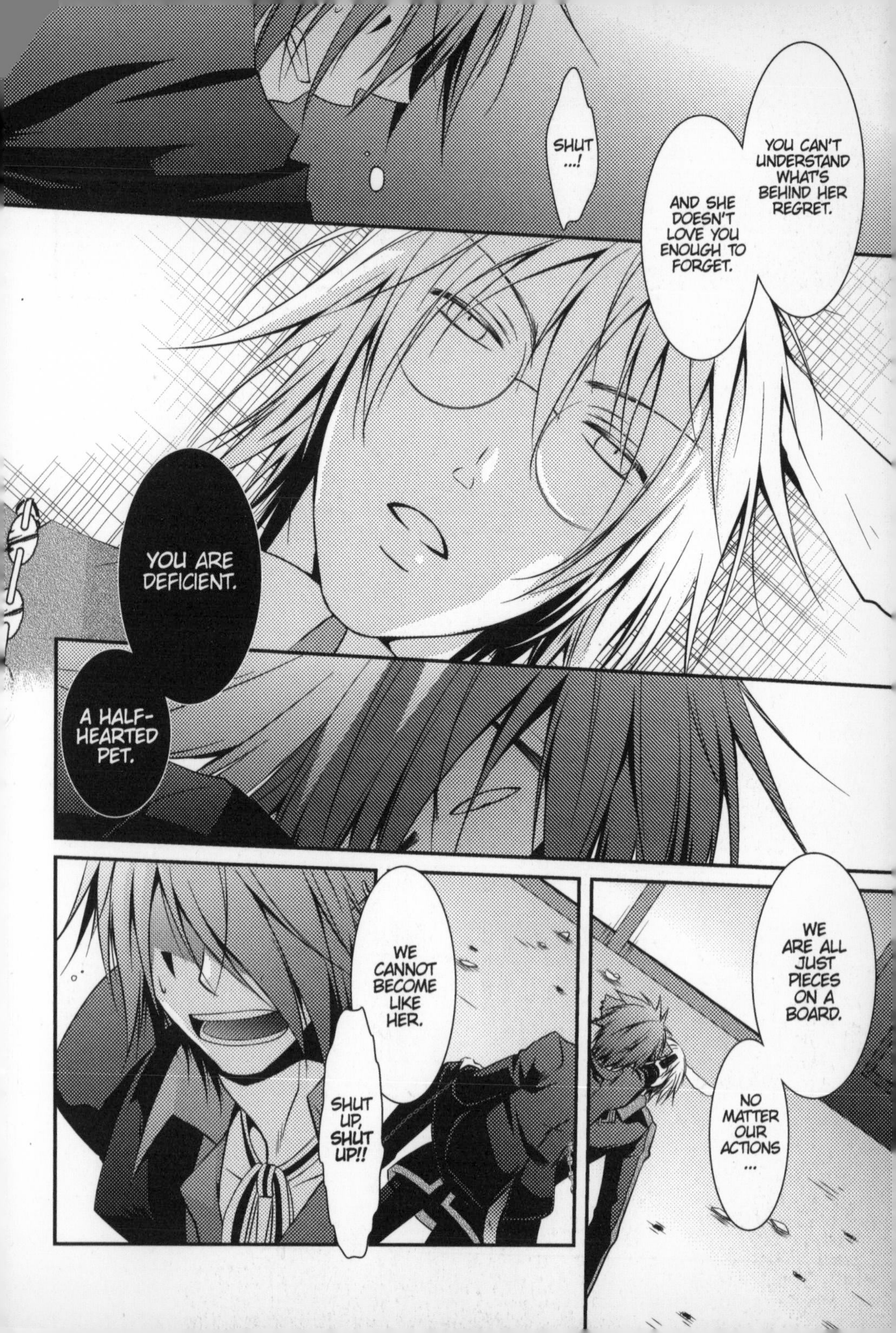
YOU CAN'T UNDERSTAND WHAT'S BEHIND HER REGRET.
AND SHE DOESN'T LOVE YOU ENOUGH TO FORGET.
SHUT ...!
YOU ARE DEFICIENT.
A HALF-HEARTED PET.
WE ARE ALL JUST PIECES ON A BOARD.
NO MATTER OUR ACTIONS ...
WE CANNOT BECOME LIKE HER.
SHUT UP, SHUT UP!!

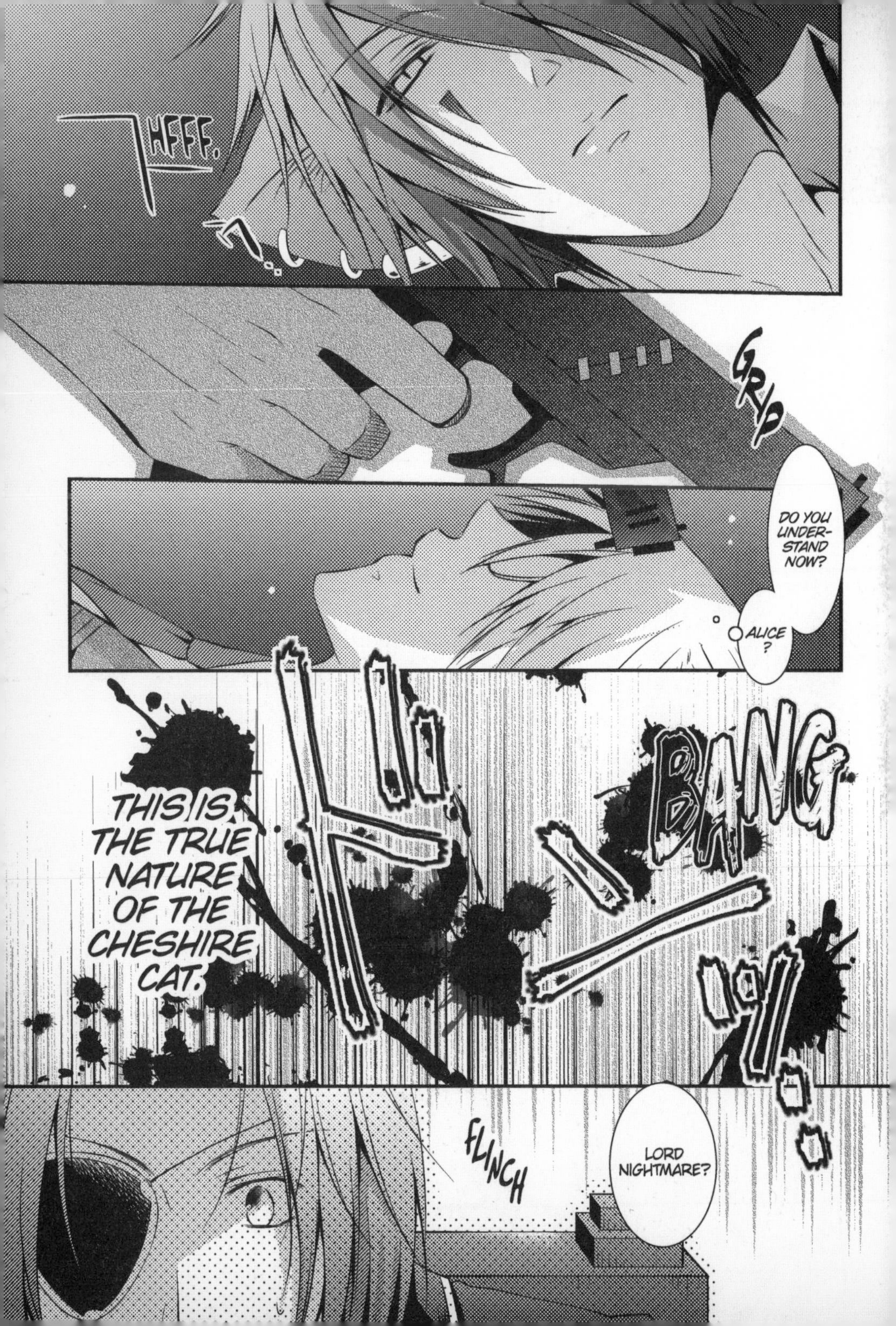
THFFF.
GRIP
DO YOU UNDER-STAND NOW?
ALICE?
BANG
THIS IS THE TRUE NATURE OF THE CHESHIRE CAT.
LORD NIGHTMARE?
FLINCH

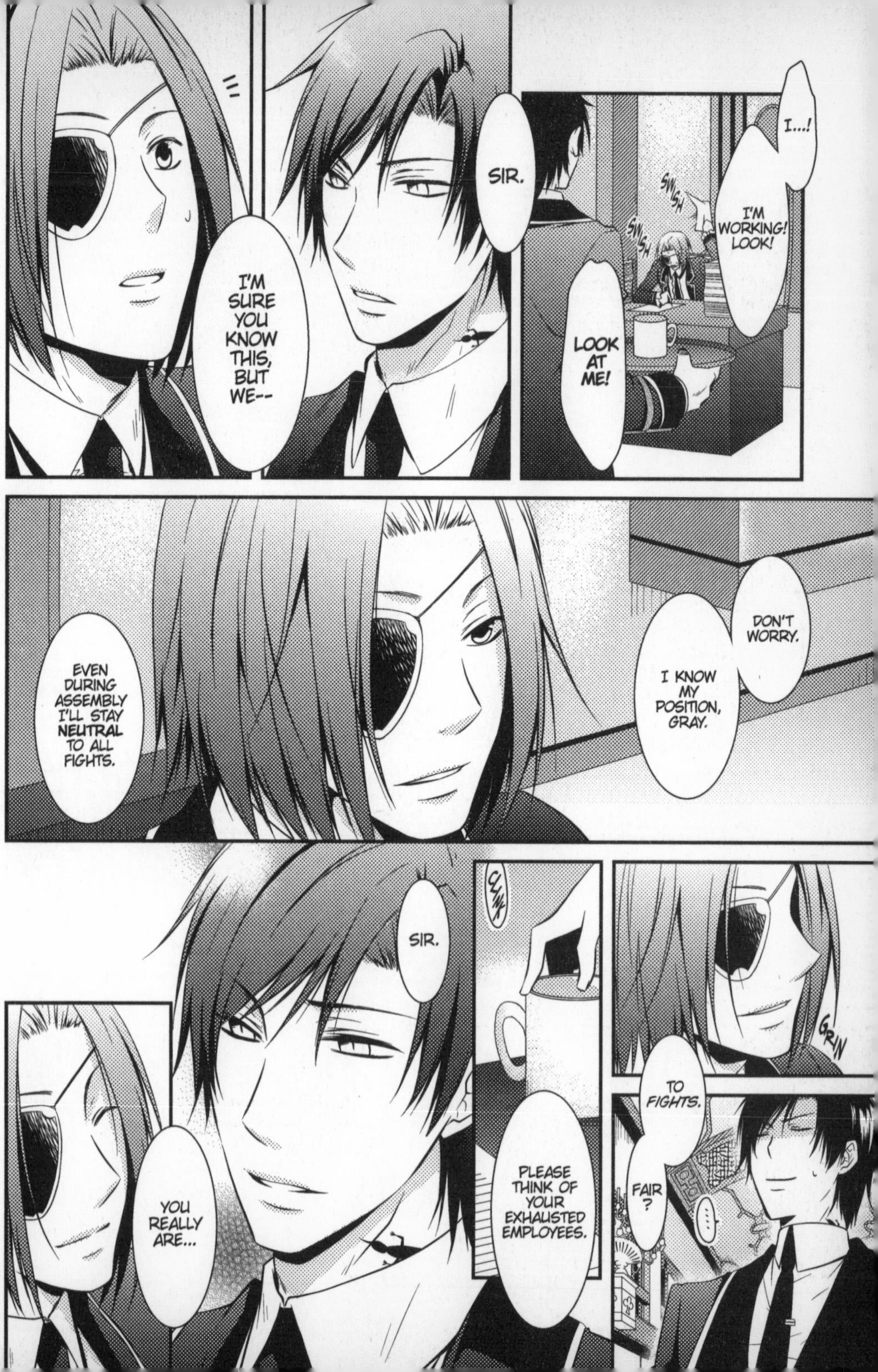
I...!
I'M WORKING! LOOK!
SWISH
SWISH
LOOK AT ME!
SIR.
I'M SURE YOU KNOW THIS, BUT WE--
DON'T WORRY.
I KNOW MY POSITION, GRAY.
EVEN DURING ASSEMBLY I'LL STAY NEUTRAL TO ALL FIGHTS.
GRIN
TO FIGHTS.
FAIR?
...
CLINK
SIR.
PLEASE THINK OF YOUR EXHAUSTED EMPLOYEES.
YOU REALLY ARE...

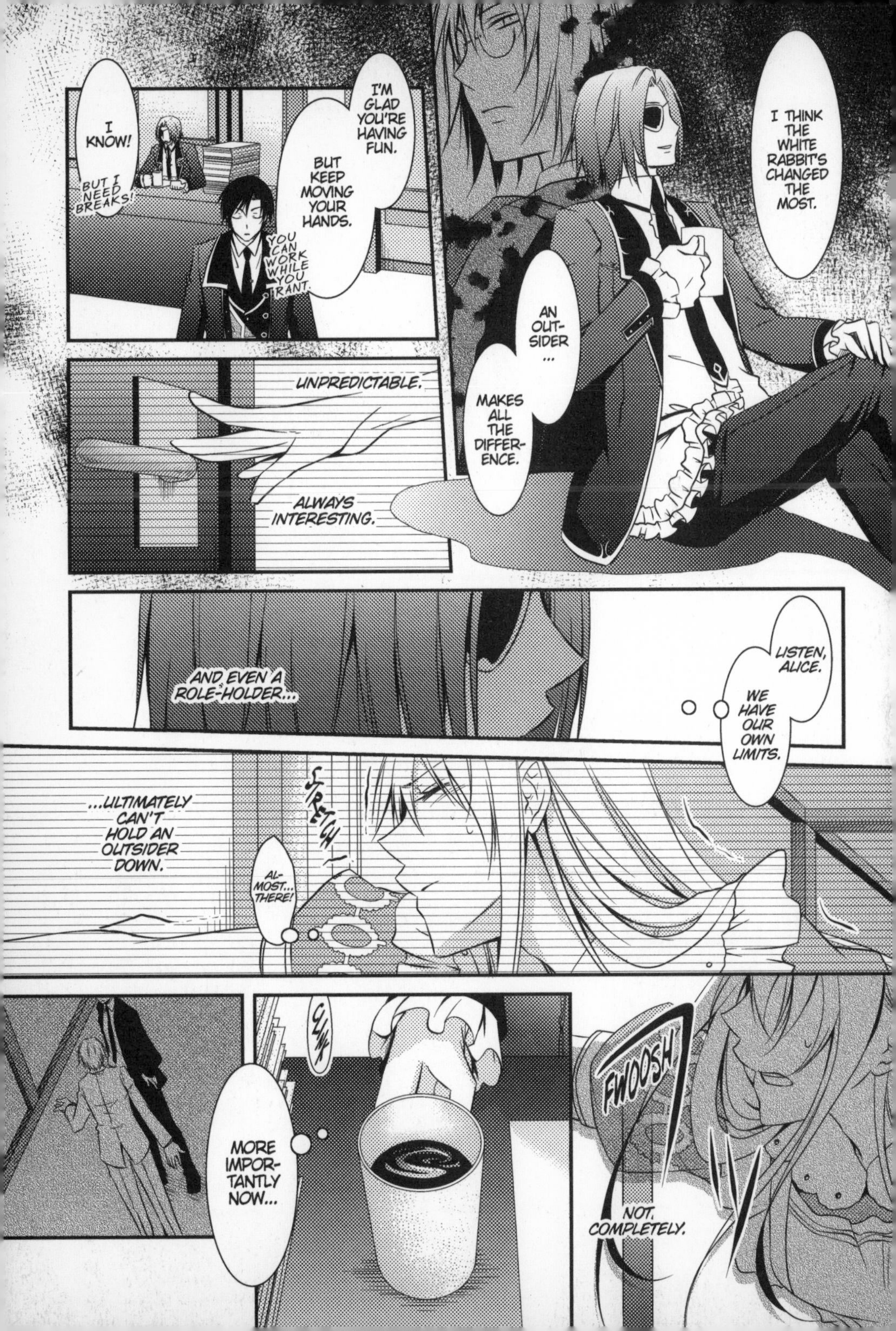
I THINK THE WHITE RABBIT'S CHANGED THE MOST.
AN OUTSIDER...
MAKES ALL THE DIFFERENCE.
I'M GLAD YOU'RE HAVING FUN.
BUT KEEP MOVING YOUR HANDS.
YOU CAN WORK WHILE YOU RANT.
I KNOW!
BUT I NEED BREAKS!
UNPREDICTABLE.
ALWAYS INTERESTING.
LISTEN, ALICE.
WE HAVE OUR OWN LIMITS.
AND EVEN A ROLE-HOLDER...
...ULTIMATELY CAN'T HOLD AN OUTSIDER DOWN.
STRETCH
AL-MOST... THERE!
FWOOSH
NOT. COMPLETELY.
CLINK
MORE IMPOR-TANTLY NOW...

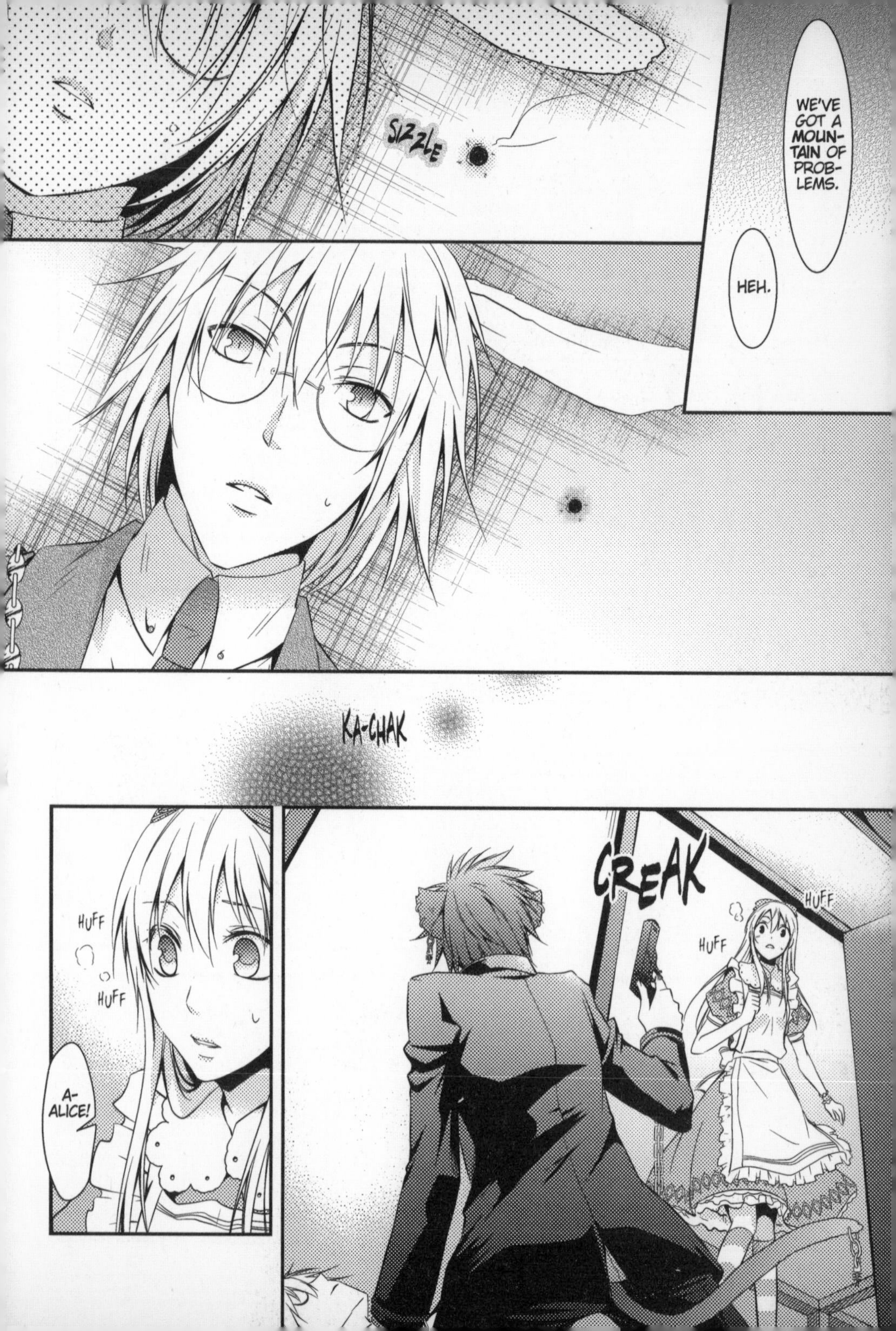
WE'VE GOT A MOUNTAIN OF PROBLEMS.
HEH.
SIZZLE
KA-CHAK
CREAK
HUFF
HUFF
HUFF
HUFF
A-ALICE!

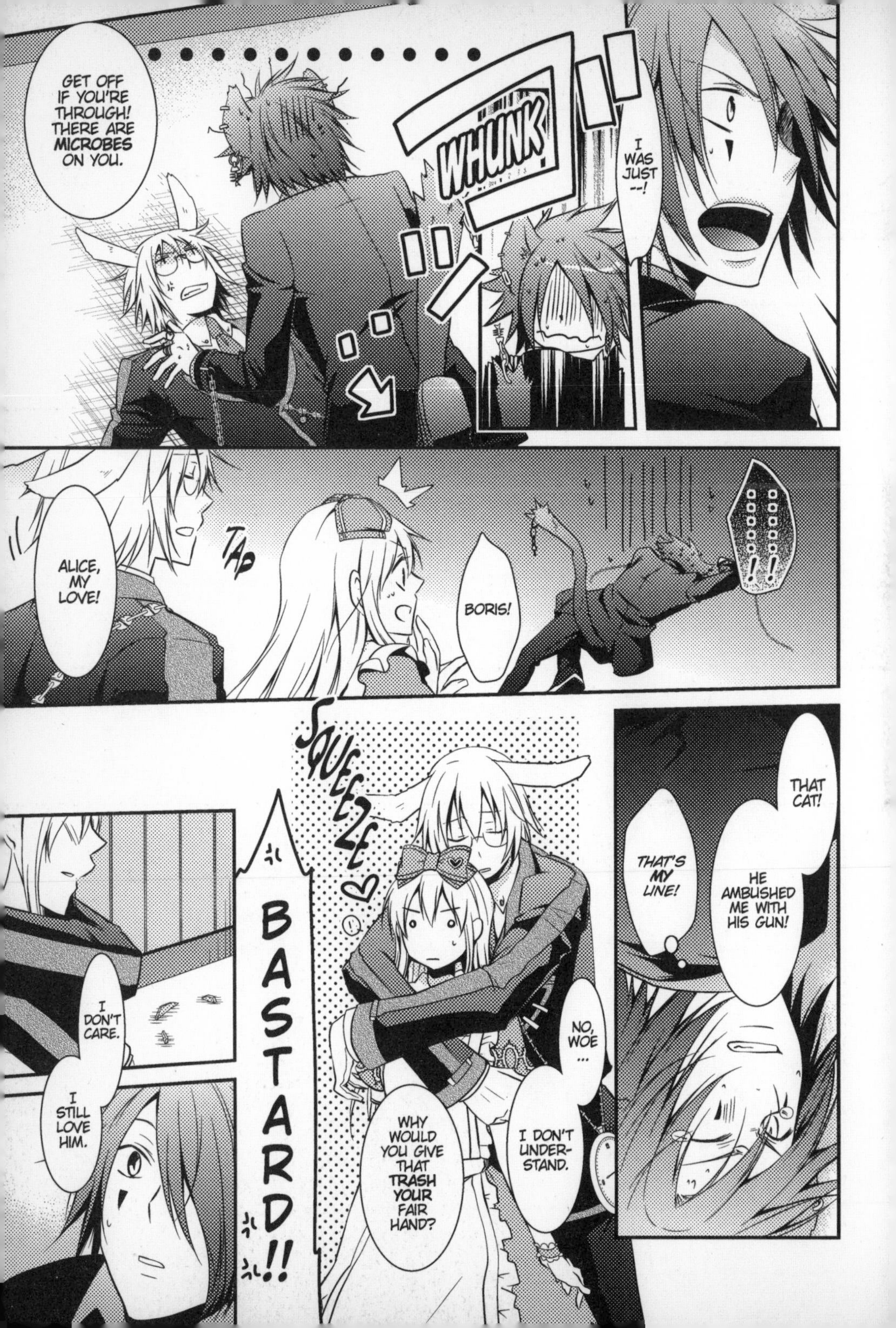

I WAS JUST --!
WHUNK
GET OFF IF YOU'RE THROUGH! THERE ARE MICROBES ON YOU.
......!!
BORIS!
TAP
ALICE, MY LOVE!
THAT CAT!
HE AMBUSHED ME WITH HIS GUN!
THAT'S MY LINE!
SQUEEZE
BASTARD!!
NO, WOE...
I DON'T UNDERSTAND.
WHY WOULD YOU GIVE THAT TRASH YOUR FAIR HAND?
I DON'T CARE.
I STILL LOVE HIM.

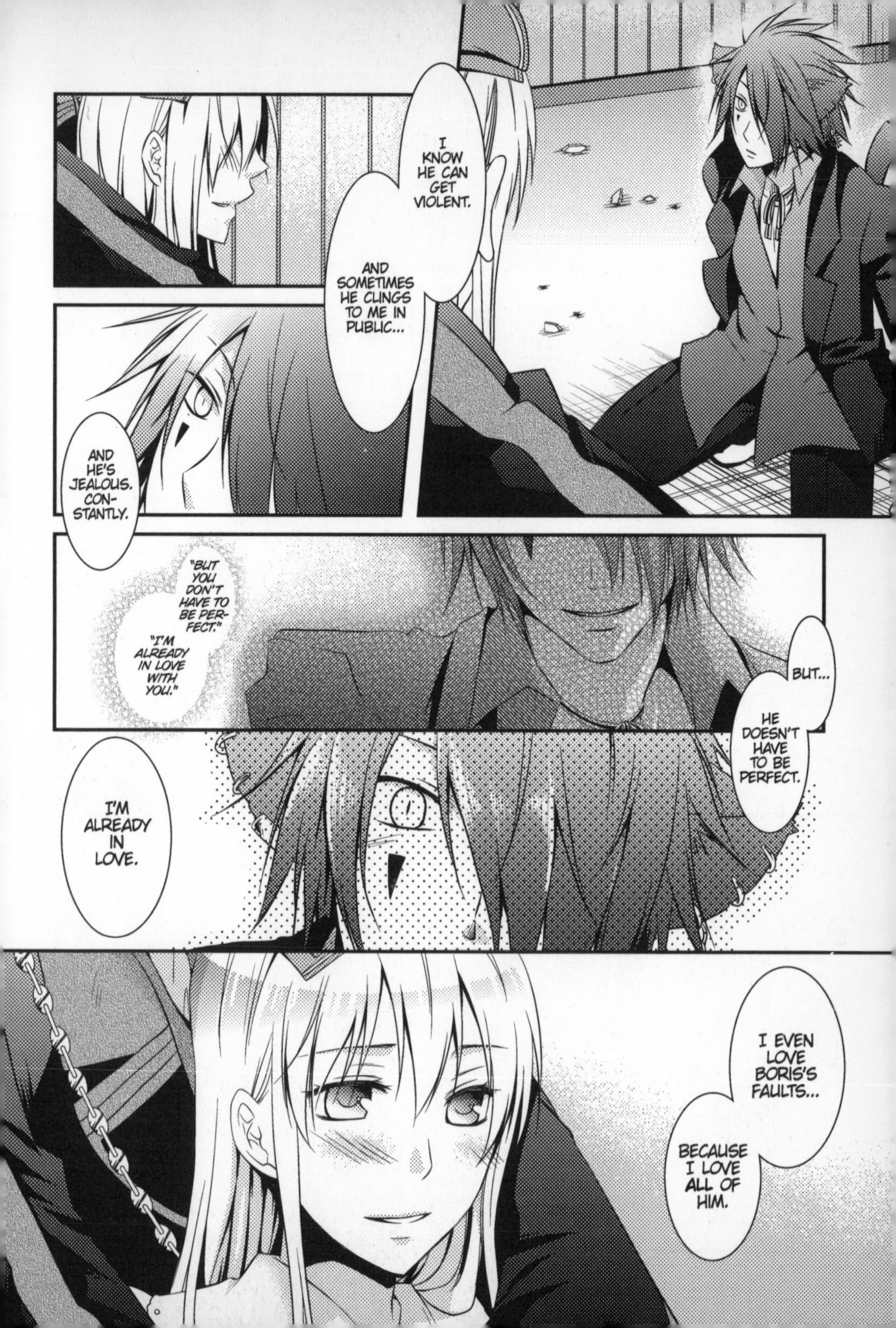
I KNOW HE CAN GET VIOLENT.
AND SOMETIMES HE CLINGS TO ME IN PUBLIC...
AND HE'S JEALOUS. CON-STANTLY.
"BUT YOU DON'T HAVE TO BE PER-FECT."
"I'M ALREADY IN LOVE WITH YOU."
BUT...
HE DOESN'T HAVE TO BE PERFECT.
I'M ALREADY IN LOVE.
I EVEN LOVE BORIS'S FAULTS...
BECAUSE I LOVE ALL OF HIM.

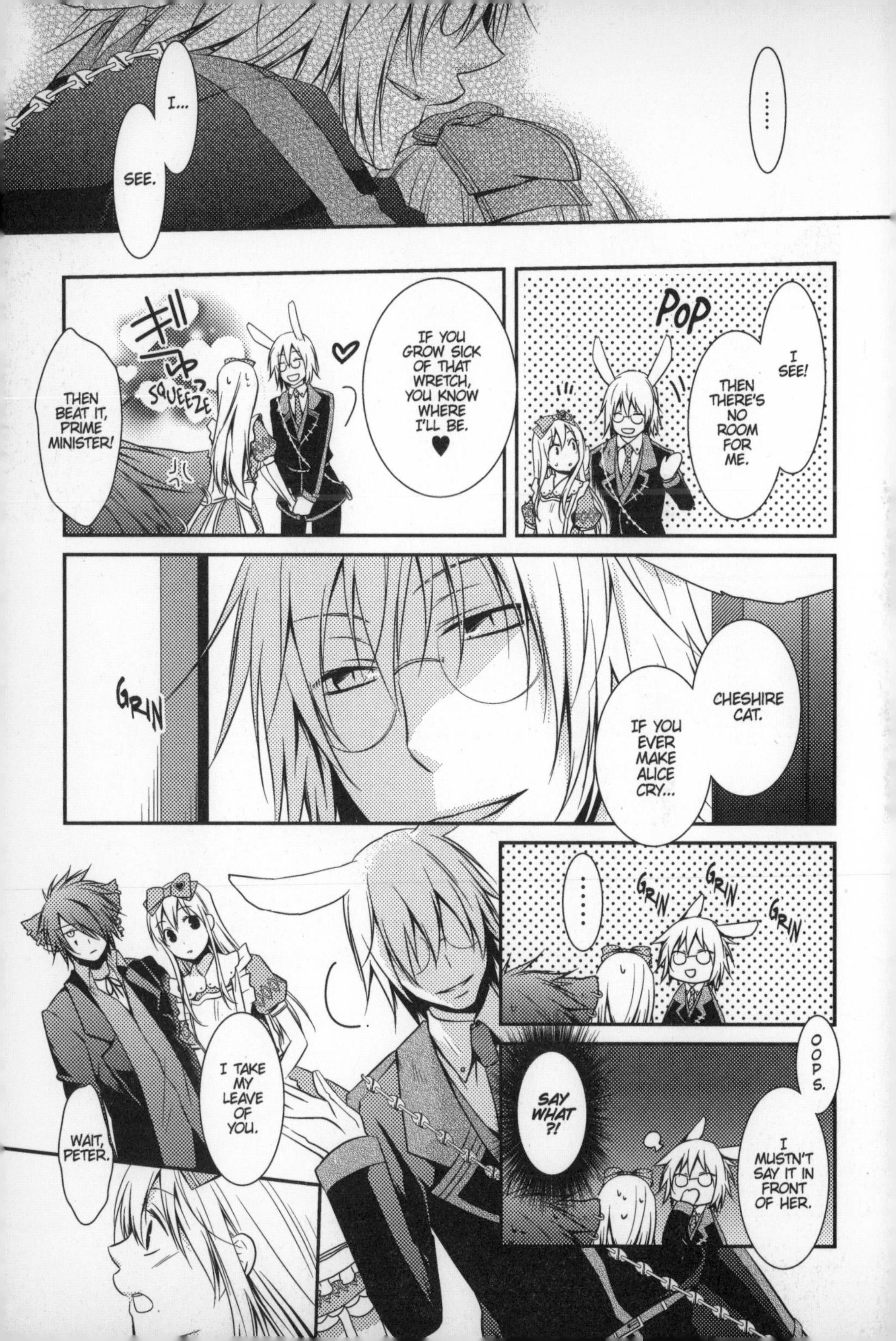
……
I...
SEE.
POP
I SEE!
THEN THERE'S NO ROOM FOR ME.
IF YOU GROW SICK OF THAT WRETCH, YOU KNOW WHERE I'LL BE. ♥
SQUEEZE
THEN BEAT IT, PRIME MINISTER!
CHESHIRE CAT.
IF YOU EVER MAKE ALICE CRY...
GRIN
……
GRIN
GRIN
GRIN
OOPS.
I MUSTN'T SAY IT IN FRONT OF HER.
SAY WHAT?!
I TAKE MY LEAVE OF YOU.
WAIT, PETER.

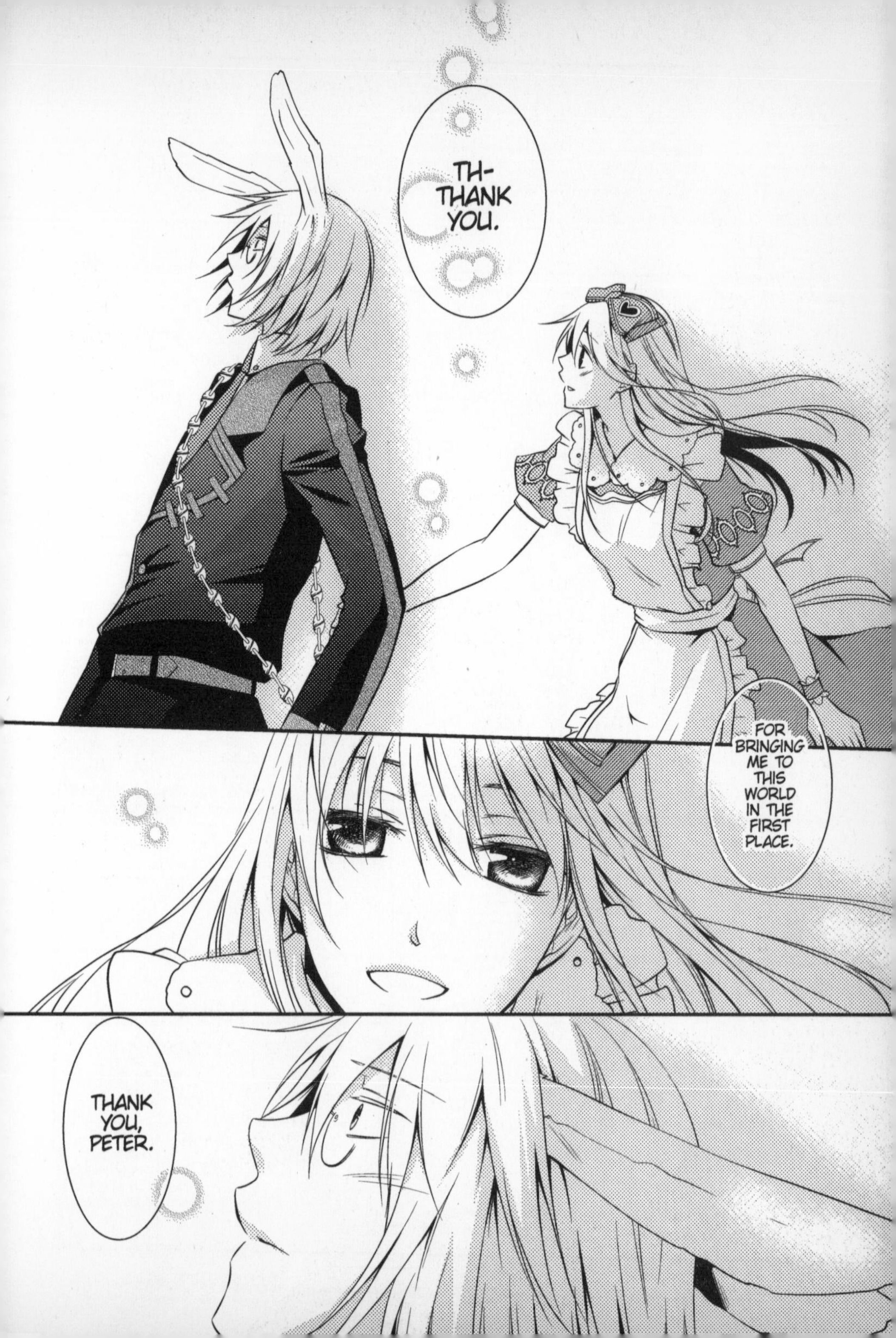
TH-
THANK
YOU.
FOR BRINGING ME TO THIS WORLD IN THE FIRST PLACE.
THANK YOU, PETER.

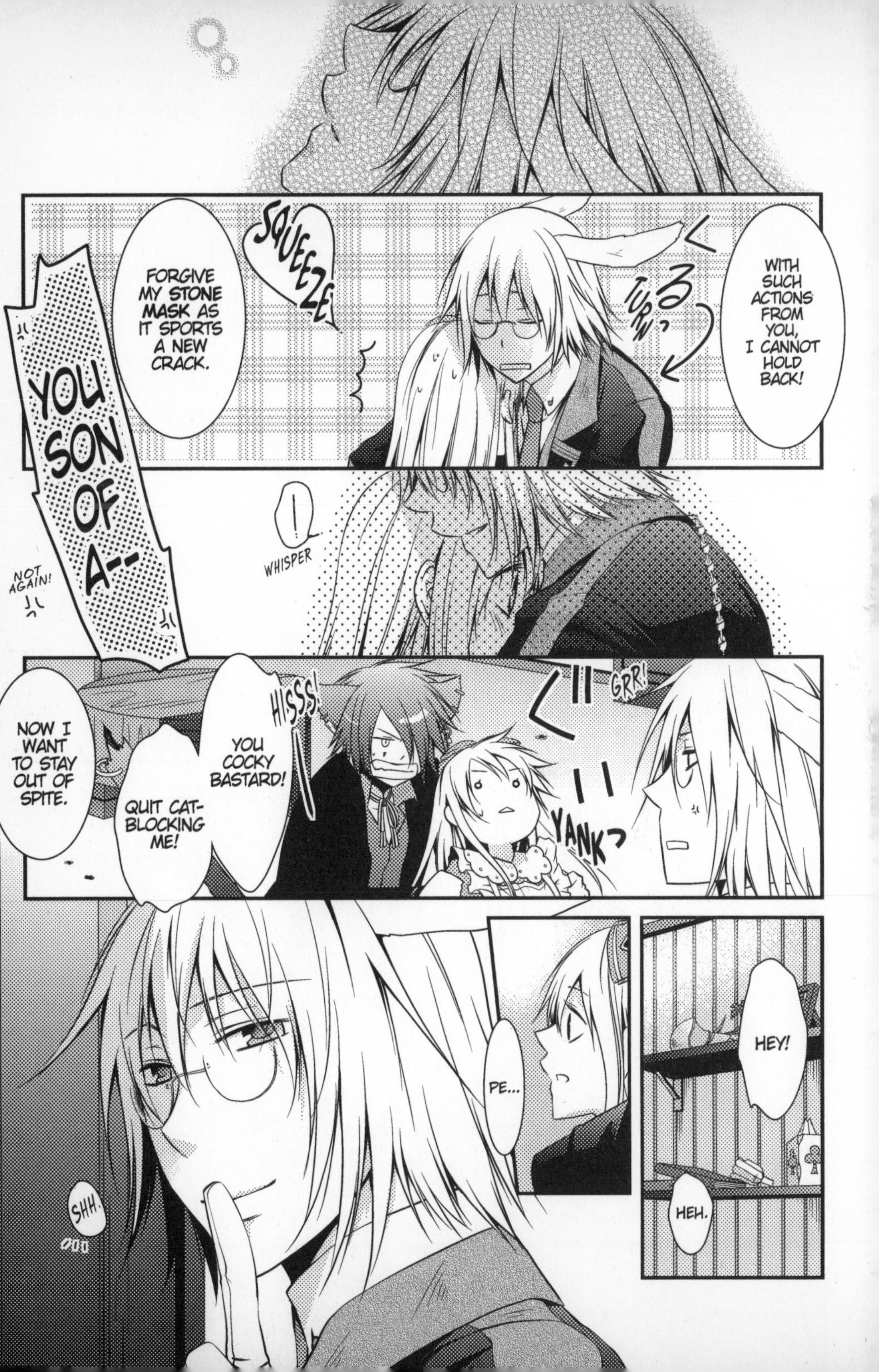
WITH SUCH ACTIONS FROM YOU, I CANNOT HOLD BACK!
くるっ
TURN
SQUEEZE
FORGIVE MY STONE MASK AS IT SPORTS A NEW CRACK.
YOU SON OF A--
!
WHISPER
NOT AGAIN!
GRR!
YANK
HISSS!
YOU COCKY BASTARD!
QUIT CAT-BLOCKING ME!
NOW I WANT TO STAY OUT OF SPITE.
HEY!
HEH.
PE...
SHH.

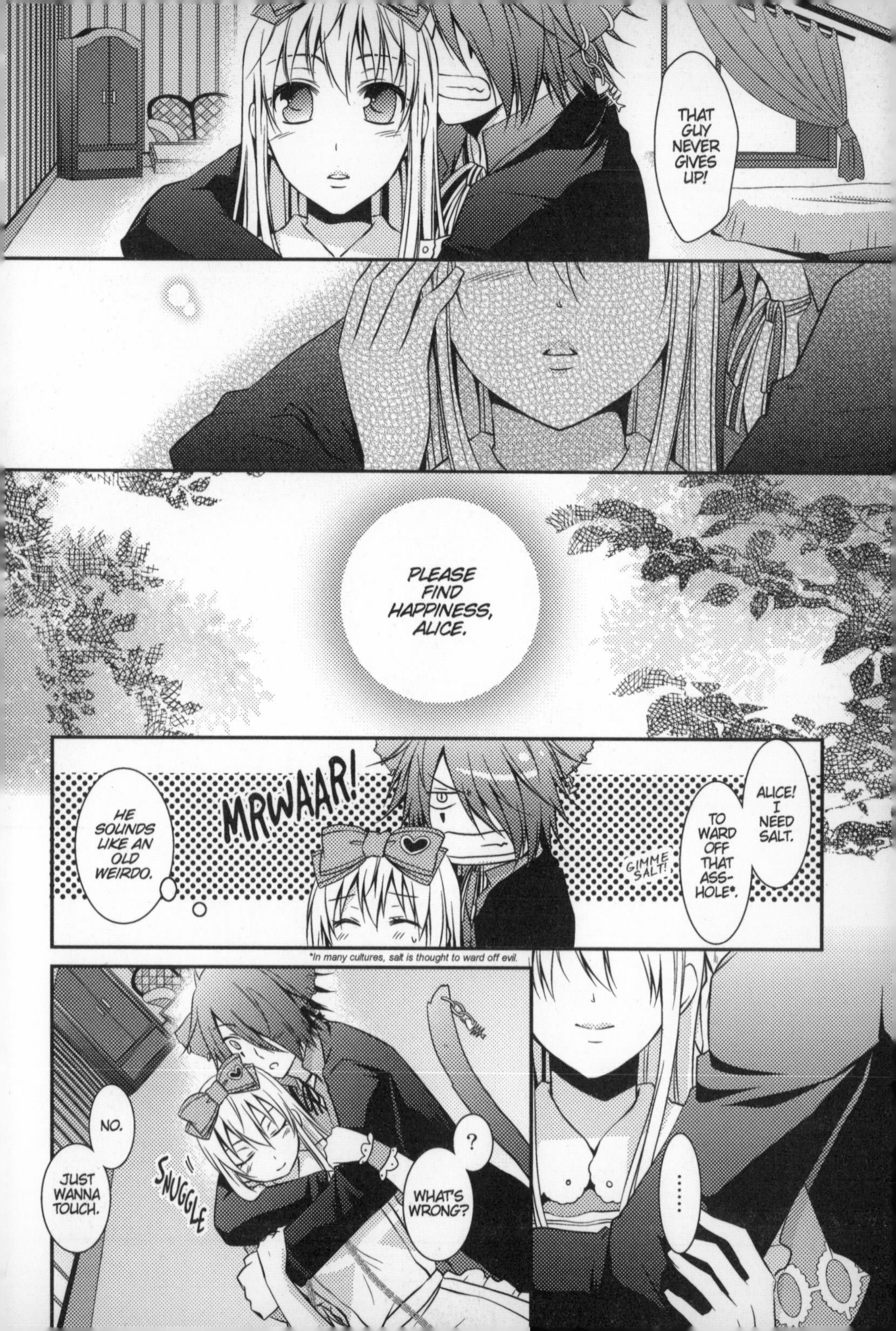
THAT GUY NEVER GIVES UP!
PLEASE FIND HAPPINESS, ALICE.
ALICE! I NEED SALT.
TO WARD OFF THAT ASS-HOLE*.
GIMME SALT!
MRWAAR!
HE SOUNDS LIKE AN OLD WEIRDO.
......
?
WHAT'S WRONG?
NO.
JUST WANNA TOUCH.
SNUGGLE
*In many cultures, salt is thought to ward off evil.

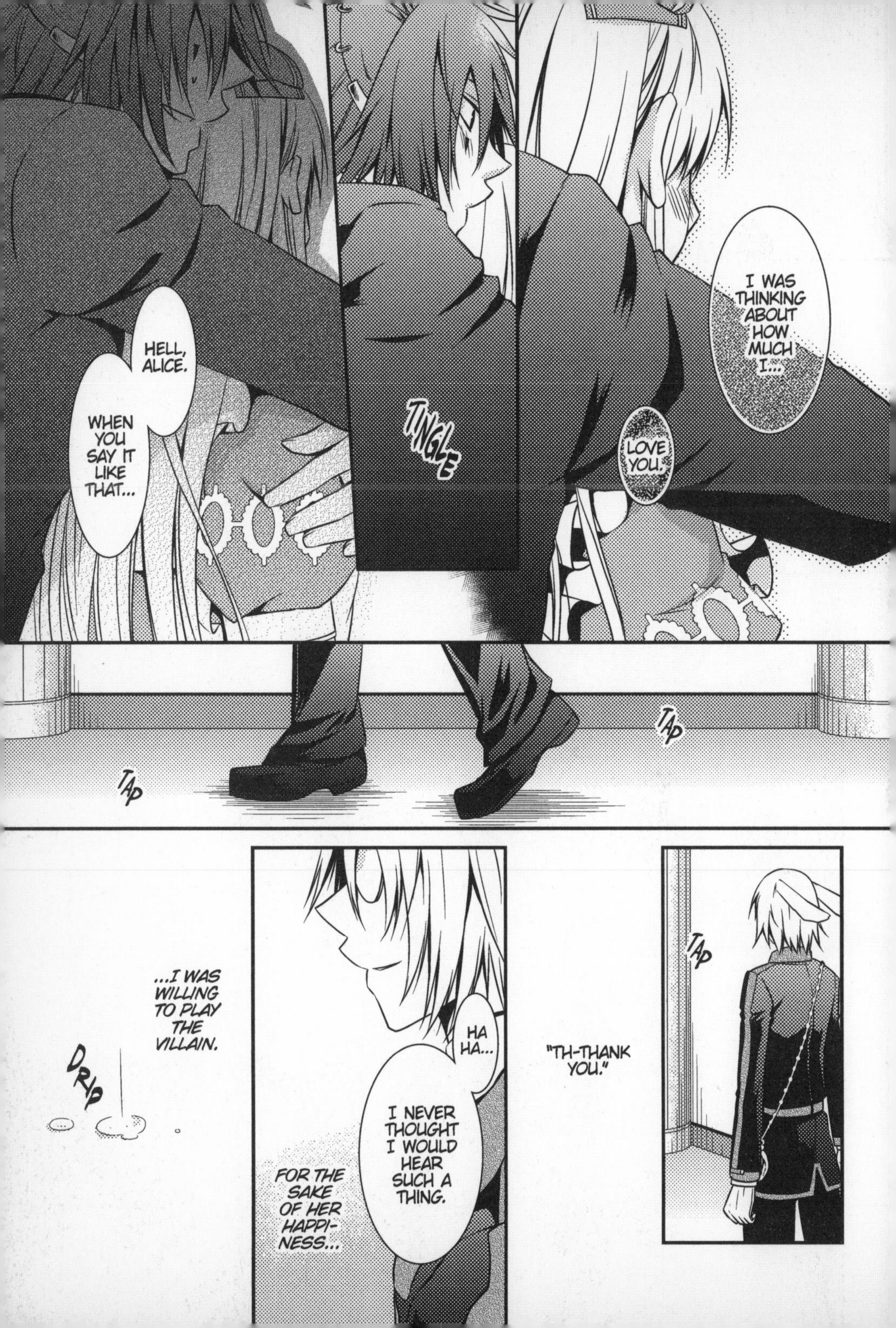
I WAS THINKING ABOUT HOW MUCH I...
LOVE YOU.
TINGLE
HELL, ALICE.
WHEN YOU SAY IT LIKE THAT...
TAP
TAP
TAP
"TH-THANK YOU."
HA HA...
I NEVER THOUGHT I WOULD HEAR SUCH A THING.
FOR THE SAKE OF HER HAPPINESS...
...I WAS WILLING TO PLAY THE VILLAIN.
DRIP

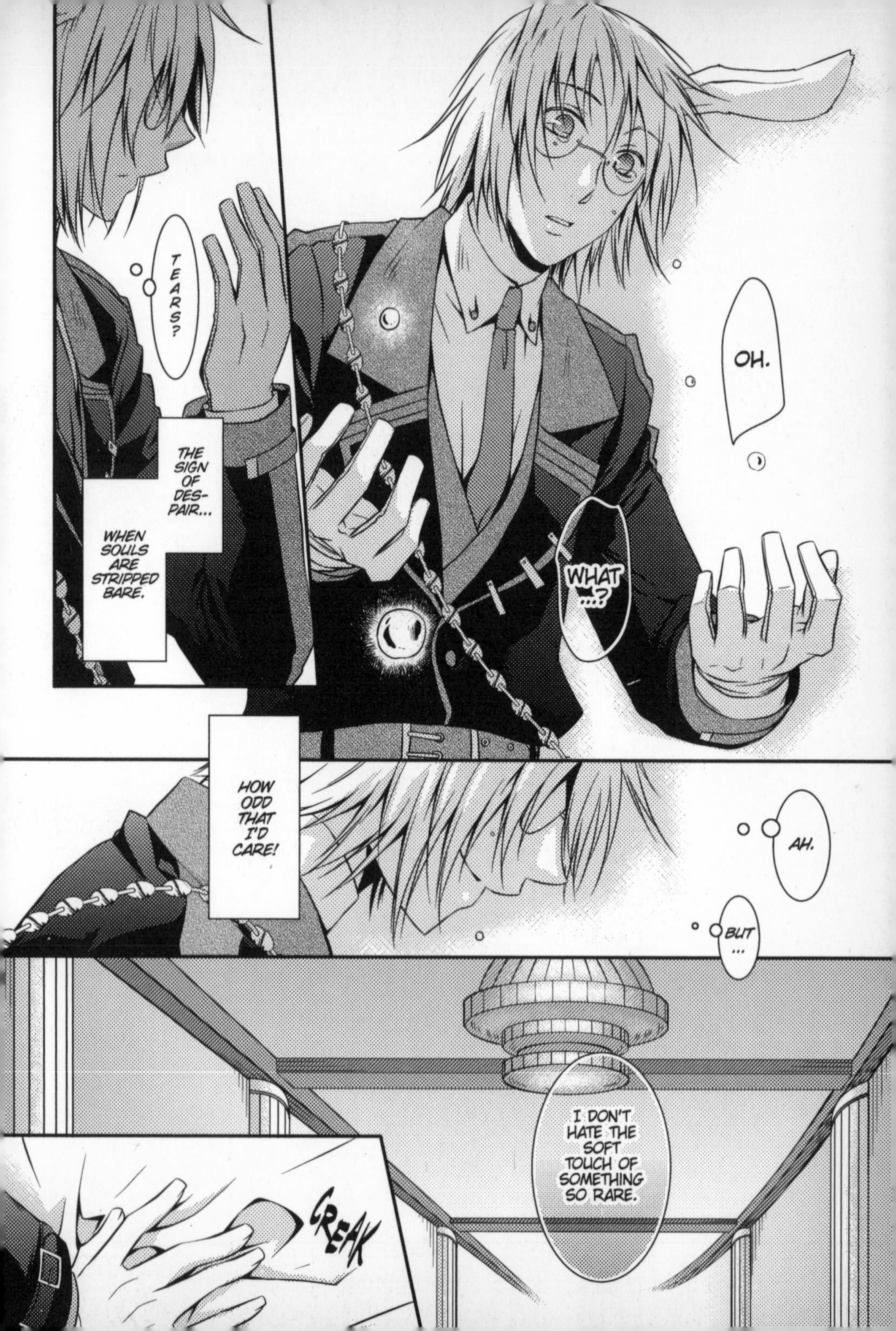
OH.
TEARS?
WHAT ...?
THE SIGN OF DESPAIR...
WHEN SOULS ARE STRIPPED BARE.
AH.
BUT ...
HOW ODD THAT I'D CARE!
I DON'T HATE THE SOFT TOUCH OF SOMETHING SO RARE.
CREAK

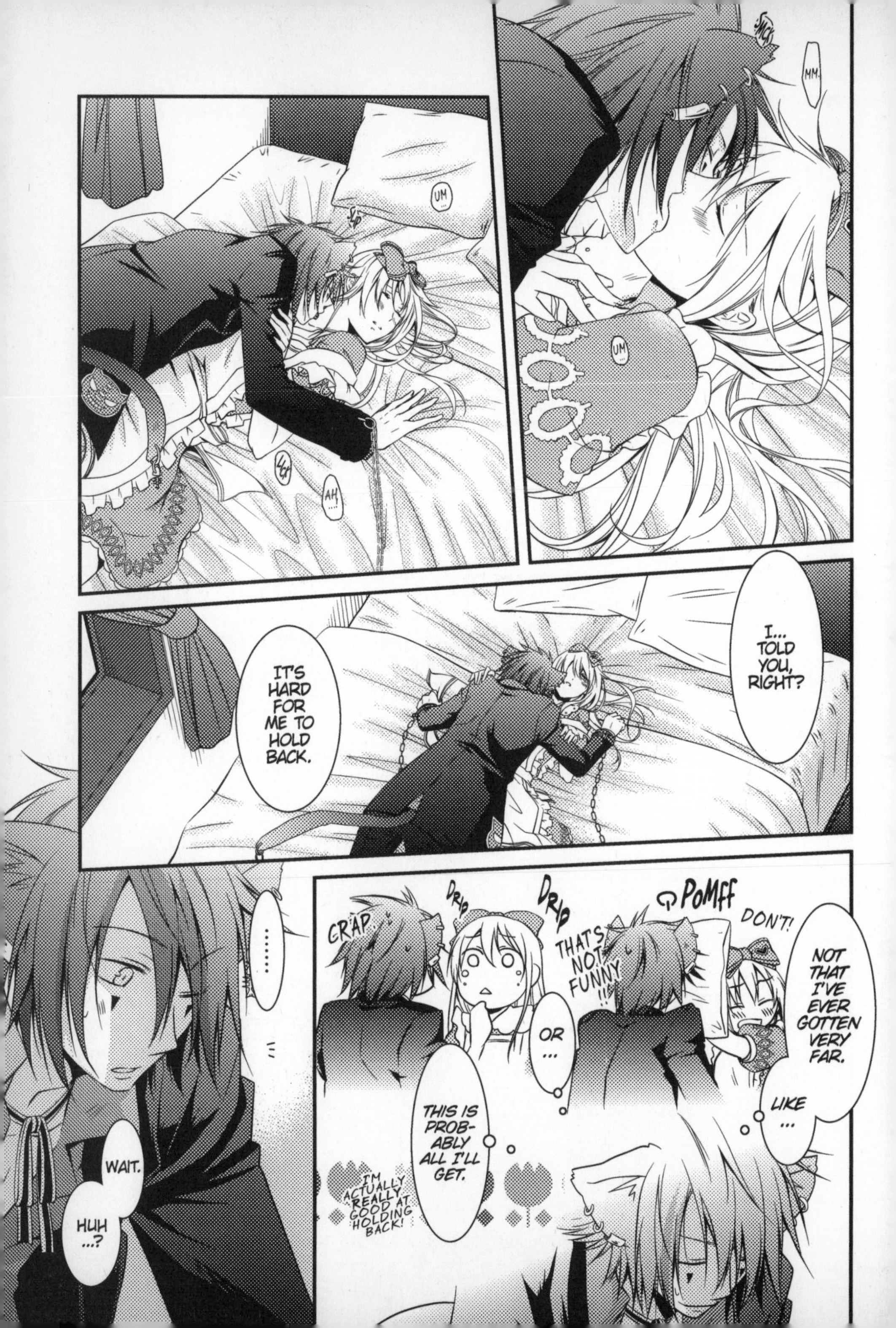
SMCK
MM.
UM...
UM...
SLP
LICK
AH...!
I... TOLD YOU, RIGHT?
IT'S HARD FOR ME TO HOLD BACK.
DON'T!
NOT THAT I'VE EVER GOTTEN VERY FAR.
POMFF
THAT'S NOT FUNNY!!
DRIP
DRIP
CRAP
LIKE...
OR...
THIS IS PROBABLY ALL I'LL GET.
I'M ACTUALLY REALLY GOOD AT HOLDING BACK!
......
WAIT.
HUH...?

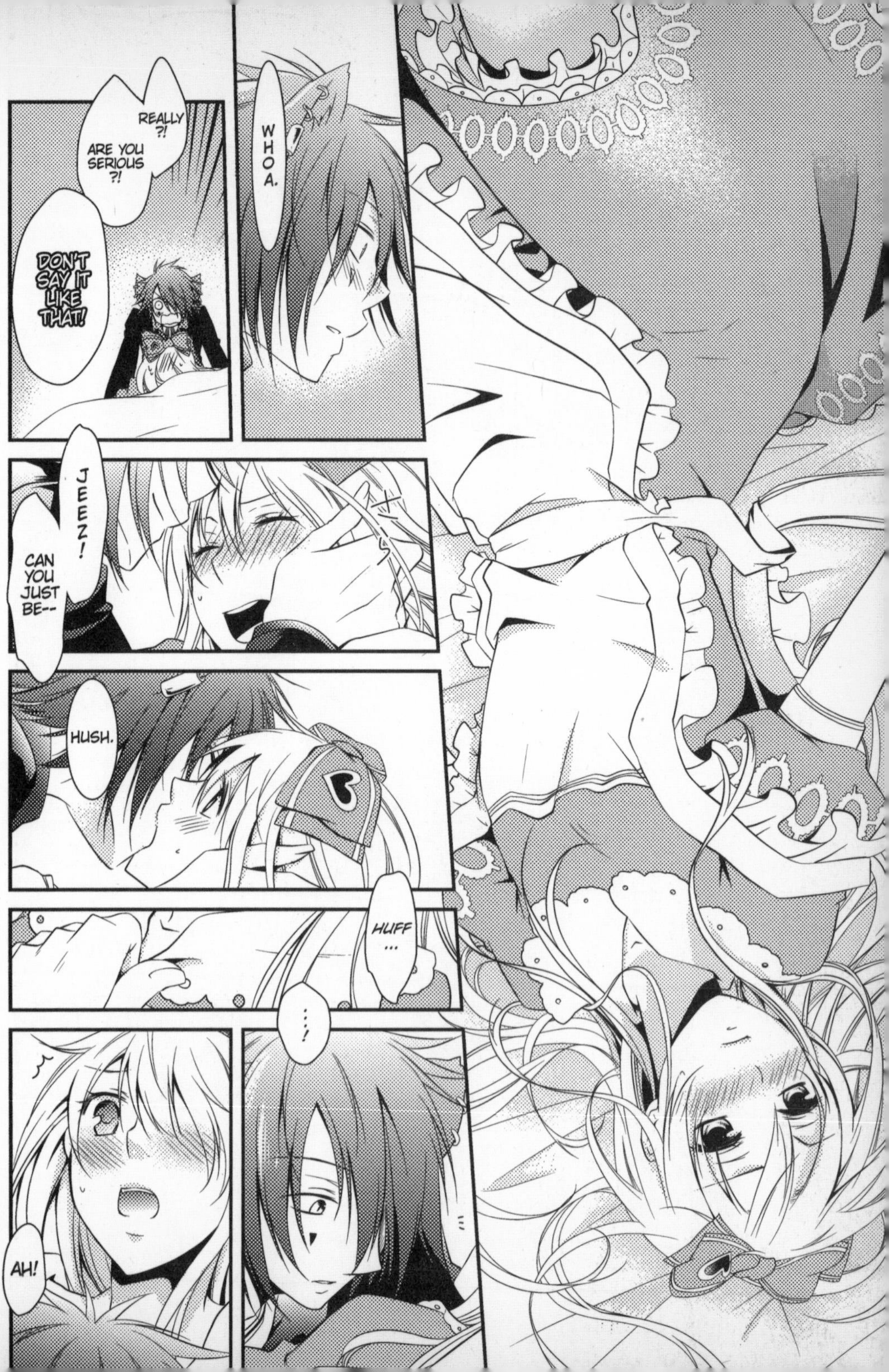
WHOA.
REALLY ?!
ARE YOU SERIOUS ?!
DON'T SAY IT LIKE THAT!
JEEZ! CAN YOU JUST BE--
HUSH.
HUFF ...
...!
AH!

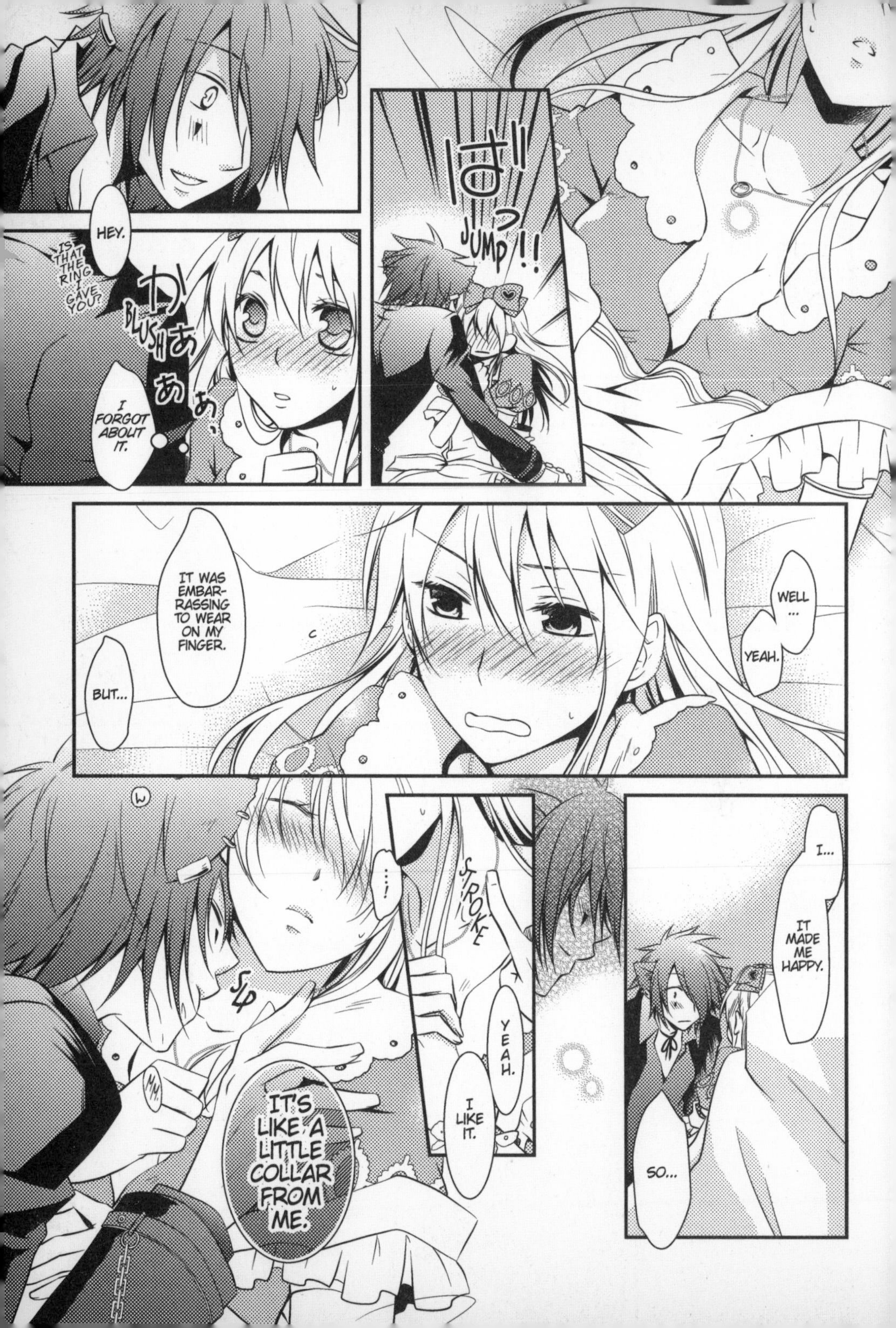
ぱっ
JUMP!!
HEY.
IS THAT THE RING I GAVE YOU?
わあああ、
BLUSH
I FORGOT ABOUT IT.
WELL...
YEAH.
IT WAS EMBARRASSING TO WEAR ON MY FINGER.
BUT...
I...
IT MADE ME HAPPY.
SO...
...!
STROKE
YEAH.
I LIKE IT.
SLP
MM.
IT'S LIKE A LITTLE COLLAR FROM ME.

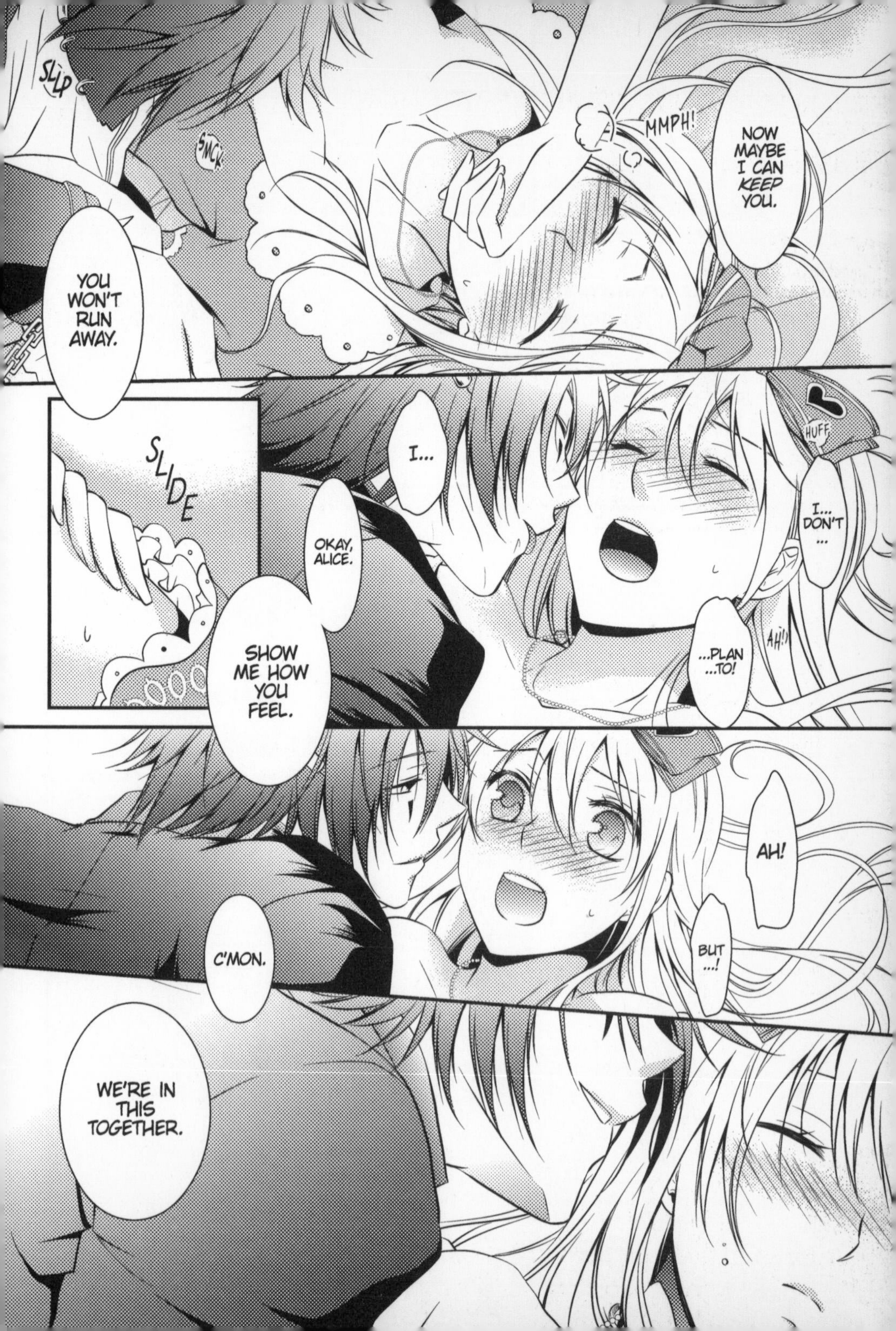
NOW MAYBE I CAN KEEP YOU.
MMPH!
SMCK
SLLP
YOU WON'T RUN AWAY.
I... DON'T ...
HUFF
AH!
...PLAN ...TO!
I...
OKAY, ALICE.
SHOW ME HOW YOU FEEL.
SLIDE
AH!
BUT ...!
C'MON.
WE'RE IN THIS TOGETHER.

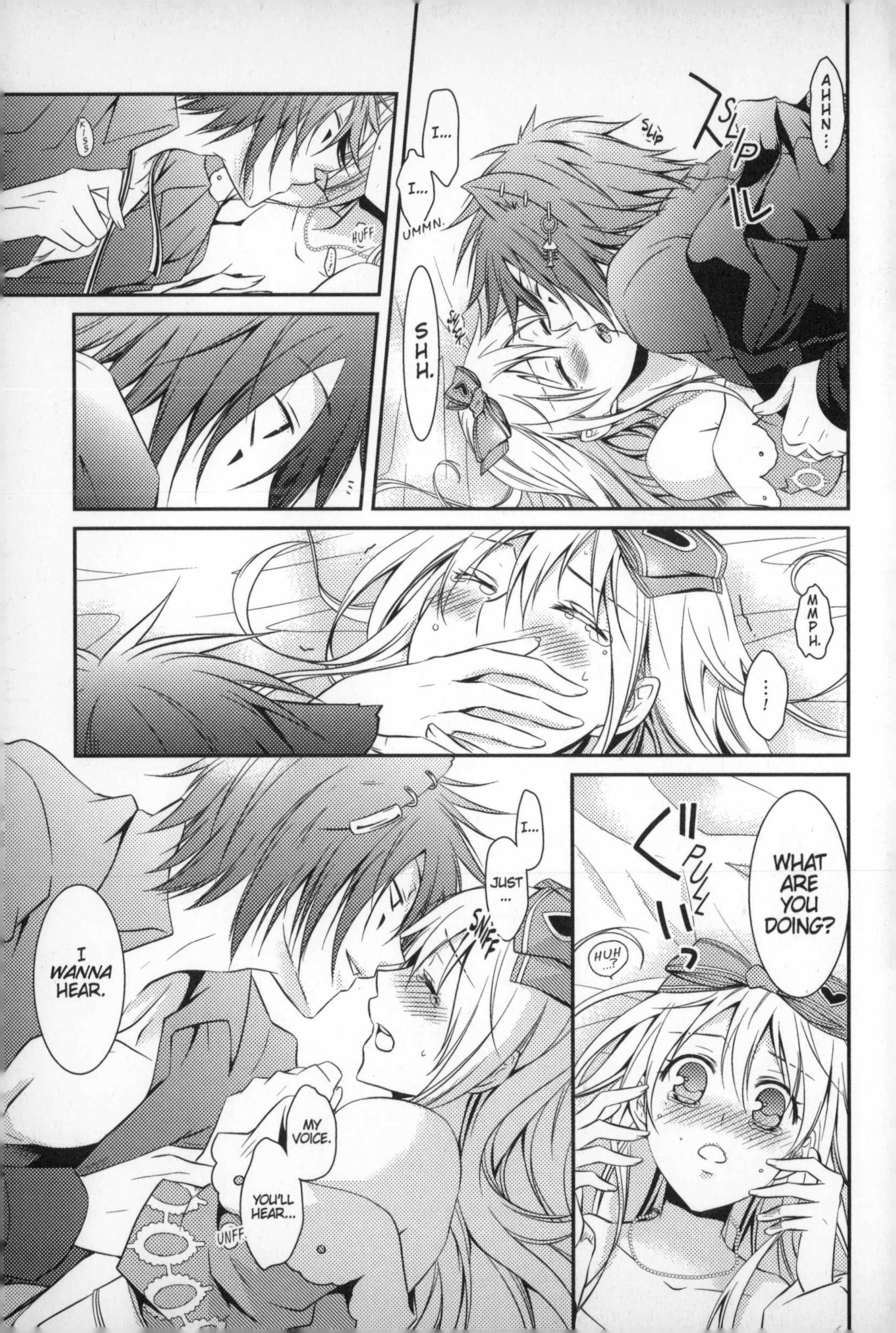
AHHN...
SLIP
SLIP
I...
I...
UMMN.
SHLICK
SHH.
HUFF
...!
KISS
MMPH.
...!
WHAT ARE YOU DOING?
PULL
HUH ...?
I... JUST ...
SNIFF
I WANNA HEAR.
MY VOICE.
YOU'LL HEAR...
UNFF.

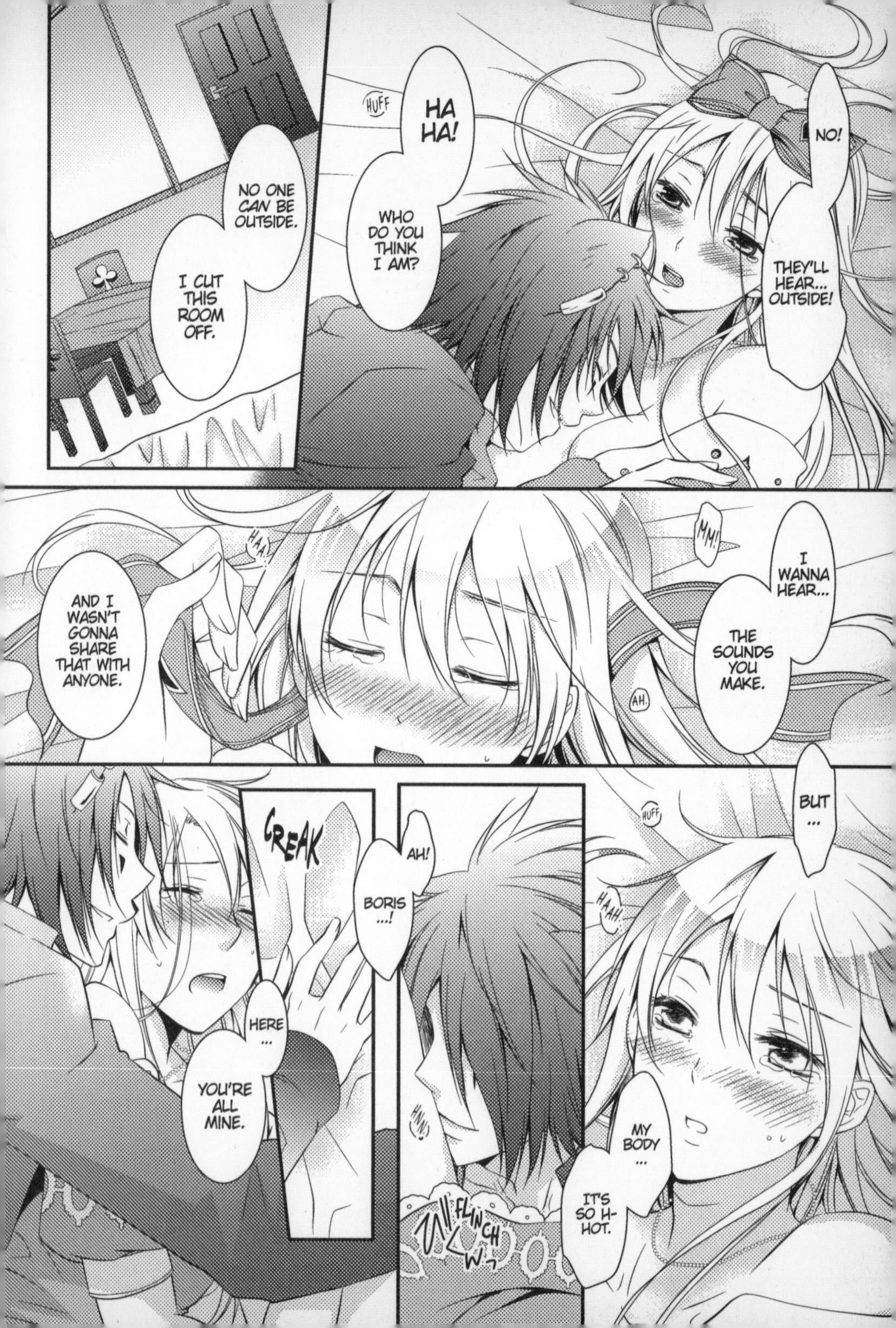
NO!
THEY'LL HEAR... OUTSIDE!
HUFF
HA HA!
WHO DO YOU THINK I AM?
NO ONE CAN BE OUTSIDE.
I CUT THIS ROOM OFF.
MM!
I WANNA HEAR...
THE SOUNDS YOU MAKE.
AH.
HAA!
AND I WASN'T GONNA SHARE THAT WITH ANYONE.
BUT ...
HUFF
HAAH
MY BODY ...
IT'S SO H-HOT.
AH!
BORIS ...!
HNN!
FLINCH
CREAK
HERE ...
YOU'RE ALL MINE.

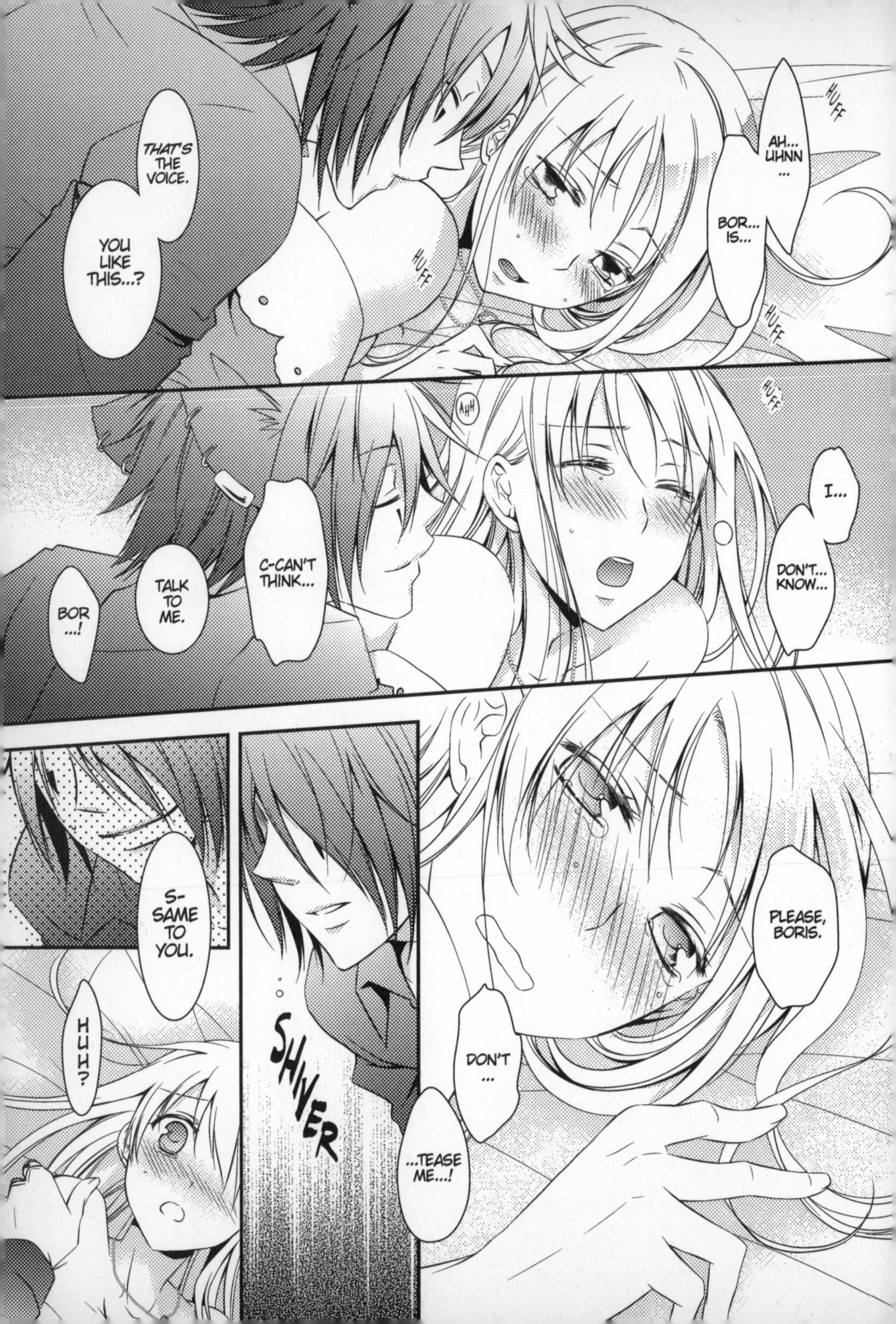
HUFF
AH... UHNN ...
BOR... IS...
HUFF
HUFF
THAT'S THE VOICE.
YOU LIKE THIS...?
HUFF
AHH
I... DON'T... KNOW...
C-CAN'T THINK...
TALK TO ME.
BOR ...!
PLEASE, BORIS.
DON'T ...
...TEASE ME...!
SHIVER
S-SAME TO YOU.
HUH?

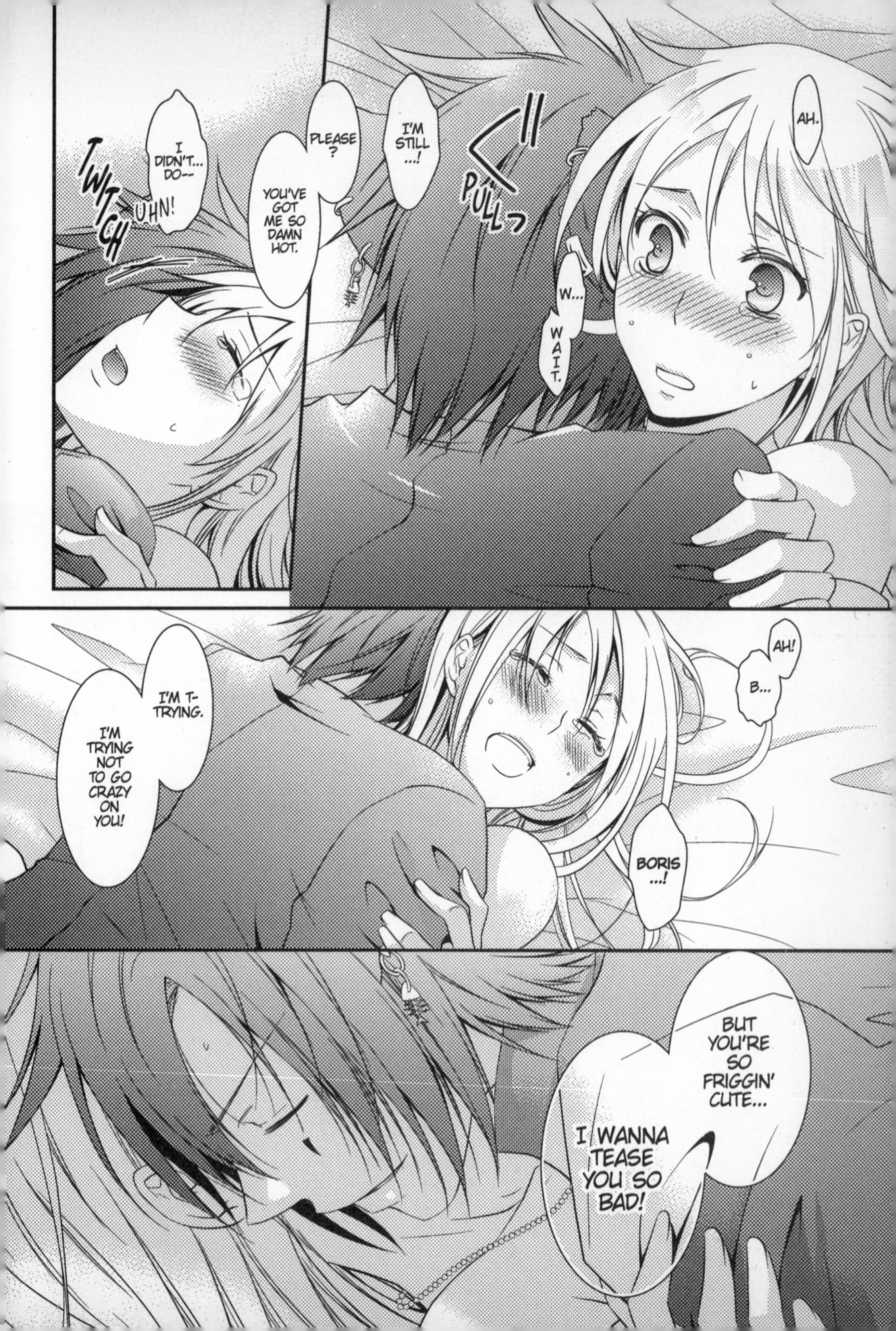
AH.
W... WAIT.
PULL
I'M STILL ...!
PLEASE?
YOU'VE GOT ME SO DAMN HOT.
I DIDN'T... DO--
TWITCH
UHN!
AH!
B...
BORIS ...!
I'M T-TRYING.
I'M TRYING NOT TO GO CRAZY ON YOU!
BUT YOU'RE SO FRIGGIN' CUTE...
I WANNA TEASE YOU SO BAD!

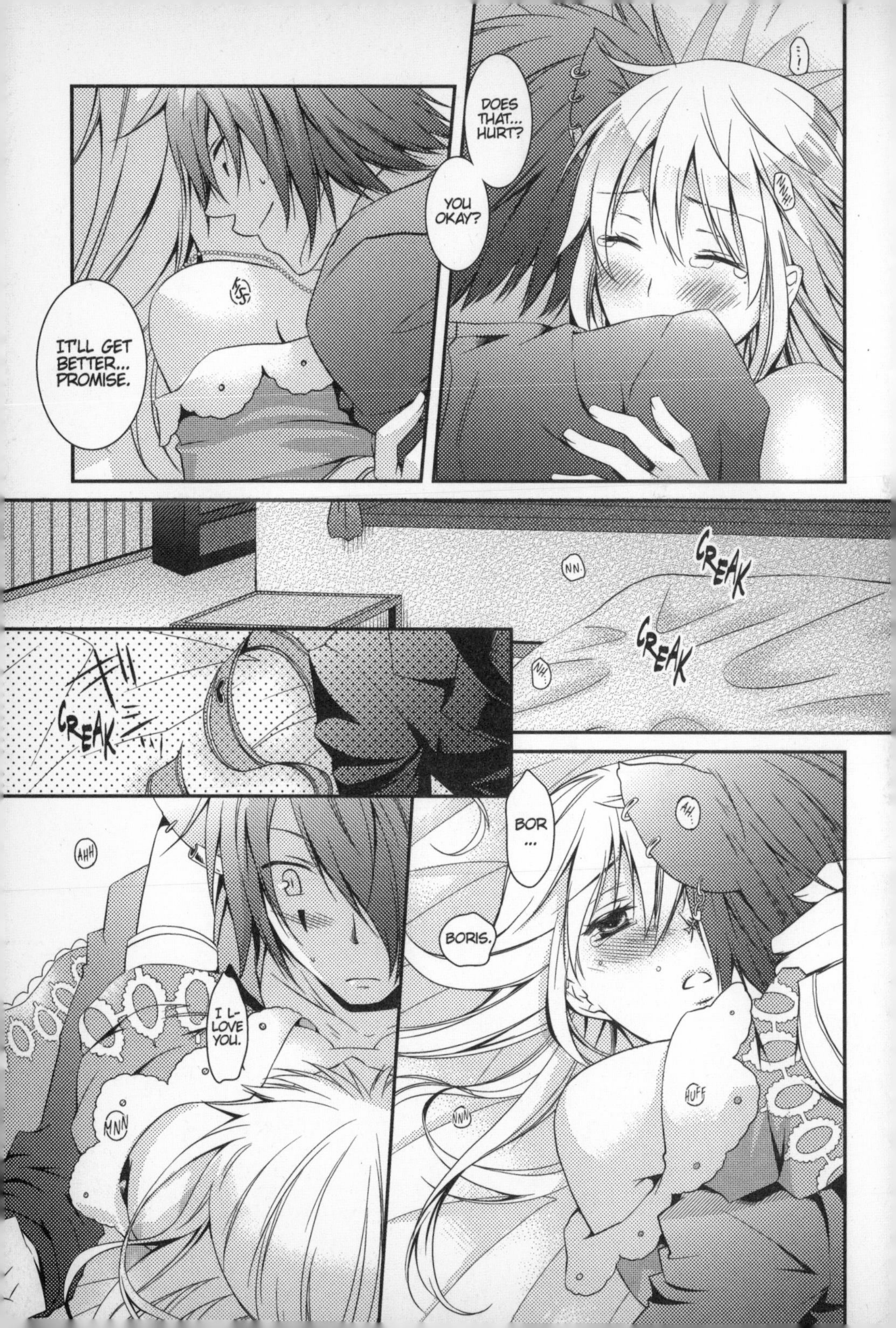
...!
DOES THAT... HURT?
YOU OKAY?
NNH!
KISS
IT'LL GET BETTER... PROMISE.
NN.
CREAK
CREAK
NH...
CREAK
BOR...
AH...
BORIS.
HUFF
NNN
AHH
I L-LOVE YOU.
MNN

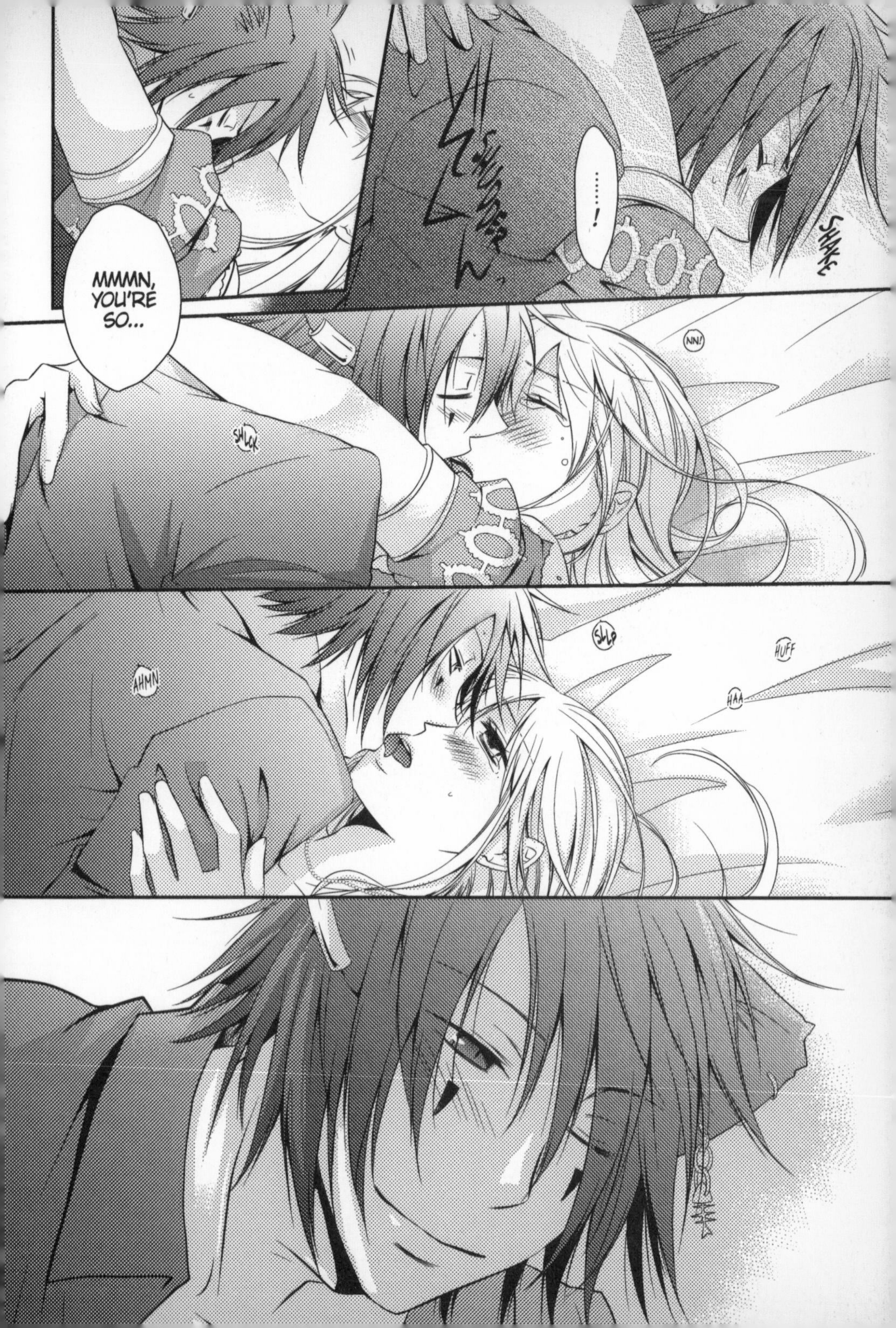
SHAKE
......!
SHUDDER
MMMN, YOU'RE SO...
NN!
SHLOK
HUFF
HAA
SLLP
AHMN

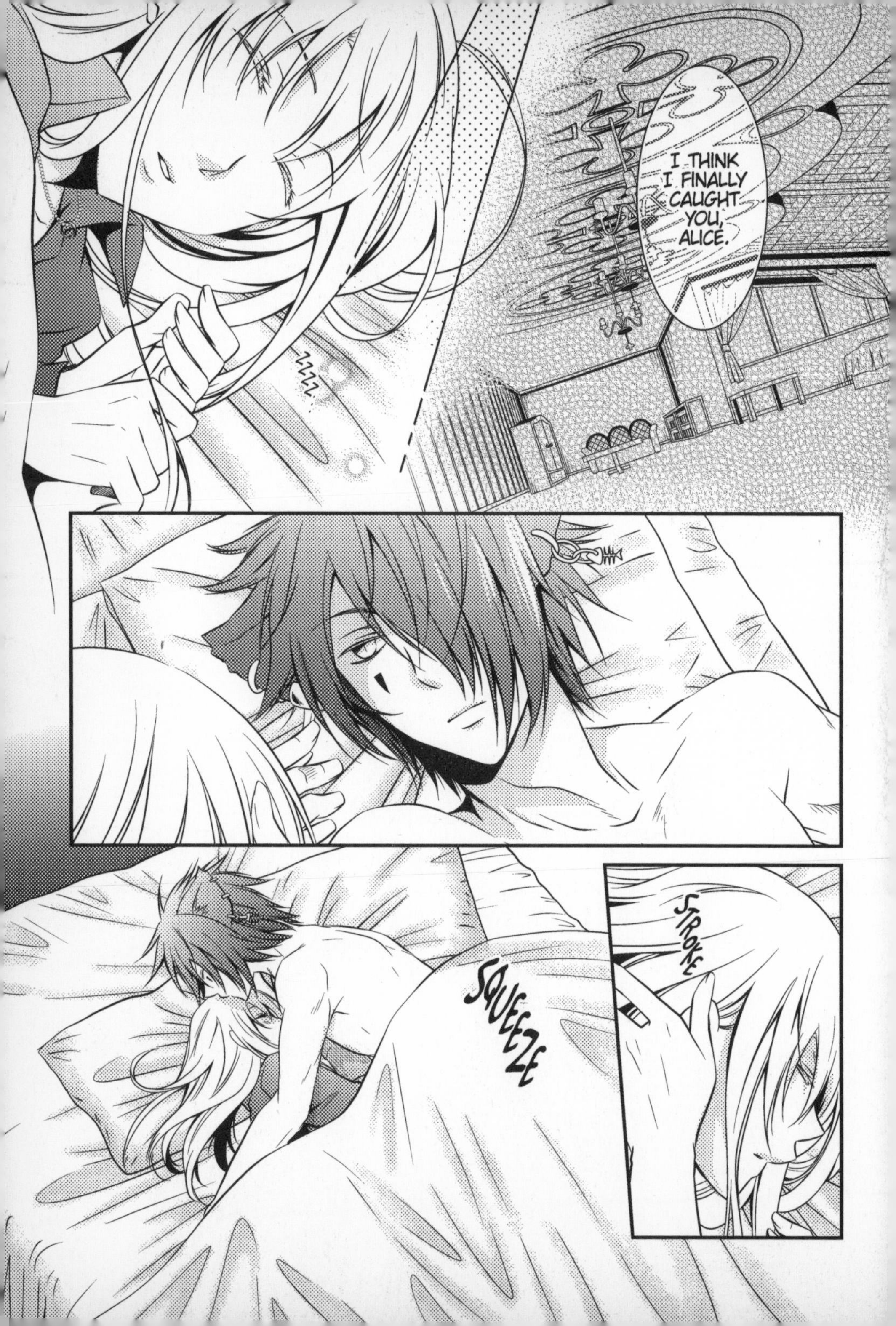
I THINK I FINALLY CAUGHT YOU, ALICE.
ZZZZZ
STROKE
SQUEEZE

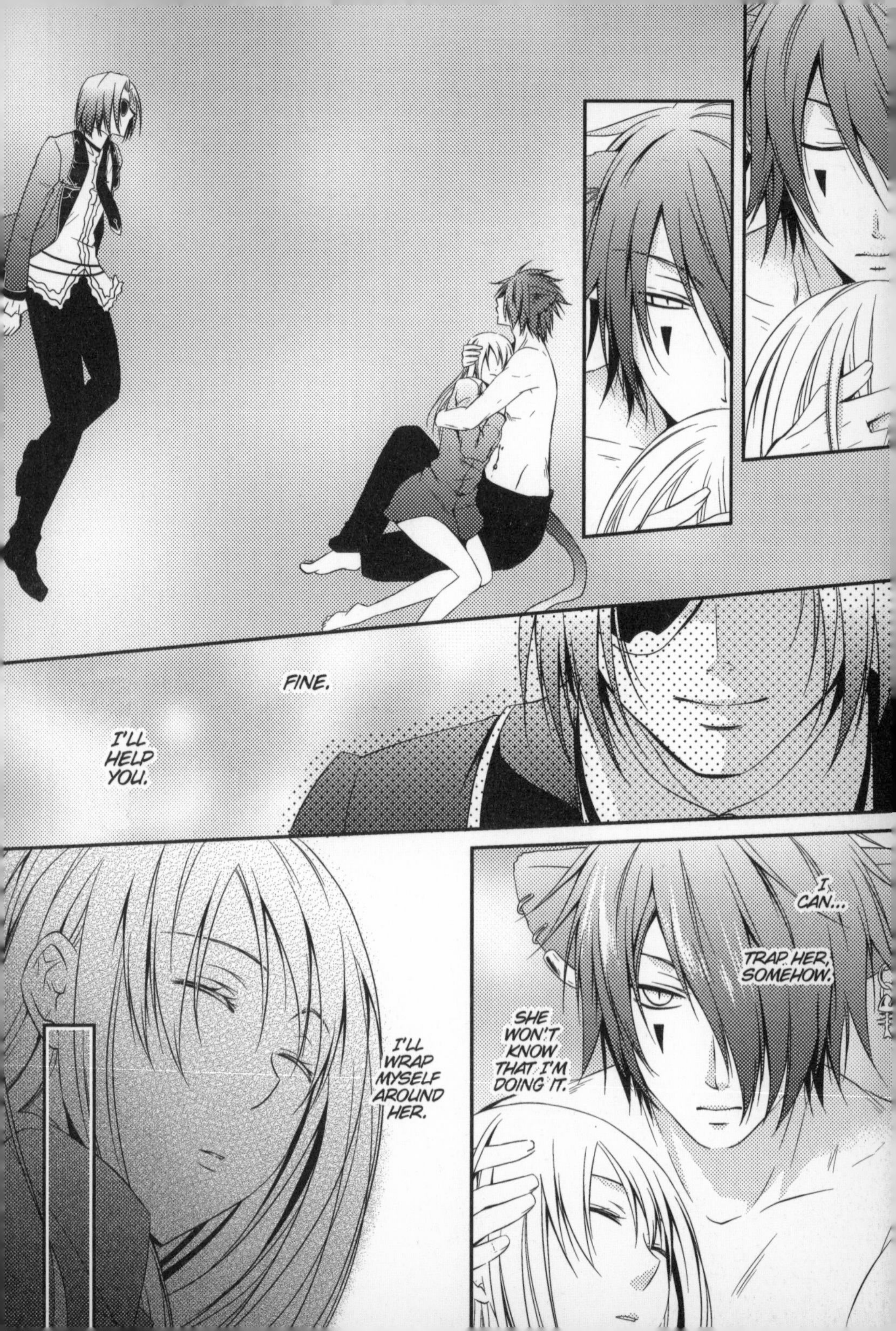
FINE.
I'LL HELP YOU.
I CAN...
TRAP HER, SOMEHOW.
SHE WON'T KNOW THAT I'M DOING IT.
I'LL WRAP MYSELF AROUND HER.

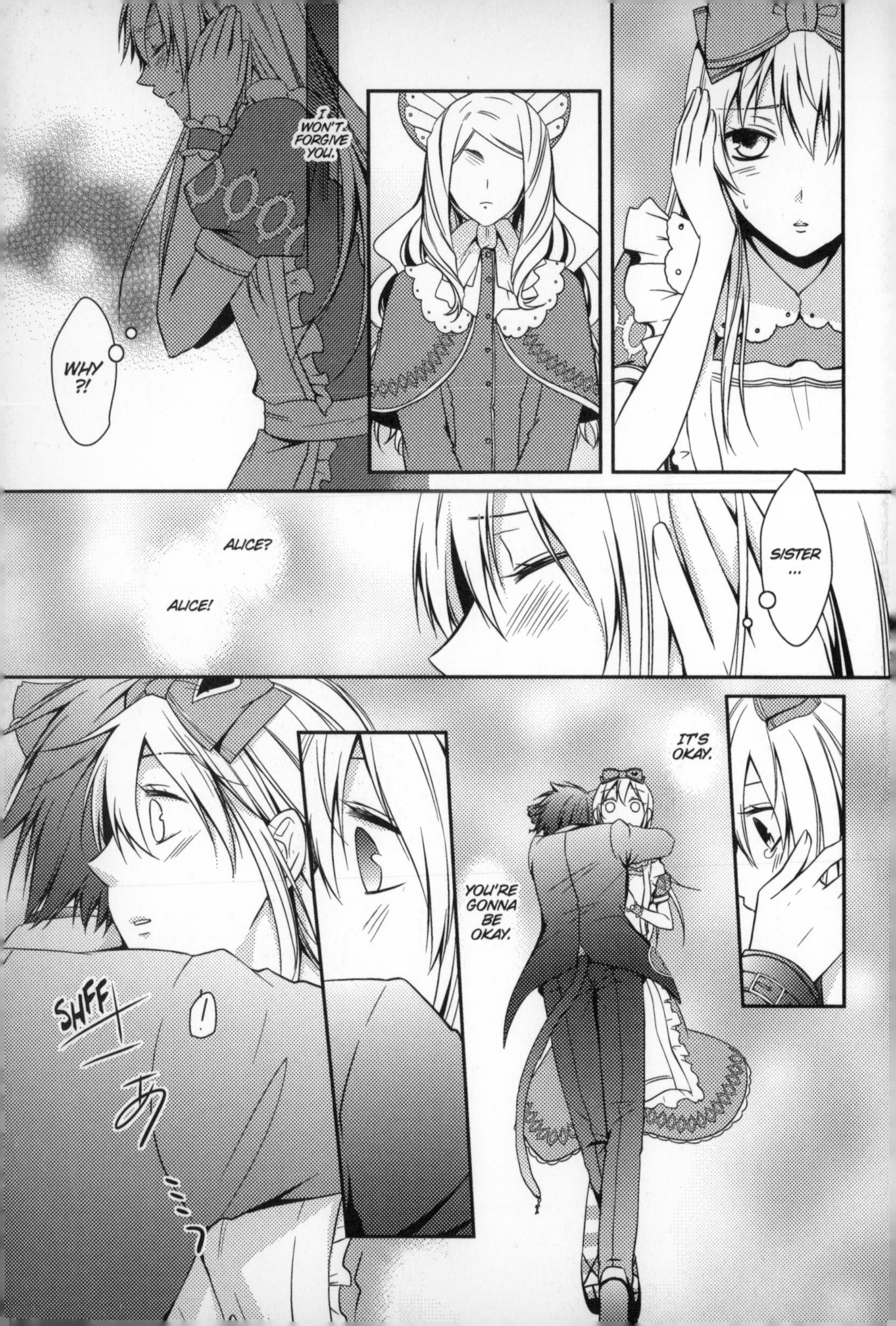
I WON'T FORGIVE YOU.
WHY?!
SISTER...
ALICE?
ALICE!
IT'S OKAY.
YOU'RE GONNA BE OKAY.
SHFF
!
あ

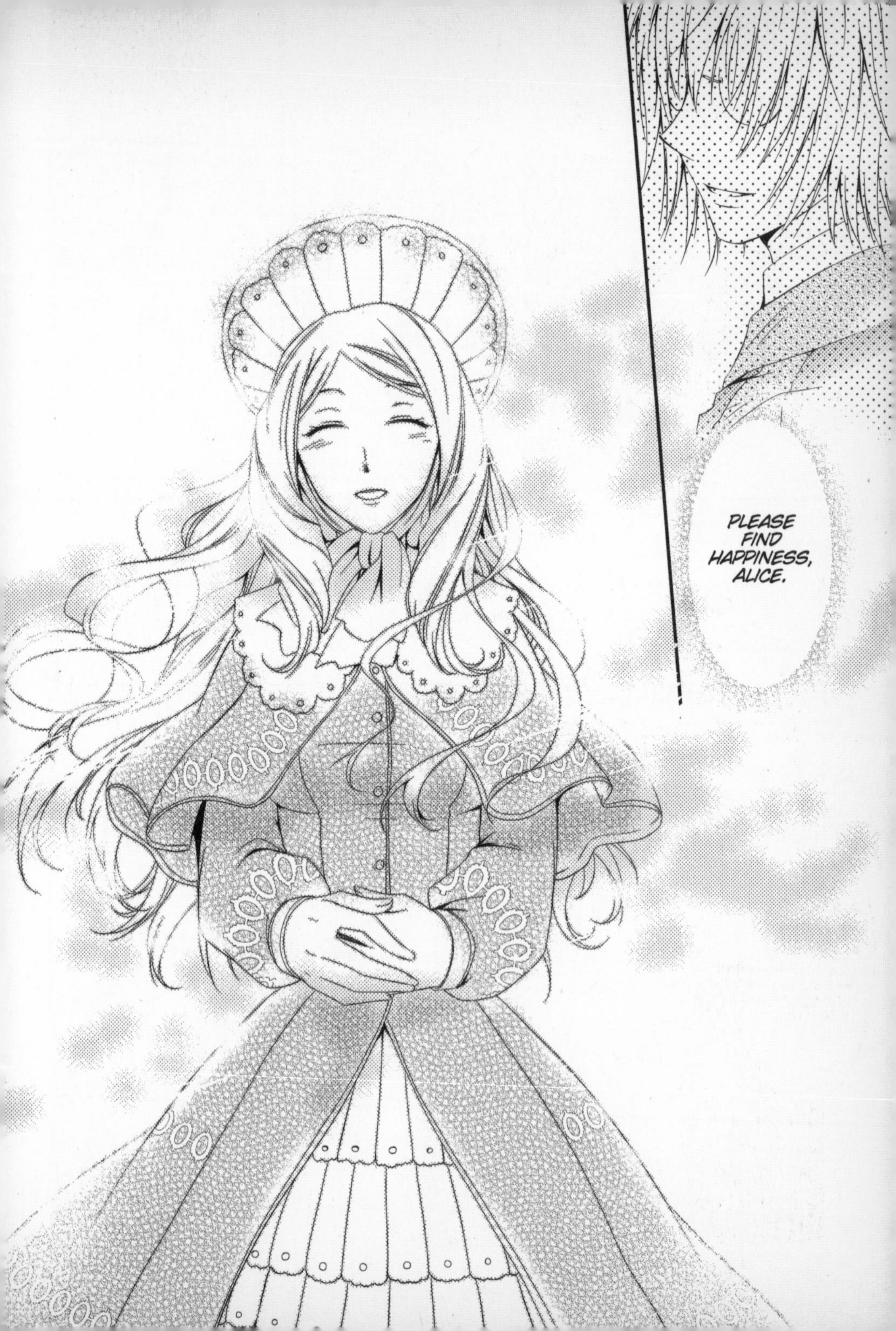
PLEASE FIND HAPPINESS, ALICE.

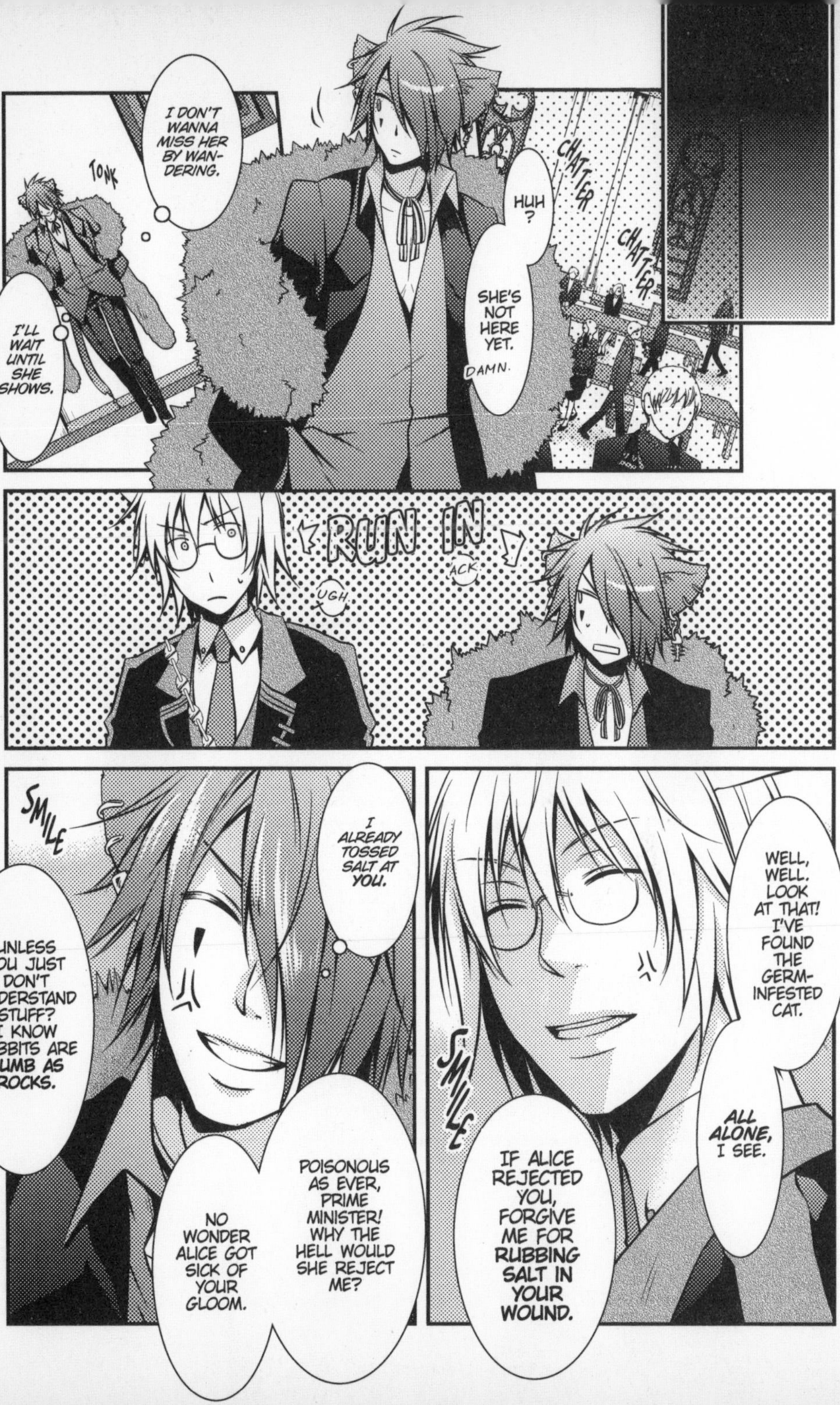
CHATTER
CHATTER
HUH?
SHE'S NOT HERE YET.
DAMN.
I DON'T WANNA MISS HER BY WAN-DERING.
TONK
I'LL WAIT UNTIL SHE SHOWS.
RUN IN
ACK
UGH
WELL, WELL. LOOK AT THAT! I'VE FOUND THE GERM-INFESTED CAT.
ALL ALONE, I SEE.
SMILE
IF ALICE REJECTED YOU, FORGIVE ME FOR RUBBING SALT IN YOUR WOUND.
I ALREADY TOSSED SALT AT YOU.
SMILE
UNLESS YOU JUST DON'T UNDERSTAND STUFF? I KNOW RABBITS ARE DUMB AS ROCKS.
POISONOUS AS EVER, PRIME MINISTER! WHY THE HELL WOULD SHE REJECT ME?
NO WONDER ALICE GOT SICK OF YOUR GLOOM.

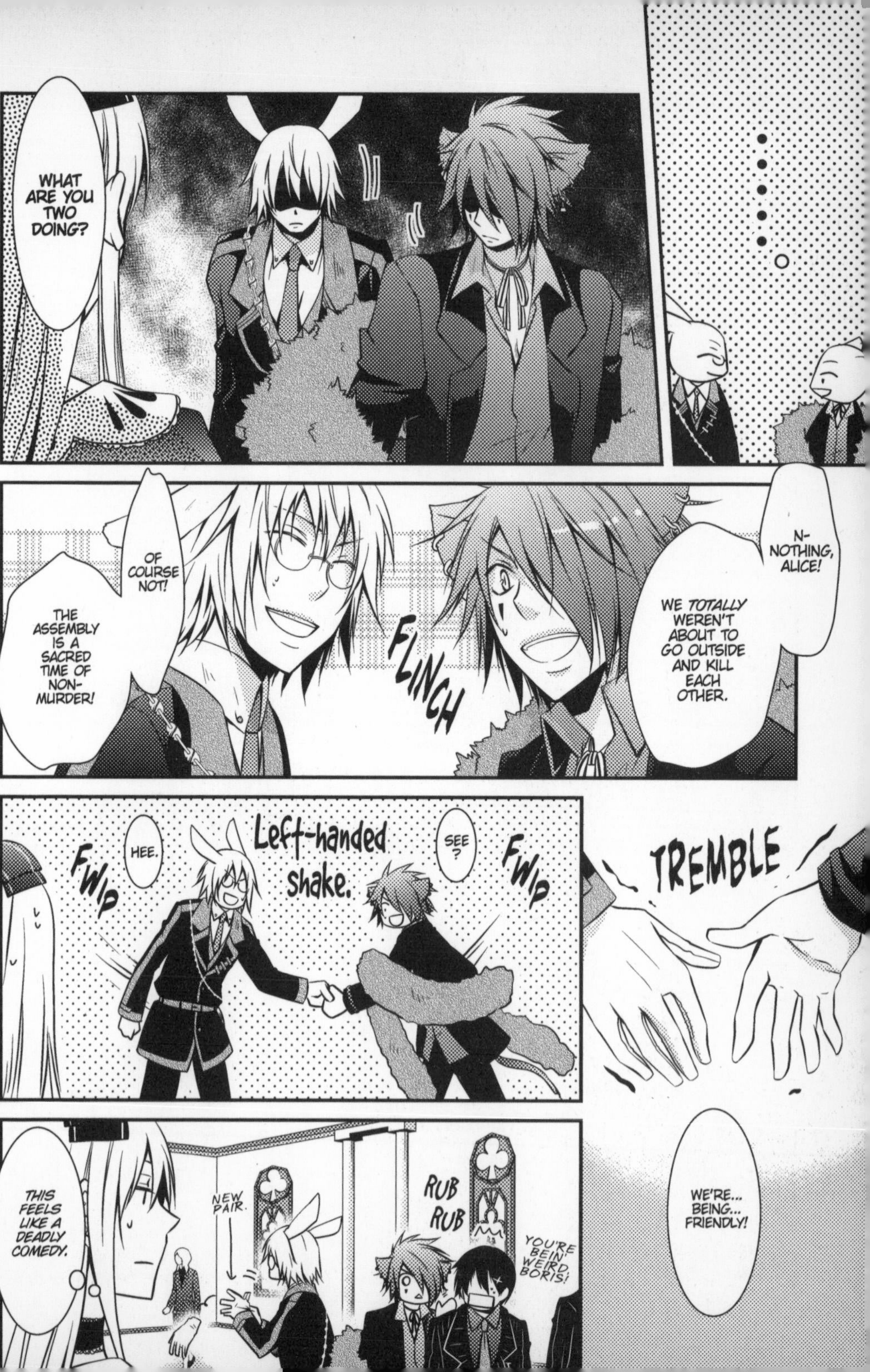
WHAT ARE YOU TWO DOING?
N-NOTHING, ALICE!
WE *TOTALLY* WEREN'T ABOUT TO GO OUTSIDE AND KILL EACH OTHER.
FLINCH
OF COURSE NOT!
THE ASSEMBLY IS A SACRED TIME OF NON-MURDER!
TREMBLE
FWIP
SEE?
Left-handed shake.
HEE.
FWIP
WE'RE... BEING... FRIENDLY!
YOU'RE BEIN' WEIRD, BORIS!
RUB RUB
NEW PAIR.
THIS FEELS LIKE A DEADLY COMEDY.

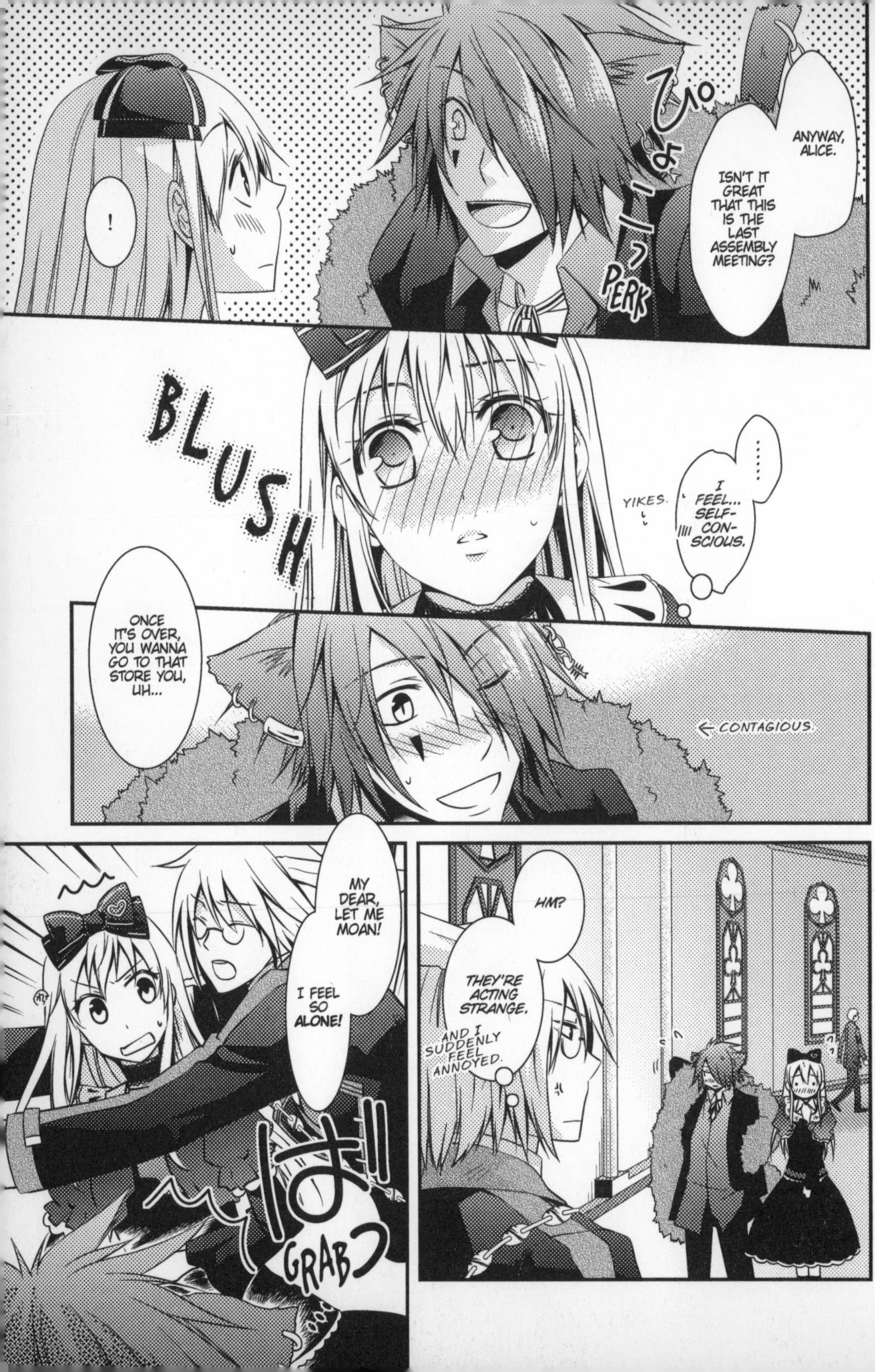
ANYWAY, ALICE.
ISN'T IT GREAT THAT THIS IS THE LAST ASSEMBLY MEETING?
PERK
!
......
I FEEL... SELF-CONSCIOUS.
YIKES.
BLUSH
← CONTAGIOUS.
ONCE IT'S OVER, YOU WANNA GO TO THAT STORE YOU, UH...
HM?
THEY'RE ACTING STRANGE.
AND I SUDDENLY FEEL ANNOYED.
MY DEAR, LET ME MOAN!
I FEEL SO ALONE!
GRAB

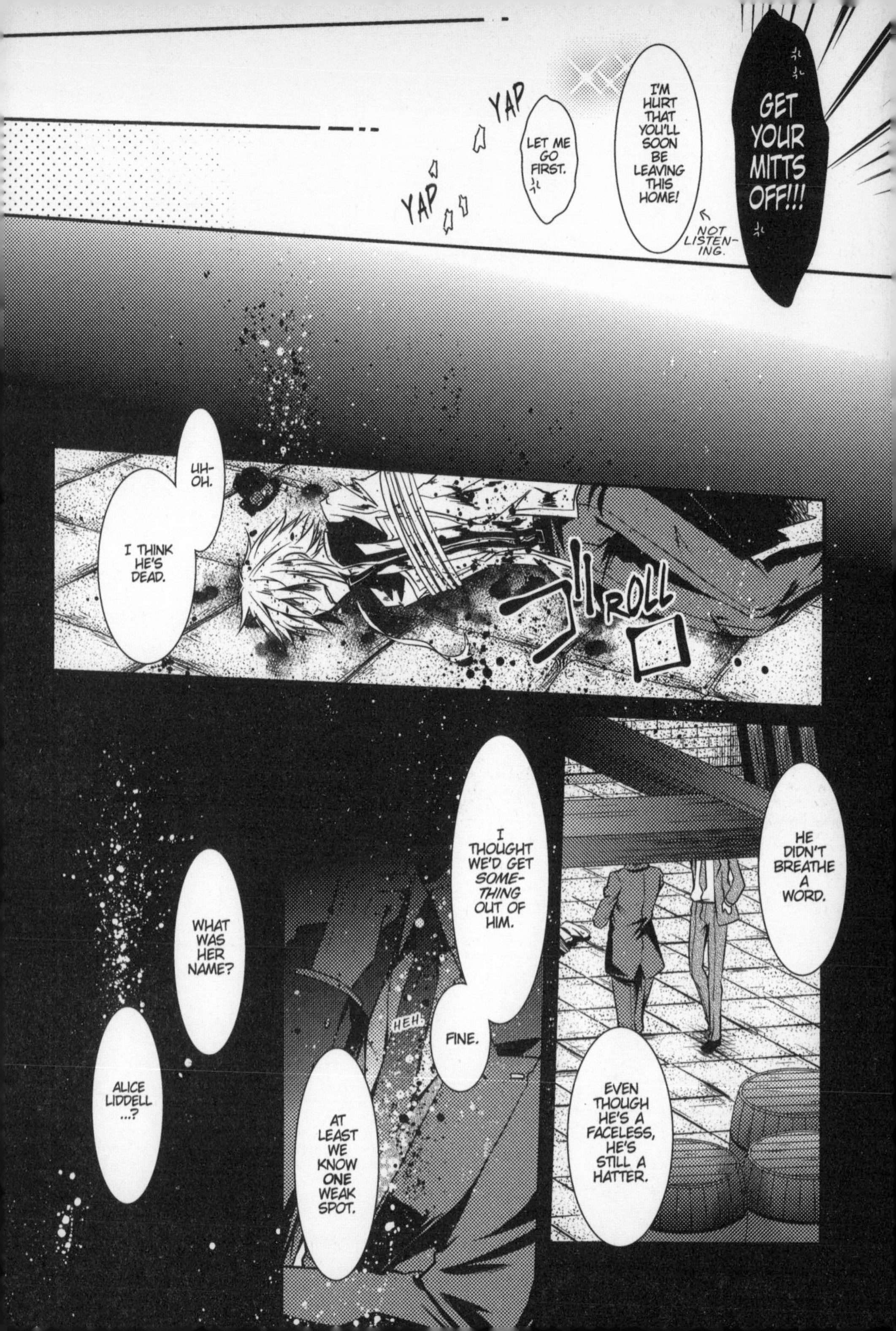
GET YOUR MITTS OFF!!!
I'M HURT THAT YOU'LL SOON BE LEAVING THIS HOME!
NOT LISTENING.
LET ME GO FIRST.
YAP
YAP
UH-OH.
I THINK HE'S DEAD.
ROLL
HE DIDN'T BREATHE A WORD.
I THOUGHT WE'D GET *SOMETHING* OUT OF HIM.
EVEN THOUGH HE'S A FACELESS, HE'S STILL A HATTER.
HEH.
FINE.
AT LEAST WE KNOW ONE WEAK SPOT.
WHAT WAS HER NAME?
ALICE LIDDELL ...?

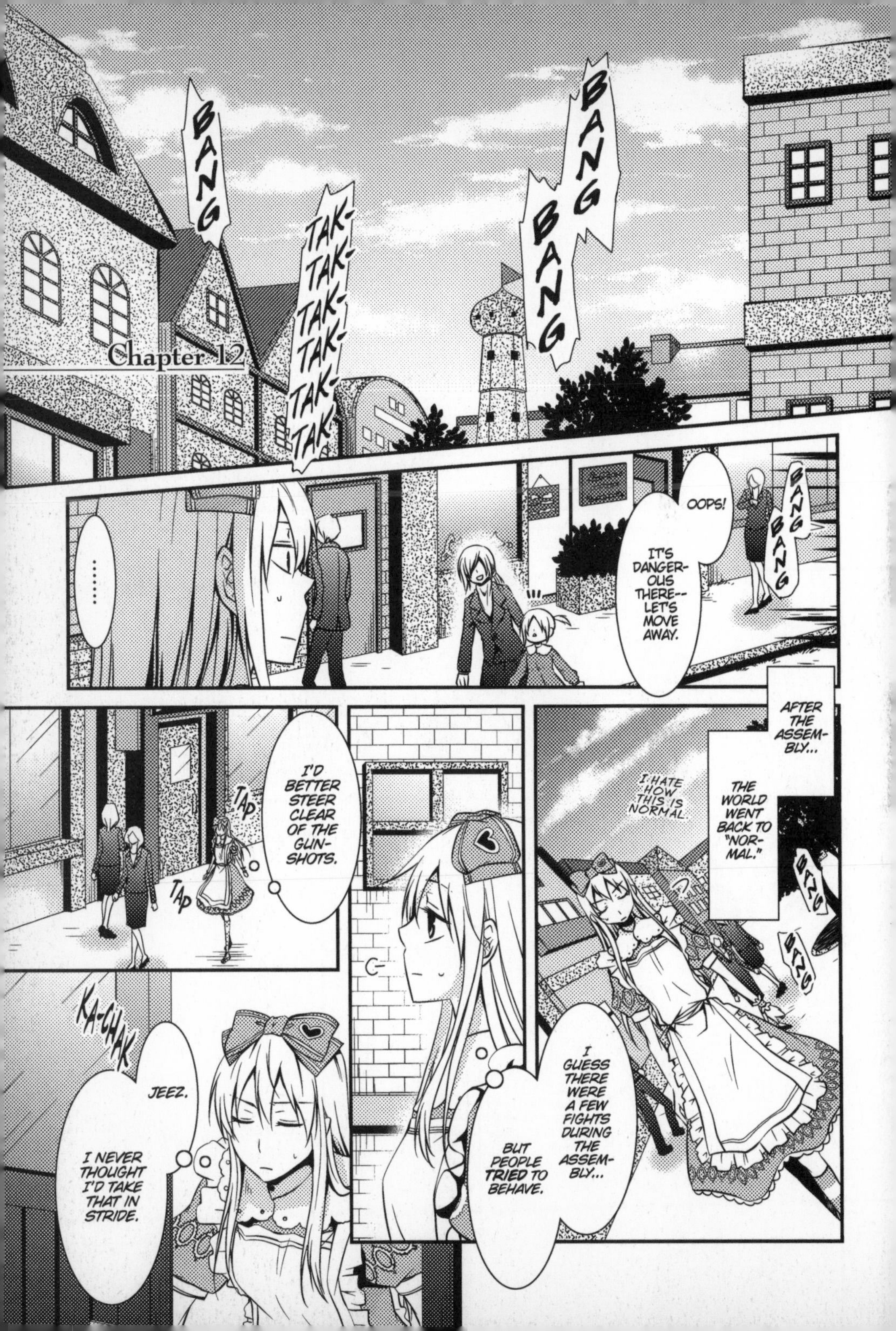
Chapter 12
BANG
BANG
BANG
TAK-TAK-TAK-TAK-TAK-TAK
BANG
BANG
BANG
OOPS!
IT'S DANGER-OUS THERE--LET'S MOVE AWAY.
......
AFTER THE ASSEM-BLY...
THE WORLD WENT BACK TO "NOR-MAL."
I HATE HOW THIS IS NORMAL.
I GUESS THERE WERE A FEW FIGHTS DURING THE ASSEM-BLY...
BUT PEOPLE TRIED TO BEHAVE.
I'D BETTER STEER CLEAR OF THE GUN-SHOTS.
TAP
TAP
KA-CHAK
JEEZ.
I NEVER THOUGHT I'D TAKE THAT IN STRIDE.

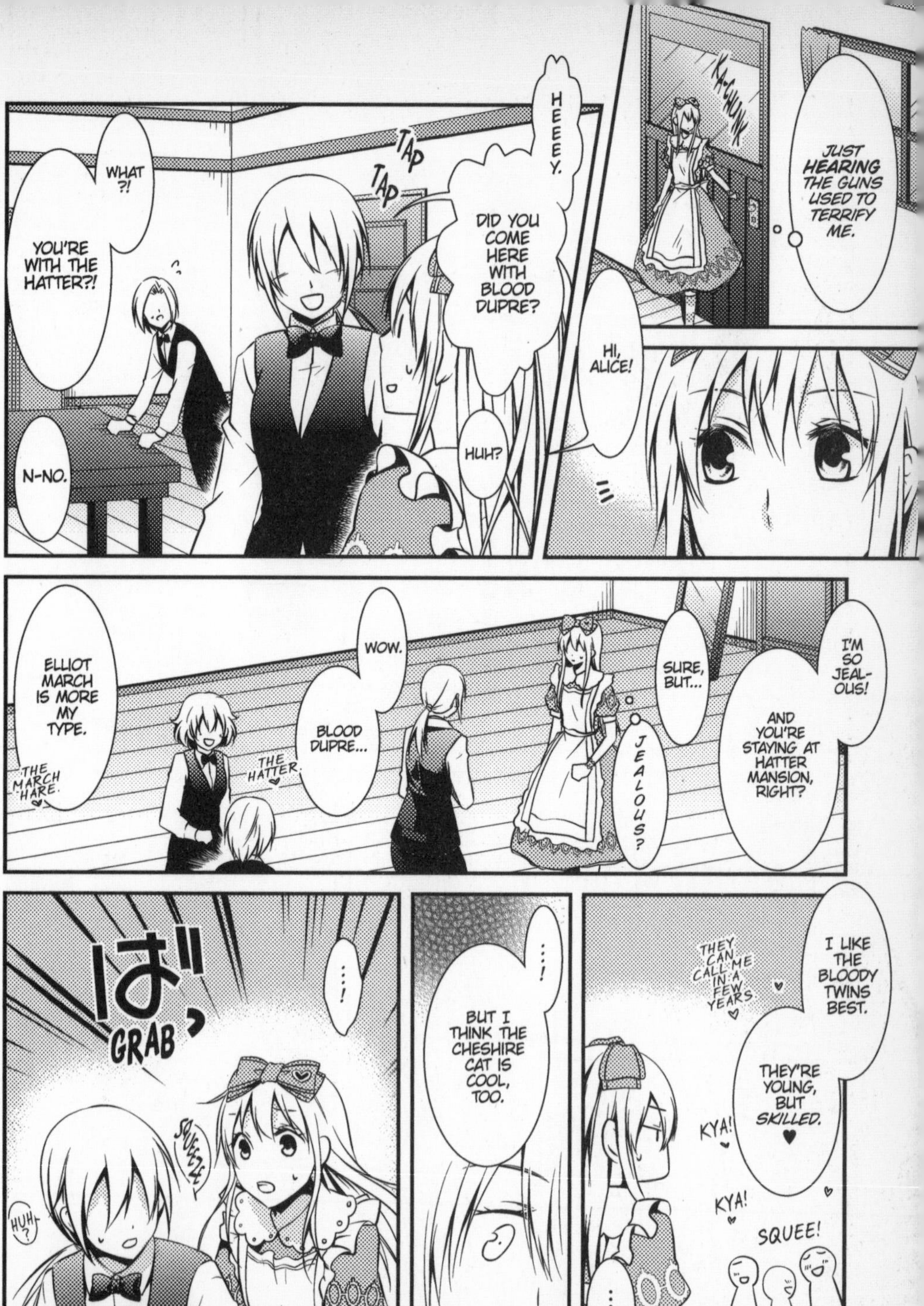
KA-CHUNK
JUST HEARING THE GUNS USED TO TERRIFY ME.
HI, ALICE!
HEEEEY.
TAP
TAP
DID YOU COME HERE WITH BLOOD DUPRE?
HUH?
WHAT?!
YOU'RE WITH THE HATTER?!
N-NO.
I'M SO JEAL-OUS!
AND YOU'RE STAYING AT HATTER MANSION, RIGHT?
SURE, BUT...
JEALOUS?
BLOOD DUPRE...
THE HATTER.
WOW.
ELLIOT MARCH IS MORE MY TYPE.
THE MARCH HARE.
I LIKE THE BLOODY TWINS BEST.
THEY CAN CALL ME IN A FEW YEARS.
THEY'RE YOUNG, BUT SKILLED.
KYA!
KYA!
SQUEE!
......
...!
BUT I THINK THE CHESHIRE CAT IS COOL, TOO.
...!
ば
GRAB
SQUEEZE
HUH-?

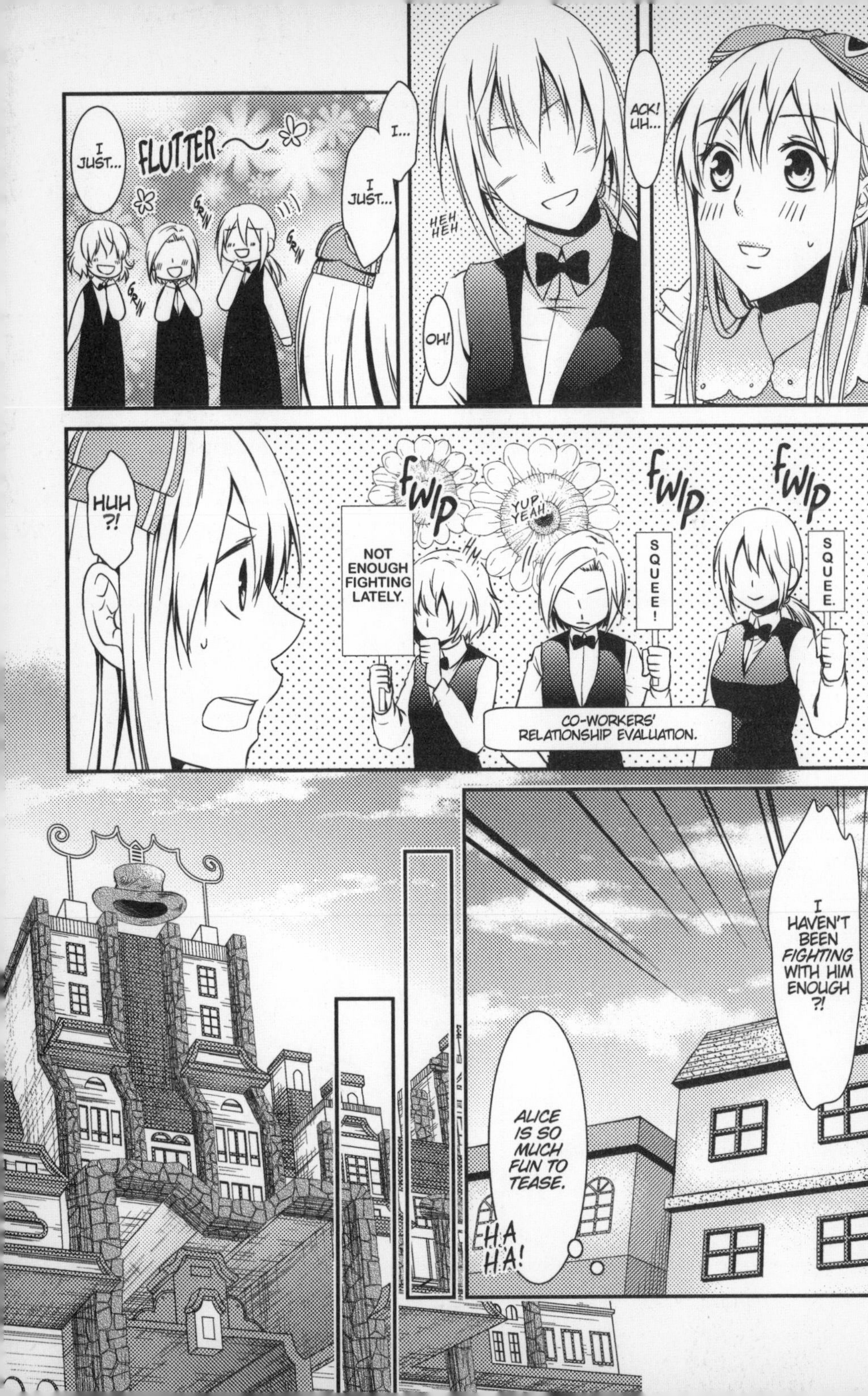
ACK! UH...
HEH HEH
OH!
I...
I JUST...
I JUST...
FLUTTER
GRIN
GRIN
GRIN
HUH?!
FWIP
SQUEE.
FWIP
SQUEE!
YUP YEAH
FWIP
NOT ENOUGH FIGHTING LATELY.
HM
CO-WORKERS' RELATIONSHIP EVALUATION.
I HAVEN'T BEEN *FIGHTING* WITH HIM ENOUGH?!
ALICE IS SO MUCH FUN TO TEASE.
HA HA!

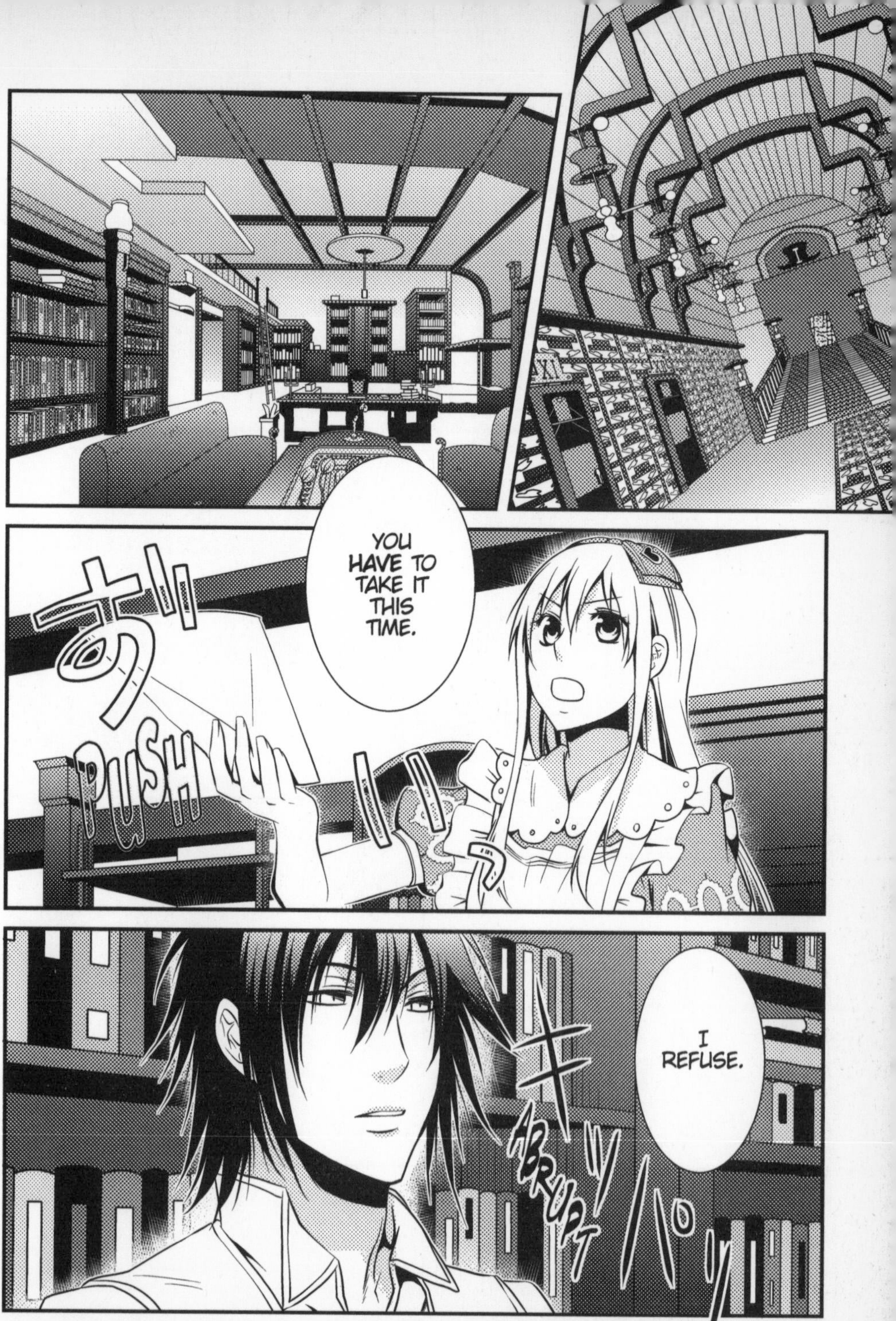
YOU HAVE TO TAKE IT THIS TIME.
PUSH
I REFUSE.
ABRUPT

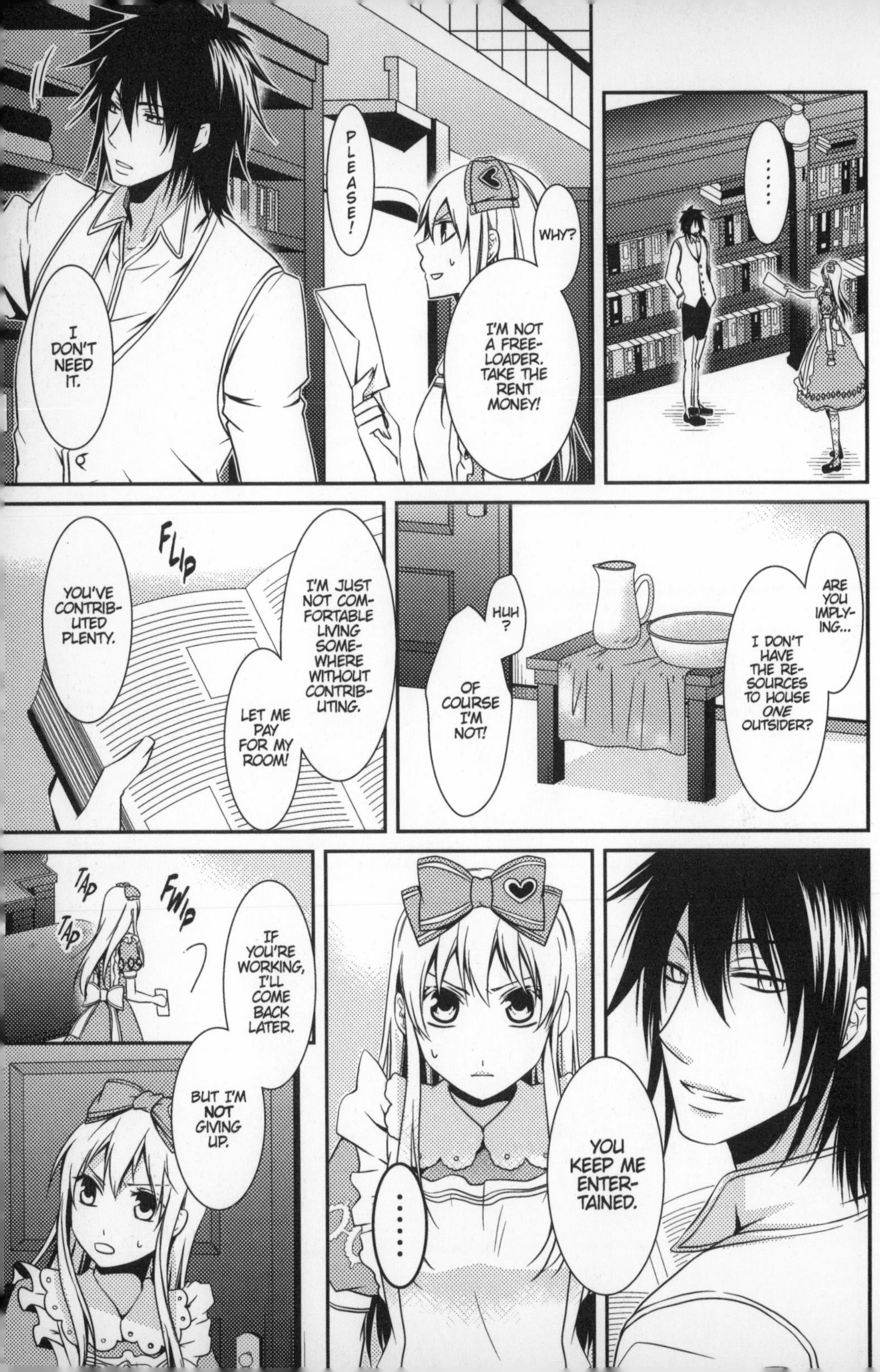
......
PLEASE!
WHY?
I'M NOT A FREE-LOADER. TAKE THE RENT MONEY!
I DON'T NEED IT.
ARE YOU IMPLYING...
I DON'T HAVE THE RE-SOURCES TO HOUSE *ONE* OUTSIDER?
HUH?
OF COURSE I'M NOT!
I'M JUST NOT COM-FORTABLE LIVING SOME-WHERE WITHOUT CONTRIB-UTING.
LET ME PAY FOR MY ROOM!
FLIP
YOU'VE CONTRIB-UTED PLENTY.
YOU KEEP ME ENTER-TAINED.
......
FWIP
TAP
TAP
IF YOU'RE WORKING, I'LL COME BACK LATER.
BUT I'M NOT GIVING UP.

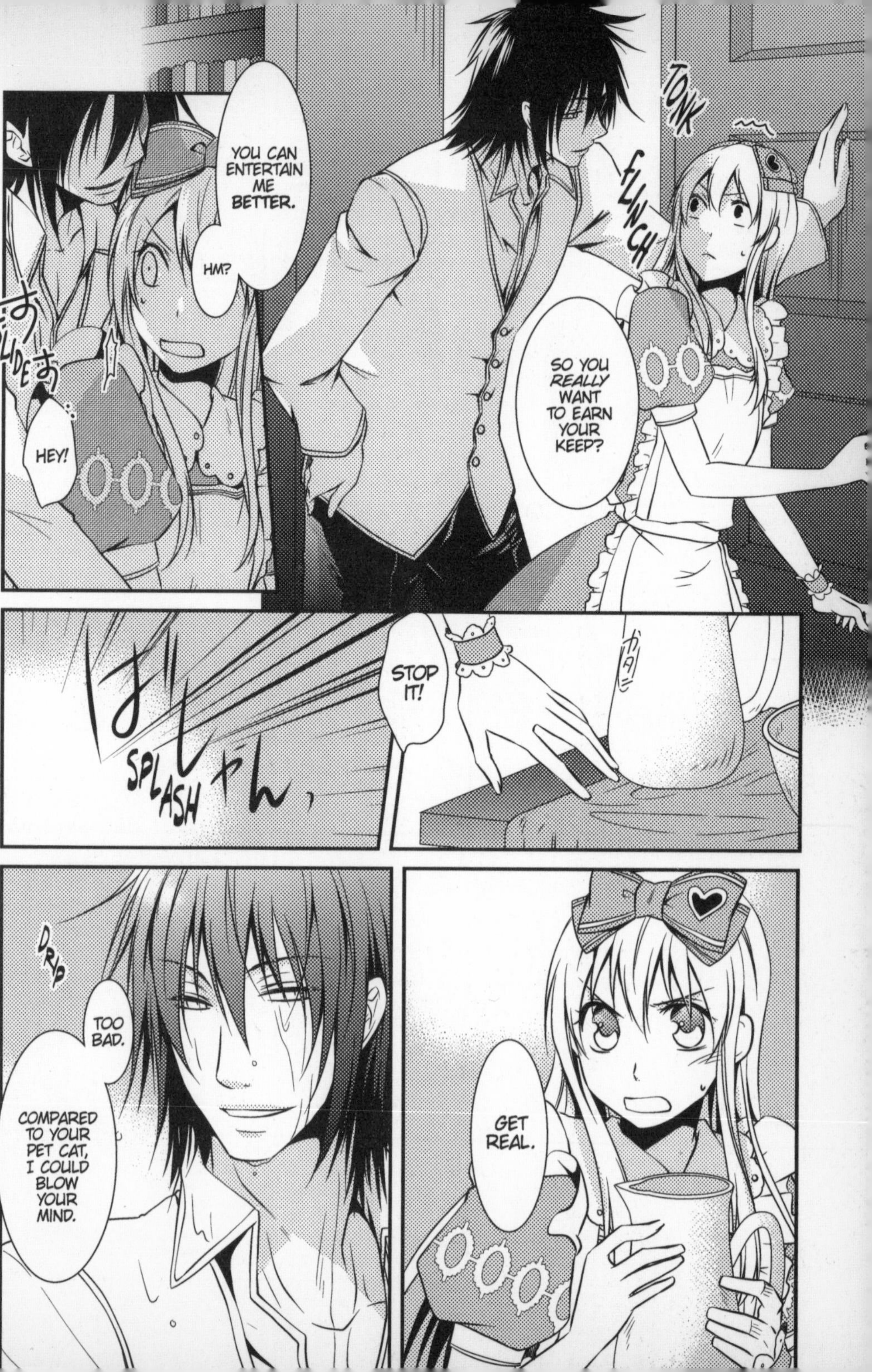
TONK
FLINCH
SO YOU REALLY WANT TO EARN YOUR KEEP?
YOU CAN ENTERTAIN ME BETTER.
HM?
SLIDE
HEY!
STOP IT!
SPLASH
GET REAL.
DRIP
TOO BAD.
COMPARED TO YOUR PET CAT, I COULD BLOW YOUR MIND.

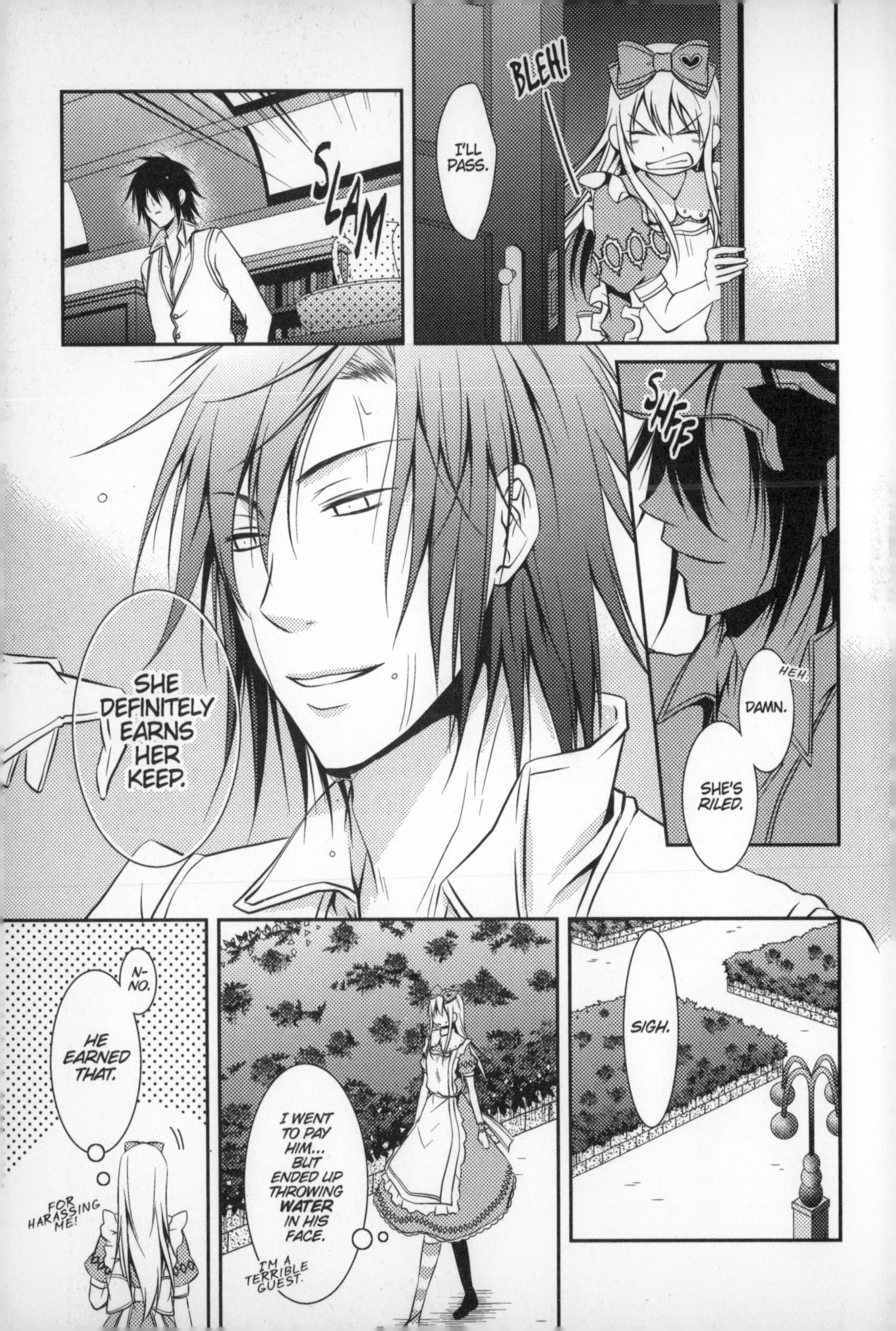
BLEH!
I'LL PASS.
SLAM
SHFF
HEH.
DAMN.
SHE'S RILED.
SHE DEFINITELY EARNS HER KEEP.
SIGH.
I WENT TO PAY HIM... BUT ENDED UP THROWING WATER IN HIS FACE.
I'M A TERRIBLE GUEST.
N-NO.
HE EARNED THAT.
FOR HARASSING ME!

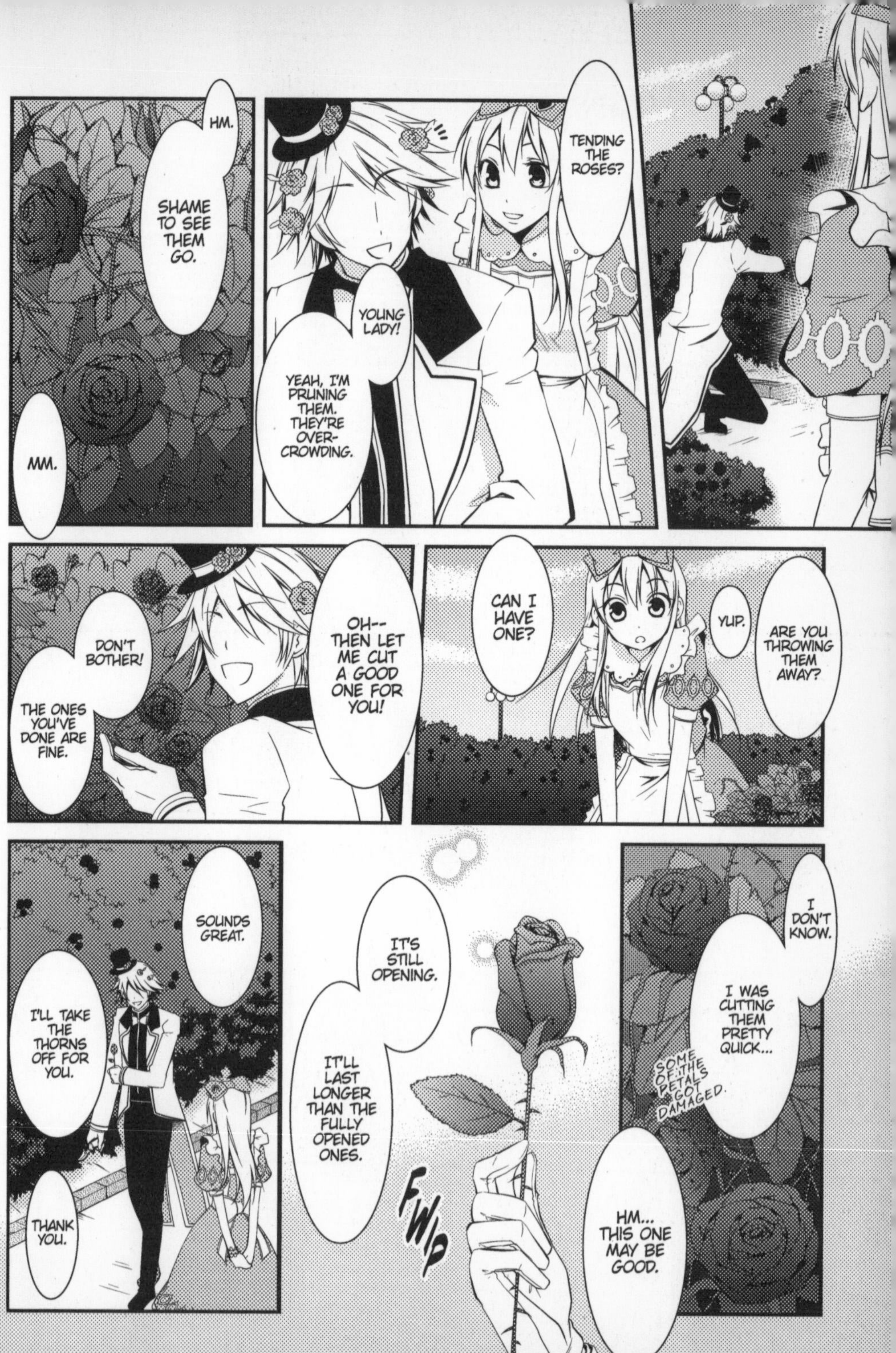
TENDING THE ROSES?
YOUNG LADY!
YEAH, I'M PRUNING THEM. THEY'RE OVER-CROWDING.
HM.
SHAME TO SEE THEM GO.
MM.
ARE YOU THROWING THEM AWAY?
YUP.
CAN I HAVE ONE?
OH-- THEN LET ME CUT A GOOD ONE FOR YOU!
DON'T BOTHER!
THE ONES YOU'VE DONE ARE FINE.
I DON'T KNOW.
I WAS CUTTING THEM PRETTY QUICK...
SOME OF THE PETALS GOT DAMAGED.
HM... THIS ONE MAY BE GOOD.
FWIP
IT'S STILL OPENING.
IT'LL LAST LONGER THAN THE FULLY OPENED ONES.
SOUNDS GREAT.
I'LL TAKE THE THORNS OFF FOR YOU.
THANK YOU.

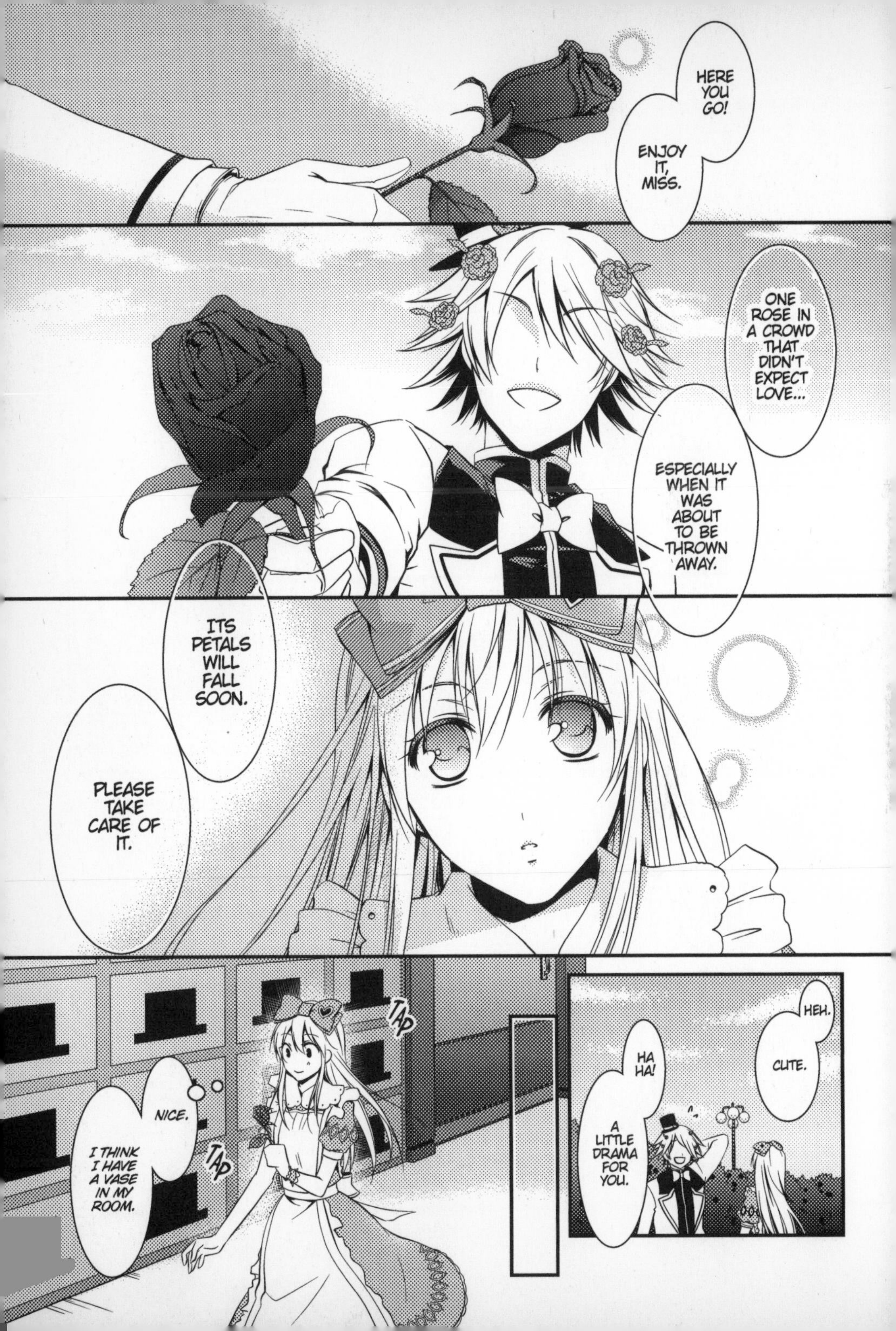
HERE YOU GO!
ENJOY IT, MISS.
ONE ROSE IN A CROWD THAT DIDN'T EXPECT LOVE...
ESPECIALLY WHEN IT WAS ABOUT TO BE THROWN AWAY.
ITS PETALS WILL FALL SOON.
PLEASE TAKE CARE OF IT.
HEH.
CUTE.
HA HA!
A LITTLE DRAMA FOR YOU.
TAP
NICE.
I THINK I HAVE A VASE IN MY ROOM.
TAP

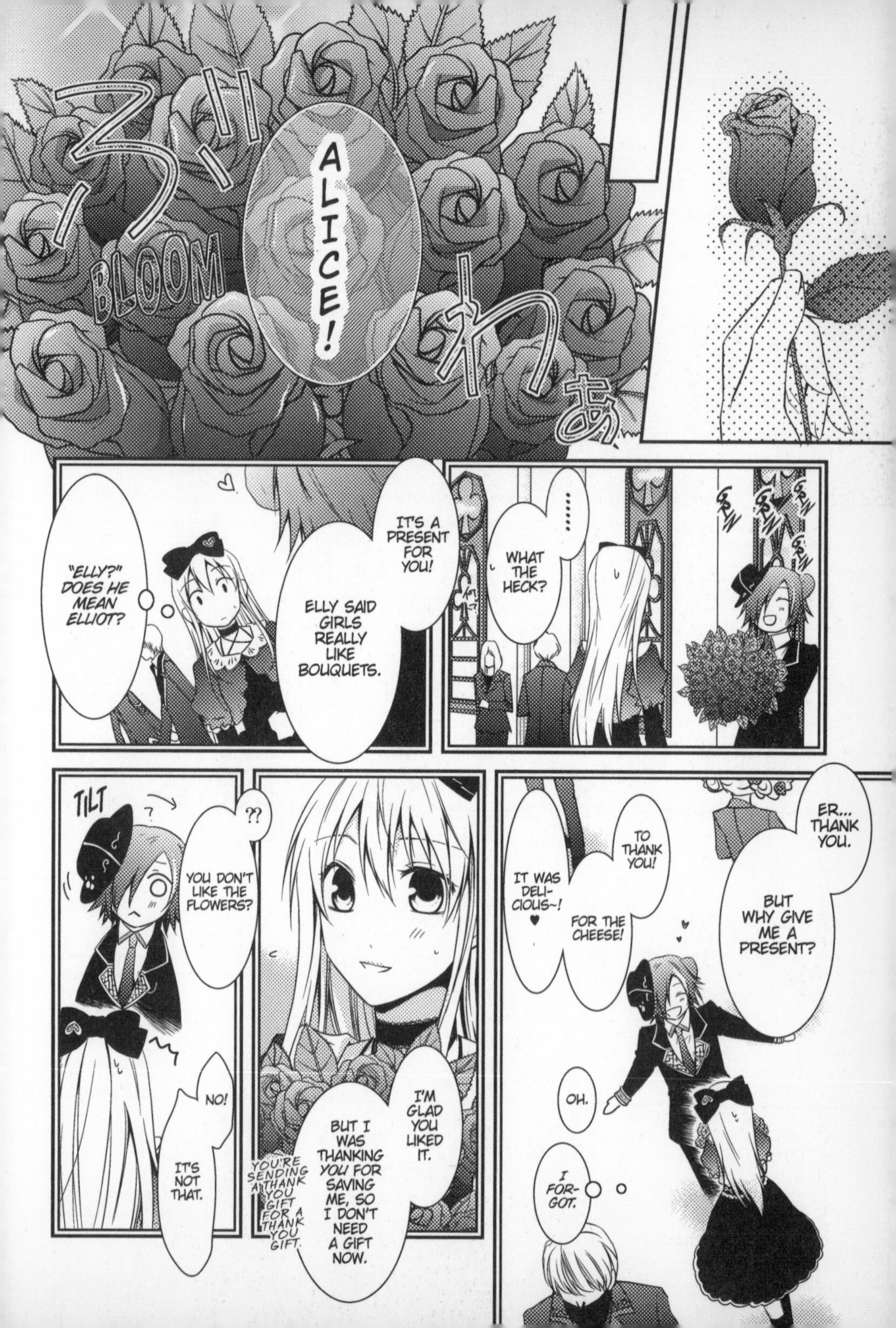
BLOOM
ALICE!
GRIN GRIN GRIN GRIN
......
WHAT THE HECK?
IT'S A PRESENT FOR YOU!
ELLY SAID GIRLS REALLY LIKE BOUQUETS.
"ELLY?" DOES HE MEAN ELLIOT?
ER... THANK YOU.
BUT WHY GIVE ME A PRESENT?
TO THANK YOU!
FOR THE CHEESE!
IT WAS DELICIOUS~!
OH.
I FOR-GOT.
I'M GLAD YOU LIKED IT.
BUT I WAS THANKING YOU FOR SAVING ME, SO I DON'T NEED A GIFT NOW.
YOU'RE SENDING A THANK YOU GIFT FOR A THANK YOU GIFT.
TILT
?
??
YOU DON'T LIKE THE FLOWERS?
NO!
IT'S NOT THAT.

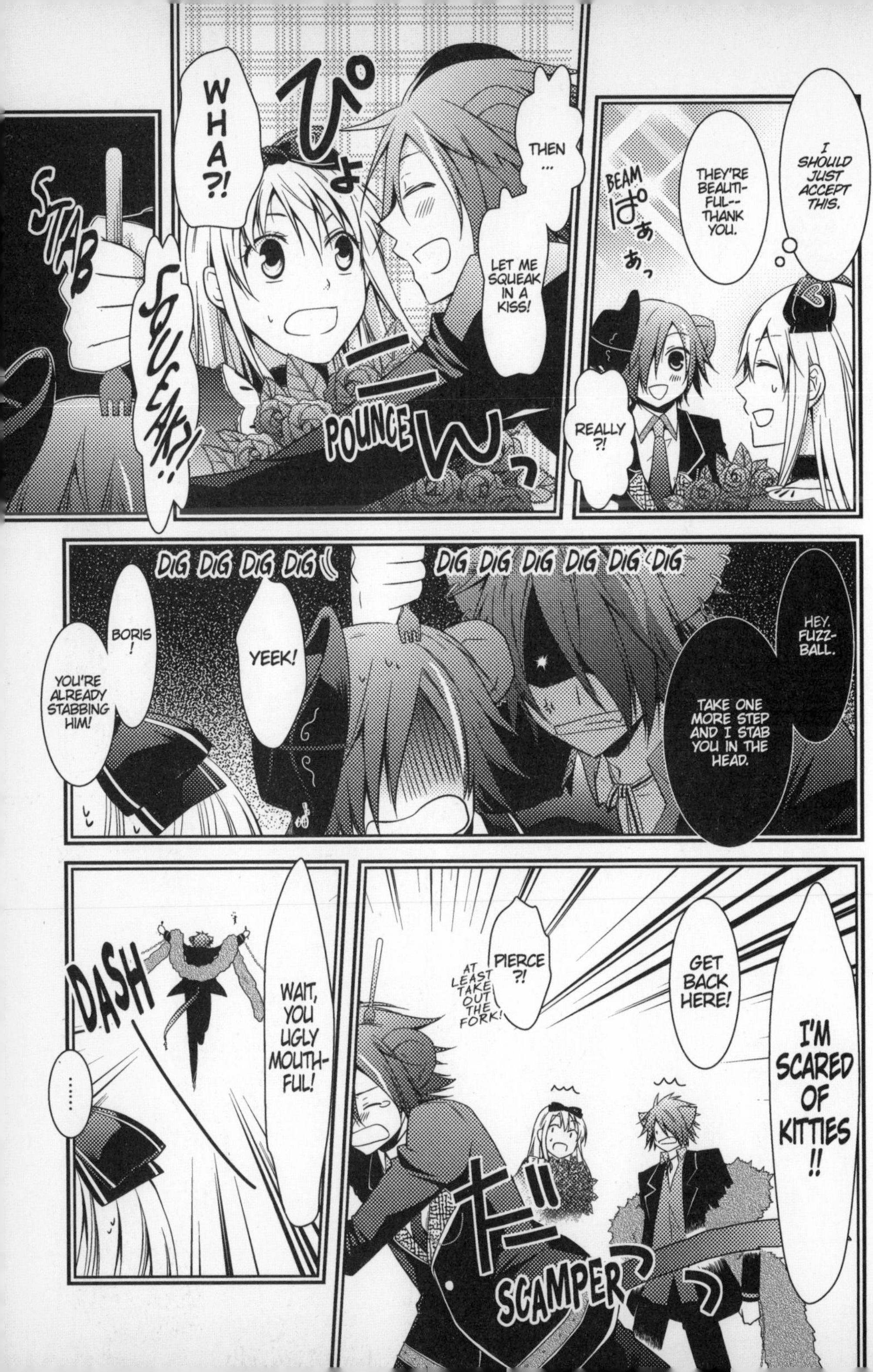
I SHOULD JUST ACCEPT THIS.
THEY'RE BEAUTIFUL--THANK YOU.
BEAM
REALLY?!
THEN ...
LET ME SQUEAK IN A KISS!
POUNCE
WHA?!
SQUEAK?!
STAB
HEY. FUZZ-BALL.
TAKE ONE MORE STEP AND I STAB YOU IN THE HEAD.
DIG DIG DIG DIG DIG DIG
YEEK!
DIG DIG DIG DIG
BORIS!
YOU'RE ALREADY STABBING HIM!
I'M SCARED OF KITTIES!!
GET BACK HERE!
PIERCE?!
AT LEAST TAKE OUT THE FORK!
SCAMPER
WAIT, YOU UGLY MOUTHFUL!
DASH
......

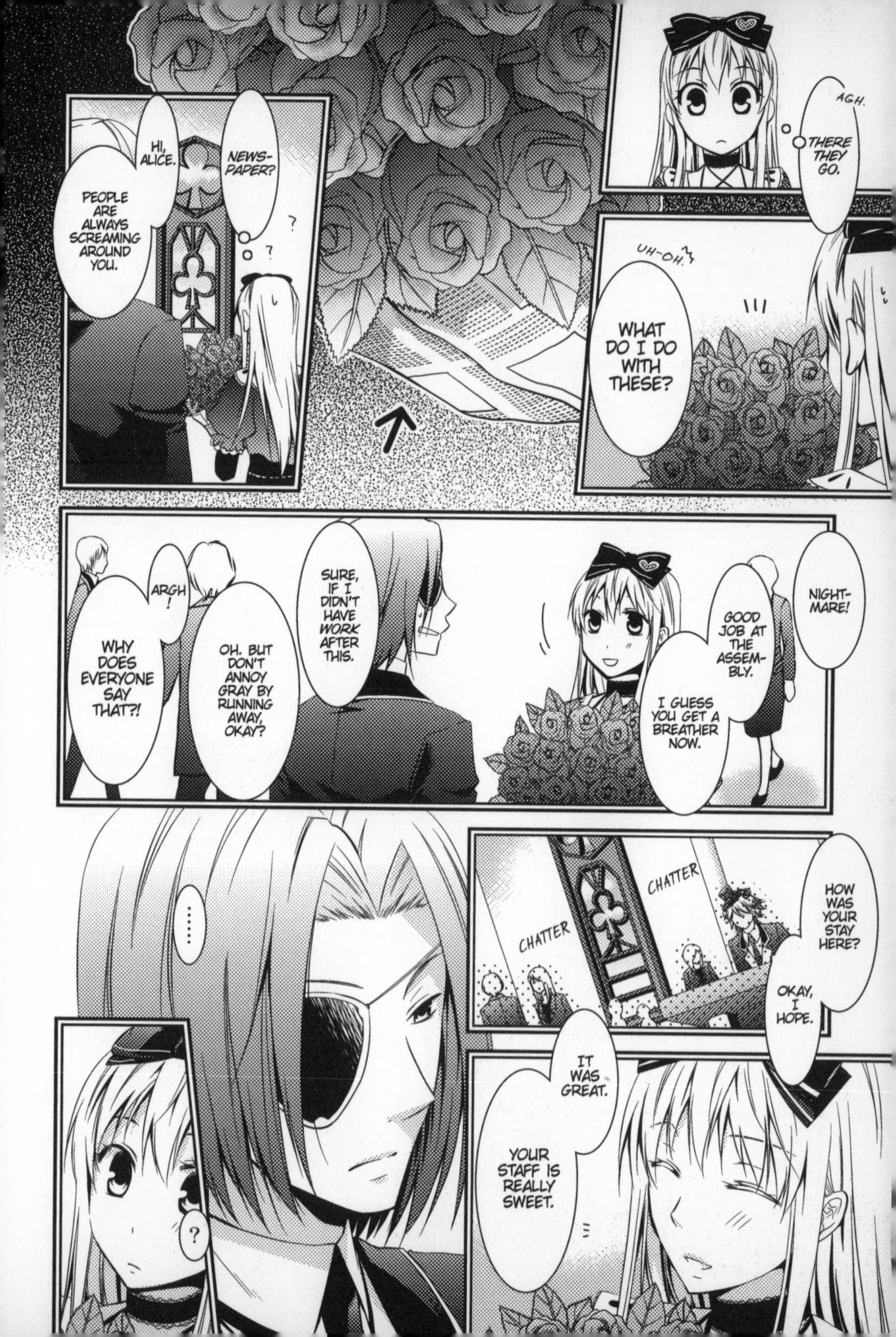

AGH.
THERE THEY GO.
UH-OH.
WHAT DO I DO WITH THESE?
NEWS-PAPER?
HI, ALICE.
PEOPLE ARE ALWAYS SCREAMING AROUND YOU.
NIGHT-MARE!
GOOD JOB AT THE ASSEM-BLY.
I GUESS YOU GET A BREATHER NOW.
SURE, IF I DIDN'T HAVE WORK AFTER THIS.
OH. BUT DON'T ANNOY GRAY BY RUNNING AWAY, OKAY?
ARGH!
WHY DOES EVERYONE SAY THAT?!
HOW WAS YOUR STAY HERE?
OKAY, I HOPE.
CHATTER
CHATTER
IT WAS GREAT.
YOUR STAFF IS REALLY SWEET.
......
?

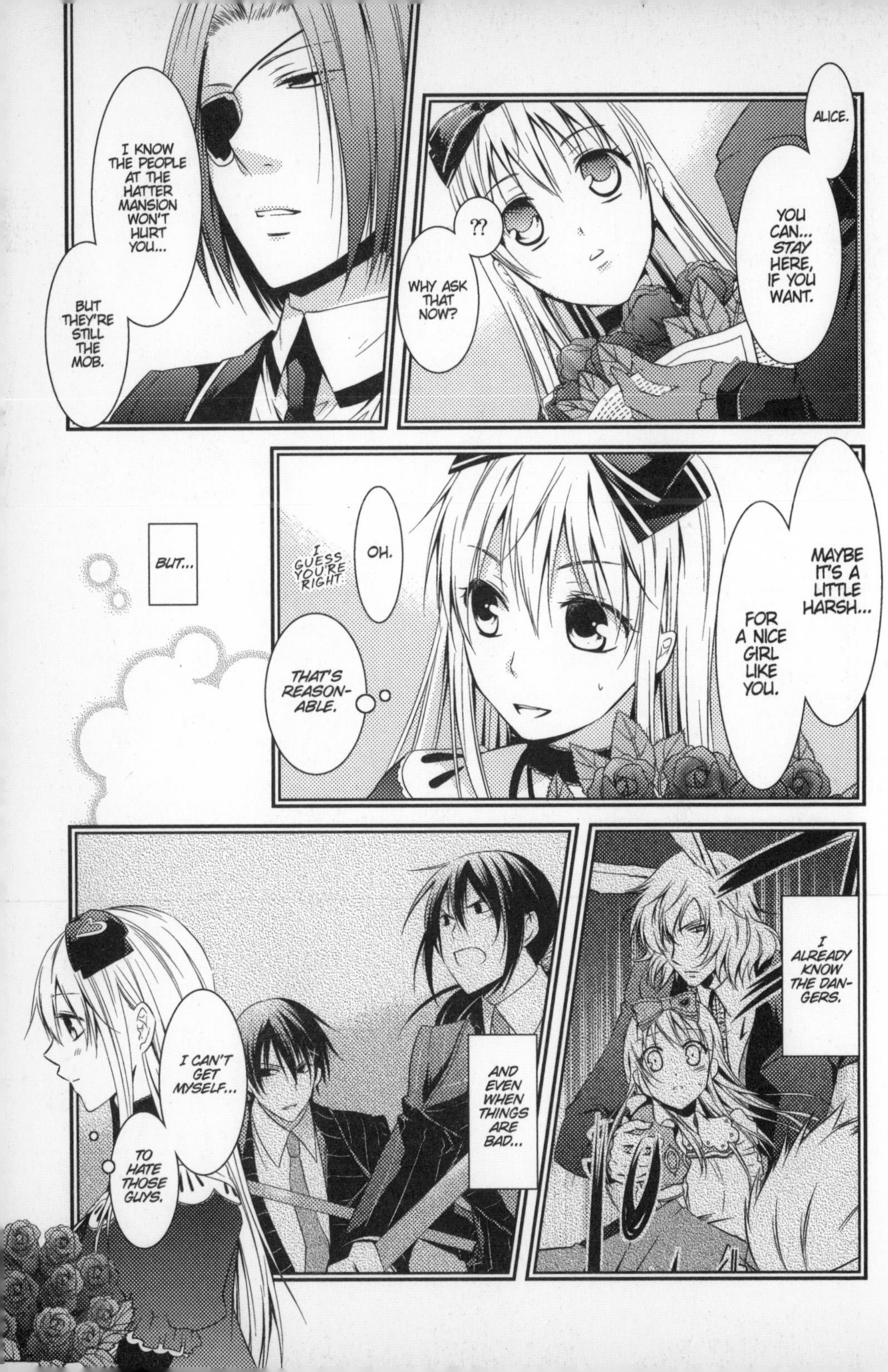
ALICE.
YOU CAN... STAY HERE, IF YOU WANT.
??
WHY ASK THAT NOW?
I KNOW THE PEOPLE AT THE HATTER MANSION WON'T HURT YOU...
BUT THEY'RE STILL THE MOB.
MAYBE IT'S A LITTLE HARSH...
FOR A NICE GIRL LIKE YOU.
OH.
I GUESS YOU'RE RIGHT.
THAT'S REASONABLE.
BUT...
I ALREADY KNOW THE DANGERS.
AND EVEN WHEN THINGS ARE BAD...
I CAN'T GET MYSELF...
TO HATE THOSE GUYS.

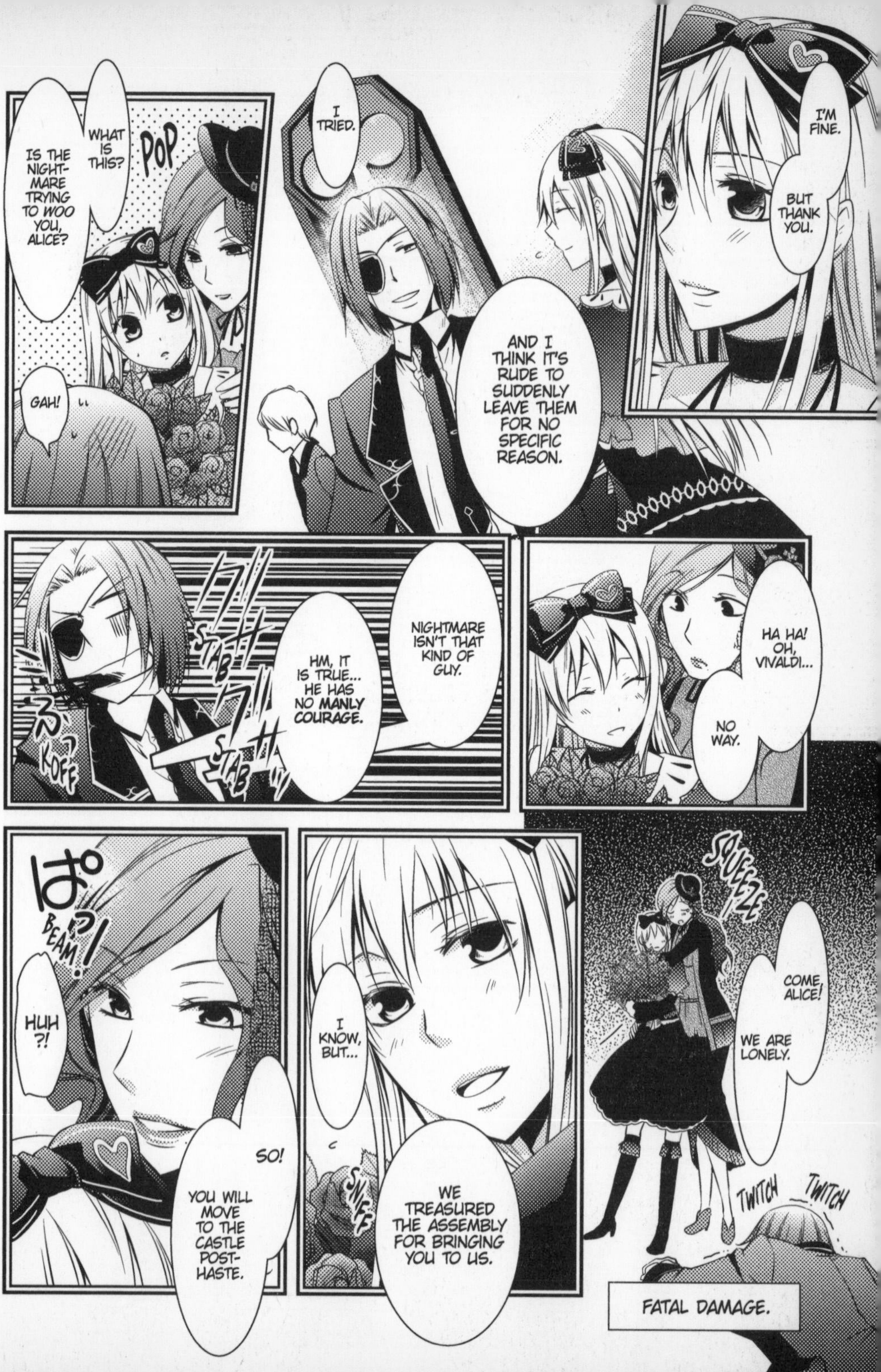
I'M FINE.
BUT THANK YOU.
I TRIED.
AND I THINK IT'S RUDE TO SUDDENLY LEAVE THEM FOR NO SPECIFIC REASON.
WHAT IS THIS?
POP
IS THE NIGHT-MARE TRYING TO WOO YOU, ALICE?
GAH!
HA HA! OH, VIVALDI...
NO WAY.
NIGHTMARE ISN'T THAT KIND OF GUY.
HM, IT IS TRUE... HE HAS NO MANLY COURAGE.
STAB
STAB
KOFF
SQUEEZE
COME, ALICE!
WE ARE LONELY.
TWITCH
TWITCH
FATAL DAMAGE.
I KNOW, BUT...
SNIFF
WE TREASURED THE ASSEMBLY FOR BRINGING YOU TO US.
ぱっ
BEAM
HUH ?!
SO!
YOU WILL MOVE TO THE CASTLE POST-HASTE.

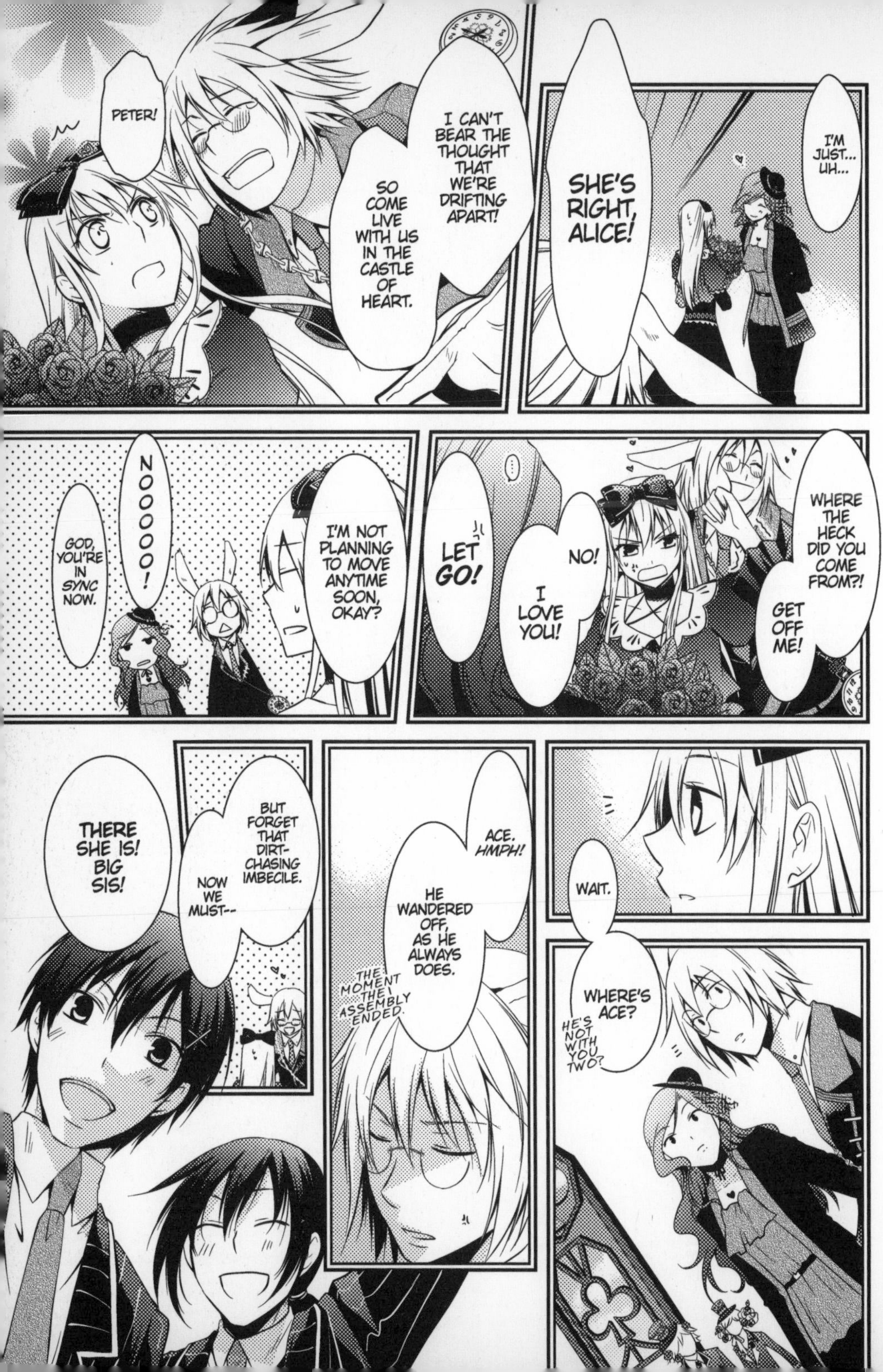
I'M JUST... UH...
SHE'S RIGHT, ALICE!
I CAN'T BEAR THE THOUGHT THAT WE'RE DRIFTING APART!
SO COME LIVE WITH US IN THE CASTLE OF HEART.
PETER!
WHERE THE HECK DID YOU COME FROM?!
GET OFF ME!
NO!
I LOVE YOU!
LET GO!
...
I'M NOT PLANNING TO MOVE ANYTIME SOON, OKAY?
NOOOOOO!
GOD, YOU'RE IN SYNC NOW.
WAIT.
WHERE'S ACE?
HE'S NOT WITH YOU TWO?
ACE. HMPH!
HE WANDERED OFF, AS HE ALWAYS DOES.
THE MOMENT THE ASSEMBLY ENDED.
BUT FORGET THAT DIRT-CHASING IMBECILE.
NOW WE MUST--
THERE SHE IS! BIG SIS!

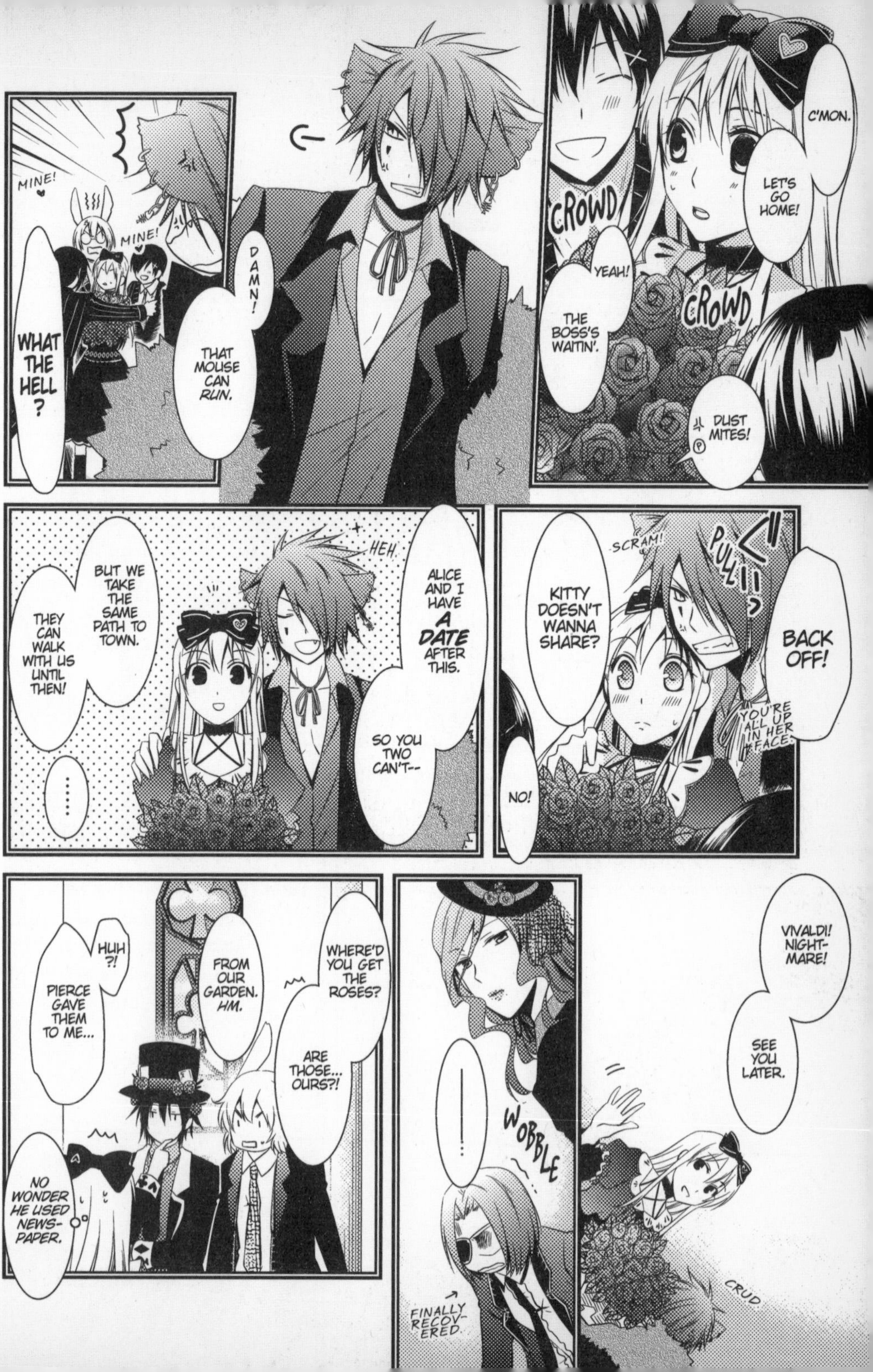
C'MON.
LET'S GO HOME!
CROWD
YEAH!
THE BOSS'S WAITIN'.
CROWD
DUST MITES!
DAMN!
THAT MOUSE CAN RUN.
MINE!
MINE!
WHAT THE HELL?
PULL
BACK OFF!
SCRAM!
KITTY DOESN'T WANNA SHARE?
YOU'RE ALL UP IN HER FACE.
NO!
HEH
ALICE AND I HAVE A DATE AFTER THIS.
SO YOU TWO CAN'T--
BUT WE TAKE THE SAME PATH TO TOWN.
THEY CAN WALK WITH US UNTIL THEN!
......
VIVALDI! NIGHTMARE!
SEE YOU LATER.
WOBBLE
CRUD
FINALLY RECOVERED.
WHERE'D YOU GET THE ROSES?
FROM OUR GARDEN. HM.
HUH?!
PIERCE GAVE THEM TO ME...
ARE THOSE... OURS?!
NO WONDER HE USED NEWSPAPER.

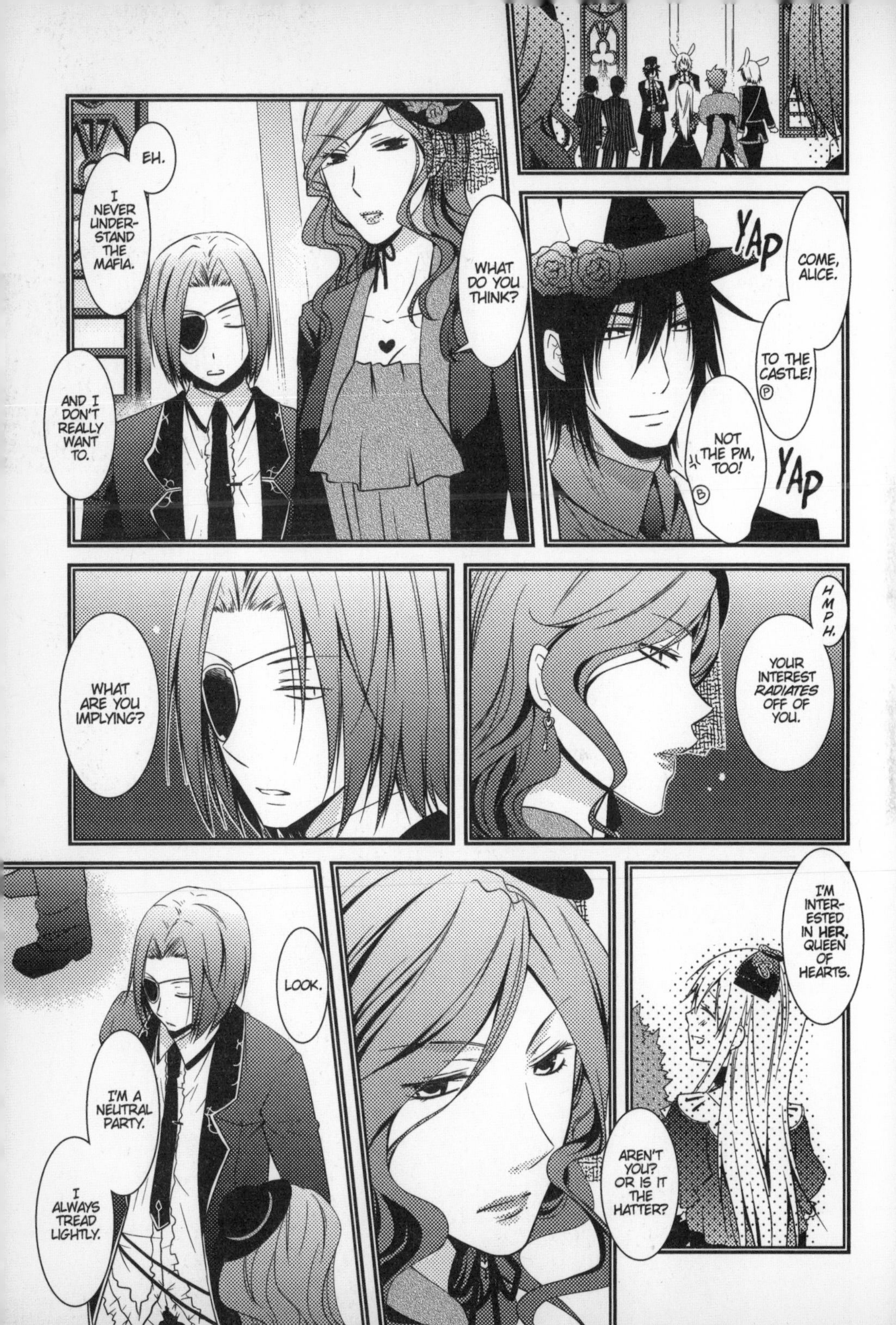

YAP
COME, ALICE.
TO THE CASTLE! (P)
NOT THE PM, TOO! (B)
YAP
WHAT DO YOU THINK?
EH.
I NEVER UNDER-STAND THE MAFIA.
AND I DON'T REALLY WANT TO.
HMPH.
YOUR INTEREST *RADIATES* OFF OF YOU.
WHAT ARE YOU IMPLYING?
I'M INTER-ESTED IN HER, QUEEN OF HEARTS.
AREN'T YOU? OR IS IT THE HATTER?
LOOK.
I'M A NEUTRAL PARTY.
I ALWAYS TREAD LIGHTLY.

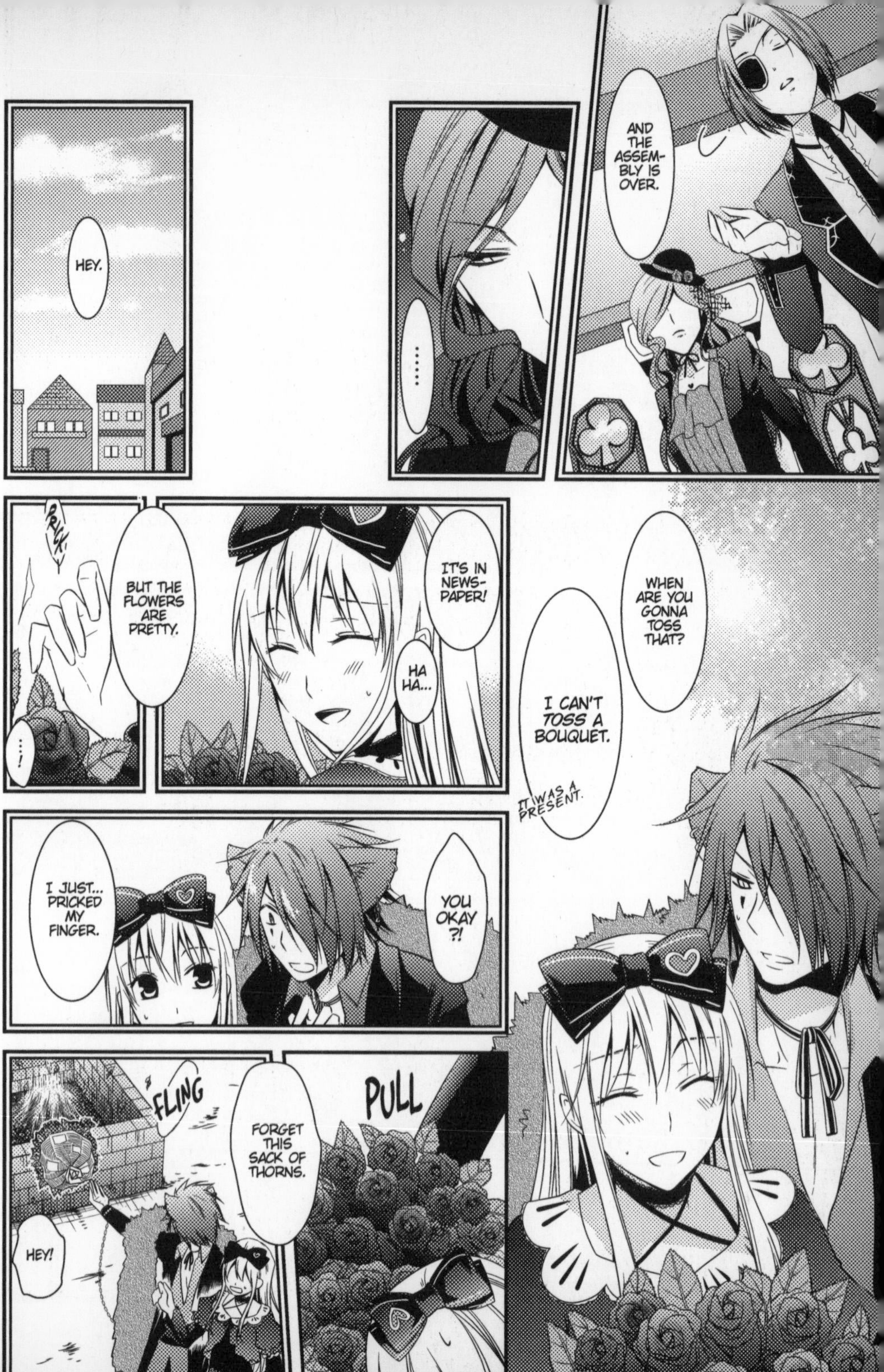
AND THE ASSEMBLY IS OVER.
......
HEY.
WHEN ARE YOU GONNA TOSS THAT?
I CAN'T *TOSS* A BOUQUET.
IT WAS A PRESENT.
IT'S IN NEWSPAPER!
HA HA...
PRICK
BUT THE FLOWERS ARE PRETTY.
...!
YOU OKAY?!
I JUST... PRICKED MY FINGER.
PULL
FLING
FORGET THIS SACK OF THORNS.
HEY!

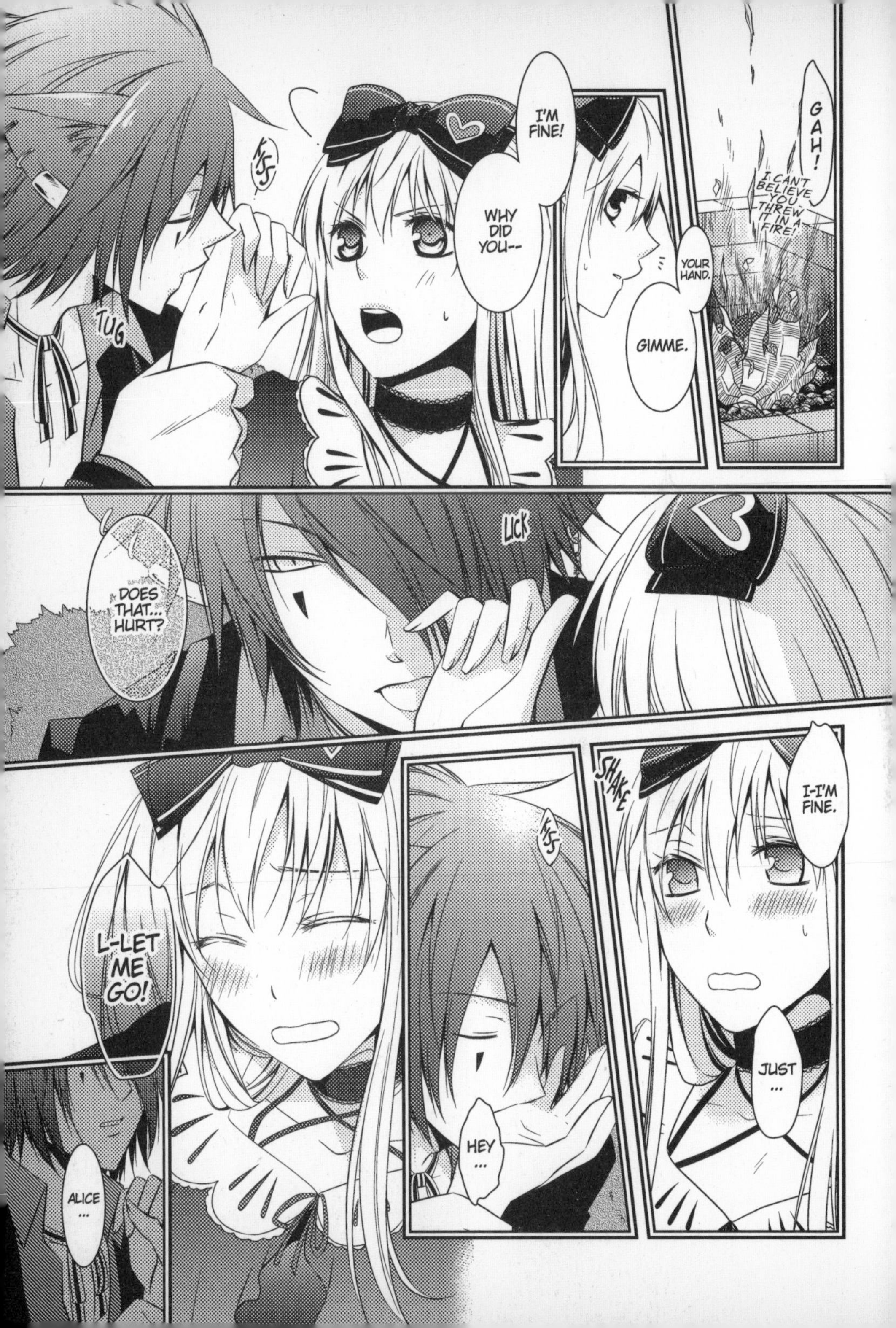
GAH!
I CAN'T BELIEVE YOU THREW IT IN A FIRE!
YOUR HAND.
I'M FINE!
GIMME.
KISS
WHY DID YOU--
TUG
LICK
DOES THAT... HURT?
SHAKE
I-I'M FINE.
JUST ...
KISS
HEY ...
L-LET ME GO!
ALICE ...

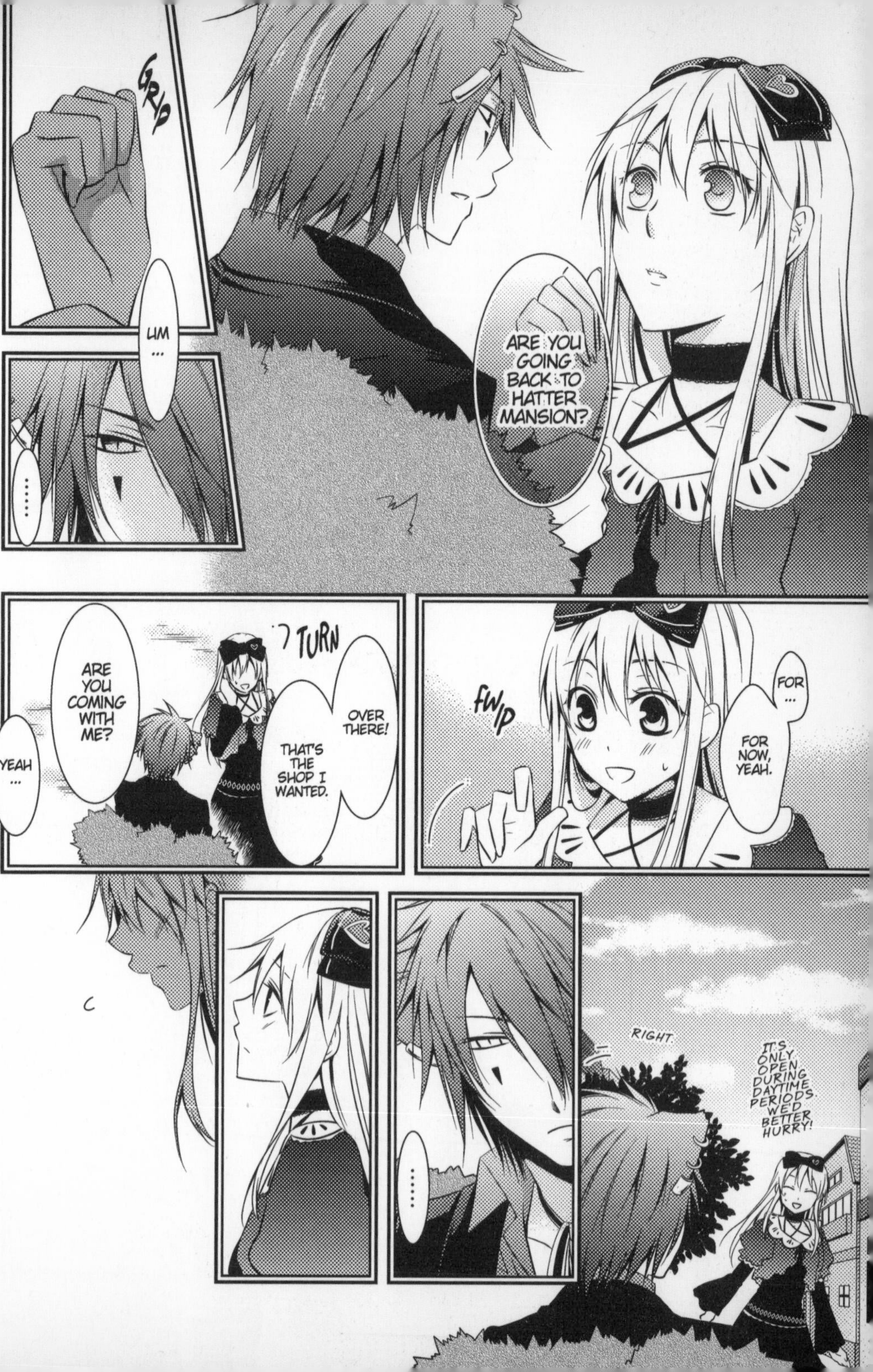
ARE YOU GOING BACK TO HATTER MANSION?
GRIP
UM ...
......
FWIP
FOR ...
FOR NOW, YEAH.
TURN
OVER THERE!
THAT'S THE SHOP I WANTED.
ARE YOU COMING WITH ME?
YEAH ...
IT'S ONLY OPEN DURING DAYTIME PERIODS. WE'D BETTER HURRY!
RIGHT.
......

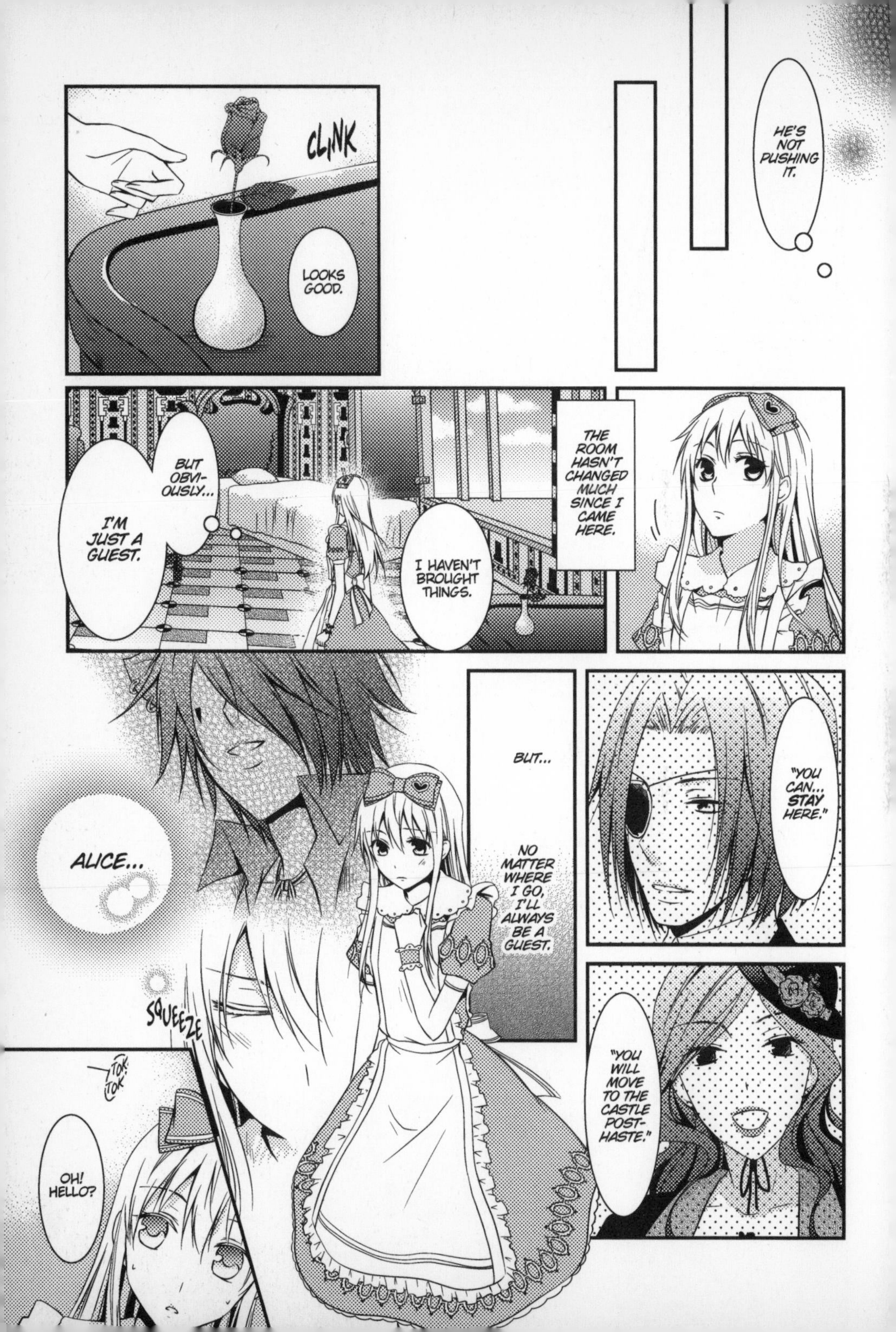
HE'S NOT PUSHING IT.
CLINK
LOOKS GOOD.
THE ROOM HASN'T CHANGED MUCH SINCE I CAME HERE.
I HAVEN'T BROUGHT THINGS.
BUT OBVI-OUSLY...
I'M JUST A GUEST.
"YOU CAN... STAY HERE."
"YOU WILL MOVE TO THE CASTLE POST-HASTE."
BUT...
NO MATTER WHERE I GO, I'LL ALWAYS BE A GUEST.
ALICE...
SQUEEZE
TOK TOK
OH! HELLO?

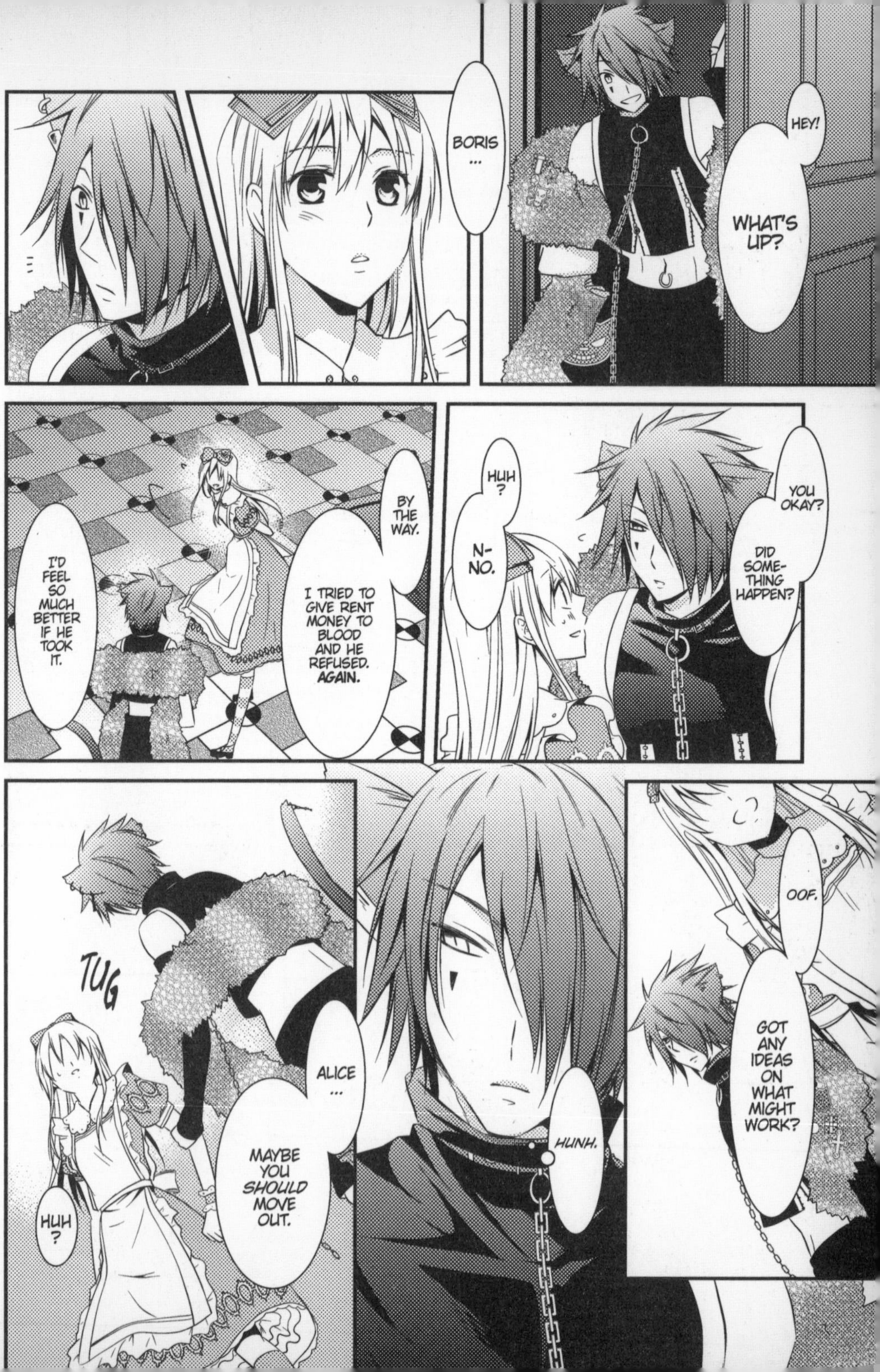
HEY!
WHAT'S UP?
BORIS ...
YOU OKAY?
DID SOMETHING HAPPEN?
HUH ?
N-NO.
BY THE WAY.
I TRIED TO GIVE RENT MONEY TO BLOOD AND HE REFUSED. **AGAIN.**
I'D FEEL SO MUCH BETTER IF HE TOOK IT.
OOF.
GOT ANY IDEAS ON WHAT MIGHT WORK?
HUNH.
ALICE ...
MAYBE YOU SHOULD MOVE OUT.
TUG
HUH ?

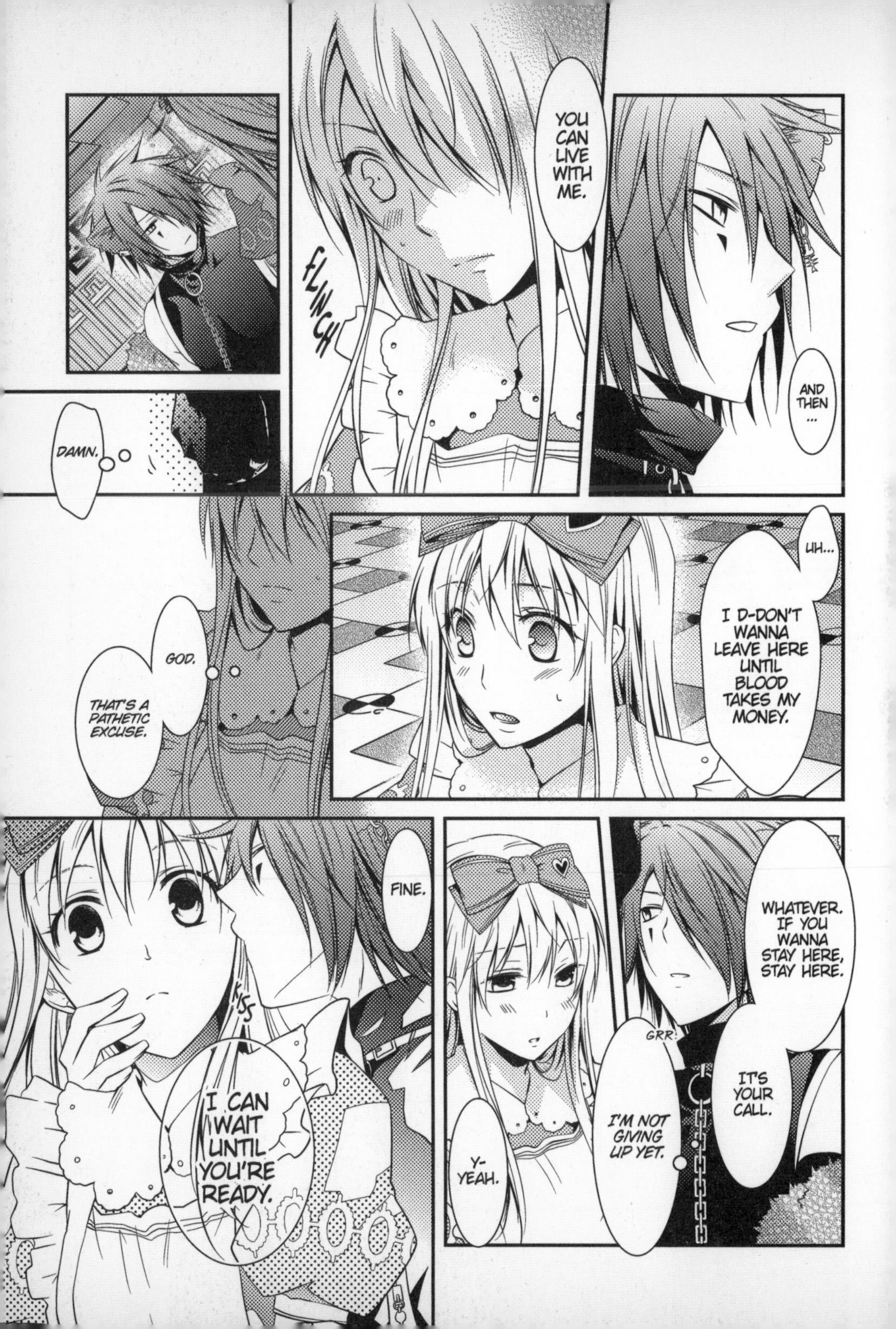
AND THEN...
YOU CAN LIVE WITH ME.
FLINCH
DAMN.
UH...
I D-DON'T WANNA LEAVE HERE UNTIL BLOOD TAKES MY MONEY.
GOD.
THAT'S A PATHETIC EXCUSE.
WHATEVER. IF YOU WANNA STAY HERE, STAY HERE.
GRR.
IT'S YOUR CALL.
I'M NOT GIVING UP YET.
Y-YEAH.
FINE.
KISS
I CAN WAIT UNTIL YOU'RE READY.

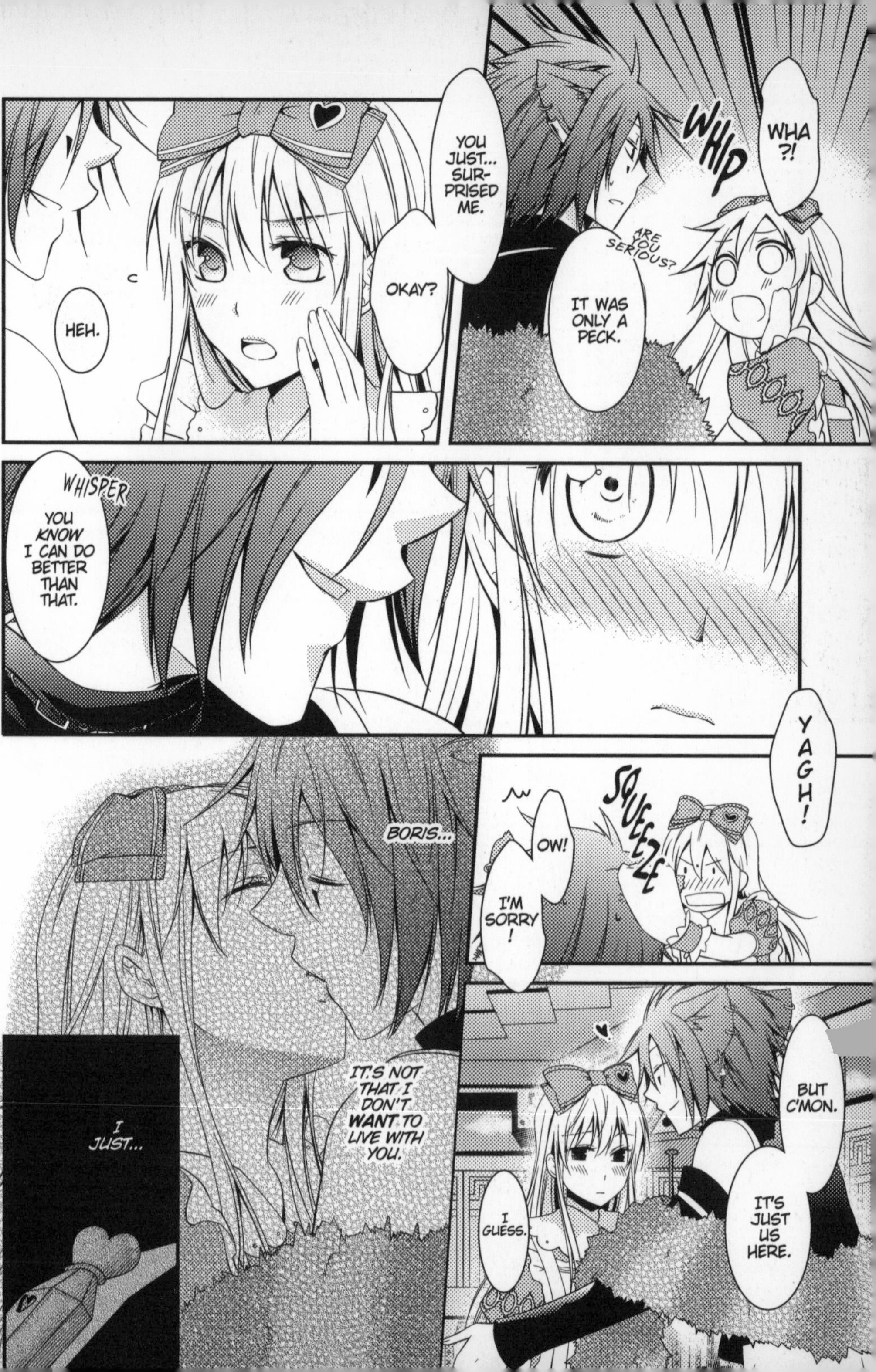
WHA ?!
WHIP
ARE YOU SERIOUS?
IT WAS ONLY A PECK.
YOU JUST... SUR-PRISED ME.
OKAY?
HEH.
WHISPER
YOU *KNOW* I CAN DO BETTER THAN THAT.
YAGH!
SQUEEZE
OW!
I'M SORRY!
BUT C'MON.
IT'S JUST US HERE.
I GUESS.
BORIS...
IT'S NOT THAT I DON'T **WANT** TO LIVE WITH YOU.
I JUST...

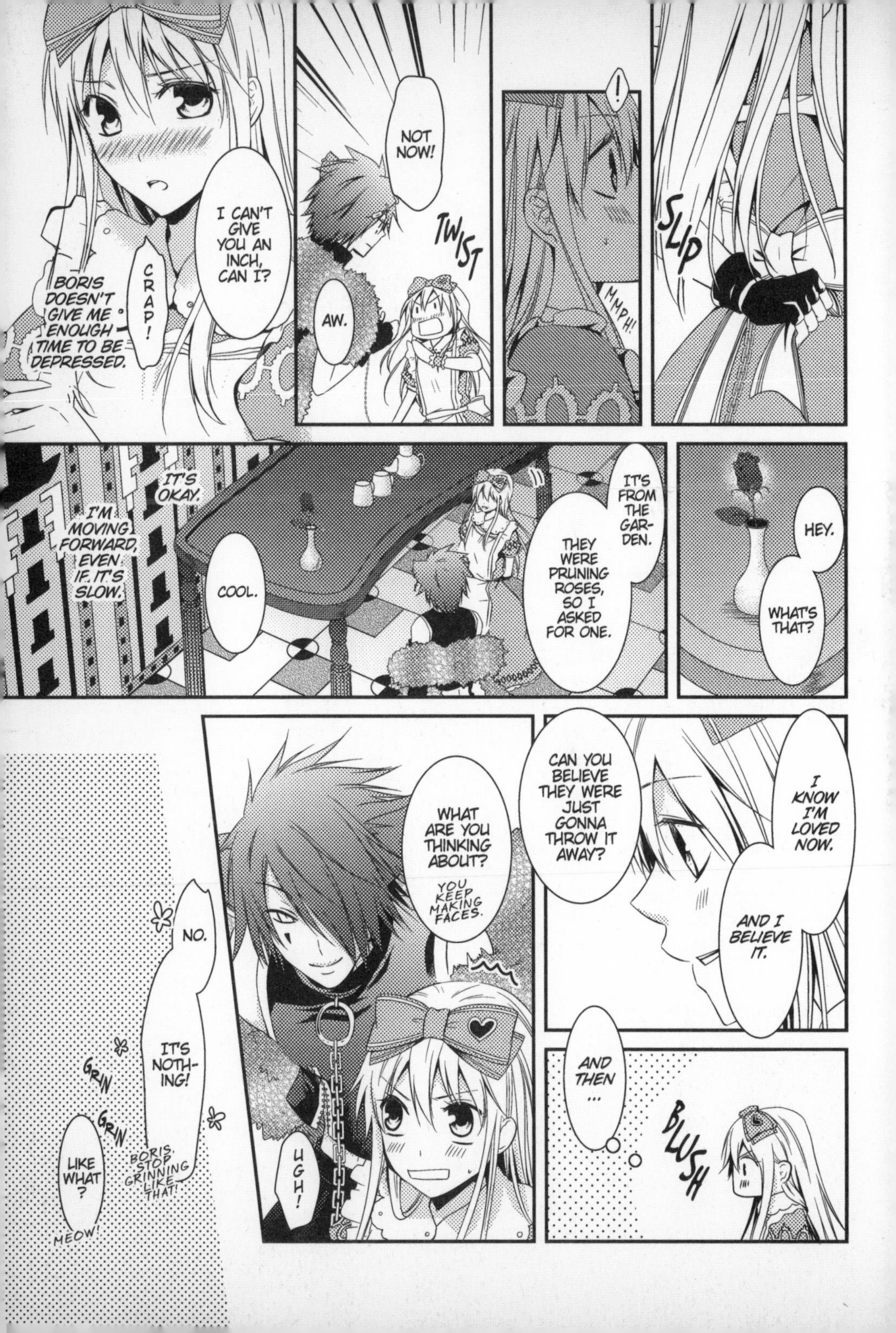
SLIP
!
MMPH!
NOT NOW!
TWIST
I CAN'T GIVE YOU AN INCH, CAN I?
AW.
CRAP!
BORIS DOESN'T GIVE ME ENOUGH TIME TO BE DEPRESSED.
HEY.
WHAT'S THAT?
IT'S FROM THE GARDEN.
THEY WERE PRUNING ROSES, SO I ASKED FOR ONE.
COOL.
IT'S OKAY.
I'M MOVING FORWARD, EVEN IF IT'S SLOW.
I KNOW I'M LOVED NOW.
CAN YOU BELIEVE THEY WERE JUST GONNA THROW IT AWAY?
AND I BELIEVE IT.
AND THEN ...
BLUSH
WHAT ARE YOU THINKING ABOUT?
YOU KEEP MAKING FACES.
NO.
IT'S NOTHING!
UGH!
GRIN
GRIN
LIKE WHAT?
BORIS. STOP GRINNING LIKE THAT!
MEOW!

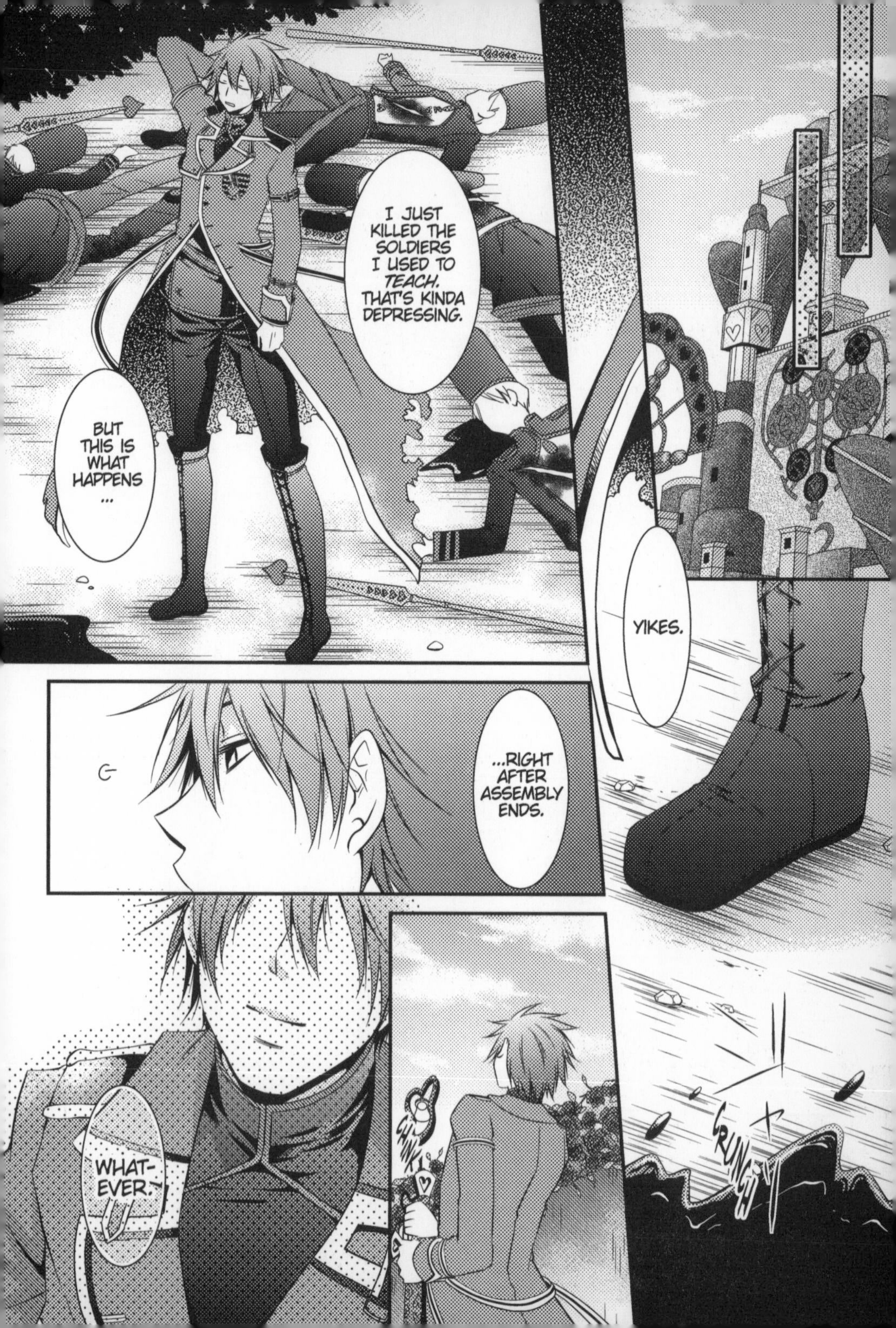

I JUST KILLED THE SOLDIERS I USED TO *TEACH*. THAT'S KINDA DEPRESSING.
BUT THIS IS WHAT HAPPENS ...
YIKES.
...RIGHT AFTER ASSEMBLY ENDS.
CRUNCH
CHINK
WHAT-EVER.

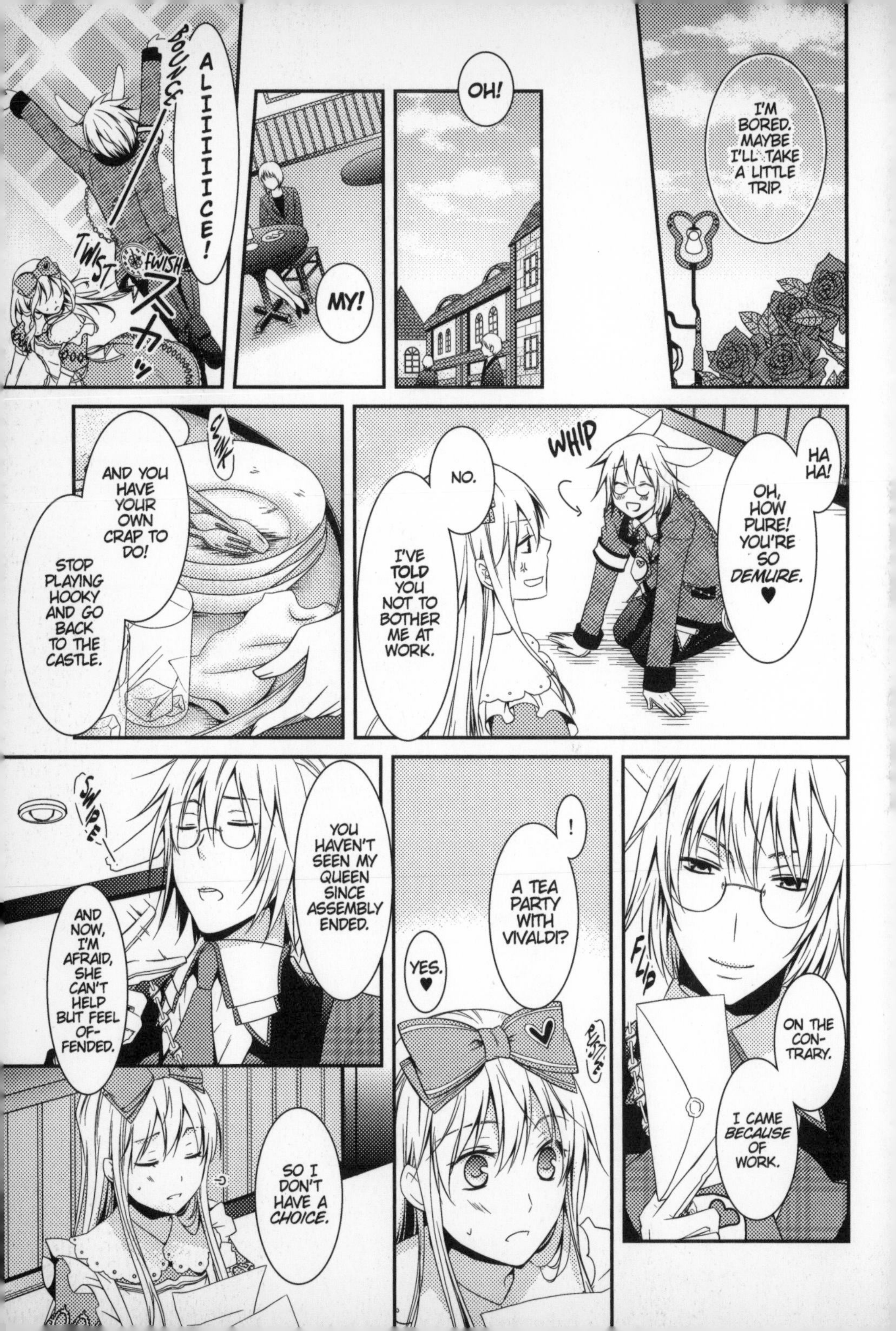
I'M BORED. MAYBE I'LL TAKE A LITTLE TRIP.
OH!
MY!
ALIIIIIICE!
BOUNCE
TWIST
FWISH
HA HA!
OH, HOW PURE! YOU'RE SO DEMURE. ♥
WHIP
NO.
I'VE TOLD YOU NOT TO BOTHER ME AT WORK.
CLINK
AND YOU HAVE YOUR OWN CRAP TO DO!
STOP PLAYING HOOKY AND GO BACK TO THE CASTLE.
ON THE CON-TRARY.
I CAME BECAUSE OF WORK.
FLIP
!
A TEA PARTY WITH VIVALDI?
YES. ♥
SWIPE
YOU HAVEN'T SEEN MY QUEEN SINCE ASSEMBLY ENDED.
AND NOW, I'M AFRAID, SHE CAN'T HELP BUT FEEL OF-FENDED.
SO I DON'T HAVE A CHOICE.

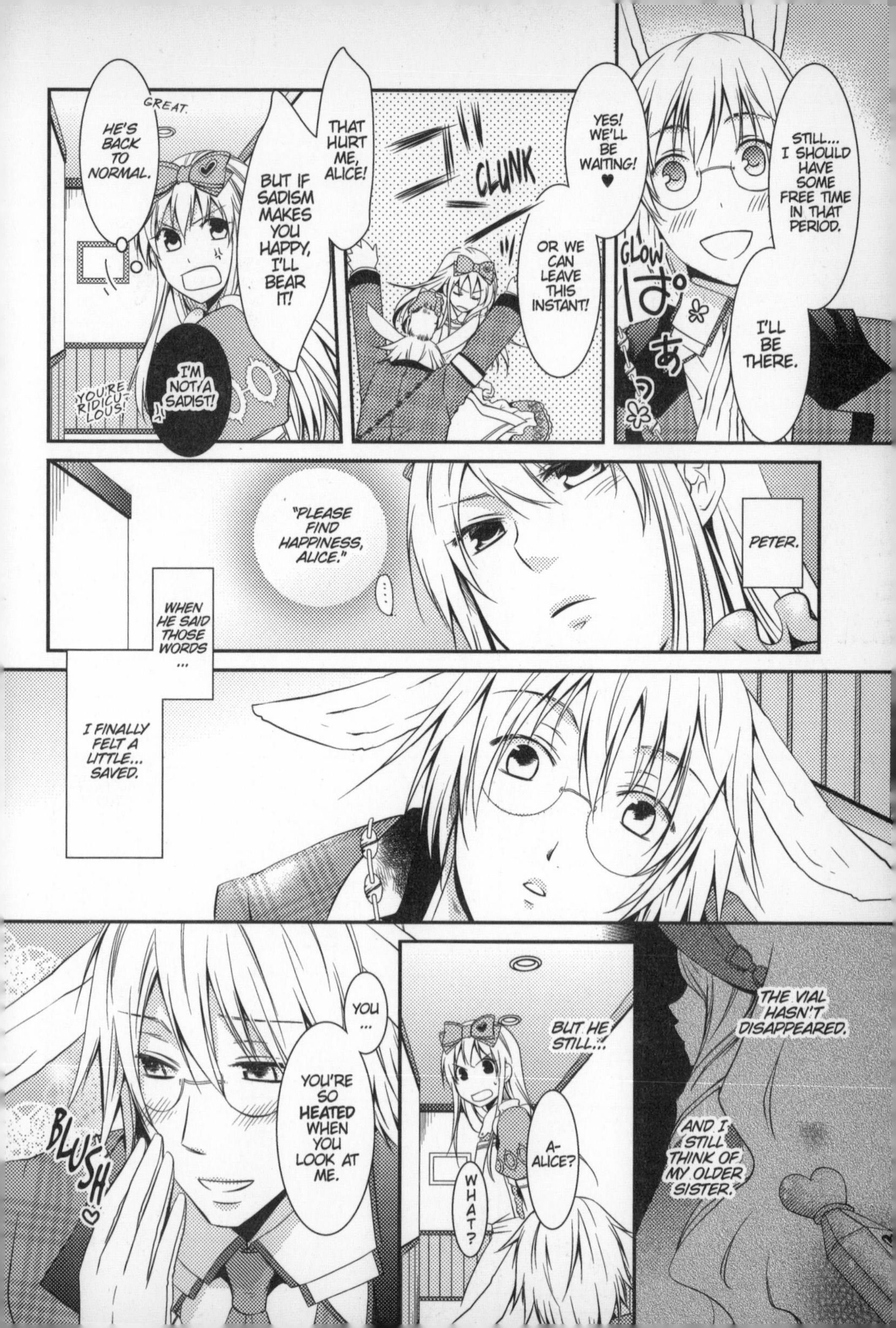
STILL... I SHOULD HAVE SOME FREE TIME IN THAT PERIOD.
I'LL BE THERE.
GLOW
ぱあっ
YES! WE'LL BE WAITING! ♥
OR WE CAN LEAVE THIS INSTANT!
CLUNK
ゴッ
THAT HURT ME, ALICE!
BUT IF SADISM MAKES YOU HAPPY, I'LL BEAR IT!
GREAT.
HE'S BACK TO NORMAL.
I'M NOT A SADIST!
YOU'RE RIDICULOUS!
PETER.
"PLEASE FIND HAPPINESS, ALICE."
...
WHEN HE SAID THOSE WORDS ...
I FINALLY FELT A LITTLE... SAVED.
THE VIAL HASN'T DISAPPEARED.
AND I STILL THINK OF MY OLDER SISTER.
BUT HE STILL...!
A-ALICE?
WHAT?
YOU ...
YOU'RE SO HEATED WHEN YOU LOOK AT ME.
BLUSH ♡

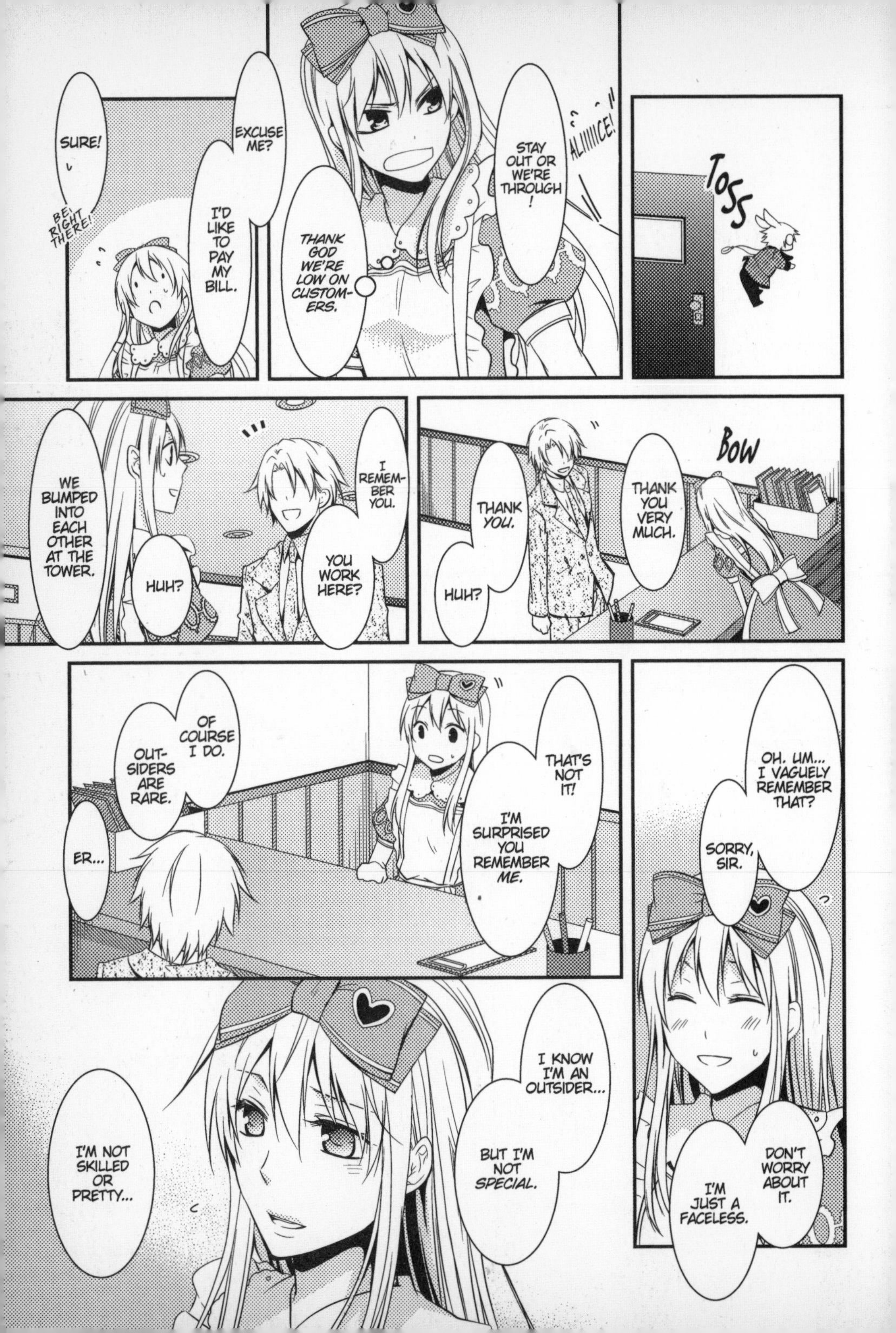

TOSS
ALIIIIICE!
STAY OUT OR WE'RE THROUGH!
THANK GOD WE'RE LOW ON CUSTOMERS.
EXCUSE ME?
I'D LIKE TO PAY MY BILL.
SURE!
BE RIGHT THERE!
BOW
THANK YOU VERY MUCH.
THANK YOU.
HUH?
I REMEMBER YOU.
YOU WORK HERE?
WE BUMPED INTO EACH OTHER AT THE TOWER.
HUH?
OH. UM... I VAGUELY REMEMBER THAT?
SORRY, SIR.
DON'T WORRY ABOUT IT.
I'M JUST A FACELESS.
THAT'S NOT IT!
I'M SURPRISED YOU REMEMBER ME.
OF COURSE I DO.
OUTSIDERS ARE RARE.
ER...
I KNOW I'M AN OUTSIDER...
BUT I'M NOT SPECIAL.
I'M NOT SKILLED OR PRETTY...

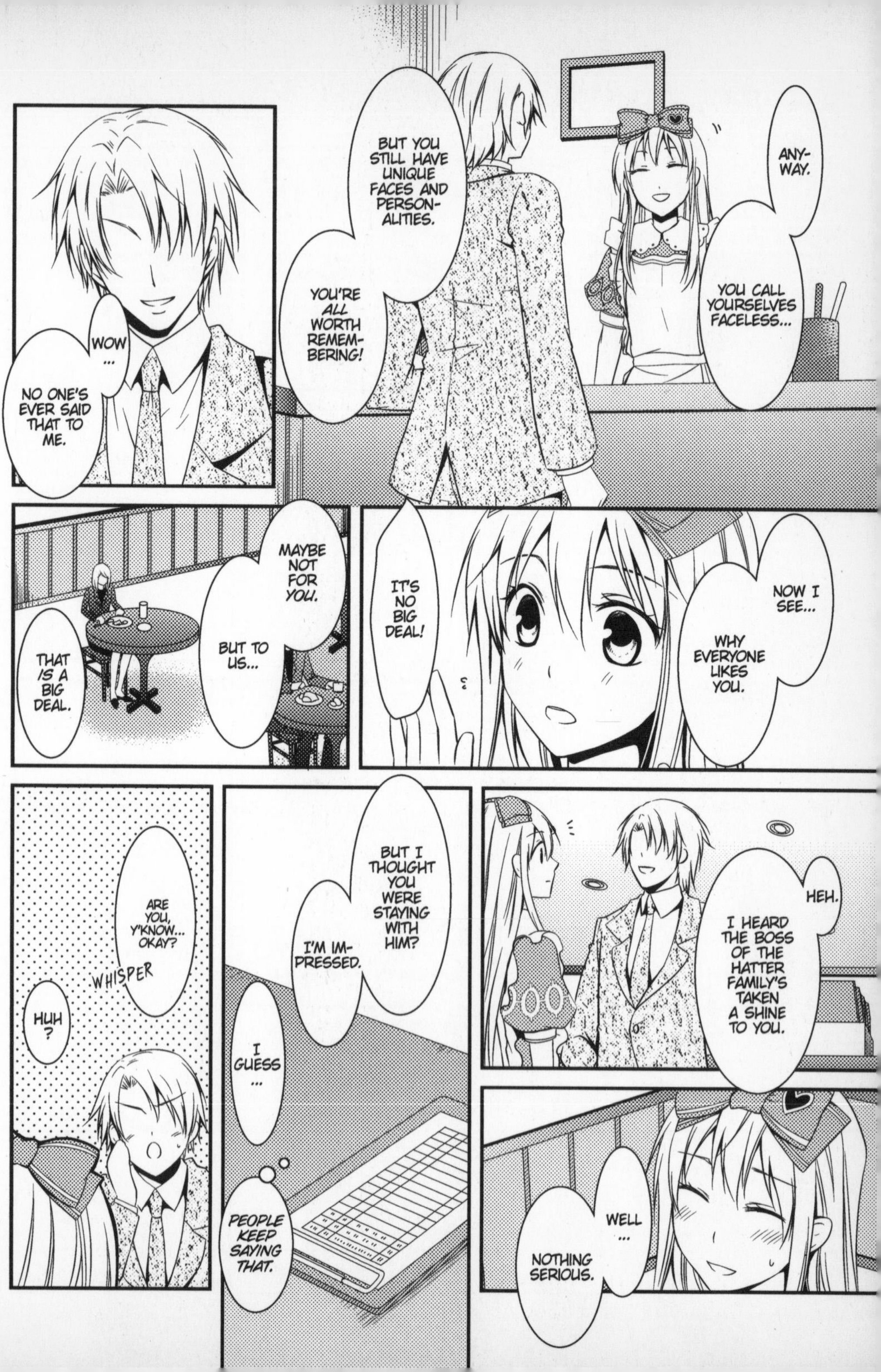
ANY-WAY.
YOU CALL YOURSELVES FACELESS...
BUT YOU STILL HAVE UNIQUE FACES AND PERSON-ALITIES.
YOU'RE ALL WORTH REMEMBERING!
WOW...
NO ONE'S EVER SAID THAT TO ME.
NOW I SEE...
WHY EVERYONE LIKES YOU.
IT'S NO BIG DEAL!
MAYBE NOT FOR YOU.
BUT TO US...
THAT IS A BIG DEAL.
HEH.
I HEARD THE BOSS OF THE HATTER FAMILY'S TAKEN A SHINE TO YOU.
WELL...
NOTHING SERIOUS.
BUT I THOUGHT YOU WERE STAYING WITH HIM?
I'M IM-PRESSED.
I GUESS...
PEOPLE KEEP SAYING THAT.
ARE YOU, Y'KNOW... OKAY?
WHISPER
HUH?

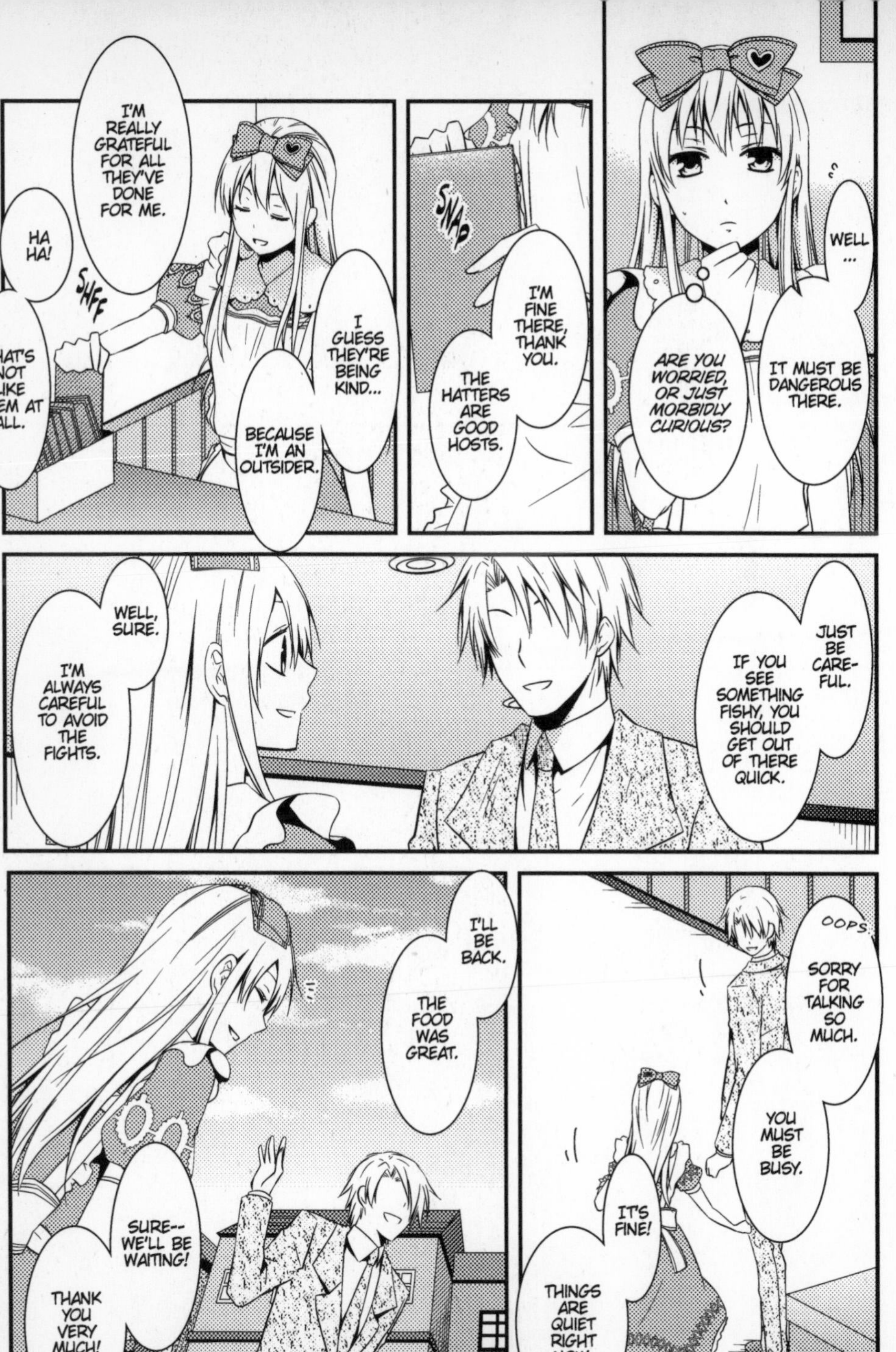
WELL ...
IT MUST BE DANGEROUS THERE.
ARE YOU WORRIED, OR JUST MORBIDLY CURIOUS?
SNAP
I'M FINE THERE, THANK YOU.
THE HATTERS ARE GOOD HOSTS.
I GUESS THEY'RE BEING KIND...
BECAUSE I'M AN OUTSIDER.
I'M REALLY GRATEFUL FOR ALL THEY'VE DONE FOR ME.
HA HA!
SHFF
THAT'S NOT LIKE THEM AT ALL.
JUST BE CAREFUL.
IF YOU SEE SOMETHING FISHY, YOU SHOULD GET OUT OF THERE QUICK.
WELL, SURE.
I'M ALWAYS CAREFUL TO AVOID THE FIGHTS.
OOPS.
SORRY FOR TALKING SO MUCH.
YOU MUST BE BUSY.
IT'S FINE!
THINGS ARE QUIET RIGHT NOW.
I'LL BE BACK.
THE FOOD WAS GREAT.
SURE-- WE'LL BE WAITING!
THANK YOU VERY MUCH!

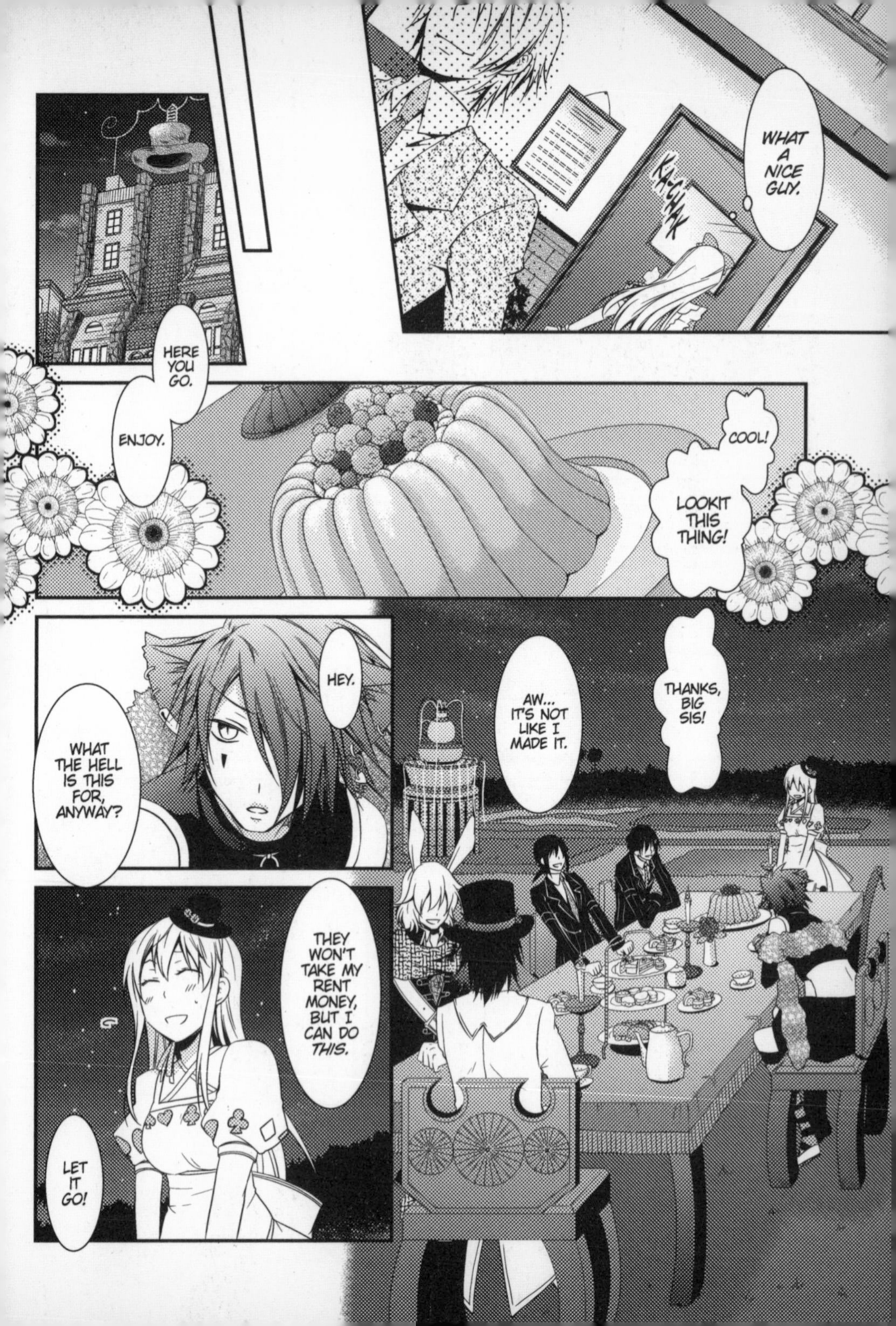
KA-CHAK
WHAT A NICE GUY.
HERE YOU GO.
ENJOY.
COOL!
LOOKIT THIS THING!
THANKS, BIG SIS!
AW... IT'S NOT LIKE I MADE IT.
HEY.
WHAT THE HELL IS THIS FOR, ANYWAY?
THEY WON'T TAKE MY RENT MONEY, BUT I CAN DO *THIS.*
LET IT GO!

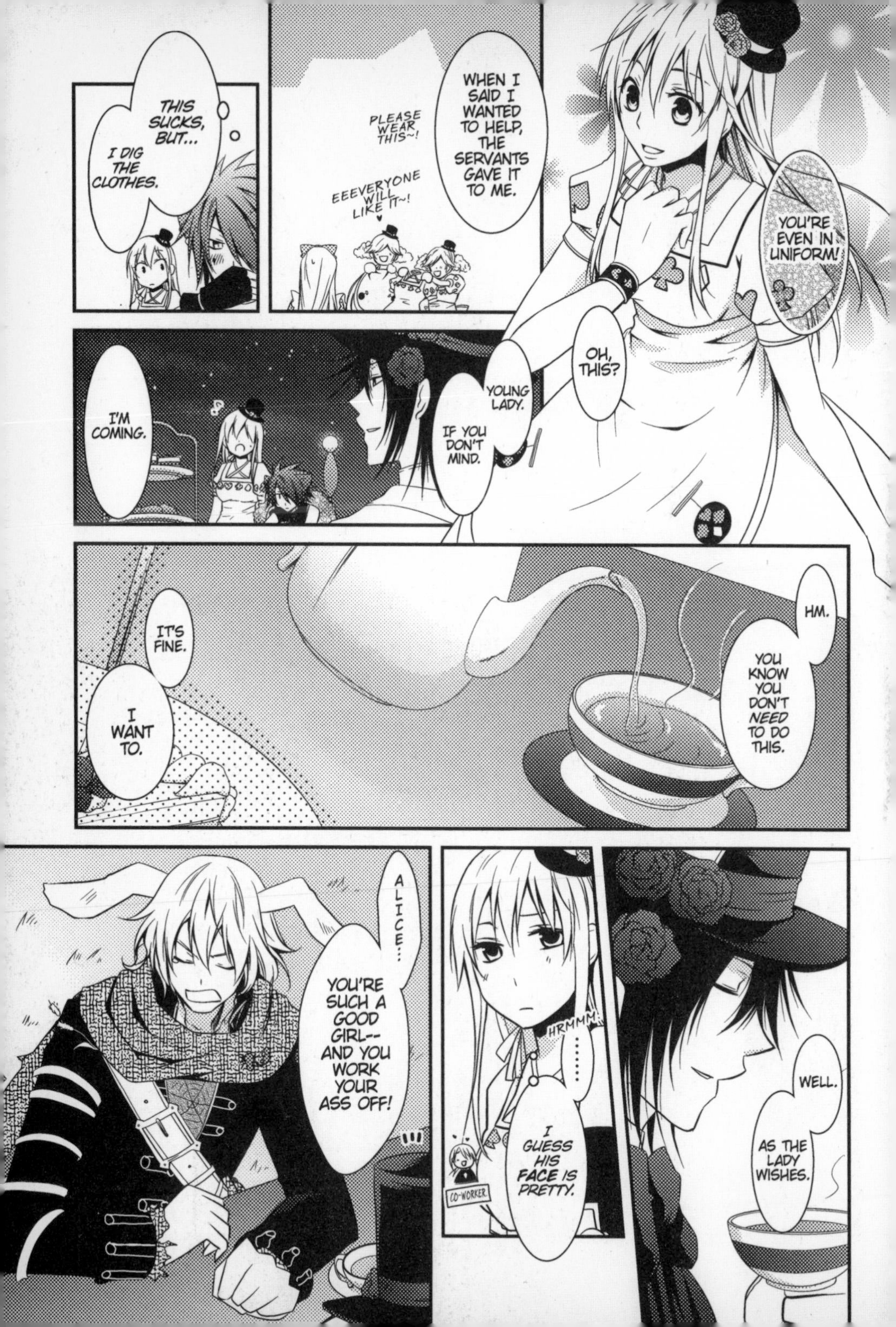
YOU'RE EVEN IN UNIFORM!
OH, THIS?
WHEN I SAID I WANTED TO HELP, THE SERVANTS GAVE IT TO ME.
PLEASE WEAR THIS~!
EEEVERYONE WILL LIKE IT~!
THIS SUCKS, BUT... I DIG THE CLOTHES.
YOUNG LADY.
IF YOU DON'T MIND.
I'M COMING.
HM.
YOU KNOW YOU DON'T NEED TO DO THIS.
IT'S FINE.
I WANT TO.
WELL.
AS THE LADY WISHES.
HRMMM.
......
I GUESS HIS FACE IS PRETTY.
CO-WORKER
ALICE...
YOU'RE SUCH A GOOD GIRL-- AND YOU WORK YOUR ASS OFF!

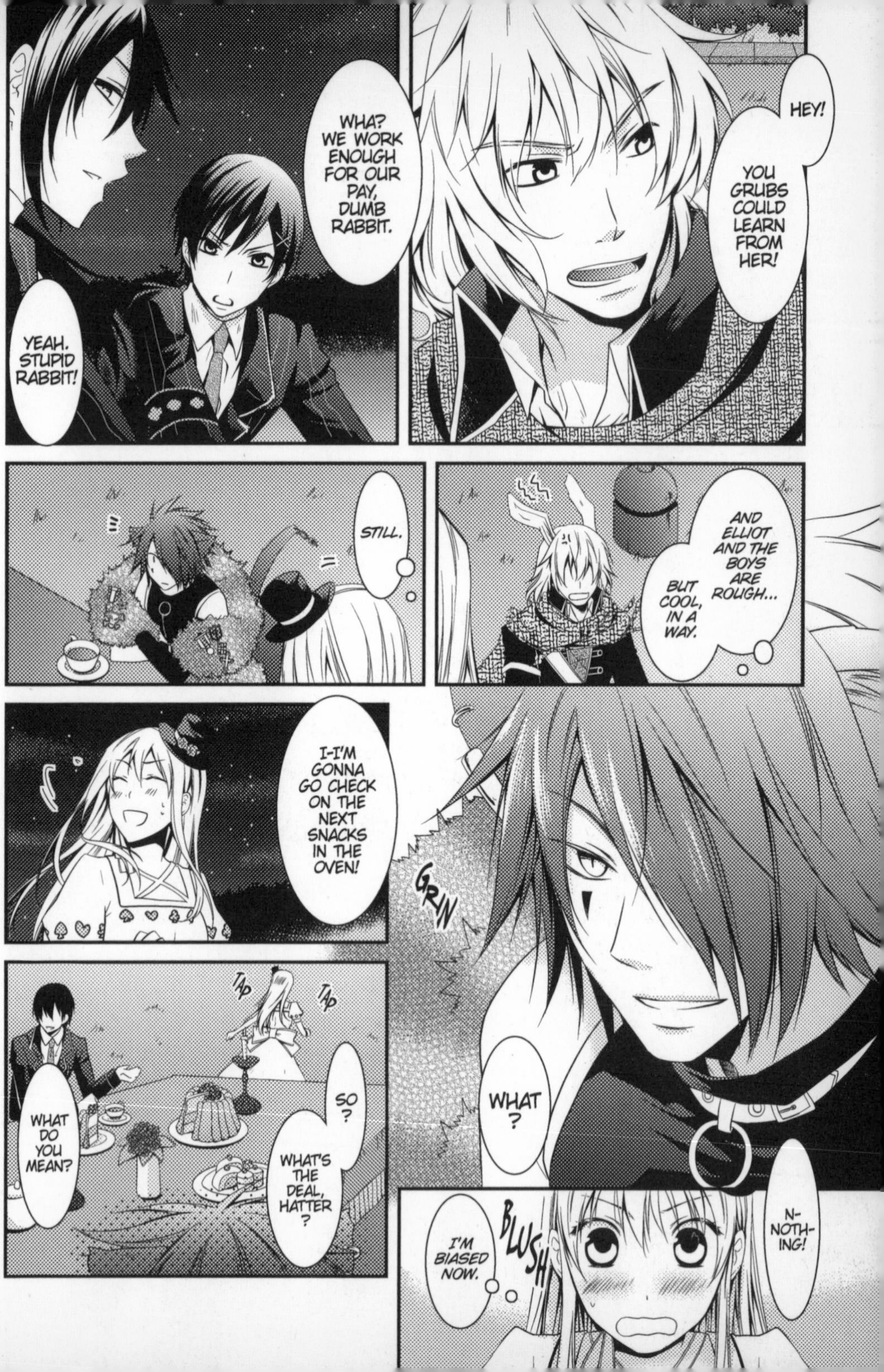
HEY!
YOU GRUBS COULD LEARN FROM HER!
WHA? WE WORK ENOUGH FOR OUR PAY, DUMB RABBIT.
YEAH. STUPID RABBIT!
AND ELLIOT AND THE BOYS ARE ROUGH...
BUT COOL, IN A WAY.
STILL.
GRIN
WHAT?
N-NOTHING!
BLUSH
I'M BIASED NOW.
I-I'M GONNA GO CHECK ON THE NEXT SNACKS IN THE OVEN!
TAP
TAP
SO?
WHAT'S THE DEAL, HATTER?
WHAT DO YOU MEAN?

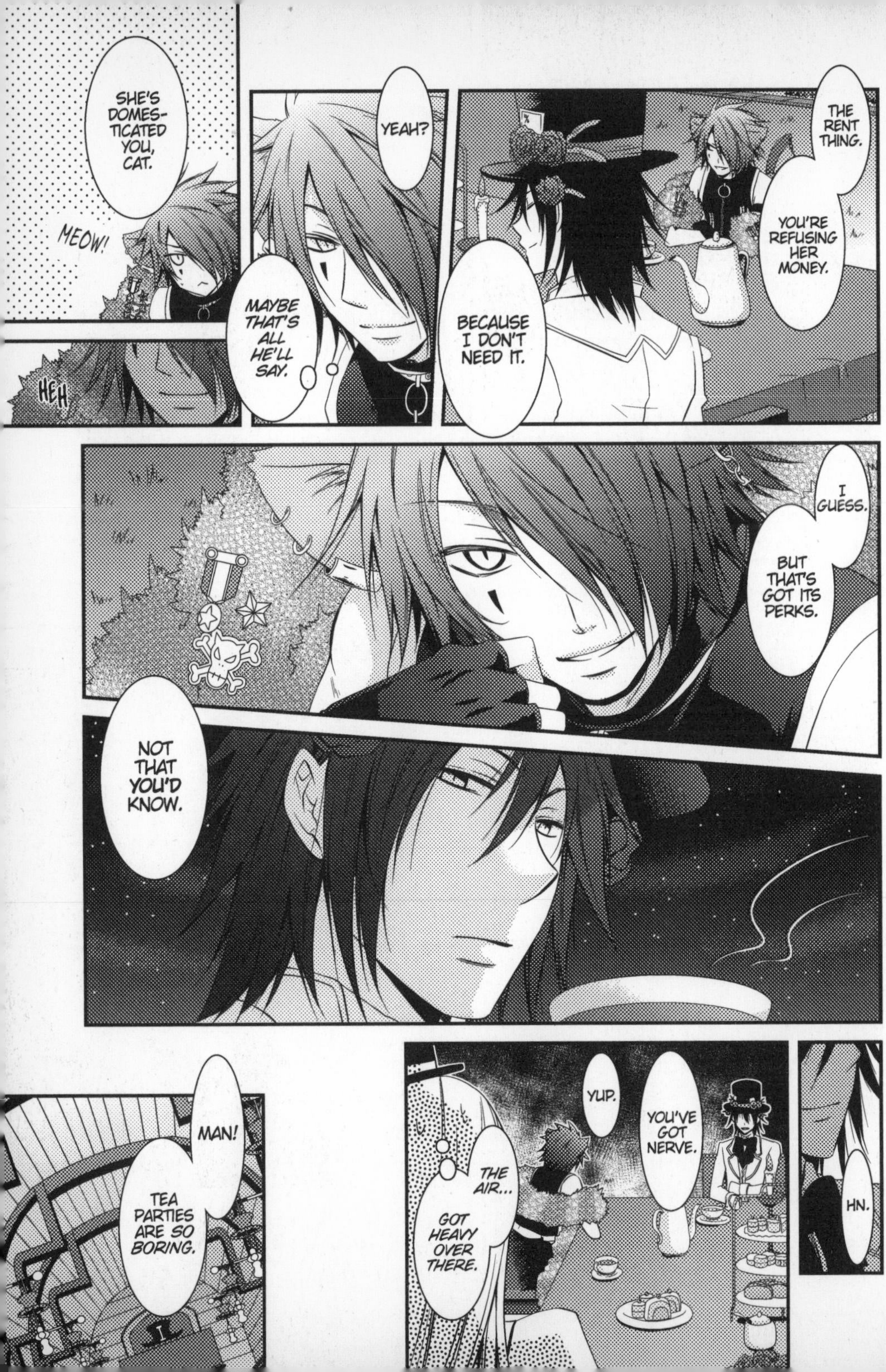
THE RENT THING.
YOU'RE REFUSING HER MONEY.
BECAUSE I DON'T NEED IT.
YEAH?
MAYBE THAT'S ALL HE'LL SAY.
SHE'S DOMES-TICATED YOU, CAT.
MEOW!
HEH
I GUESS.
BUT THAT'S GOT ITS PERKS.
NOT THAT YOU'D KNOW.
HN.
YOU'VE GOT NERVE.
YUP.
THE AIR...
GOT HEAVY OVER THERE.
MAN!
TEA PARTIES ARE SO BORING.

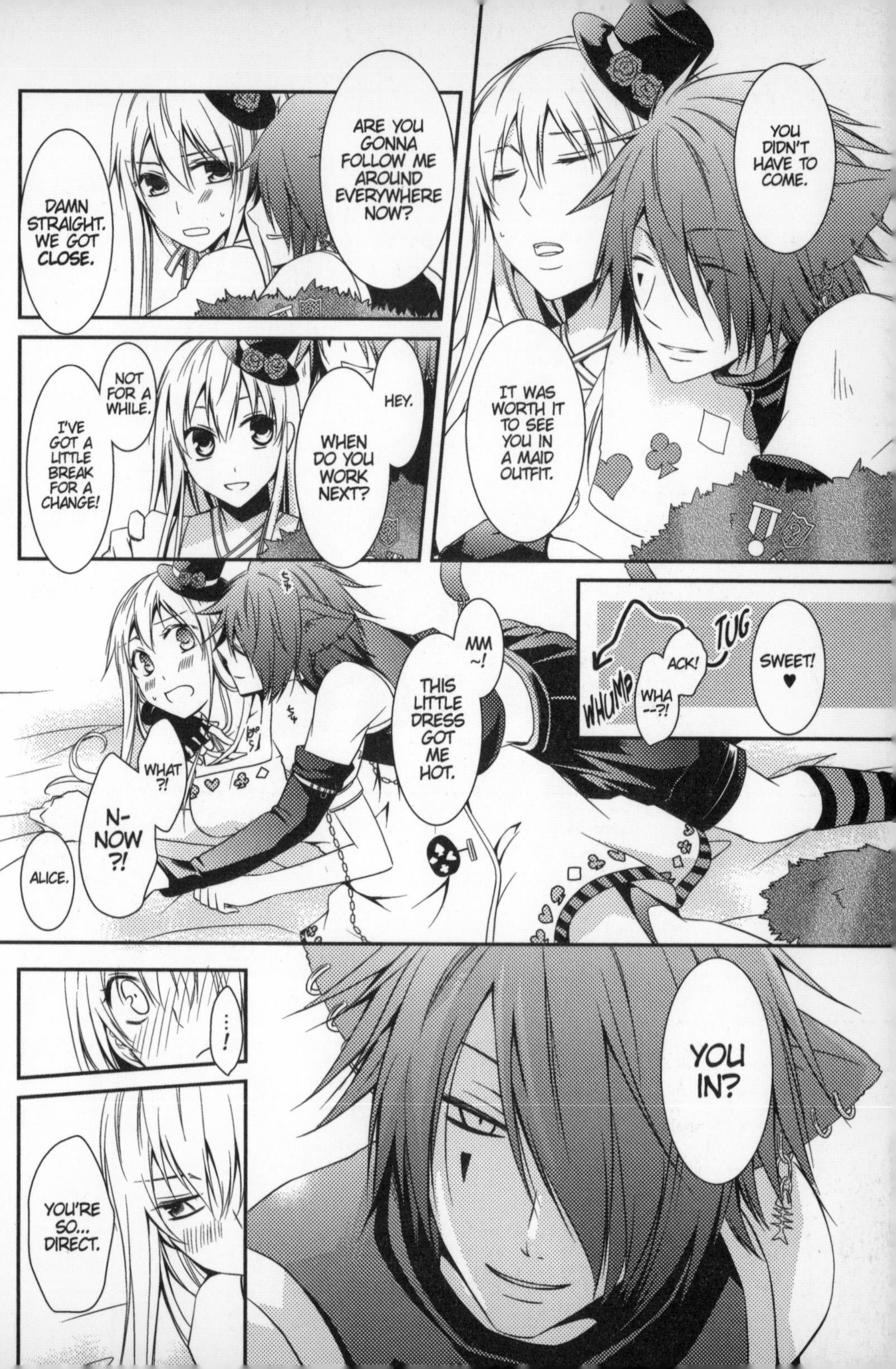
YOU DIDN'T HAVE TO COME.
IT WAS WORTH IT TO SEE YOU IN A MAID OUTFIT.
ARE YOU GONNA FOLLOW ME AROUND EVERYWHERE NOW?
DAMN STRAIGHT. WE GOT CLOSE.
HEY.
WHEN DO YOU WORK NEXT?
NOT FOR A WHILE.
I'VE GOT A LITTLE BREAK FOR A CHANGE!
SWEET! ♥
TUG
ACK!
WHA--?!
WHUMP
MM~!
THIS LITTLE DRESS GOT ME HOT.
WHAT?!
N-NOW?!
ALICE.
YOU IN?
...!
YOU'RE SO... DIRECT.

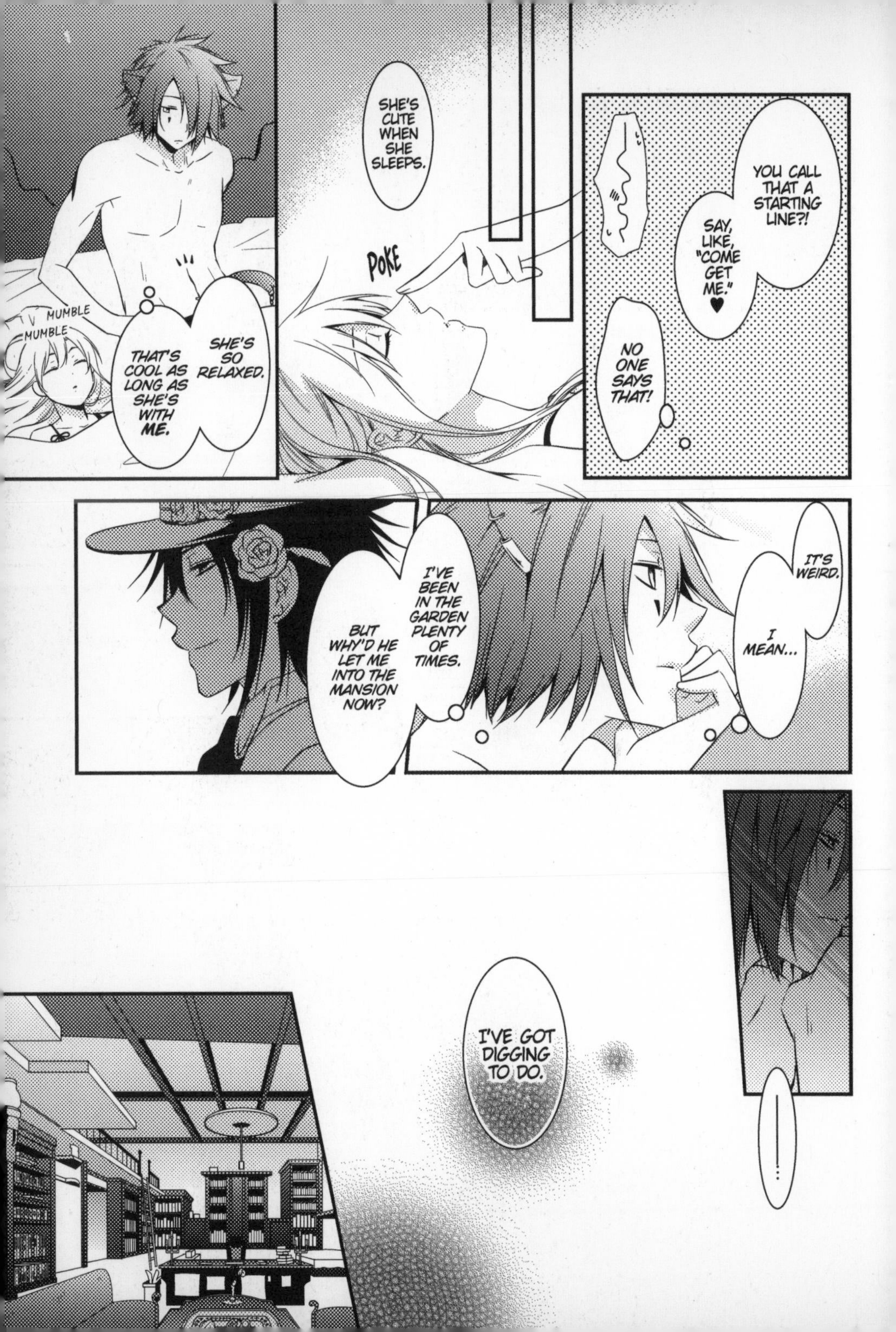
YOU CALL THAT A STARTING LINE?!
SAY, LIKE, "COME GET ME." ♥
NO ONE SAYS THAT!
SHE'S CUTE WHEN SHE SLEEPS.
POKE
SHE'S SO RELAXED.
THAT'S COOL AS LONG AS SHE'S WITH ME.
MUMBLE
MUMBLE
IT'S WEIRD.
I MEAN...
I'VE BEEN IN THE GARDEN PLENTY OF TIMES.
BUT WHY'D HE LET ME INTO THE MANSION NOW?
......!
I'VE GOT DIGGING TO DO.

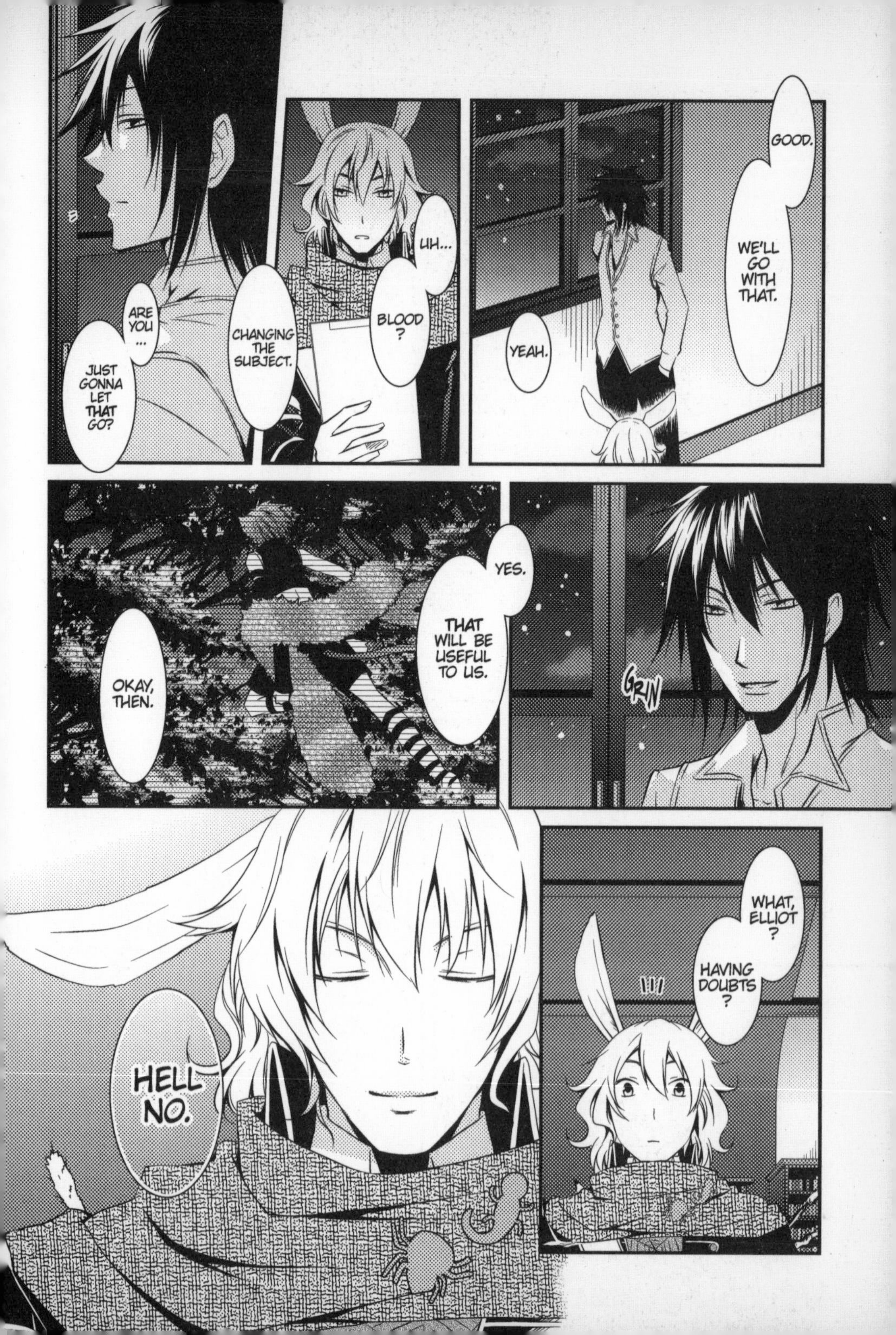
GOOD.
WE'LL GO WITH THAT.
YEAH.
UH...
BLOOD?
CHANGING THE SUBJECT.
ARE YOU ...
JUST GONNA LET THAT GO?
GRIN
YES.
THAT WILL BE USEFUL TO US.
OKAY, THEN.
WHAT, ELLIOT?
HAVING DOUBTS?
!!!
HELL NO.

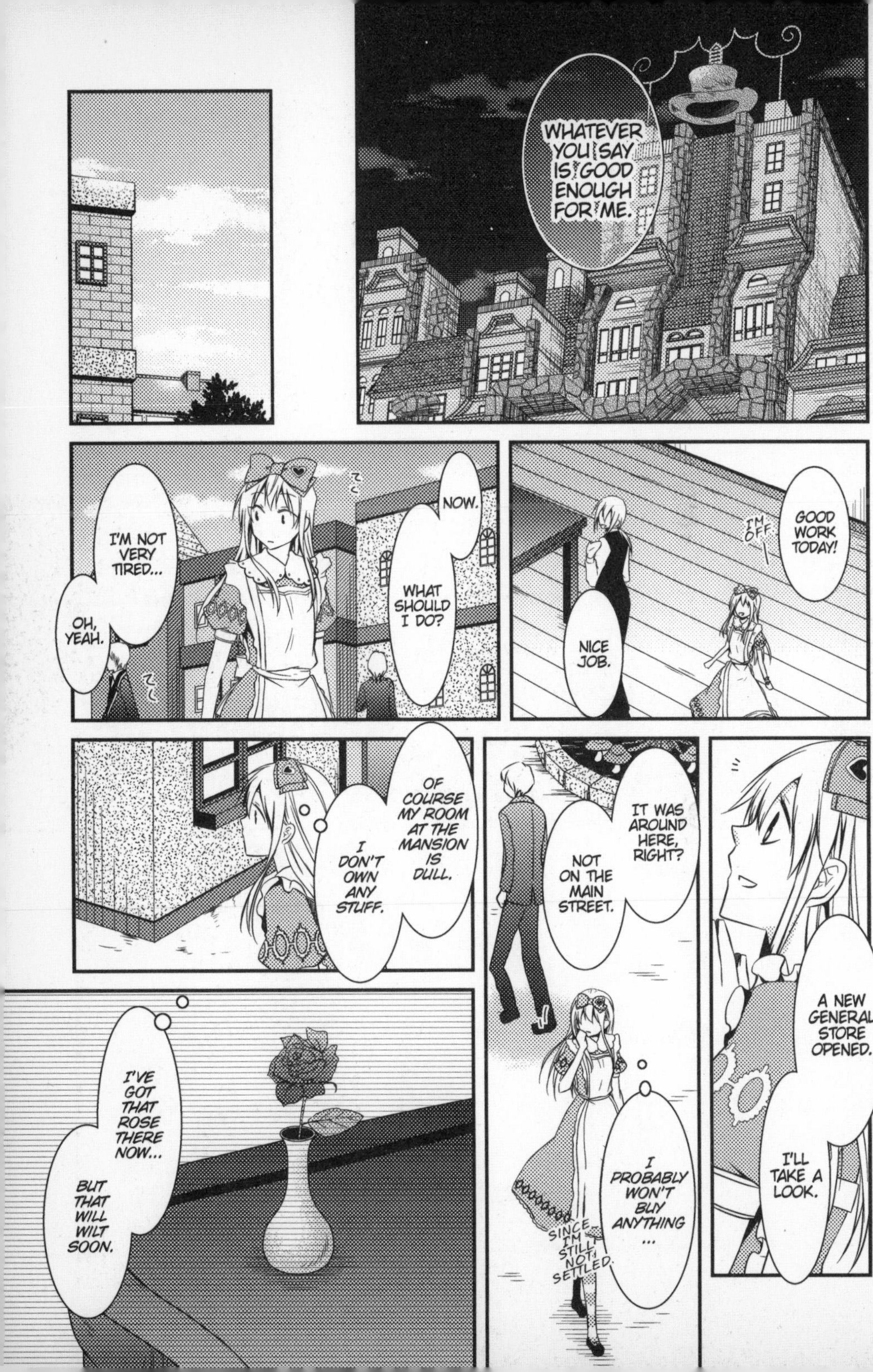
WHATEVER YOU SAY IS GOOD ENOUGH FOR ME.
GOOD WORK TODAY!
I'M OFF—
NICE JOB.
NOW.
WHAT SHOULD I DO?
I'M NOT VERY TIRED...
OH, YEAH.
A NEW GENERAL STORE OPENED.
I'LL TAKE A LOOK.
IT WAS AROUND HERE, RIGHT?
NOT ON THE MAIN STREET.
I PROBABLY WON'T BUY ANYTHING...
SINCE I'M STILL NOT SETTLED.
OF COURSE MY ROOM AT THE MANSION IS DULL.
I DON'T OWN ANY STUFF.
I'VE GOT THAT ROSE THERE NOW...
BUT THAT WILL WILT SOON.

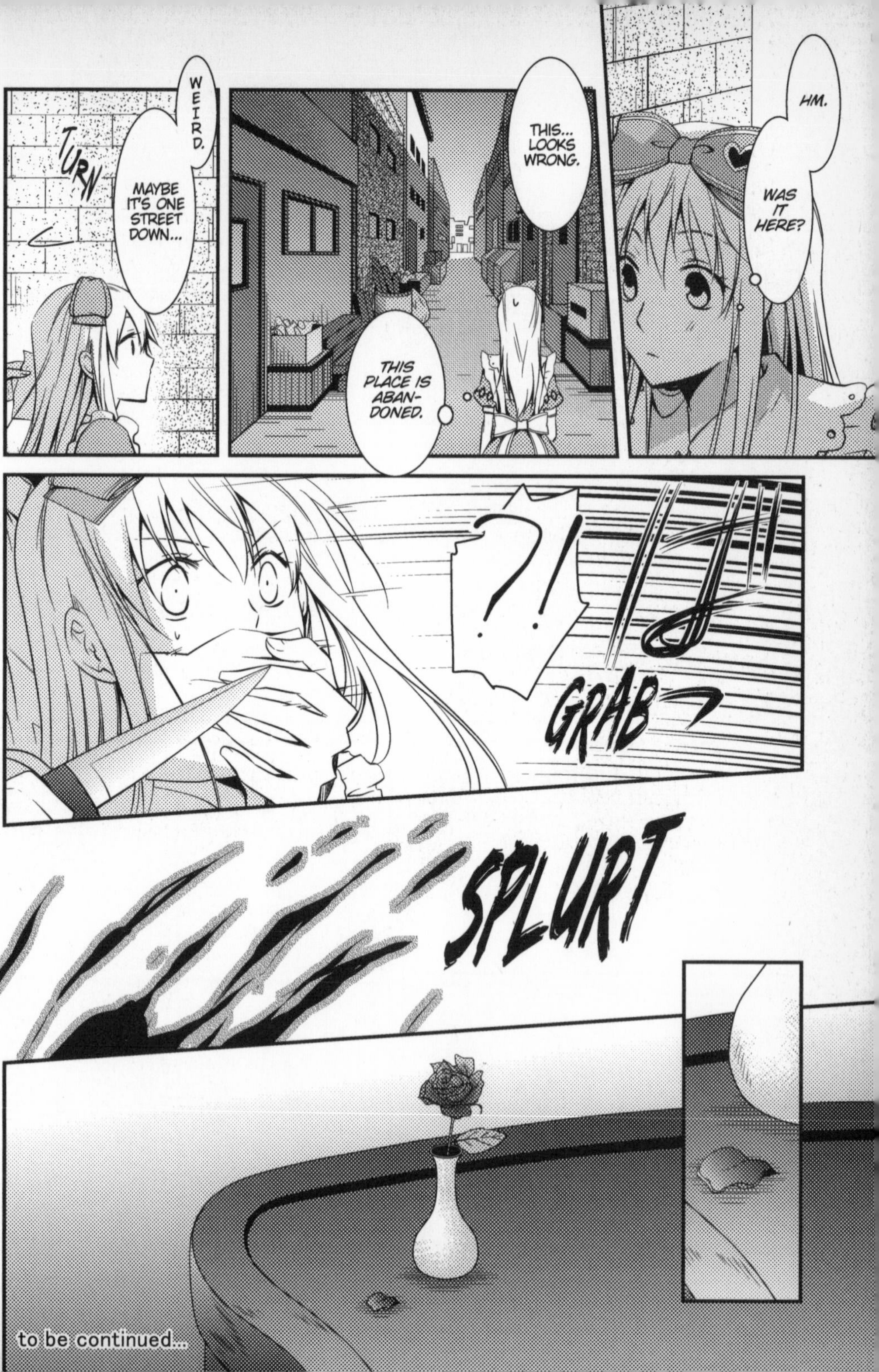
HM.
WAS IT HERE?
THIS... LOOKS WRONG.
THIS PLACE IS ABANDONED.
WEIRD.
MAYBE IT'S ONE STREET DOWN...
TURN
?!
GRAB
SPLURT
to be continued...

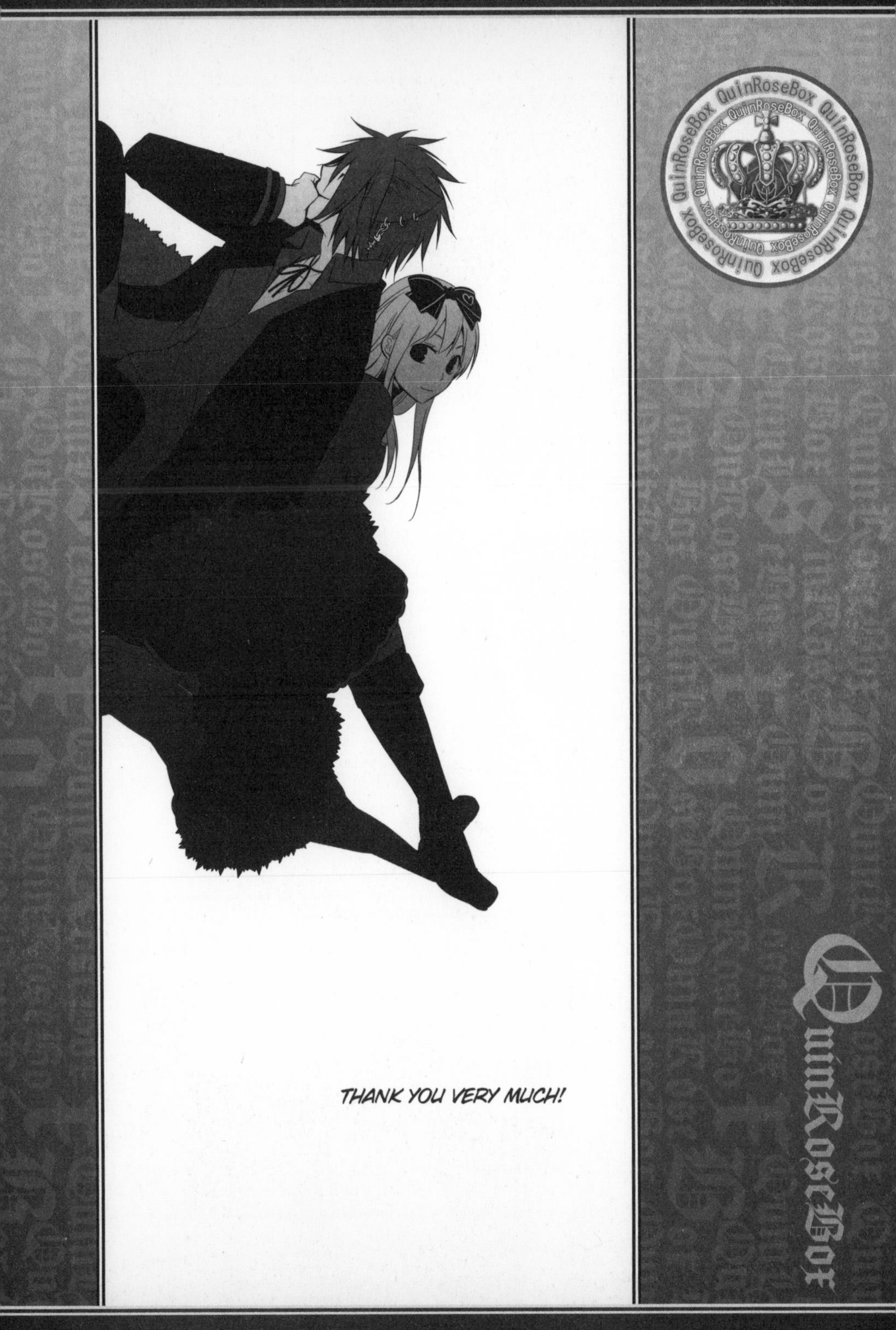
QuinRoseBox
THANK YOU VERY MUCH!
QuinRoseBox

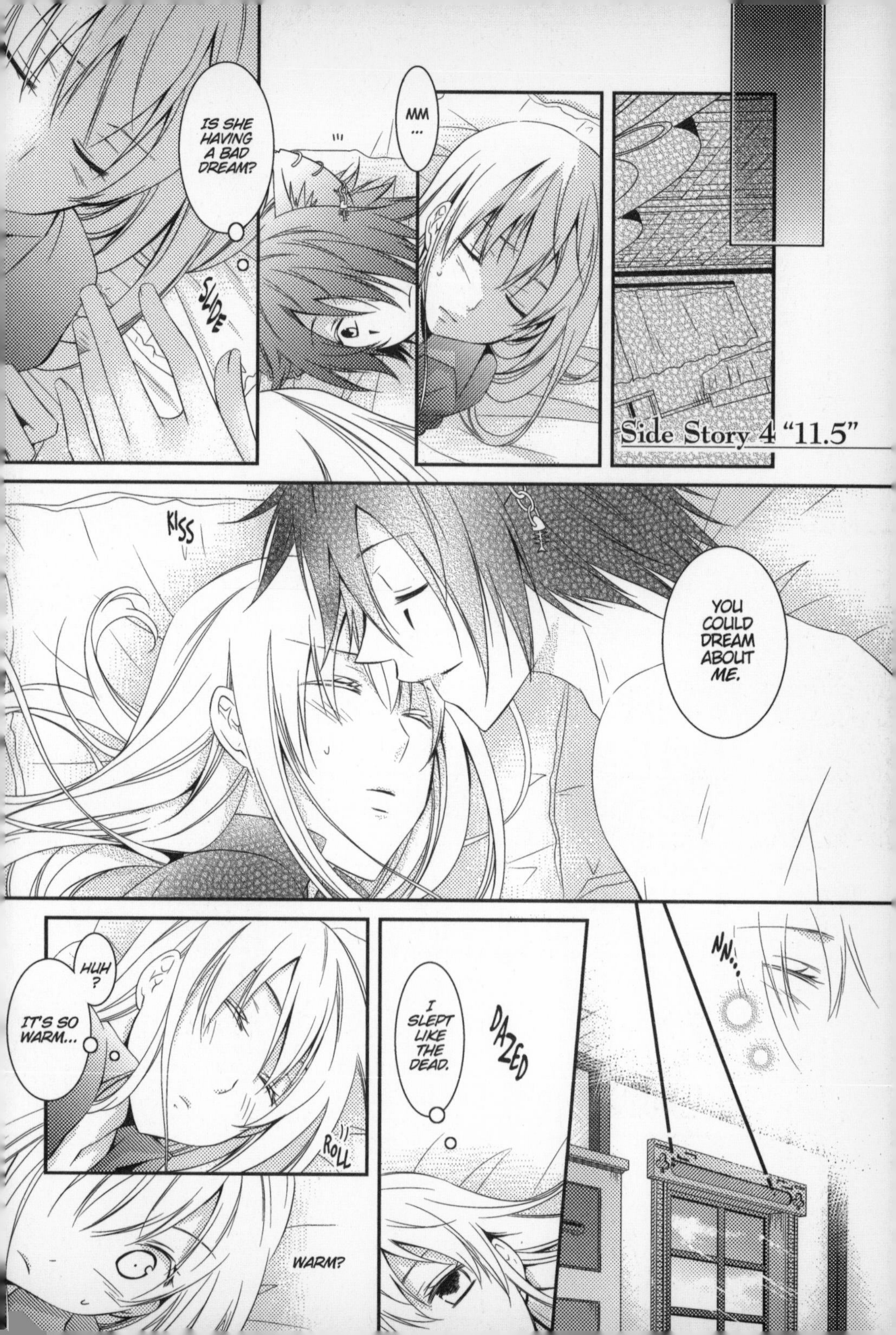
Side Story 4 "11.5"
MM ...
IS SHE HAVING A BAD DREAM?
SLIDE
YOU COULD DREAM ABOUT ME.
KISS
NN...
DAZED
I SLEPT LIKE THE DEAD.
HUH?
IT'S SO WARM...
ROLL
WARM?

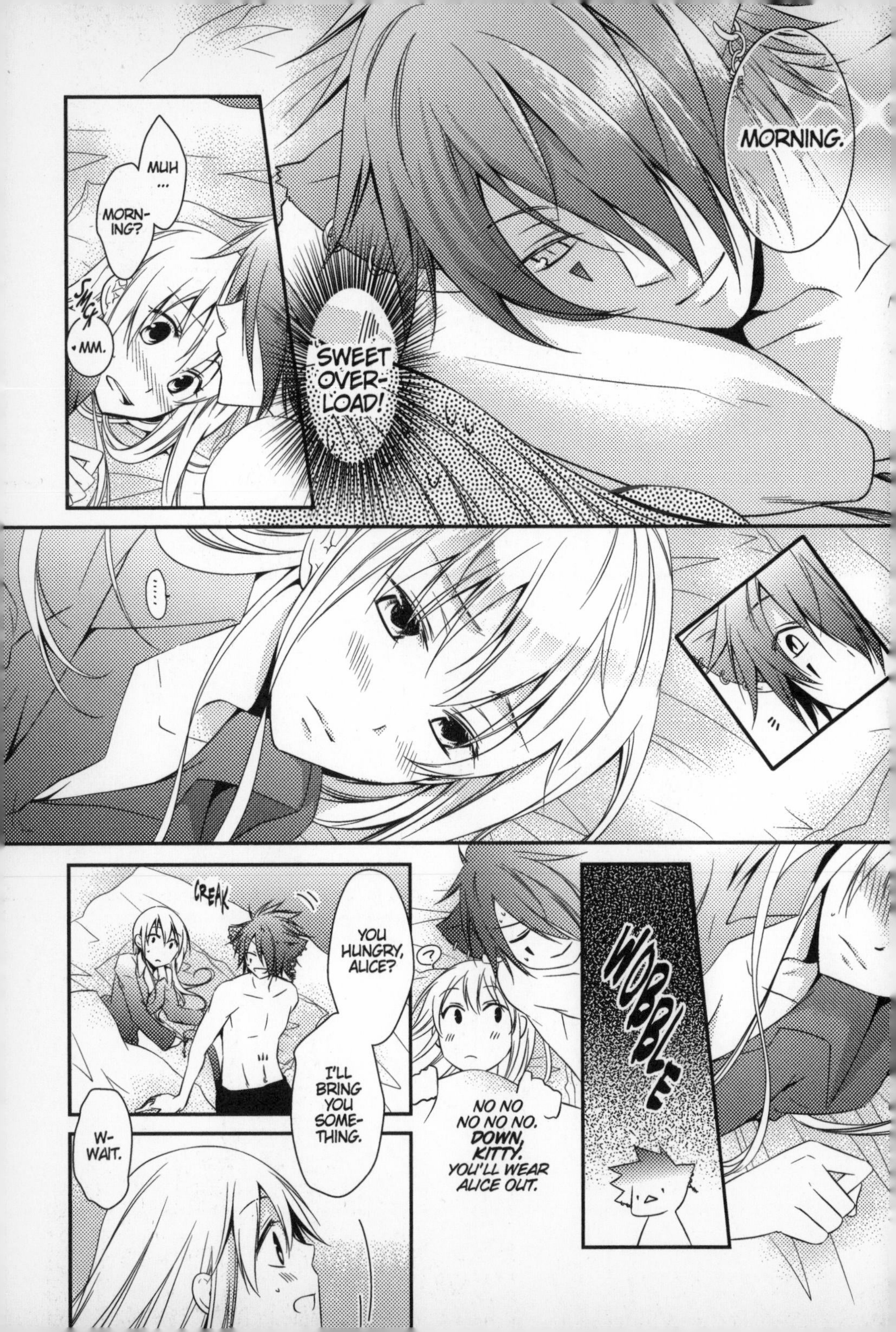

MORNING.
SWEET OVER-LOAD!
MUH ... MORN-ING?
SMCK
♥MM.
.....
WOBBLE
NO NO NO NO NO. DOWN, KITTY. YOU'LL WEAR ALICE OUT.
CREAK
YOU HUNGRY, ALICE?
?
I'LL BRING YOU SOME-THING.
W-WAIT.

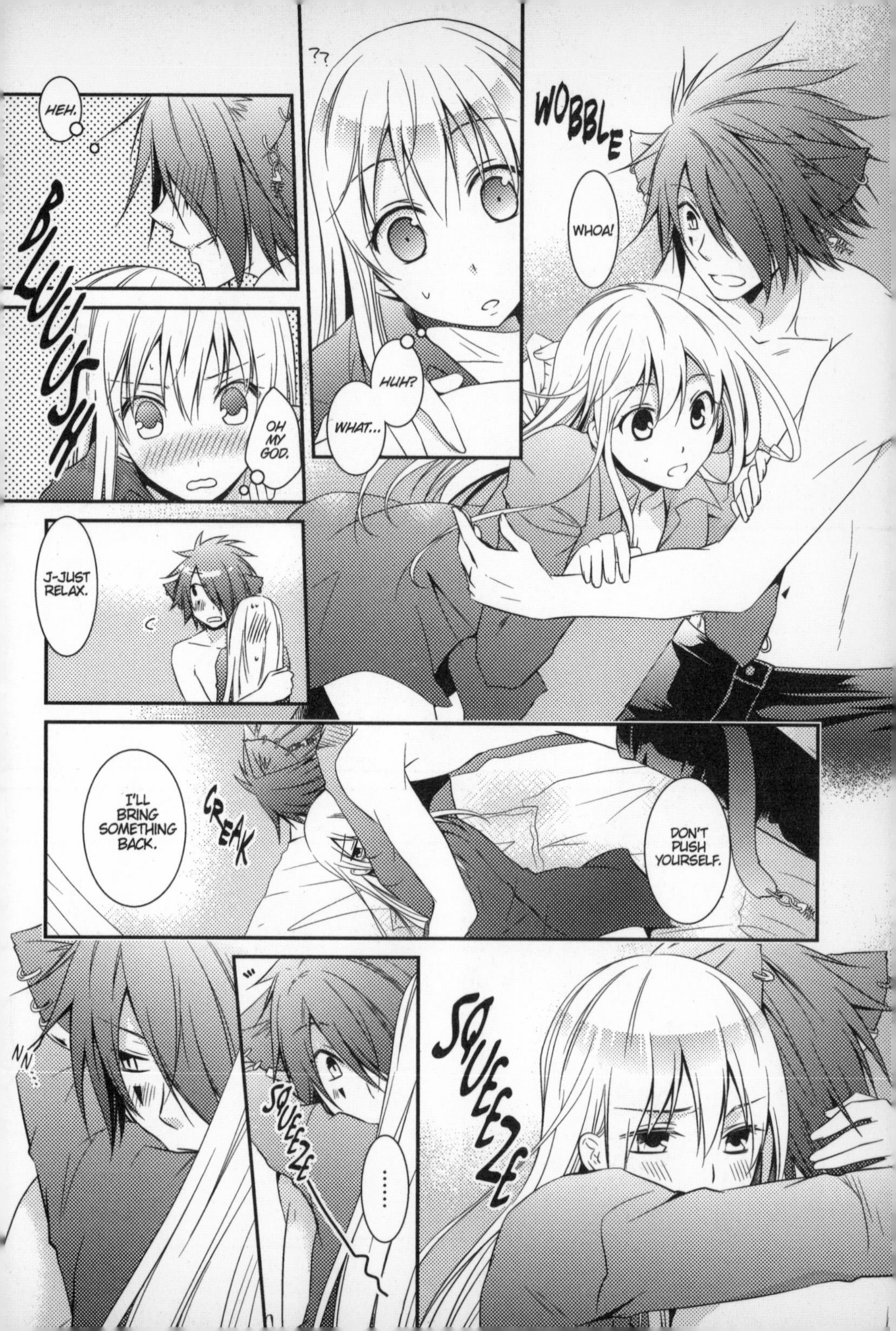
WOBBLE
WHOA!
??
HUH?
WHAT...
HEH.
BLUUUSH
OH MY GOD.
J-JUST RELAX.
DON'T PUSH YOURSELF.
CREAK
I'LL BRING SOMETHING BACK.
SQUEEZE
...
SQUEEZE
......
NN

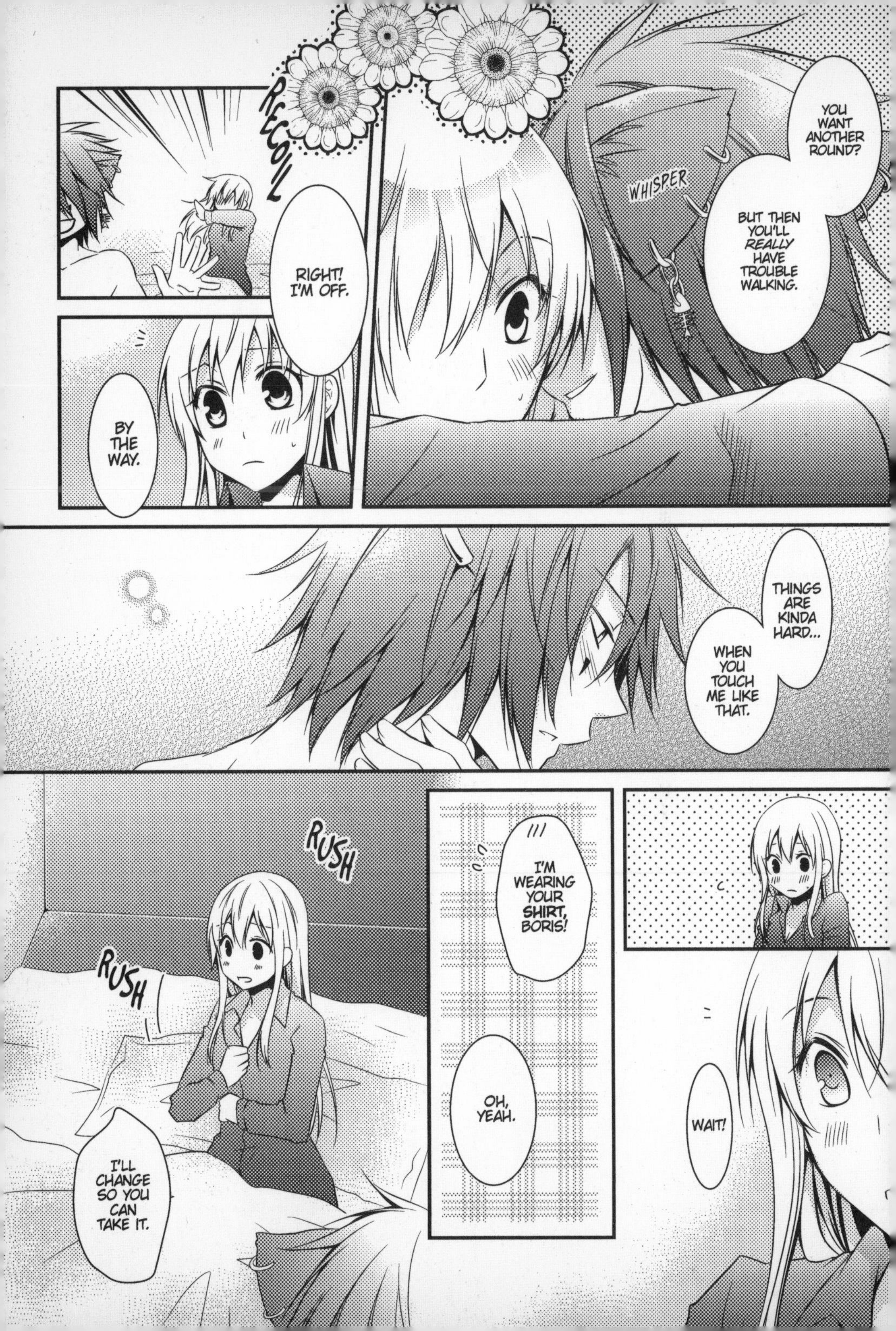
YOU WANT ANOTHER ROUND?
WHISPER
BUT THEN YOU'LL *REALLY* HAVE TROUBLE WALKING.
RECOIL
RIGHT! I'M OFF.
BY THE WAY.
THINGS ARE KINDA HARD...
WHEN YOU TOUCH ME LIKE THAT.
WAIT!
I'M WEARING YOUR SHIRT, BORIS!
OH, YEAH.
RUSH
RUSH
I'LL CHANGE SO YOU CAN TAKE IT.

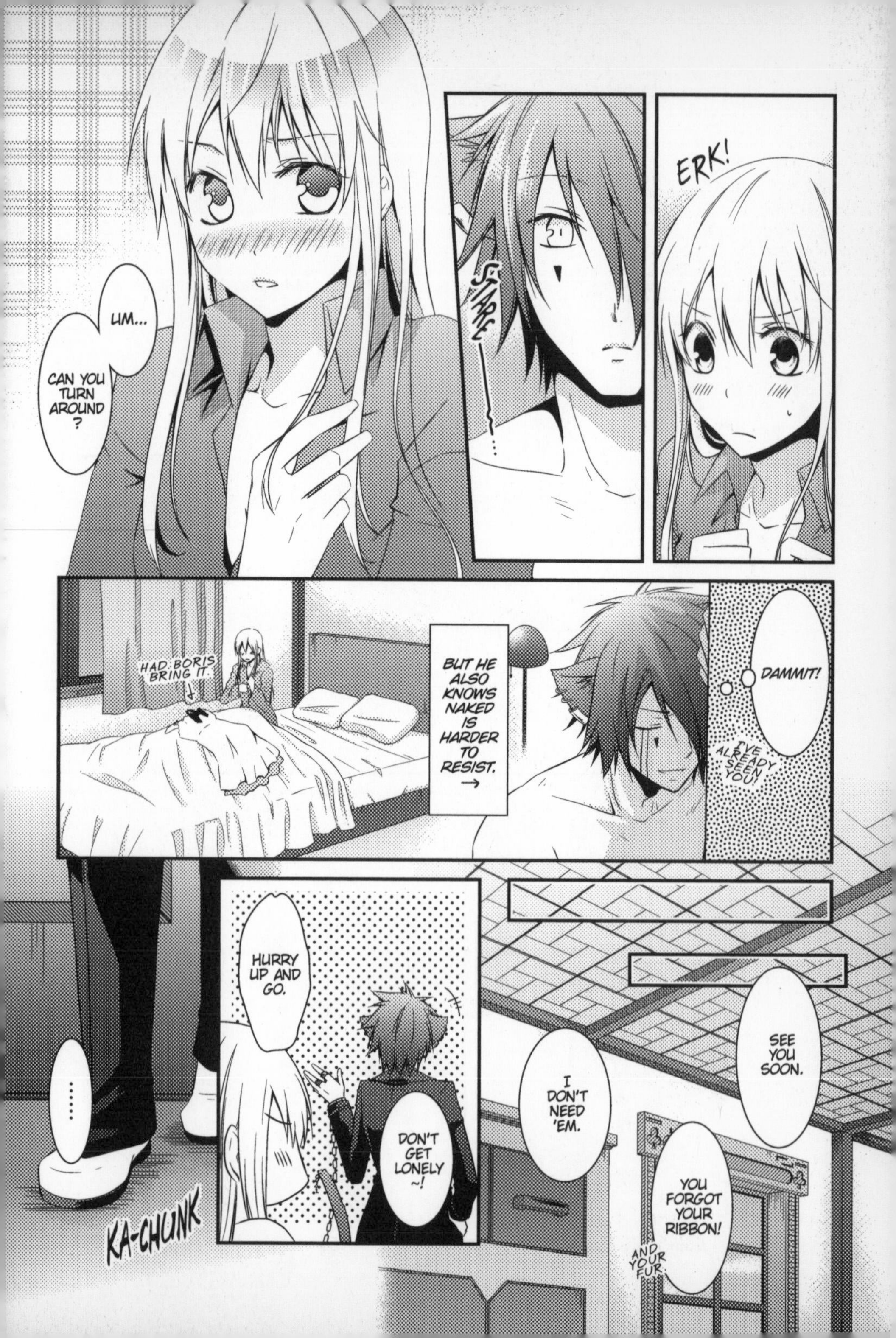
ERK!
STARE——...
UM...
CAN YOU TURN AROUND?
DAMMIT!
I'VE ALREADY SEEN YOU!
BUT HE ALSO KNOWS NAKED IS HARDER TO RESIST. →
HAD BORIS BRING IT.
SEE YOU SOON.
YOU FORGOT YOUR RIBBON!
AND YOUR FUR.
I DON'T NEED 'EM.
HURRY UP AND GO.
DON'T GET LONELY ~!
KA-CHUNK
......

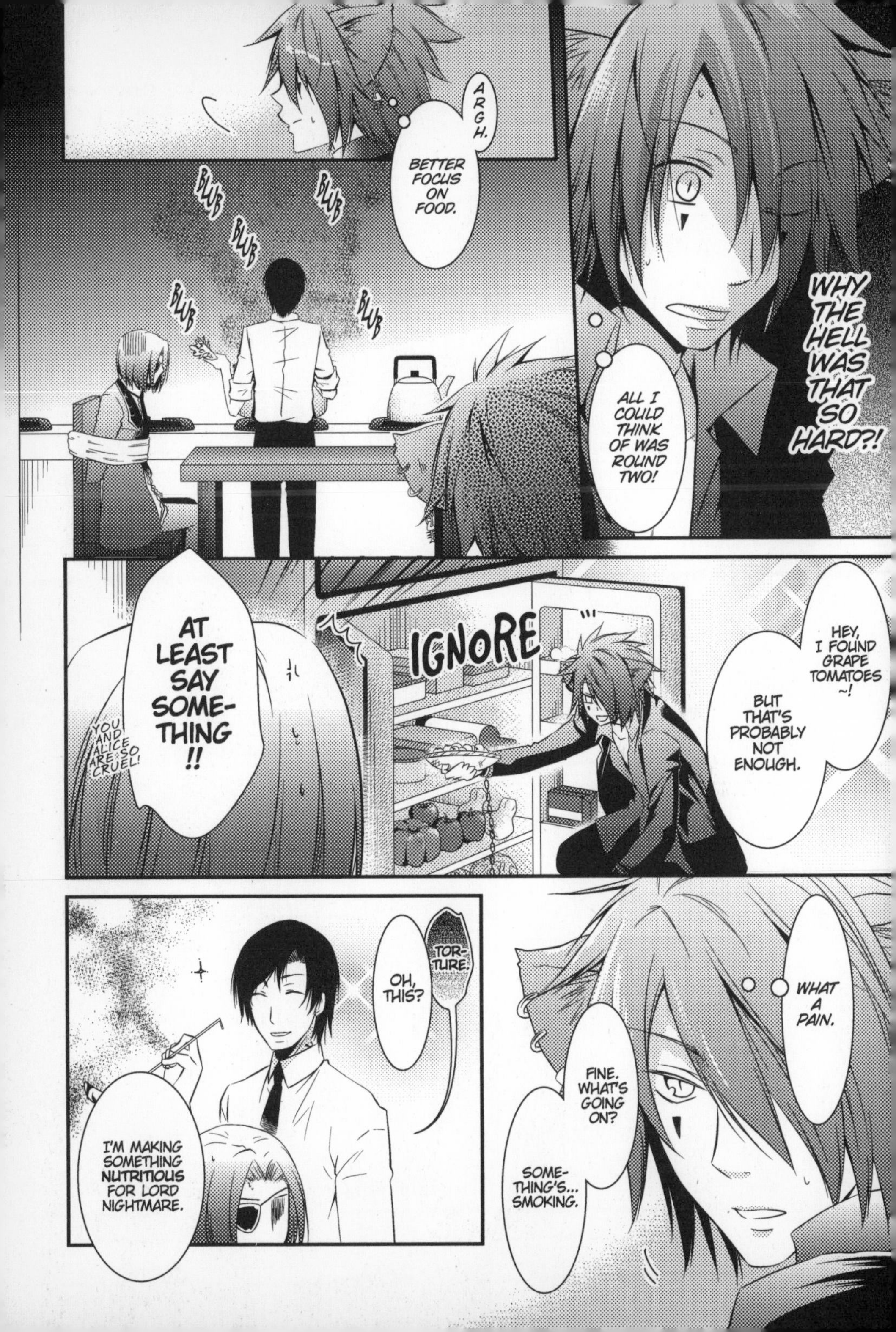
WHY THE HELL WAS THAT SO HARD?!
ALL I COULD THINK OF WAS ROUND TWO!
ARGH.
BETTER FOCUS ON FOOD.
BLUB
BLUB
BLUB
BLUB
BLUB
HEY, I FOUND GRAPE TOMATOES ~!
BUT THAT'S PROBABLY NOT ENOUGH.
IGNORE
AT LEAST SAY SOME-THING!!
YOU AND ALICE ARE SO CRUEL!
WHAT A PAIN.
FINE. WHAT'S GOING ON?
SOME-THING'S... SMOKING.
OH, THIS?
TOR-TURE.
I'M MAKING SOMETHING NUTRITIOUS FOR LORD NIGHTMARE.

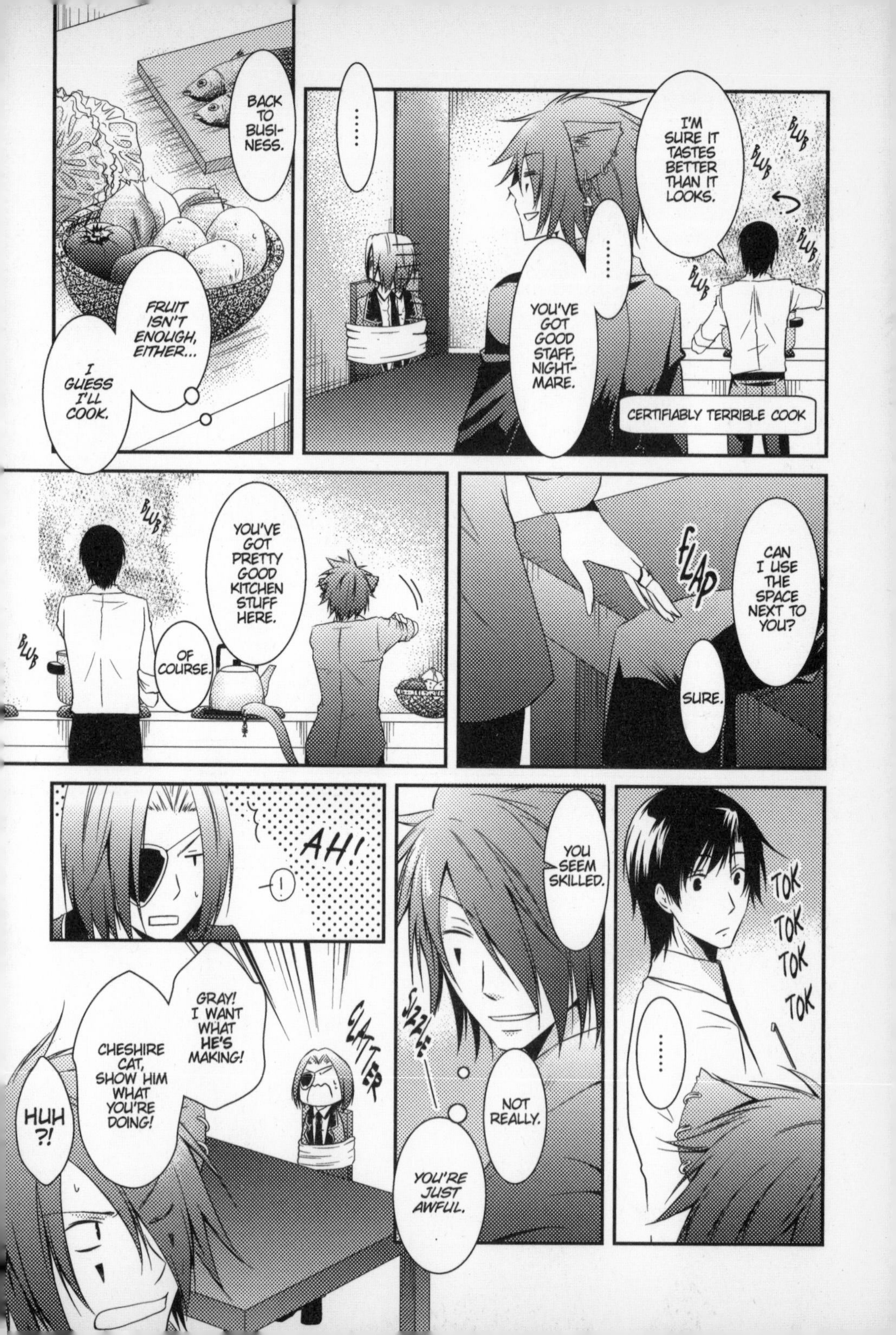

I'M SURE IT TASTES BETTER THAN IT LOOKS.
BLUB
BLUB
BLUB
BLUB
......
YOU'VE GOT GOOD STAFF, NIGHTMARE.
CERTIFIABLY TERRIBLE COOK
......
BACK TO BUSINESS.
FRUIT ISN'T ENOUGH, EITHER...
I GUESS I'LL COOK.
FLAP
CAN I USE THE SPACE NEXT TO YOU?
SURE.
YOU'VE GOT PRETTY GOOD KITCHEN STUFF HERE.
BLUB
OF COURSE.
BLUB
TOK
TOK
TOK
TOK
......
YOU SEEM SKILLED.
NOT REALLY.
SIZZLE
YOU'RE JUST AWFUL.
AH!
!
GRAY! I WANT WHAT HE'S MAKING!
CLATTER
CHESHIRE CAT, SHOW HIM WHAT YOU'RE DOING!
HUH?!

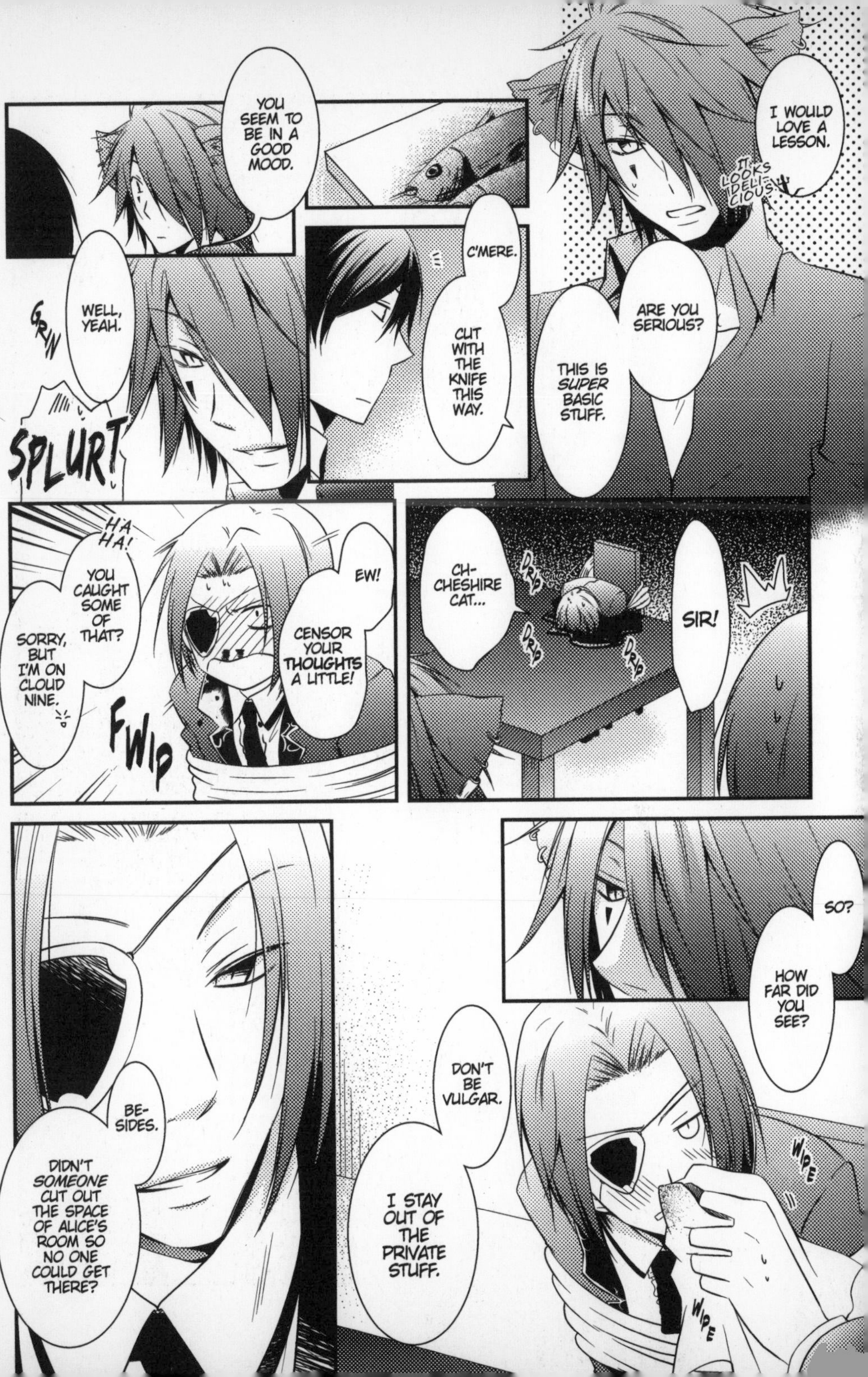
I WOULD LOVE A LESSON.
IT LOOKS DELICIOUS
ARE YOU SERIOUS?
THIS IS SUPER BASIC STUFF.
YOU SEEM TO BE IN A GOOD MOOD.
C'MERE.
CUT WITH THE KNIFE THIS WAY.
WELL, YEAH.
GRIN
SPLURT!
SIR!
CH-CHESHIRE CAT...
DRIP
DRIP
DRIP
EW!
CENSOR YOUR THOUGHTS A LITTLE!
HA HA!
YOU CAUGHT SOME OF THAT?
SORRY, BUT I'M ON CLOUD NINE.
FWIP
SO?
HOW FAR DID YOU SEE?
DON'T BE VULGAR.
I STAY OUT OF THE PRIVATE STUFF.
WIPE
WIPE
BE-SIDES.
DIDN'T SOMEONE CUT OUT THE SPACE OF ALICE'S ROOM SO NO ONE COULD GET THERE?

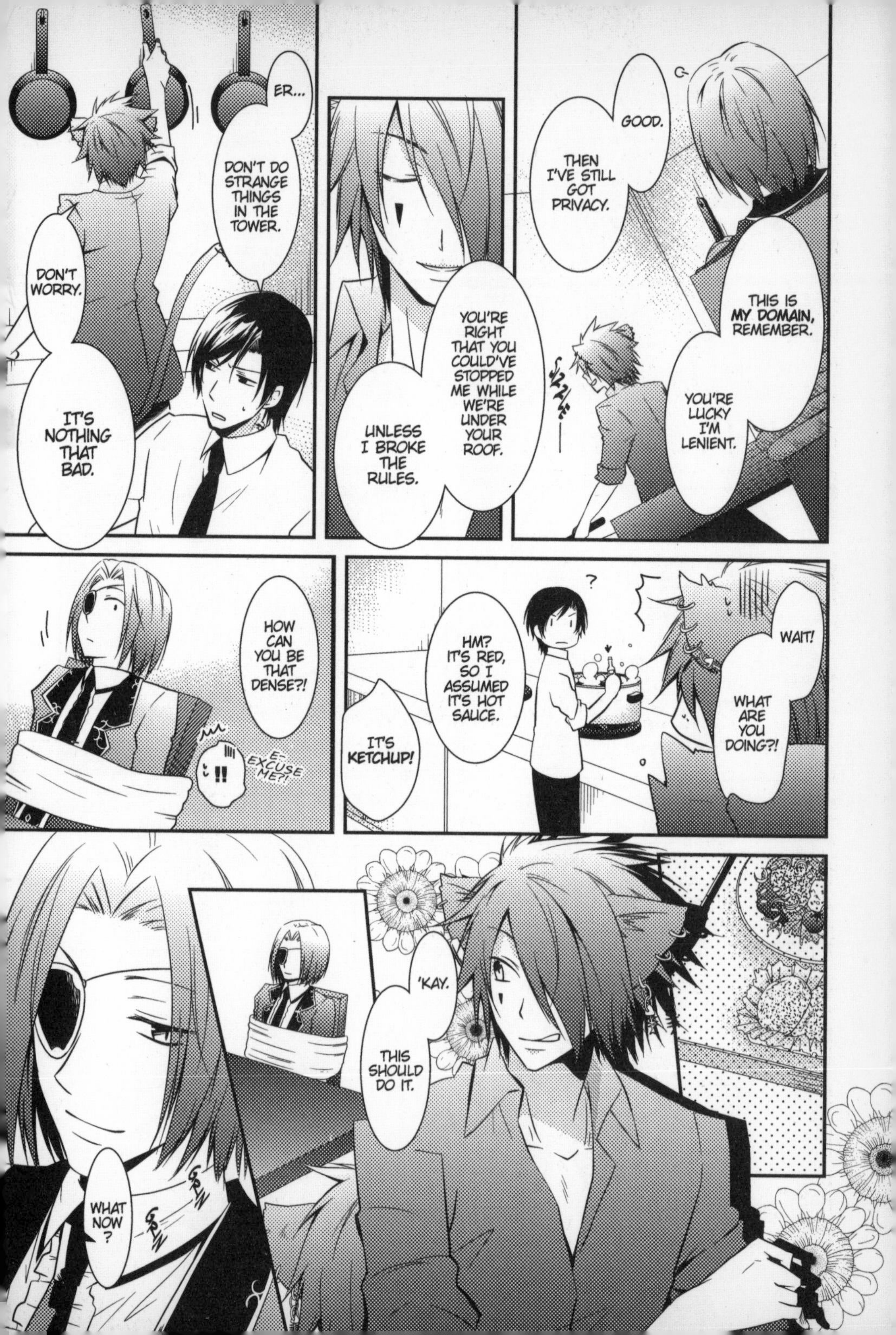
GOOD.
THEN I'VE STILL GOT PRIVACY.
THIS IS MY DOMAIN, REMEMBER.
YOU'RE LUCKY I'M LENIENT.
YOU'RE RIGHT THAT YOU COULD'VE STOPPED ME WHILE WE'RE UNDER YOUR ROOF.
UNLESS I BROKE THE RULES.
ER...
DON'T DO STRANGE THINGS IN THE TOWER.
DON'T WORRY.
IT'S NOTHING THAT BAD.
WAIT!
WHAT ARE YOU DOING?!
HM? IT'S RED, SO I ASSUMED IT'S HOT SAUCE.
IT'S KETCHUP!
HOW CAN YOU BE THAT DENSE?!
E-EXCUSE ME?!
'KAY.
THIS SHOULD DO IT.
GRIN
GRIN
WHAT NOW?

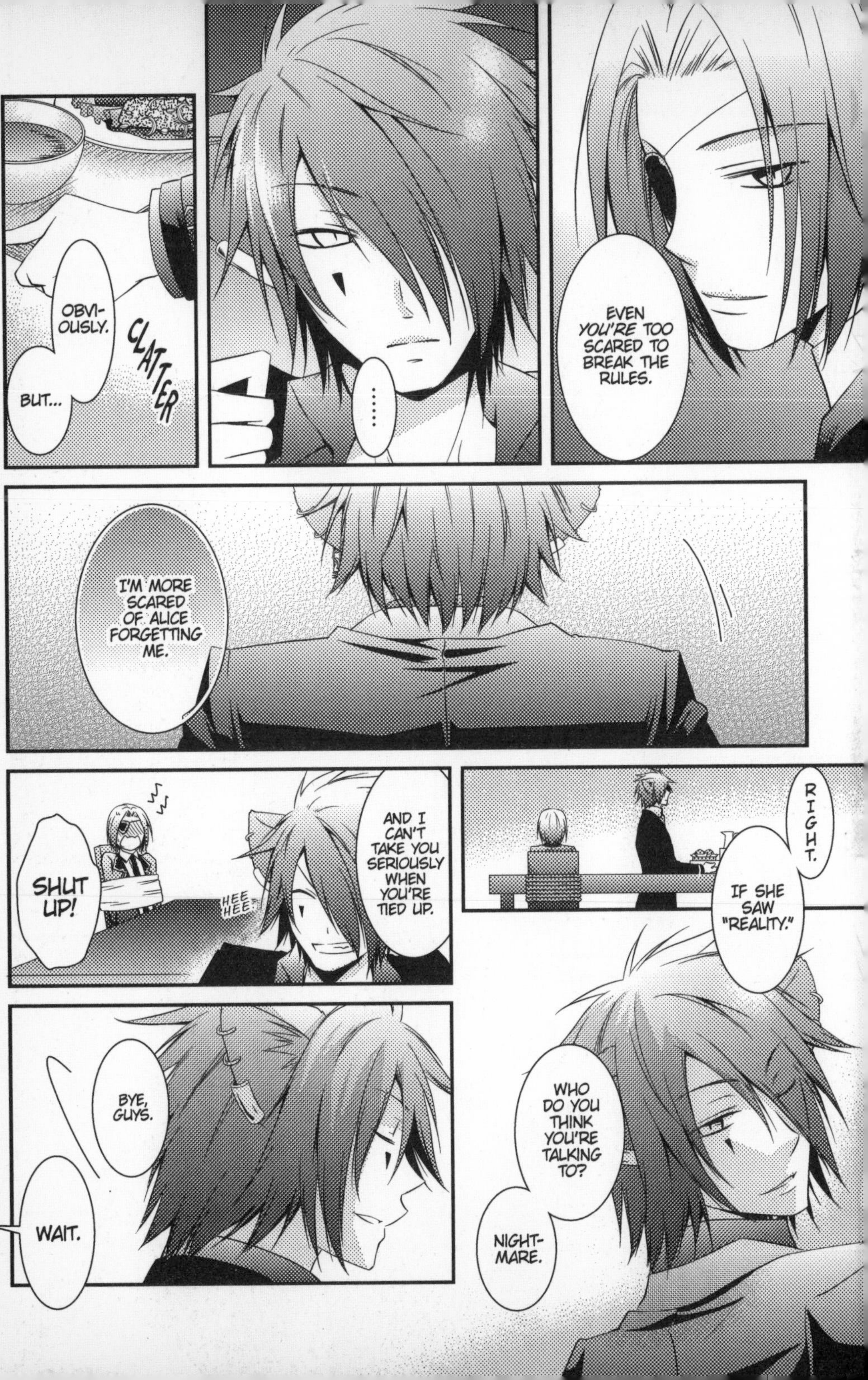
EVEN YOU'RE TOO SCARED TO BREAK THE RULES.
......
OBVI-OUSLY.
CLATTER
BUT...
I'M MORE SCARED OF ALICE FORGETTING ME.
RIGHT.
IF SHE SAW "REALITY."
AND I CAN'T TAKE YOU SERIOUSLY WHEN YOU'RE TIED UP.
HEE HEE
SHUT UP!
WHO DO YOU THINK YOU'RE TALKING TO?
NIGHT-MARE.
BYE, GUYS.
WAIT.

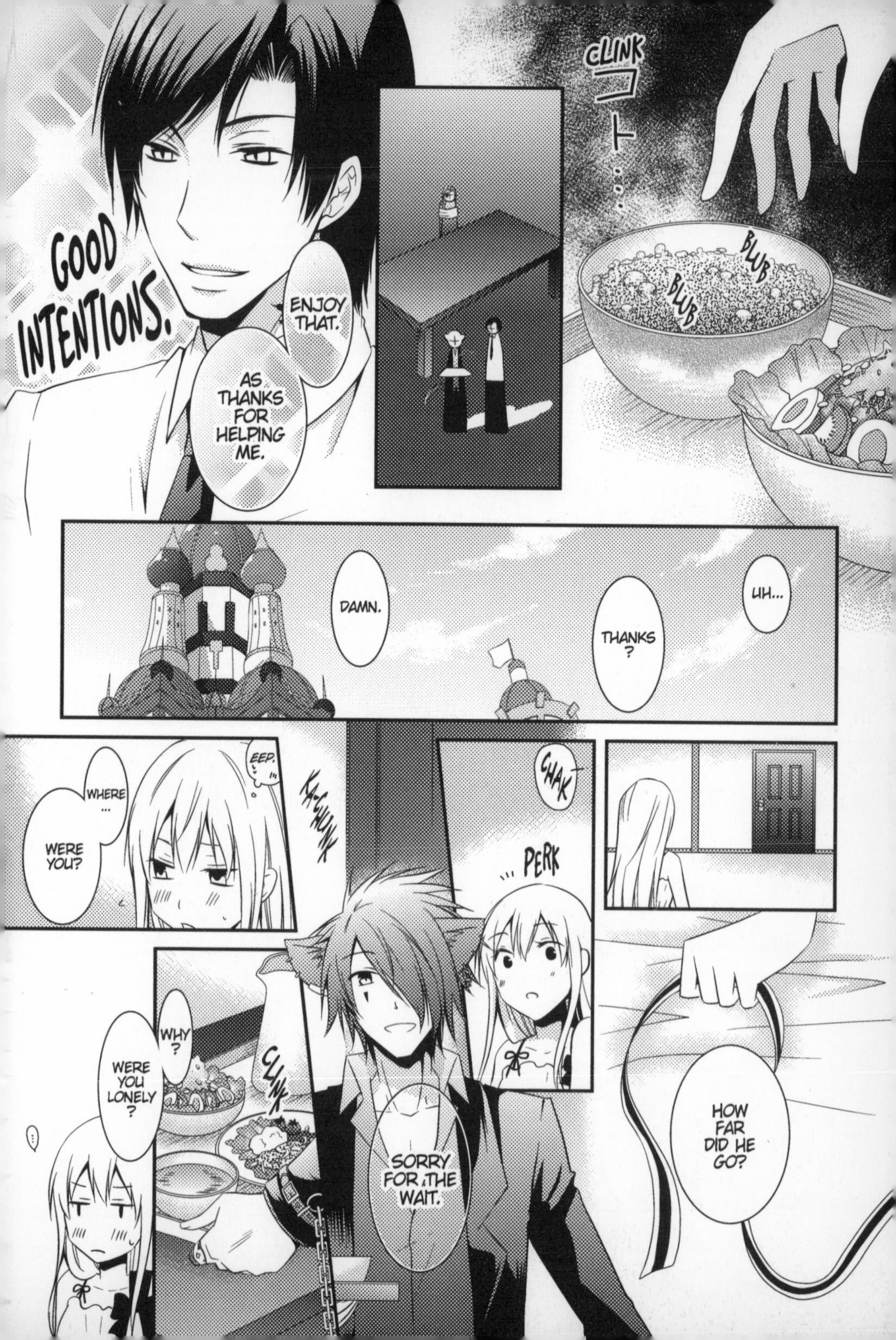
CLINK
コト…
BLUB
BLUB
ENJOY THAT.
AS THANKS FOR HELPING ME.
GOOD INTENTIONS.
UH...
THANKS?
DAMN.
CHAK
... PERK
EEP.
KA-CHUNK
WHERE ... WERE YOU?
HOW FAR DID HE GO?
CLINK
SORRY FOR THE WAIT.
WHY?
WERE YOU LONELY?
...

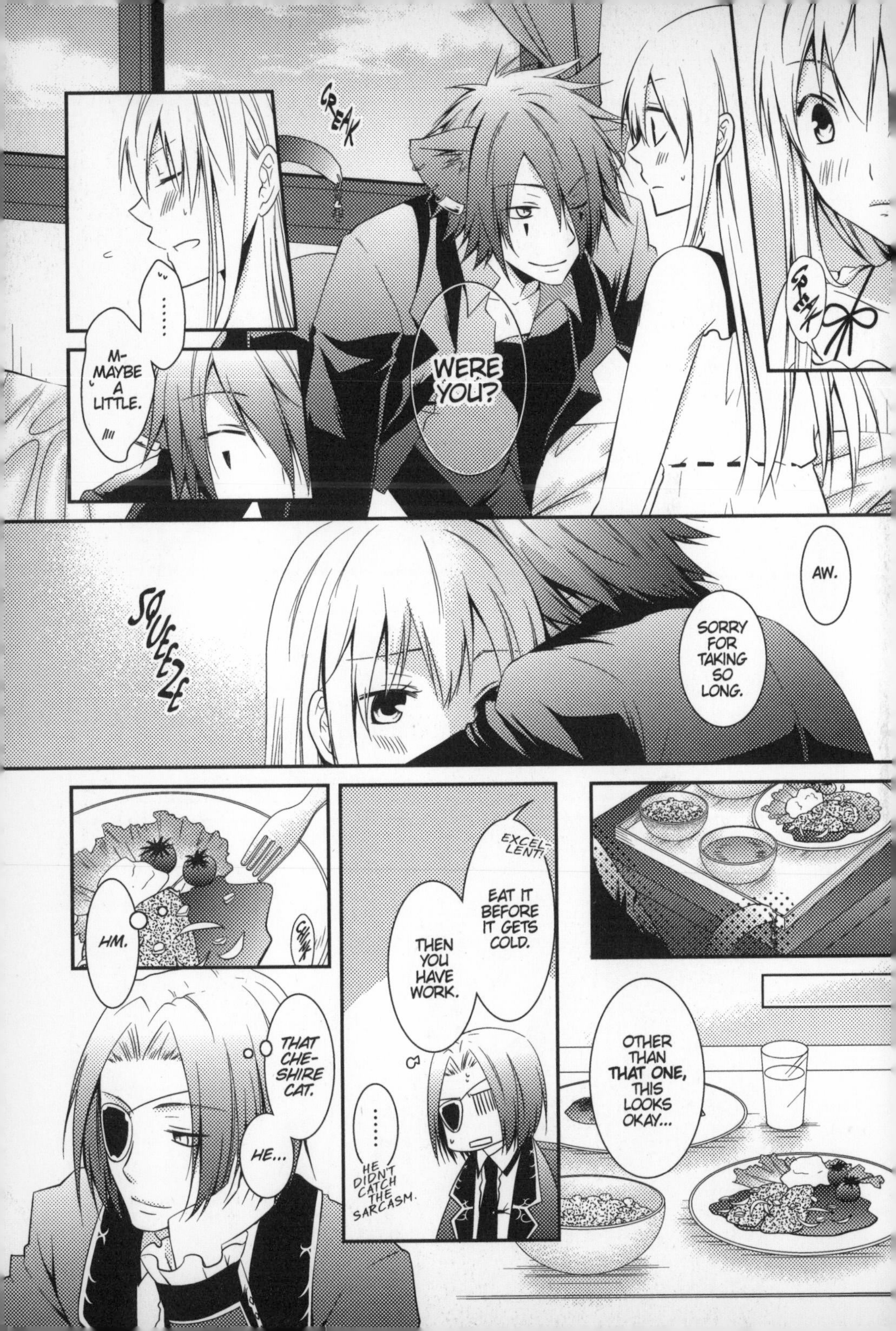
CREAK
CREAK
WERE YOU?
......
M-MAYBE A LITTLE.
AW.
SORRY FOR TAKING SO LONG.
SQUEEZE
OTHER THAN THAT ONE, THIS LOOKS OKAY...
EXCEL-LENT!
EAT IT BEFORE IT GETS COLD.
THEN YOU HAVE WORK.
......
HE DIDN'T CATCH THE SARCASM.
CHINK
HM.
THAT CHE-SHIRE CAT.
HE...

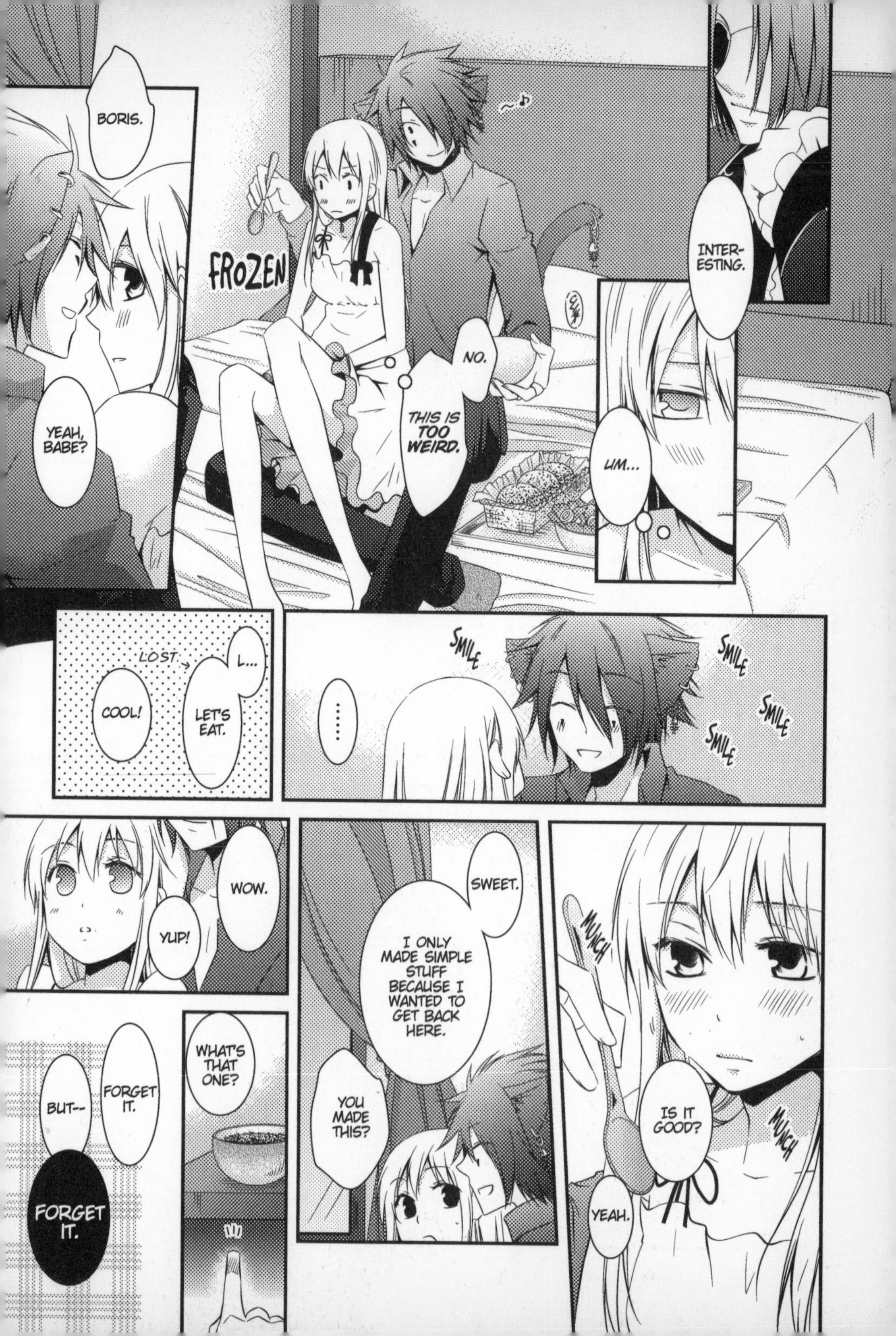
INTER-ESTING.
UM...
~♪
FROZEN
NO.
THIS IS TOO WEIRD.
BORIS.
YEAH, BABE?
SMILE
SMILE
SMILE
SMILE
......
L...
LET'S EAT.
LOST →
COOL!
MUNCH
IS IT GOOD?
MUNCH
YEAH.
SWEET.
I ONLY MADE SIMPLE STUFF BECAUSE I WANTED TO GET BACK HERE.
YOU MADE THIS?
WOW.
YUP!
WHAT'S THAT ONE?
FORGET IT.
BUT--
FORGET IT.

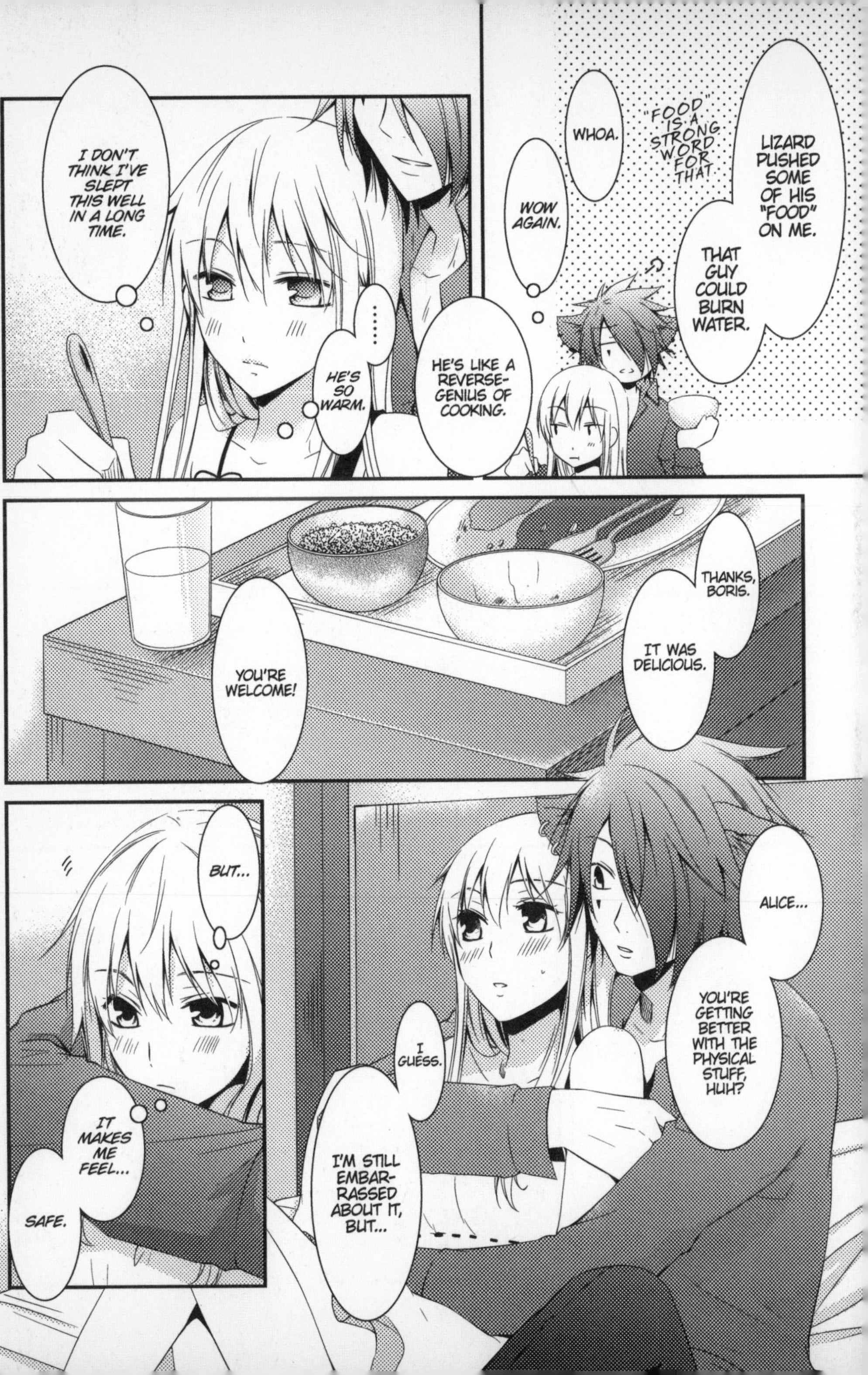
LIZARD PUSHED SOME OF HIS "FOOD" ON ME.
"FOOD" IS A STRONG WORD FOR THAT.
THAT GUY COULD BURN WATER.
WHOA.
WOW AGAIN.
HE'S LIKE A REVERSE-GENIUS OF COOKING.
I DON'T THINK I'VE SLEPT THIS WELL IN A LONG TIME.
......
HE'S SO WARM.
THANKS, BORIS.
IT WAS DELICIOUS.
YOU'RE WELCOME!
ALICE...
YOU'RE GETTING BETTER WITH THE PHYSICAL STUFF, HUH?
I GUESS.
I'M STILL EMBARRASSED ABOUT IT, BUT...
BUT...
IT MAKES ME FEEL...
SAFE.

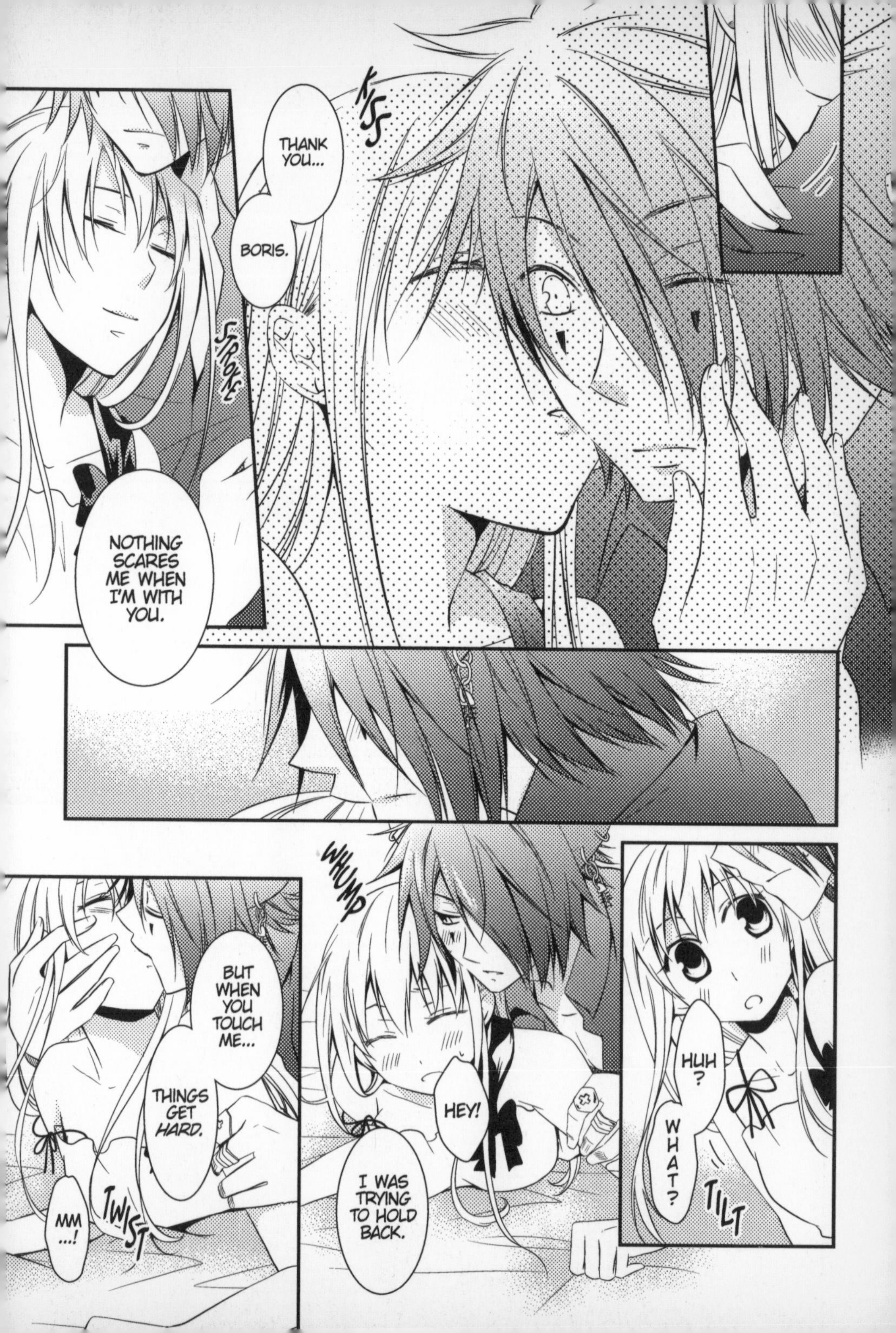
KISS
THANK YOU...
BORIS.
STROKE
NOTHING SCARES ME WHEN I'M WITH YOU.
HUH?
WHAT?
TILT
WHUMP
HEY!
I WAS TRYING TO HOLD BACK.
BUT WHEN YOU TOUCH ME...
THINGS GET *HARD*.
TWIST
MM...!

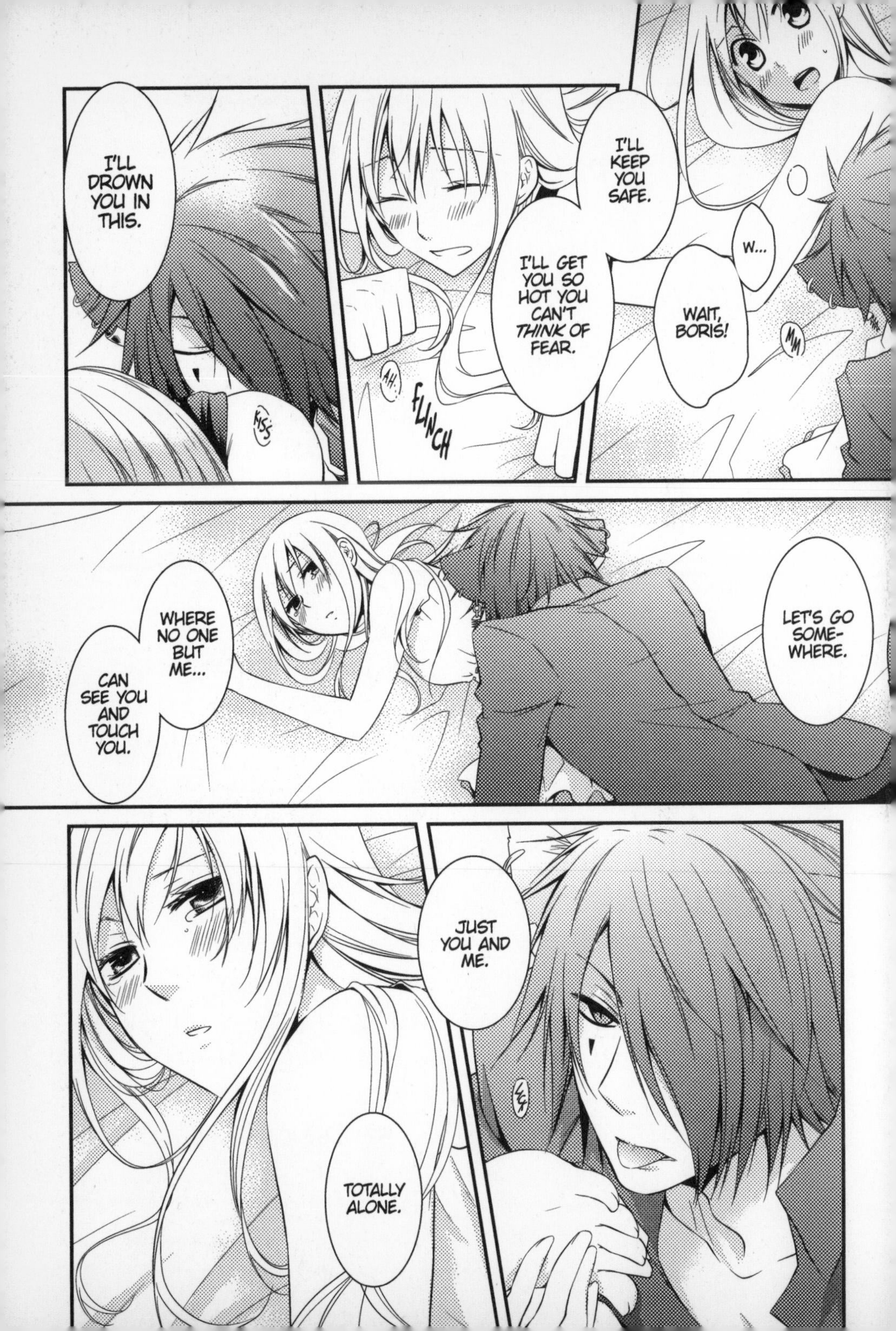
W...
WAIT, BORIS!
MM
I'LL KEEP YOU SAFE.
I'LL GET YOU SO HOT YOU CAN'T *THINK* OF FEAR.
AH
FLINCH
I'LL DROWN YOU IN THIS.
KISS
LET'S GO SOME-WHERE.
WHERE NO ONE BUT ME...
CAN SEE YOU AND TOUCH YOU.
JUST YOU AND ME.
TOTALLY ALONE.

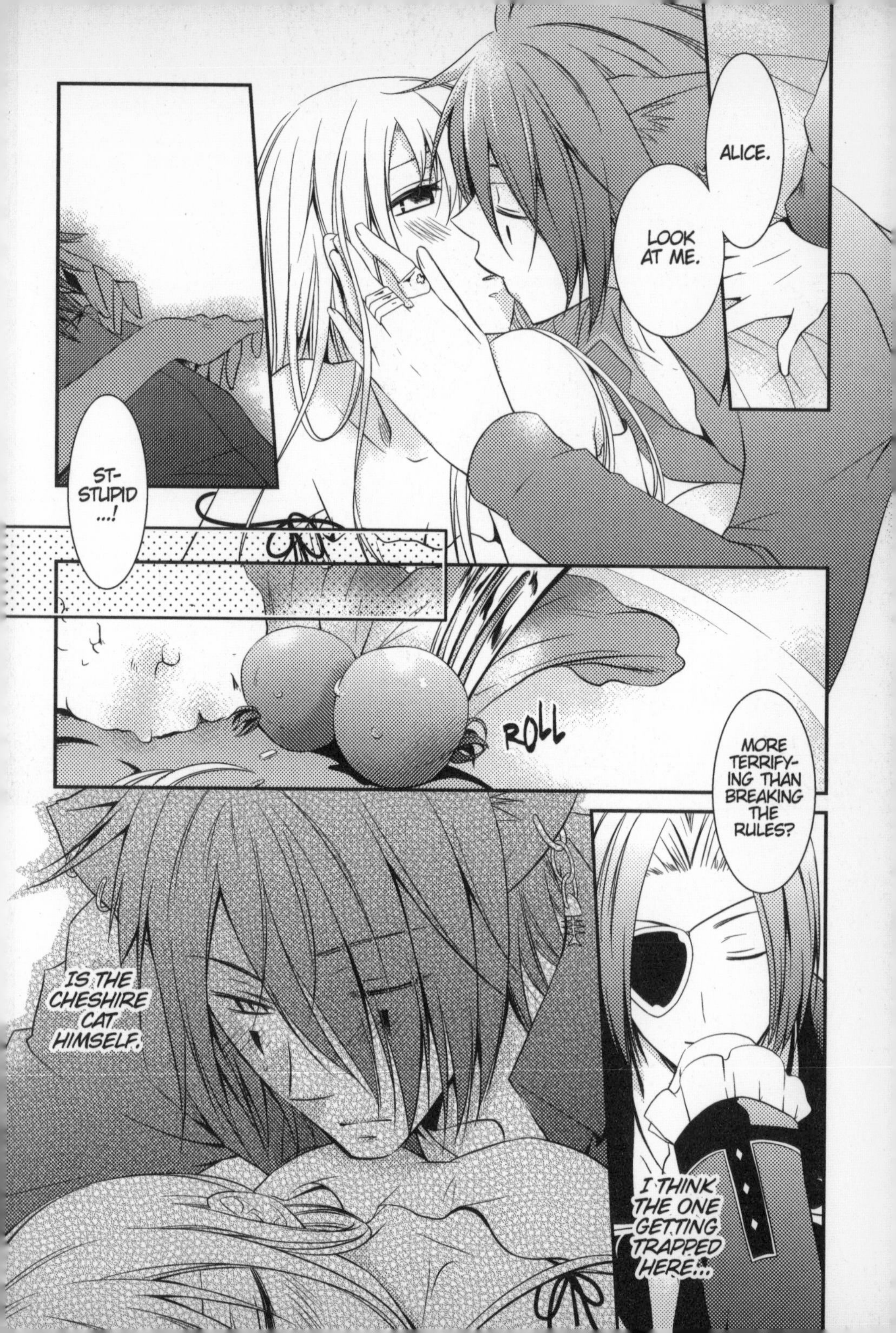
ALICE.
LOOK AT ME.
ST-STUPID ...!
ROLL
MORE TERRIFY-ING THAN BREAKING THE RULES?
I THINK THE ONE GETTING TRAPPED HERE...
IS THE CHESHIRE CAT HIMSELF.

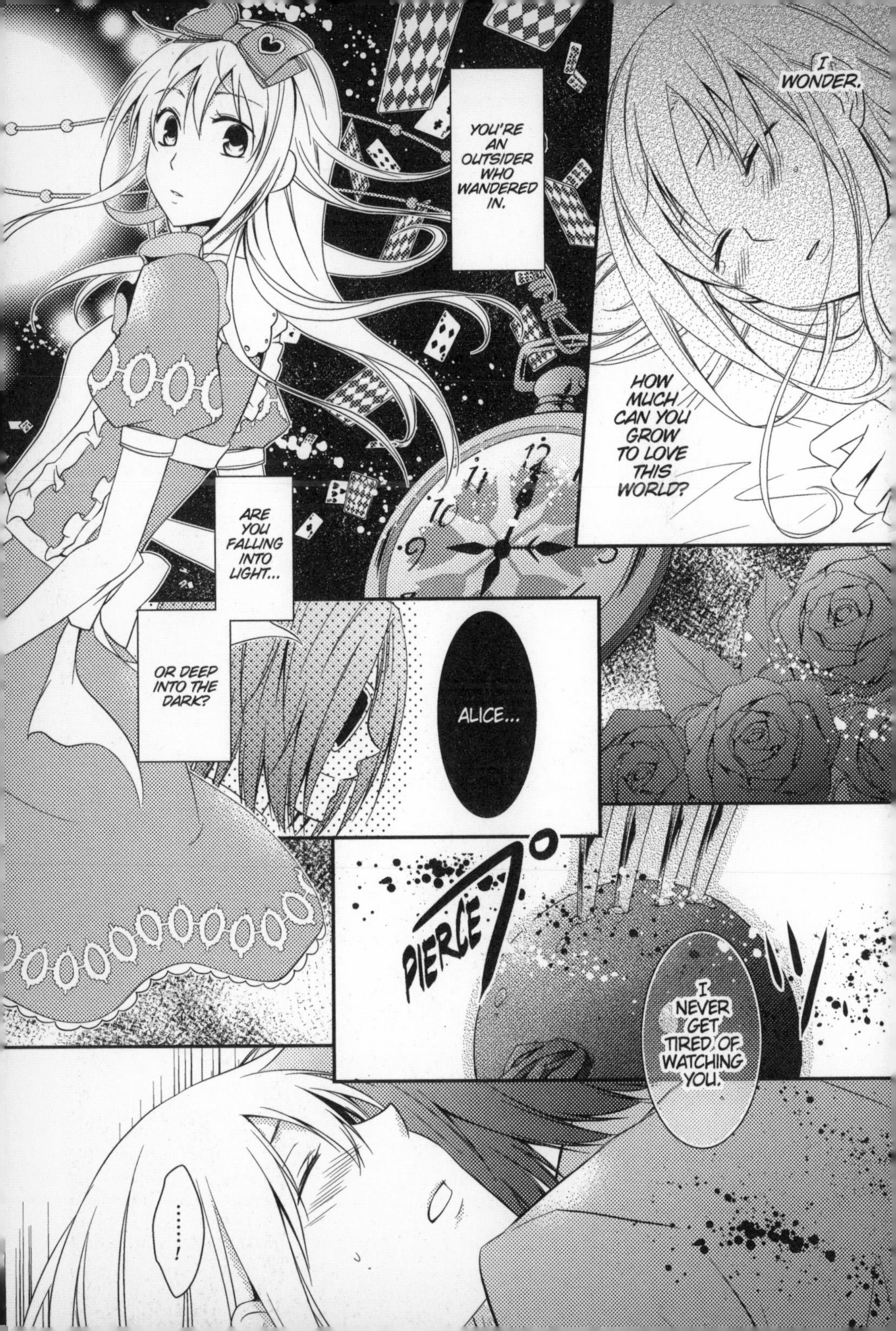
I WONDER.
HOW MUCH CAN YOU GROW TO LOVE THIS WORLD?
YOU'RE AN OUTSIDER WHO WANDERED IN.
ARE YOU FALLING INTO LIGHT...
OR DEEP INTO THE DARK?
ALICE...
PIERCE
I NEVER GET TIRED OF WATCHING YOU.
......!

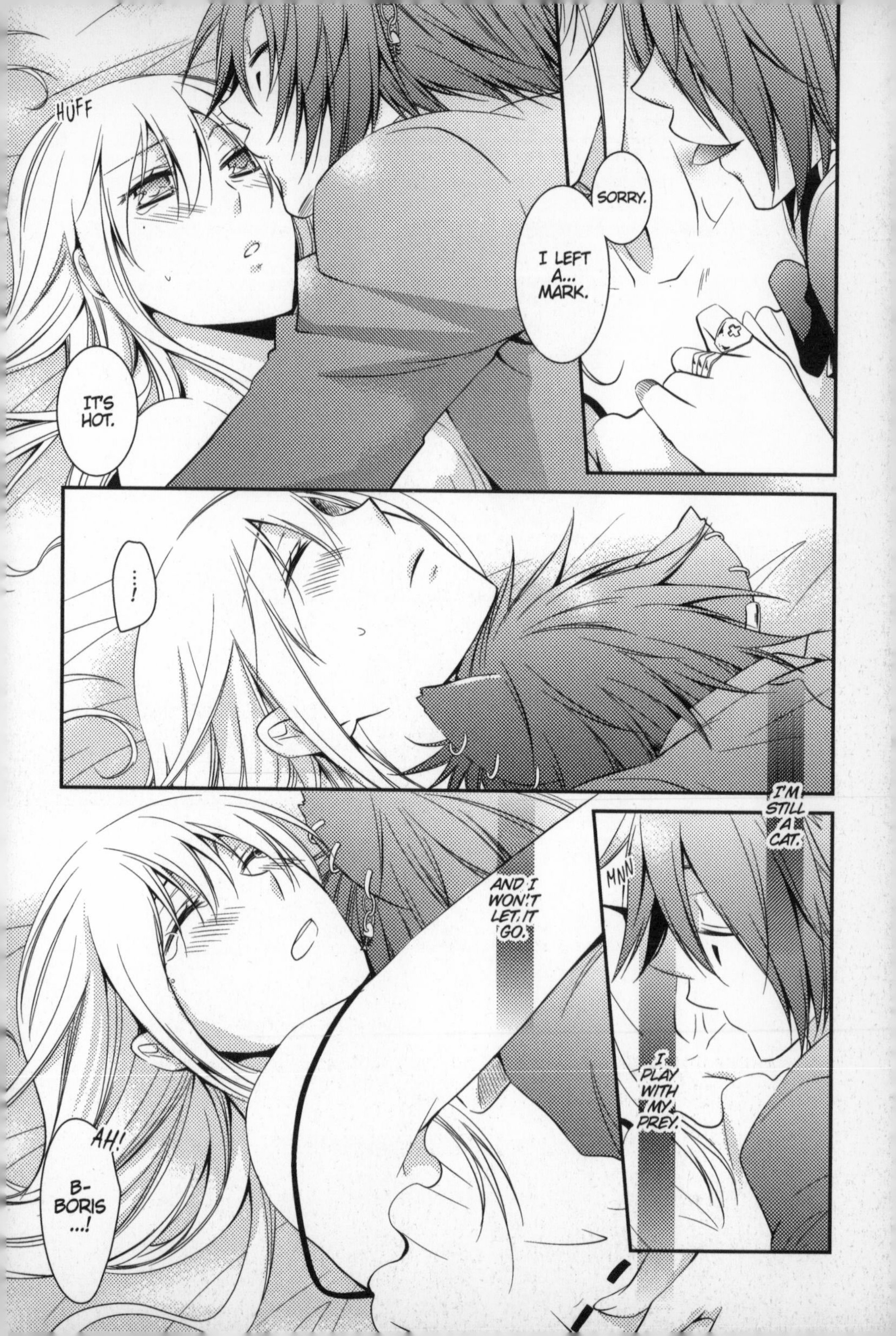
SORRY.
I LEFT A... MARK.
HUFF
IT'S HOT.
...!
I'M STILL A CAT.
MNN
I PLAY WITH MY PREY.
AND I WON'T LET IT GO.
AH!
B-BORIS ...!

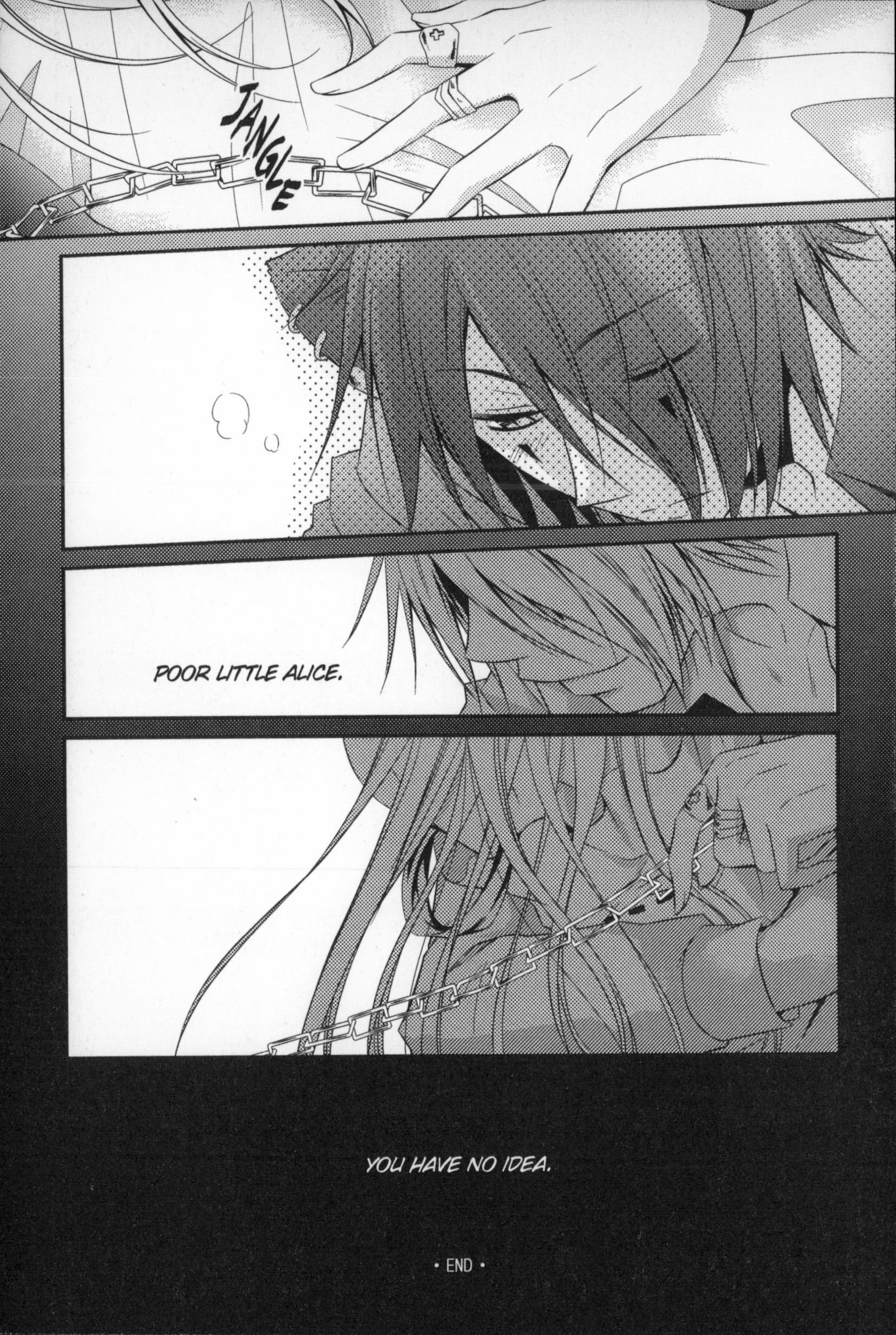
JANGLE
POOR LITTLE ALICE.
YOU HAVE NO IDEA.
• END •

CHESHIRE CAT WALTZ VOL. 4 - POST-MORTEM

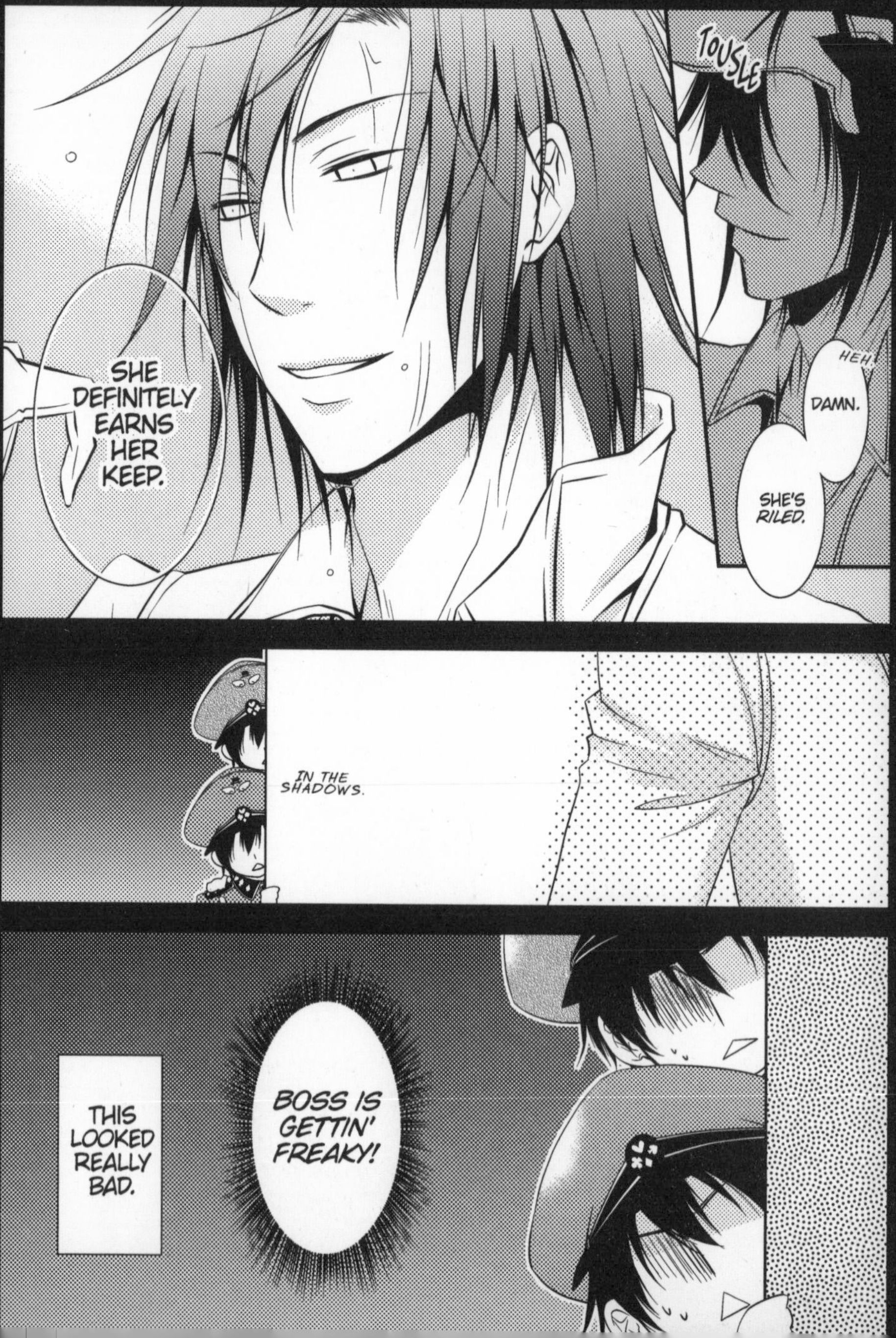
TOUSLE
HEH.
DAMN.
SHE'S RILED.
SHE DEFINITELY EARNS HER KEEP.
IN THE SHADOWS.
BOSS IS GETTIN' FREAKY!
THIS LOOKED REALLY BAD.

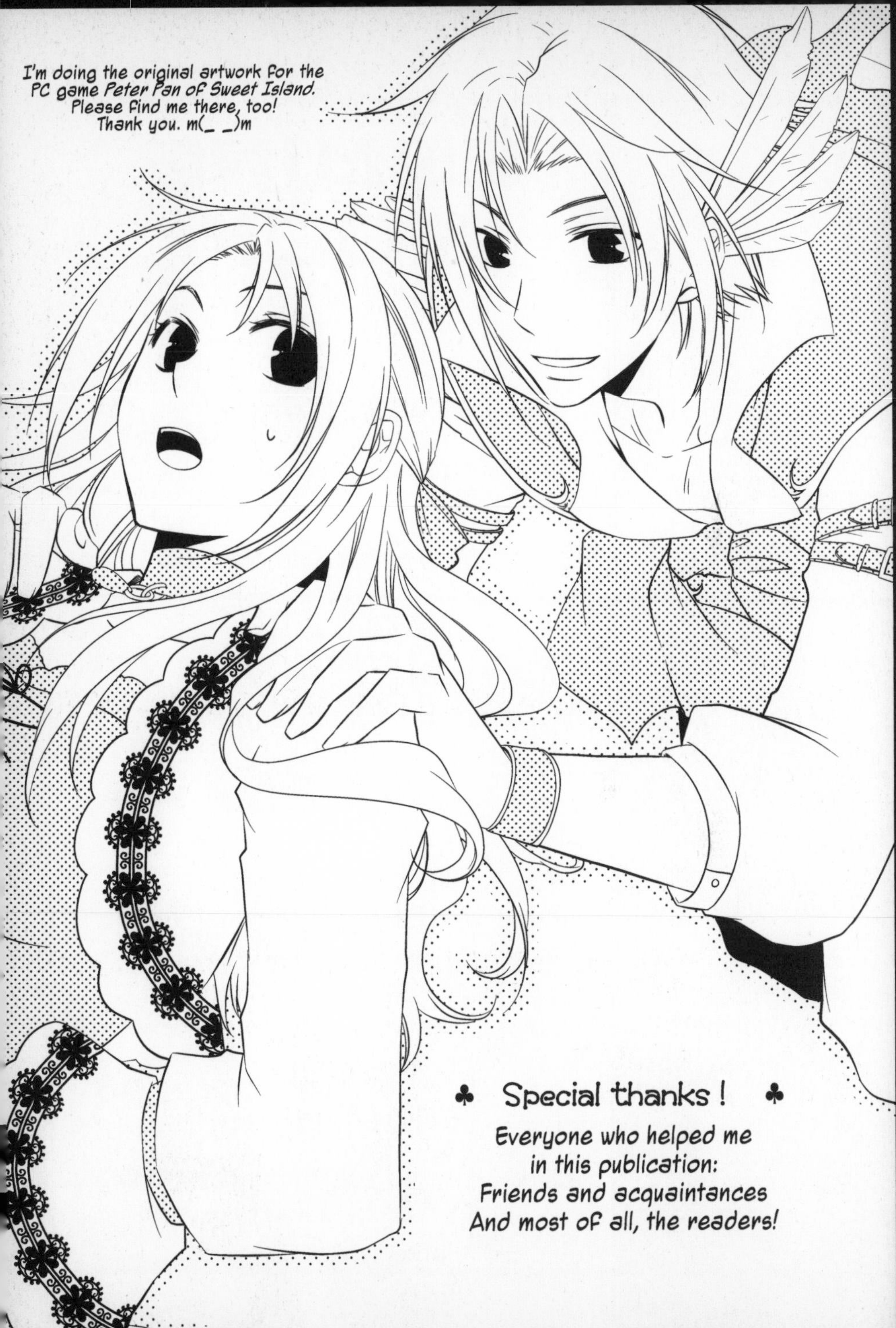
I'm doing the original artwork for the PC game *Peter Pan of Sweet Island.* Please find me there, too! Thank you. m(_ _)m
♣ Special thanks ! ♣
Everyone who helped me in this publication: Friends and acquaintances And most of all, the readers!

COMING SOON

APRIL 2013
Crimson Empire Vol. 1

MAY 2013
Alice in the Country of Joker:
Circus and Liar's Game Vol. 2

JUNE 2013
Alice in the Country of Clover:
Cheshire Cat Waltz Vol. 5

JULY 2013
Alice in the Country of Clover:
Ace of Hearts

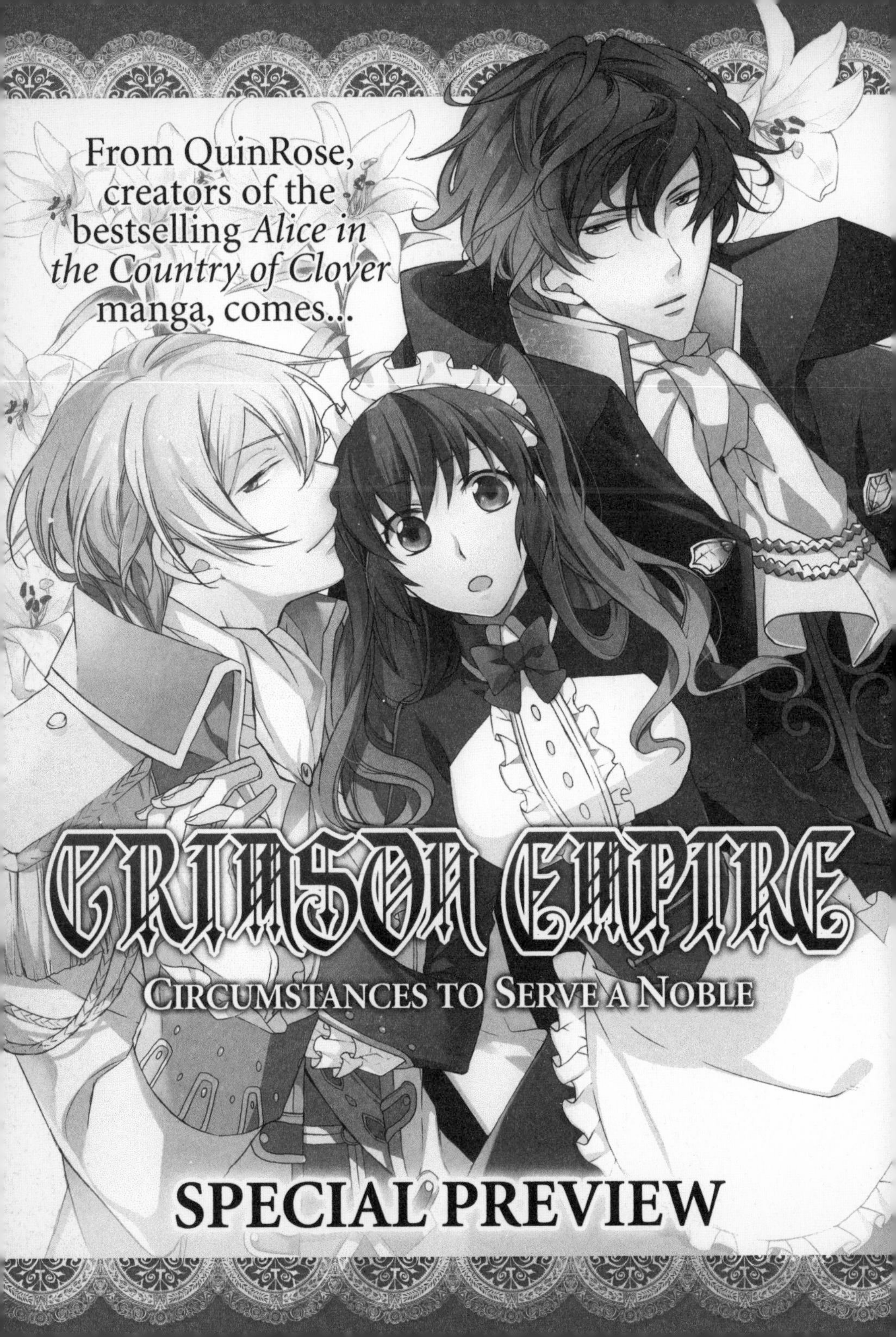
From QuinRose, creators of the bestselling *Alice in the Country of Clover* manga, comes...
CRIMSON EMPIRE
CIRCUMSTANCES TO SERVE A NOBLE
SPECIAL PREVIEW

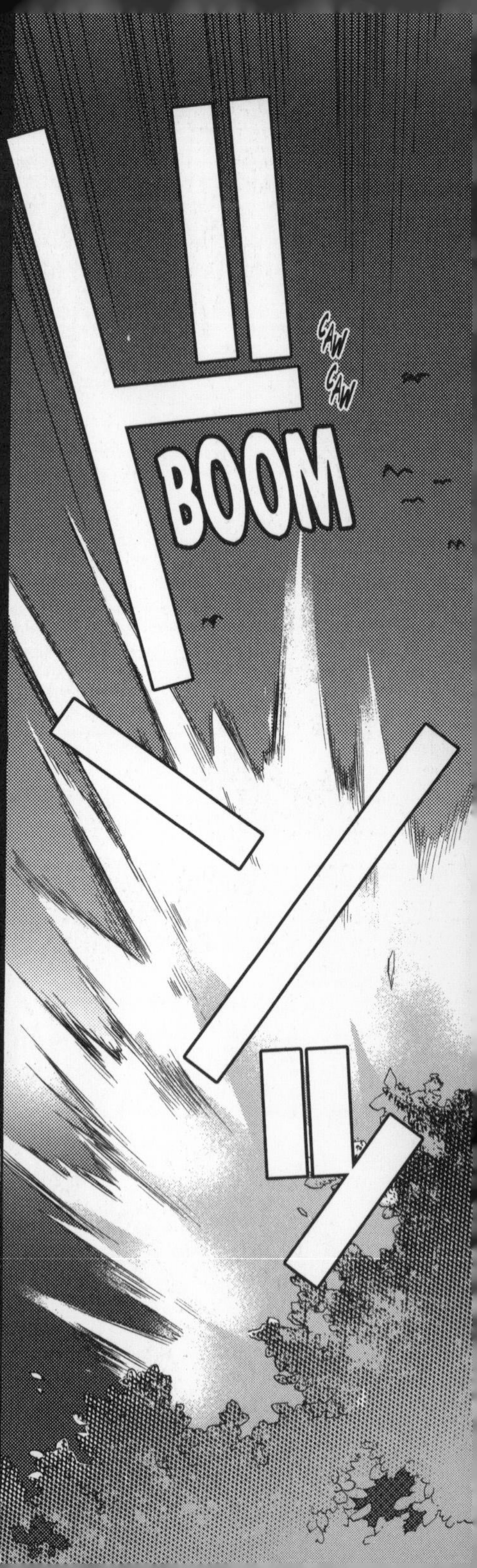
CAW CAW
BOOM
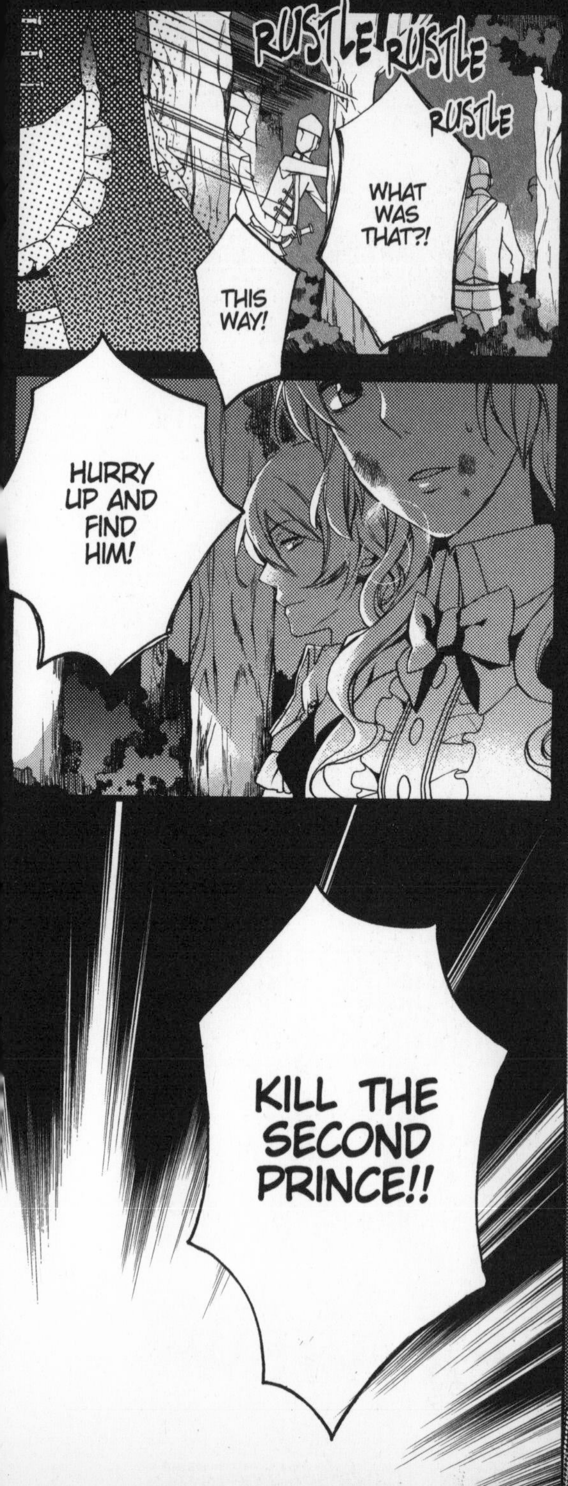
RUSTLE RUSTLE
RUSTLE
WHAT WAS THAT?!
THIS WAY!
HURRY UP AND FIND HIM!
KILL THE SECOND PRINCE!!

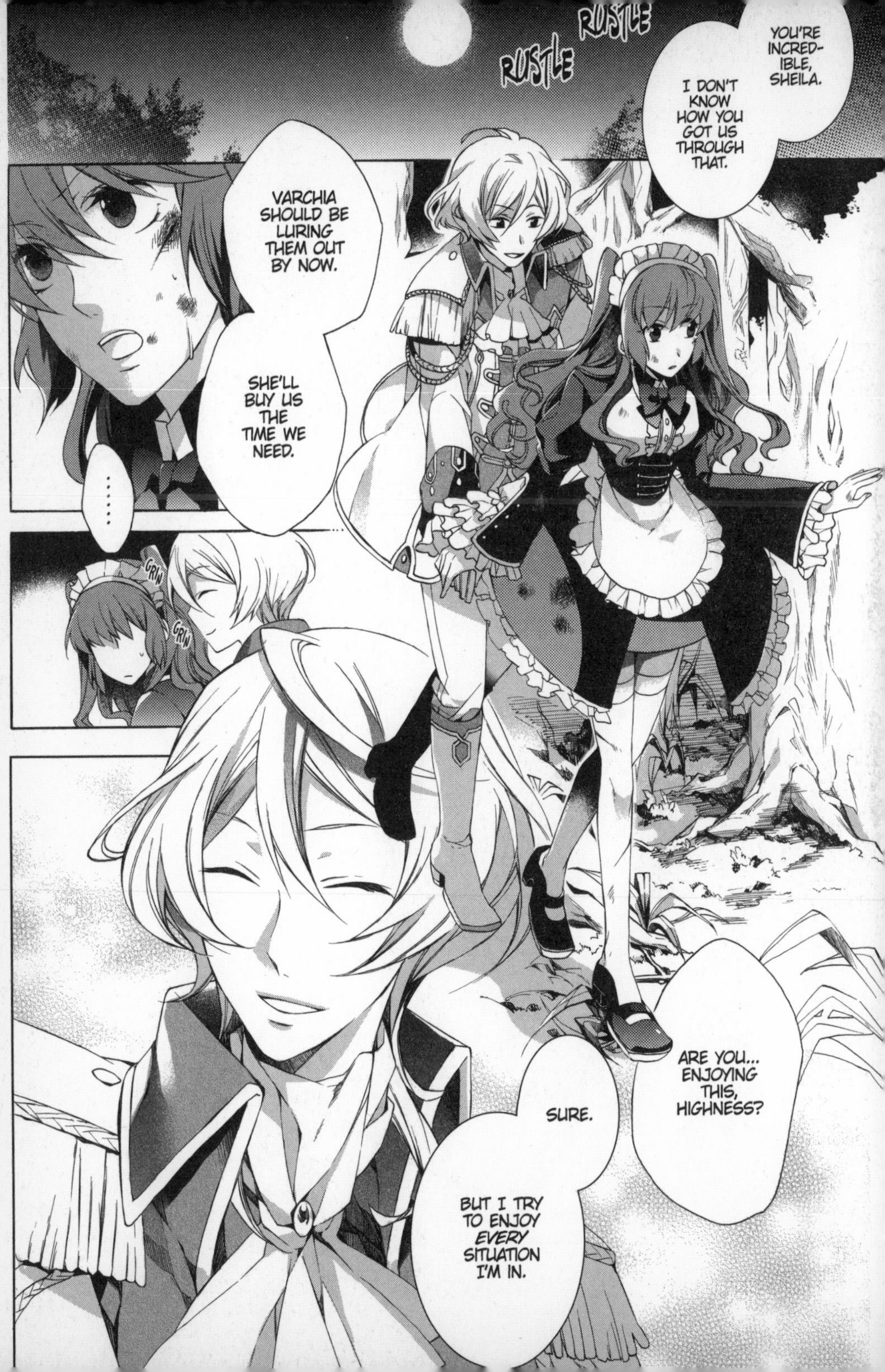

RUSTLE
RUSTLE
YOU'RE INCREDIBLE, SHEILA.
I DON'T KNOW HOW YOU GOT US THROUGH THAT.
VARCHIA SHOULD BE LURING THEM OUT BY NOW.
SHE'LL BUY US THE TIME WE NEED.
......
GRIN
GRIN
ARE YOU... ENJOYING THIS, HIGHNESS?
SURE.
BUT I TRY TO ENJOY *EVERY* SITUATION I'M IN.

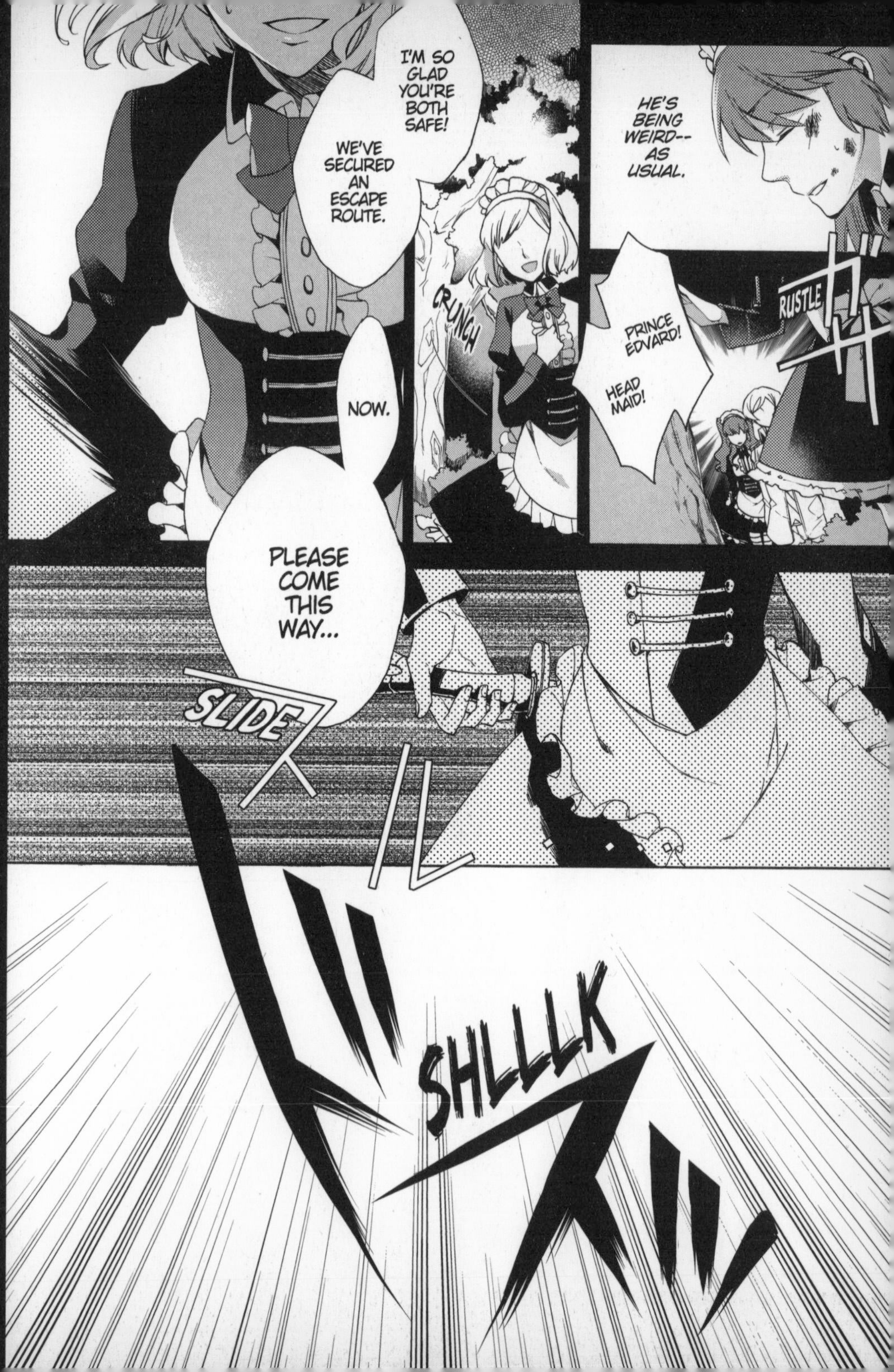
HE'S BEING WEIRD-- AS USUAL.
RUSTLE
PRINCE EDVARD!
HEAD MAID!
I'M SO GLAD YOU'RE BOTH SAFE!
CRUNCH
WE'VE SECURED AN ESCAPE ROUTE.
NOW.
PLEASE COME THIS WAY...
SLIDE
SHLLLK

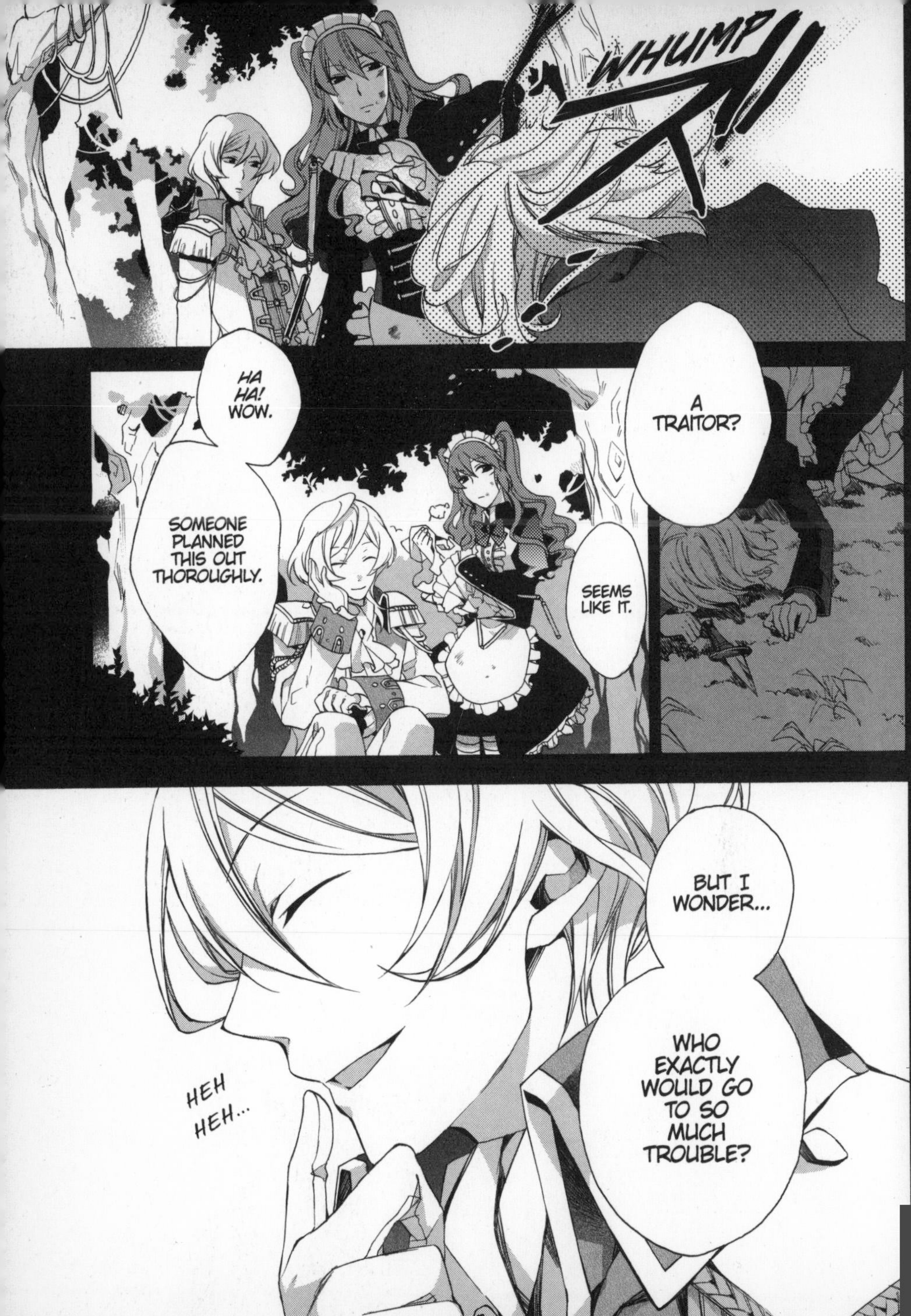
WHUMP
A TRAITOR?
SEEMS LIKE IT.
HA HA! WOW.
SOMEONE PLANNED THIS OUT THOROUGHLY.
BUT I WONDER...
WHO EXACTLY WOULD GO TO SO MUCH TROUBLE?
HEH HEH...

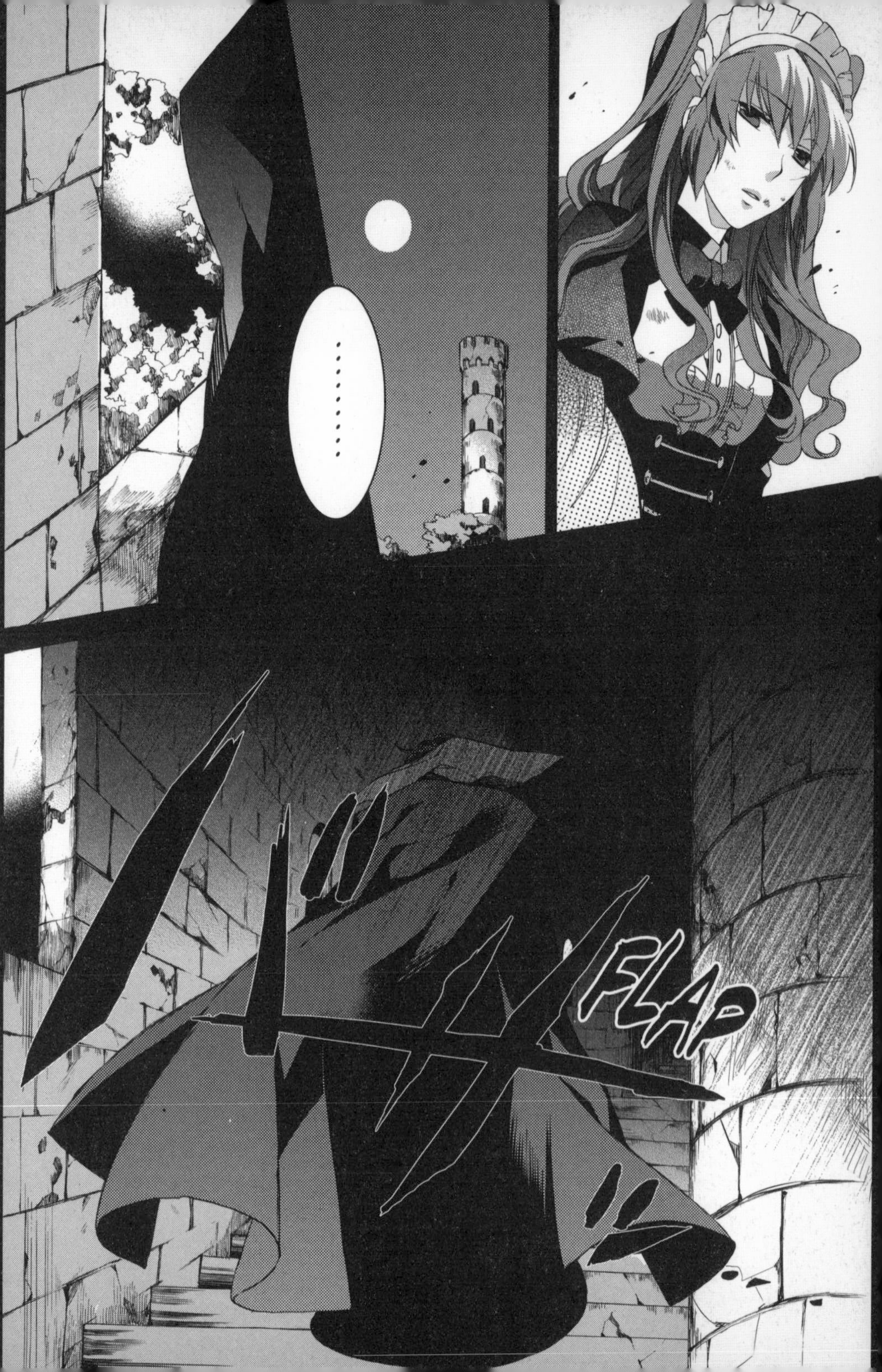
......
FLAP

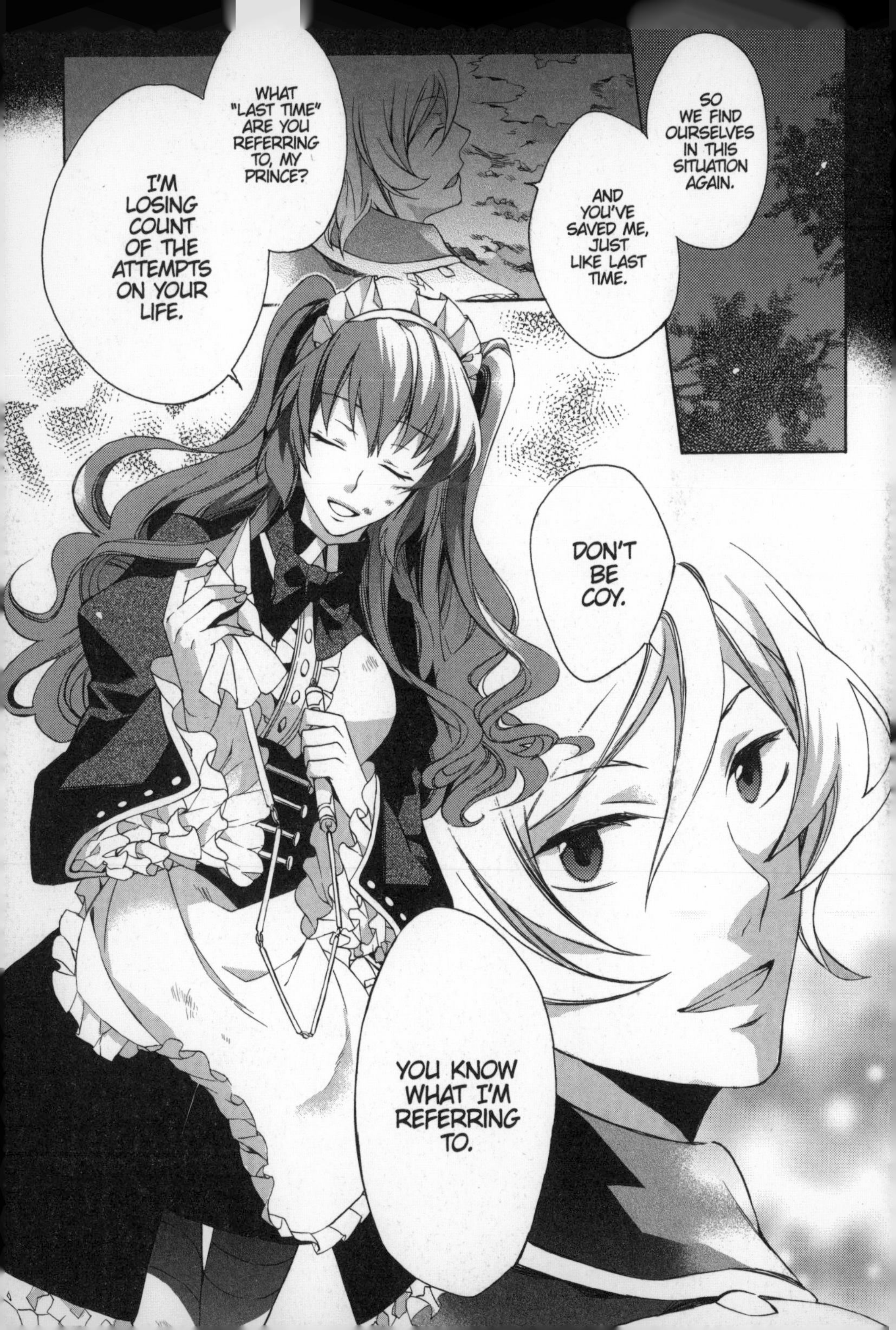
SO WE FIND OURSELVES IN THIS SITUATION AGAIN.
AND YOU'VE SAVED ME, JUST LIKE LAST TIME.
WHAT "LAST TIME" ARE YOU REFERRING TO, MY PRINCE?
I'M LOSING COUNT OF THE ATTEMPTS ON YOUR LIFE.
DON'T BE COY.
YOU KNOW WHAT I'M REFERRING TO.

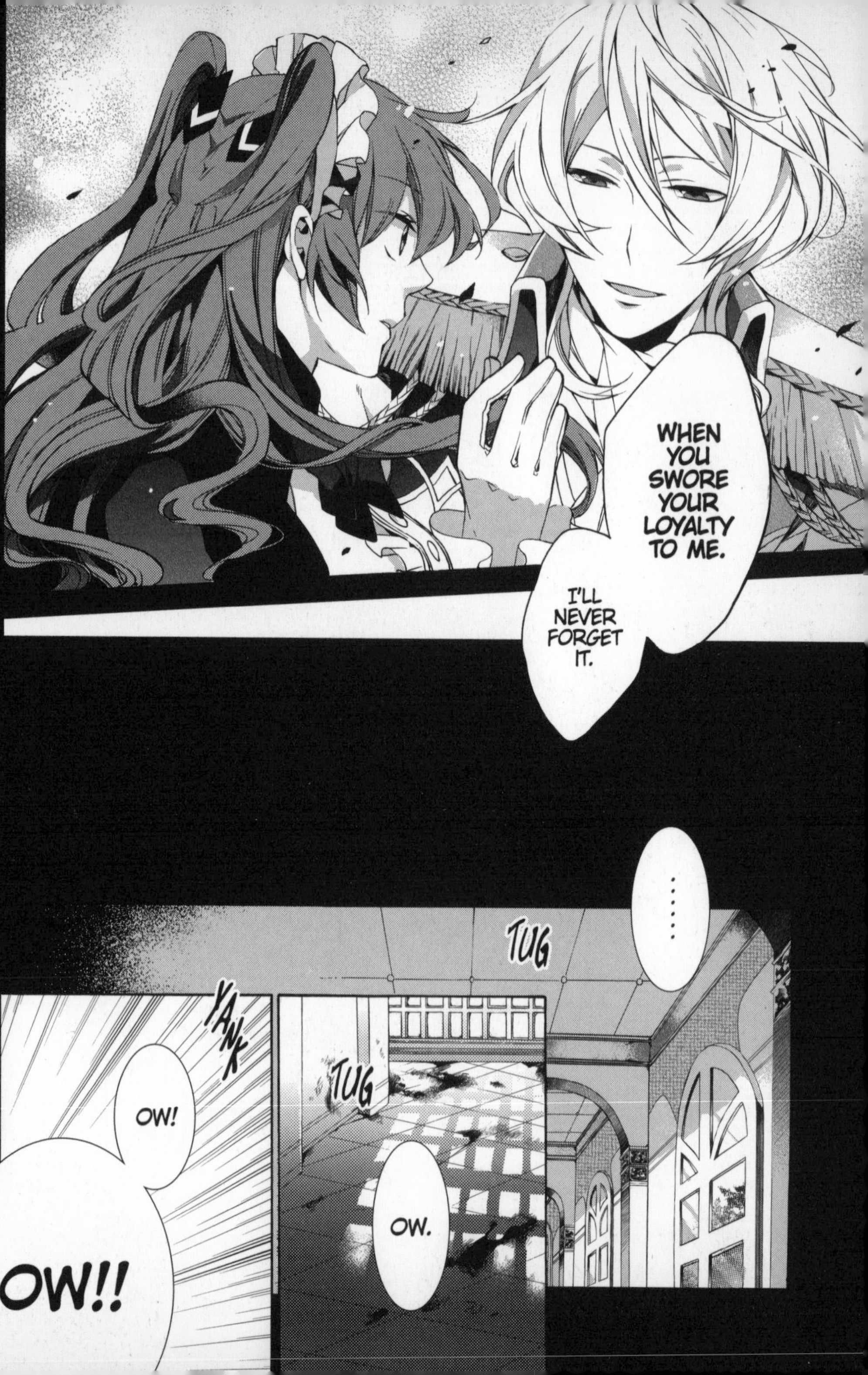
WHEN YOU SWORE YOUR LOYALTY TO ME.
I'LL NEVER FORGET IT.
......
TUG
TUG
OW.
YANK
OW!
OW!!

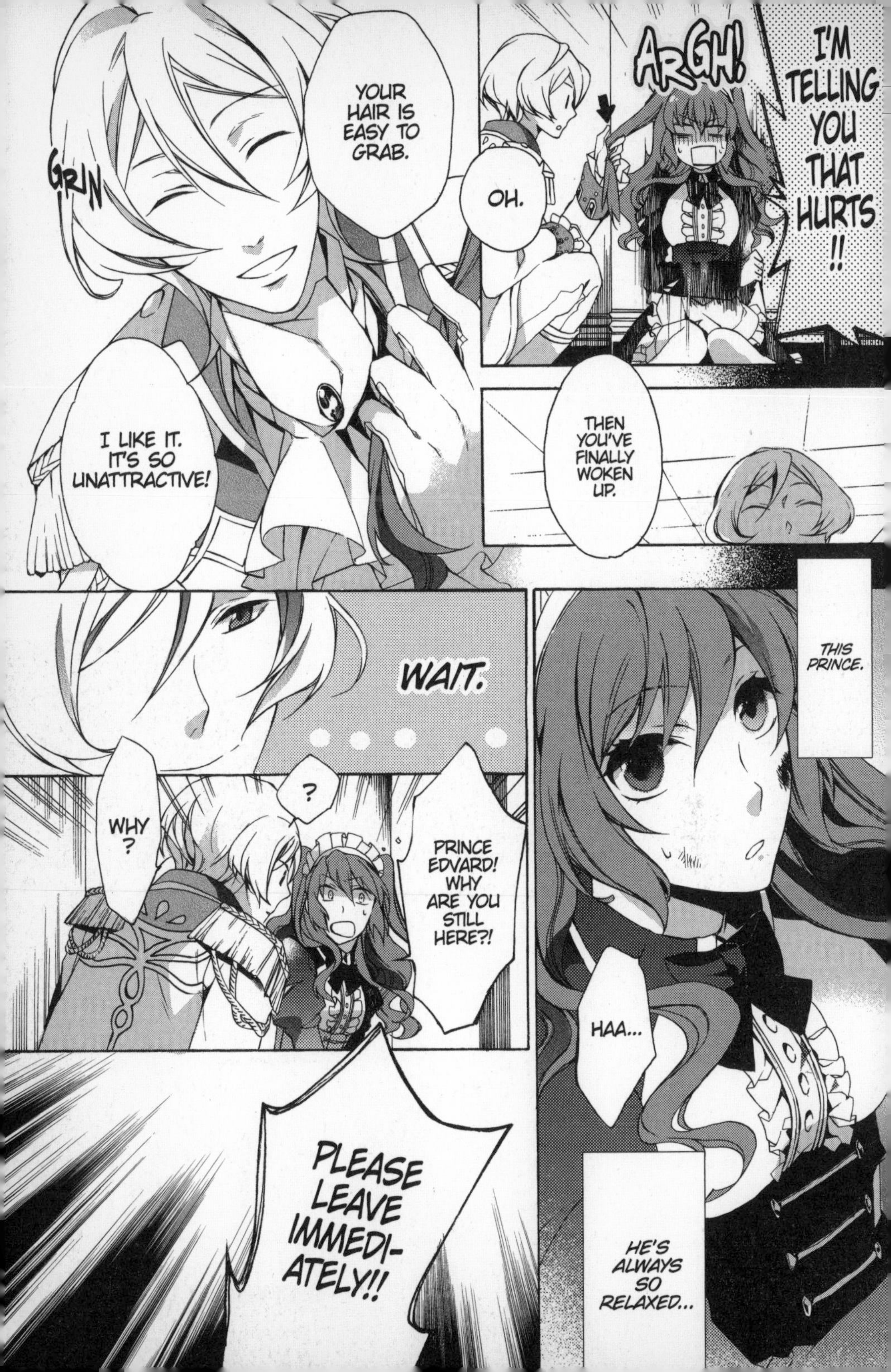
ARGH!
I'M TELLING YOU THAT HURTS!!
OH.
THEN YOU'VE FINALLY WOKEN UP.
YOUR HAIR IS EASY TO GRAB.
GRIN
I LIKE IT. IT'S SO UNATTRACTIVE!
THIS PRINCE.
HAA...
HE'S ALWAYS SO RELAXED...
WAIT.
. . . .
PRINCE EDVARD! WHY ARE YOU STILL HERE?!
?
WHY ?
PLEASE LEAVE IMMEDI-ATELY!!

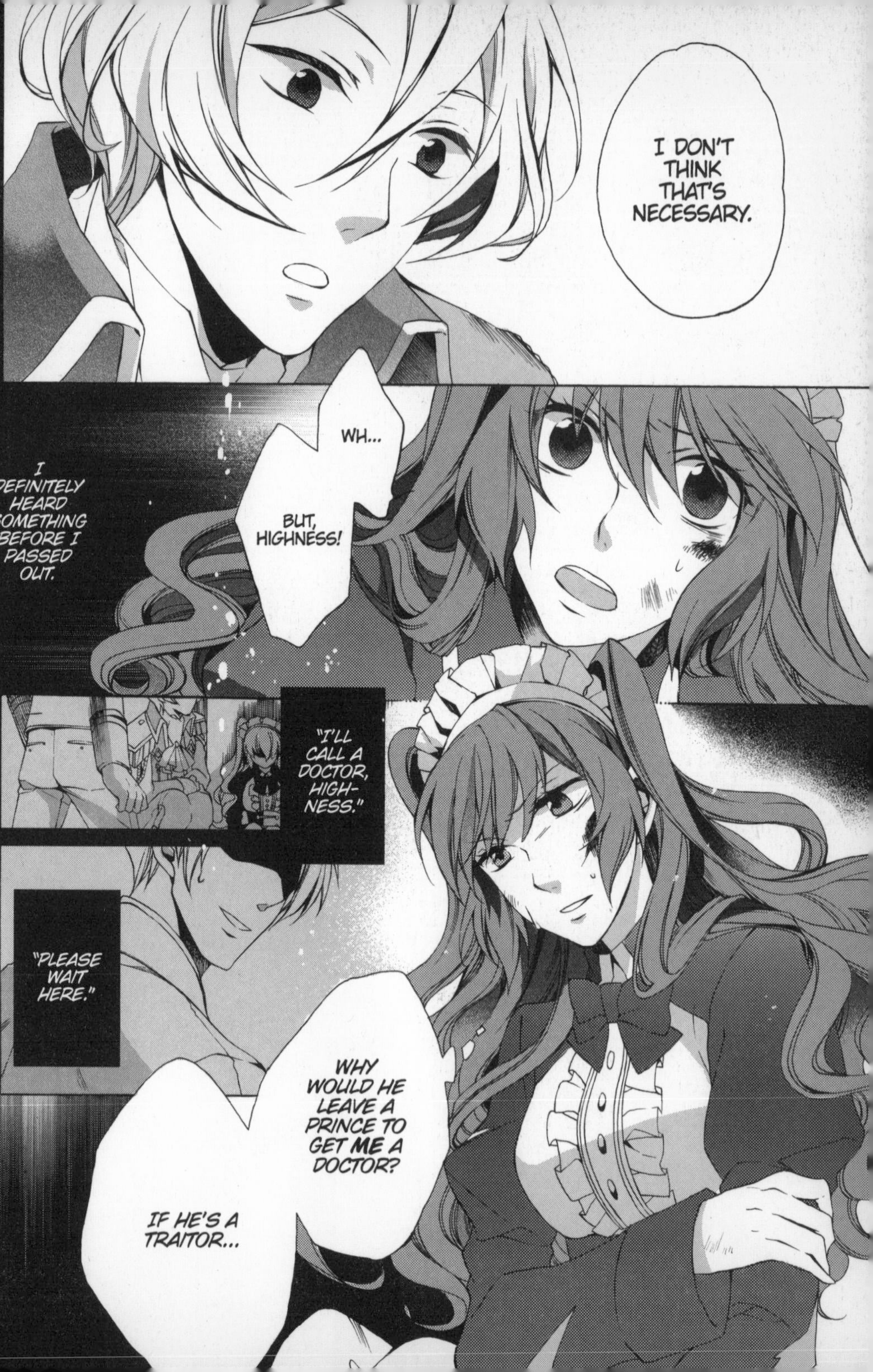
I DON'T THINK THAT'S NECESSARY.
WH...
BUT, HIGHNESS!
I DEFINITELY HEARD SOMETHING BEFORE I PASSED OUT.
"I'LL CALL A DOCTOR, HIGHNESS."
"PLEASE WAIT HERE."
WHY WOULD HE LEAVE A PRINCE TO GET **ME** A DOCTOR?
IF HE'S A TRAITOR...

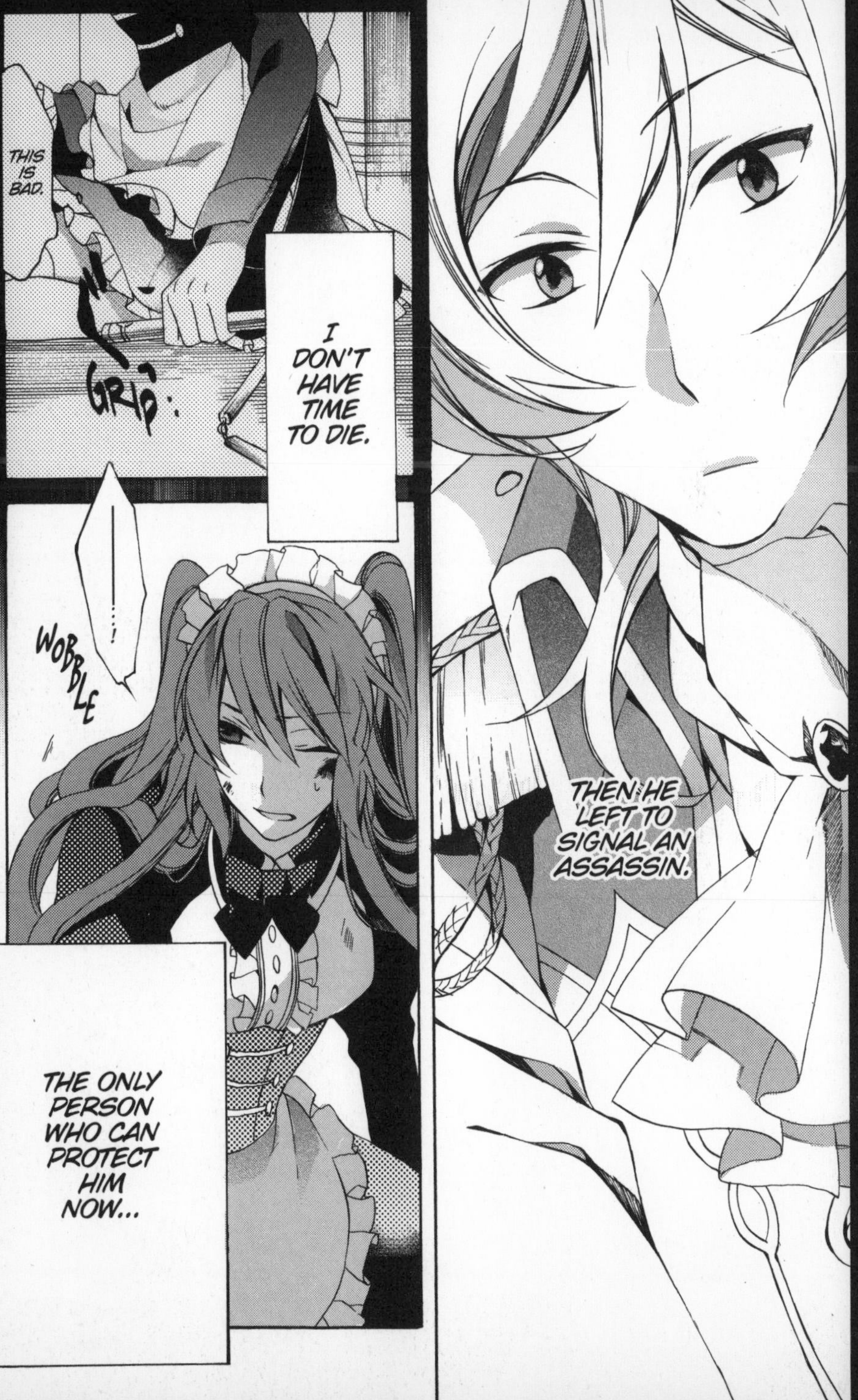
THEN HE LEFT TO SIGNAL AN ASSASSIN.
THIS IS BAD.
GRIP
I DON'T HAVE TIME TO DIE.
WOBBLE
THE ONLY PERSON WHO CAN PROTECT HIM NOW...

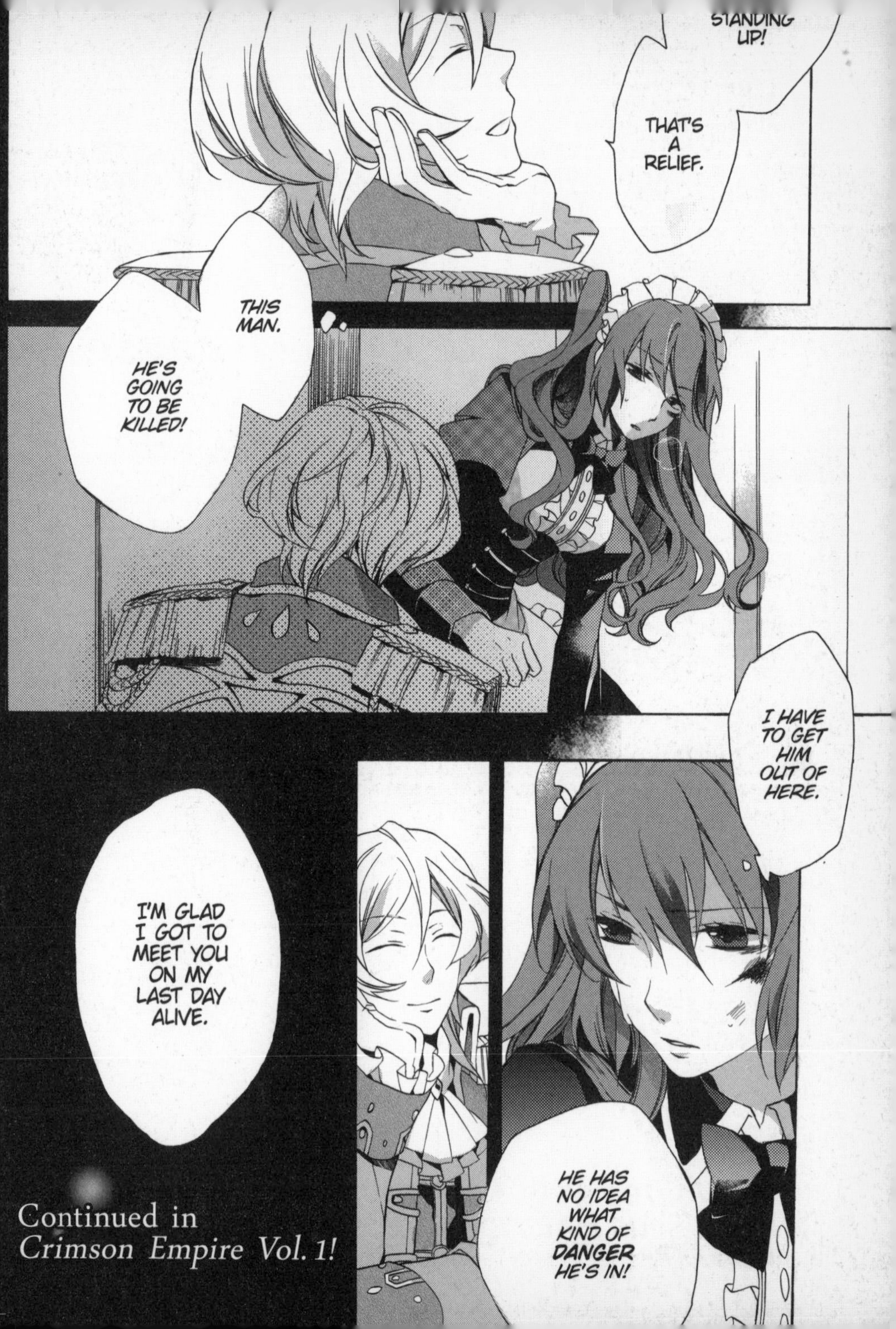
STANDING UP!
THAT'S A RELIEF.
THIS MAN.
HE'S GOING TO BE KILLED!
I HAVE TO GET HIM OUT OF HERE.
HE HAS NO IDEA WHAT KIND OF DANGER HE'S IN!
I'M GLAD I GOT TO MEET YOU ON MY LAST DAY ALIVE.

Continued in *Crimson Empire Vol. 1!*

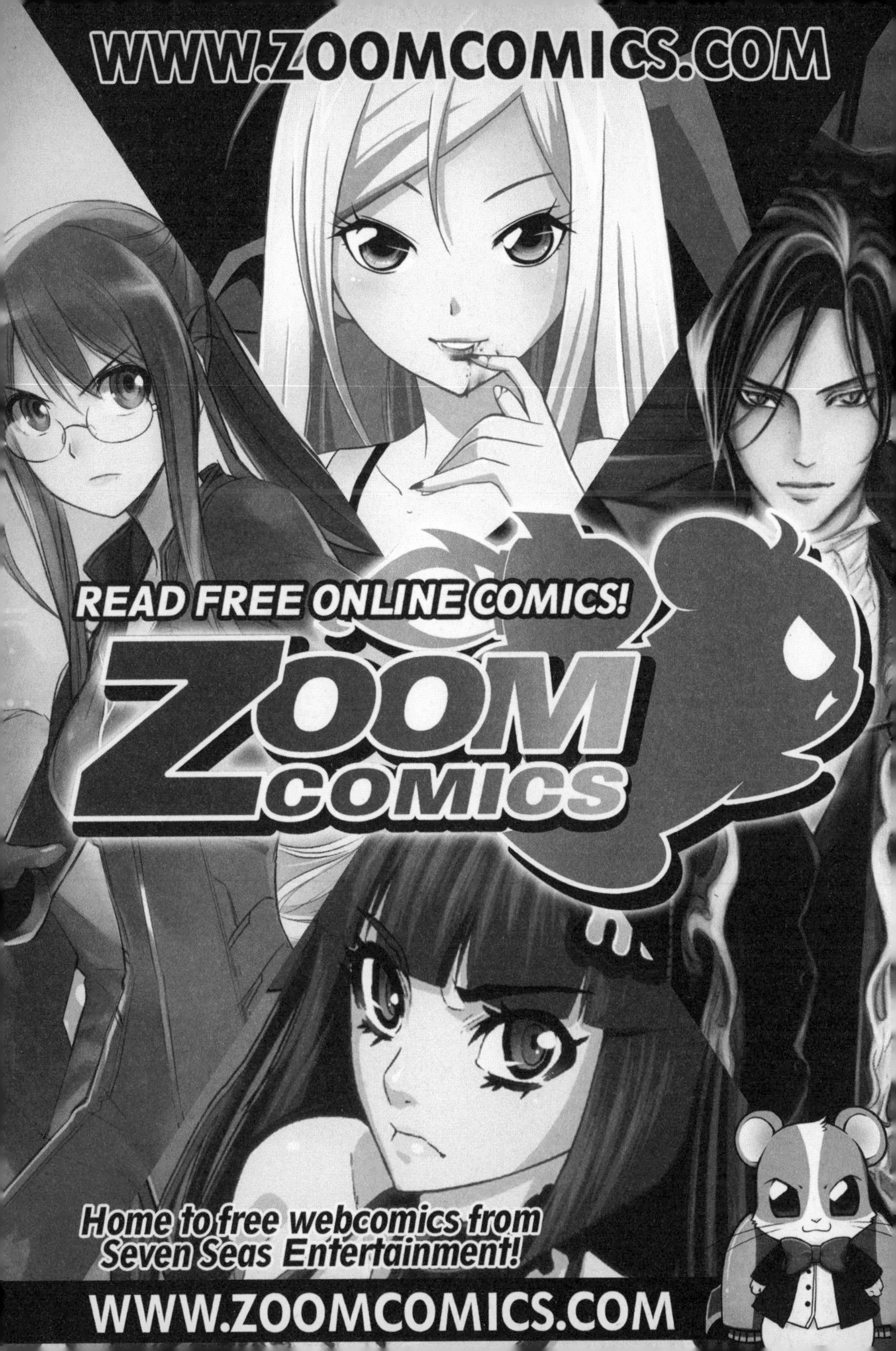

WWW.ZOOMCOMICS.COM
READ FREE ONLINE COMICS!
ZOOM COMICS
Home to free webcomics from Seven Seas Entertainment!
WWW.ZOOMCOMICS.COM

Experience all that *SEVEN SEAS* has to offer!

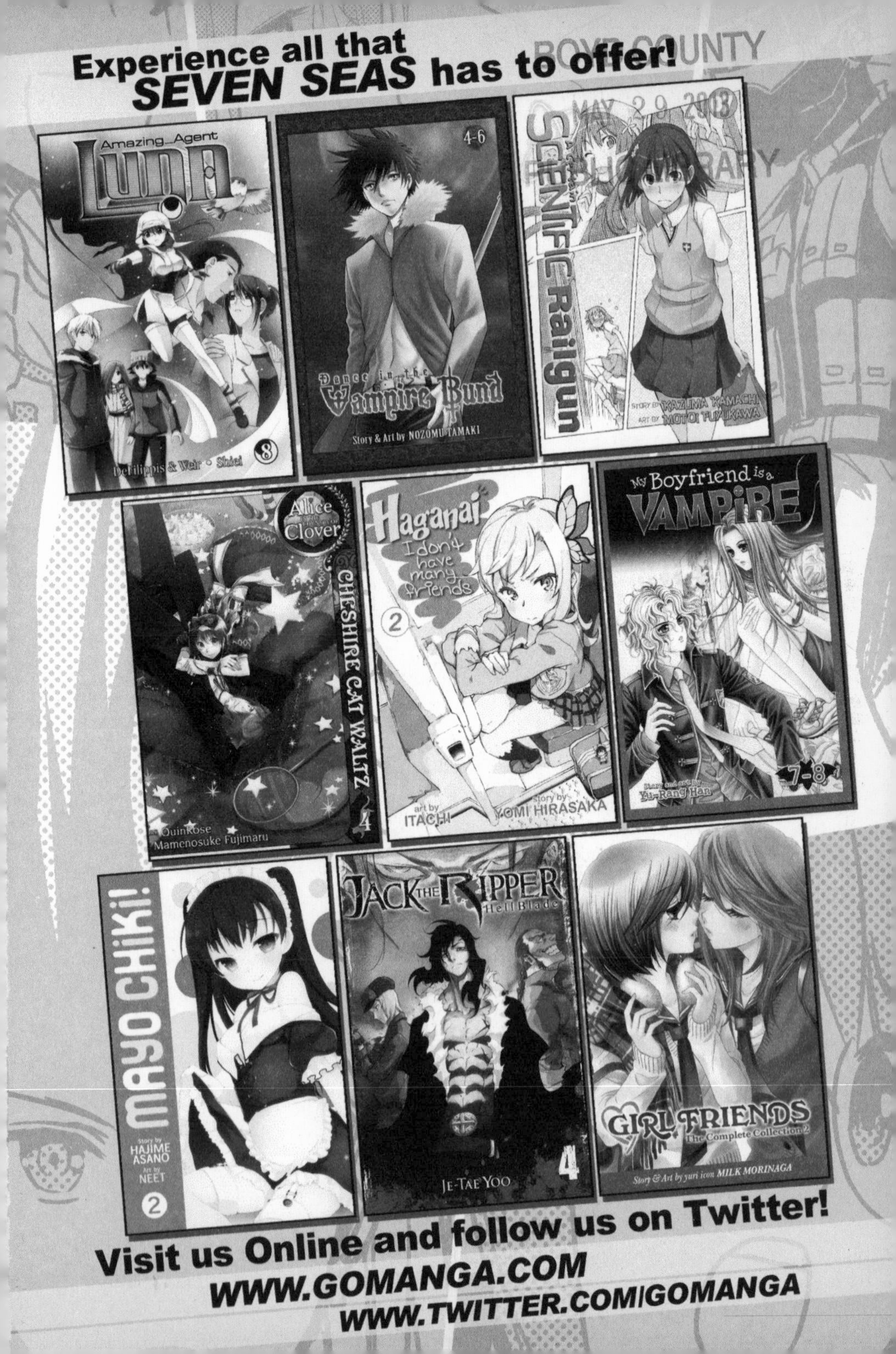
Amazing Agent Luna
8
DeFilippis & Weir • Shiei
4-6
Dance in the Vampire Bund
Story & Art by NOZOMU TAMAKI
Scientific Railgun
STORY BY KAZUMA KAMACHI
ART BY MOTOI FUYUKAWA
Alice in the Country of Clover
CHESHIRE CAT WALTZ
4
QuinRose
Mamenosuke Fujimaru
Haganai
I don't have many friends
2
art by ITACHI
Story by YOMI HIRASAKA
My Boyfriend is a VAMPIRE
7-8
Story and art by Yu-Rang Han
MAYO CHIKI!
Story by HAJIME ASANO
Art by NEET
2
JACK THE RIPPER
Hell Blade
JE-TAE YOO
4
GIRL FRIENDS
The Complete Collection 2
Story & Art by yuri icon MILK MORINAGA

Visit us Online and follow us on Twitter!

WWW.GOMANGA.COM

WWW.TWITTER.COM/GOMANGA